THE UNMAKING OF THE MEDIEVAL CHRISTIAN COSMOS 1500–1760

From Solid Heavens to Boundless Æther

Woodcut engraving of the medieval Christian cosmos in Jan Glogowezyk (Johannes Glogoviensis, d. 1507), *Introductorium Compendiosum in Tractatum Spere materialis magistri Joannis de Sacrobosco*, Cracow, 1506, f.br. Photograph courtesy of the James Ford Bell Library, University of Minnesota.

At the top: the Empyrean with Christ surrounded by the Saints and the Angels. The two empty bands below represent the Supercelestial Waters and the *Primum Mobile*. Thereafter: the sphere of the fixed stars (the Zodiac), the planetary spheres of Saturn, Jupiter, Mars, the Sun, Venus, Mercury, and the Moon, followed by the elementary spheres of the fire, of the air, of the water and of the earth. Figures representing the four winds puff their cheeks in the corners.

THE UNMAKING OF THE MEDIEVAL CHRISTIAN COSMOS, 1500–1760

From Solid Heavens
to Boundless Æther

W.G.L. Randles

Ashgate

Aldershot • Brookfield USA • Singapore • Sydney

© W.G.L. Randles, 1999

All rights reserved. No part of this publication may be reproduced, stored in a retrieval system, or transmitted in any form or by any means, electronic, mechanical, photocopying, recording, or otherwise without the prior permission of the publisher.

The author has asserted his right under the Copyright, Designs and Patents Act, 1988, to be identified as the Author of this work.

Published by
Ashgate Publishing Limited
Gower House, Croft Road
Aldershot
Hants GU11 3HR
United Kingdom

Ashgate Publishing Company
Old Post Road
Brookfield
Vermont 05036-9704
USA

British Library Cataloguing-in-Publication data

Randles, W.G.L.
   The unmaking of the medieval Christian cosmos, 1500–1760 : from solid heavens to boundless æther
   1.Creation 2.Creation – Philosophy 3.Cosmology, Medieval
   4.Creationism – Europe – History
   I.Title
   231.7'652'094'0903

Library of Congress Cataloging-in-Publication data

Randles, W.G.L.
   The unmaking of the medieval Christian cosmos, 1500–1760 : from solid heavens to boundless æther / W.G.L. Randles.
   Includes bibliographical references and index.
   1. Astronomy – Religious aspects – Catholic Church – History of doctrines. 2. Catholic Church – Doctrines. I. Title.
   BX1795.A82R36 1999
   261.5'5—dc21   98-39359
                    CIP

ISBN 1 84014 624 9

Typeset in Caslon by Manton Typesetters, 5–7 Eastfield Road, Louth, Lincs.
Printed and bound in Great Britain by MPG Books Ltd, Bodmin, Cornwall

Contents

List of illustrations		vi
Acknowledgements		viii
Introduction		x
1.	The medieval foundations of the Christian cosmos	1
2.	Renaissance and Reformation challenges to the medieval cosmos and the response of the Counter-Reformation	32
3.	The challenge of applied optics	58
4.	The reception of new astronomical evidence	80
5.	The challenge of infinity	106
6.	The Empyrean in the late Renaissance and the Baroque age	133
7.	The cosmos in university textbooks	151
8.	The impact of Cartesianism and Copernicanism and the end of the medieval cosmos	183
Conclusion		219
Bibliography		224
Index		263

List of illustrations

1. The medieval Ptolemaic universe in Juan de Celaya (c.1490–1558), *Expositio magistri ioannis de Celaya Valentini in quattuor libros de celo & mundi Aristotelis cum questionibus eiusdem*, Paris, 1518, f.xlii^r [=f.xxxviii^r]. Photo: Bibliothèque Mazarine, Paris.
   The Empyrean heaven is shown folllowed by the *Primum Mobile*, by the Aqueous or Crystalline heaven, by the Firmament of the Fixed Stars, by the heavens of Saturn, of Jupiter, of Mars, of the Sun, of Mercury, of Venus and of the Moon. Thereafter: the elementary spheres of the fire, the air, the water and the earth.   13
2. Engraving of Robert Bellarmine, S.J. (1542–1621). Photo: Bibliothèque Nationale, Paris.   45
3. Tycho Brahe (1546–1601). Engraving in Tycho Brahe, *Epistolarum astronomicarum libri*, edn Frankfurt, 1610, frontispiece. Photo: Bibliothèque Nationale, Paris.   65
4. The type of instrument used by Tycho Brahe to measure solar and stellar refraction. Engraving in Joan Blaeu, *Le Grand Atlas ou Cosmographie Blaviane*, Amsterdam, 1663, vol.I. Photo: Bibliothèque Nationale, Paris.   66
5. Engraving of Christoph Clavius, S.J. (1538–1612). Photo: Bibliothèque Nationale, Paris.   91
6. The Tychonic geo-heliocentric astronomical system first expounded by Tycho Brahe, *De Mundi Ætherei Recentioribus Phænomenis liber secundus*, Uraniborg, 1588. The Supercelestial Waters and the Empyrean were dropped by Tycho, but were later restored by the Jesuits. Diagram in Melchior Cornäus, S.J. (1598–1665), *Curriculum philosophiæ peripateticæ*, Herbipoli, [Würzburg], 1657, p.528. Photo: Bibliothèque Municipale de Bordeaux. The earth is shown in the centre of the universe with the sphere of the fixed stars concentric to it. Above them are the Supercelestial Waters and above them the Empyrean. The planets revolve round the sun which itself revolves round the earth. Jupiter is shown with its satellites.   96

7. The Copernican heliocentric astronomical system first expounded by Nicolaus Copernicus (1473–1543), *De Revolutionibus orbium cælestium libri VI*, Nuremberg, 1543. Diagram in Melchior Cornäus, S.J. (1598–1665), *Curriculum philosophiæ peripateticæ* (Herbipoli [Würzburg], 1657, p.527, Photo: Bibliothèque Municipale de Bordeaux.

The sun is placed, not as Copernicus had placed it *near* the centre of the universe, but as Kepler had put it, at the centre; the planets are shown with their periodic times of revolution and Jupiter is shown with its satellites. The Empyrean and the Supercelestial Waters were omitted by Copernicus. 134

Acknowledgements

The earlier chapters of this work were researched at the *Bibliothèque Nationale* in Paris, while I was attached to the *Ecole Pratique des Hautes Etudes, VIe Section* (later to become the *Ecole des Hautes Etudes en Sciences Sociales*). I owe profound gratitude to the late Professor Léon Bourdon of the Sorbonne for his help in the translation of the difficult Renaissance texts on which these chapters are based. Without his aid and the benefit of his unrivalled command of Latin, this book would never have taken the form it has. I nevertheless take full responsibility for the translations as they stand. Professor Pierre Costabel of the *Centre Koyré* was also good enough to give me occasional valuable and well-timed comments on the natural philosophical meanings in some of these texts.

My colleagues at the *Observatoire de Paris*, Michel-Pierre Lerner, Isabelle Pantin and Alain Segonds have been constant in making available their expert counsel and critical rigour. My especial gratitude goes to Michel-Pierre Lerner for his much-valued comments on the manuscript. His readiness to share his extensive knowledge of Renaissance astronomy and his familiarity with Italy and its libraries greatly facilitated my analysis of Italian writers.

The remaining chapters of the work were written in the Bordeaux region, when in 1991 under the aegis of Professor Joseph Perez, its founder and first Director, I became attached to the *Maison des Pays Ibériques* at the University of Bordeaux III. My colleagues at this unique little research institute, Professors Bernard Lavallé, Jean-Pierre Dedieu and François Guichard, offered me an hospitable welcome and much kindness. My sincere thanks for their attentive help go to the staff of the University Library of the University of Bordeaux III and especially to those responsible for the rapid and efficient inter-library loan service.

The Bordeaux Municipal Library's extraordinarily rich holdings of works of the sixteenth and seventeenth centuries provided the greater part of the research resources for more than half the book. My warmest gratitude is expressed to Madame Hélène de Bellaigue, *Conservateur de la Salle du Patrimoine*, for her ever-ready help in tracking down information on obscure research problems and for obtaining microfilms and photocopies of works in other provincial libraries through her many professional contacts in them. The cheerful helpfulness of her staff made working there an experience rarely encountered elsewhere.

For the sections on Spain, Professor Victor Navarro Brotóns of the University of Valencia is thanked for his kindness in forwarding to me copies of his works and articles, especially on Tosca. To Professor François Lopez of the University of Bordeaux III, I am grateful for his counsel and help on seventeenth- and eighteenth-century Spain.

For the sections on Portugal, I remember the spontaneous kindness of the late Professor Luís de Albuquerque of the University of Coimbra in introducing me to the work of Borri. Gratitude is expressed to Dr Inácio Guerreiro for his kindness in obtaining for me photocopies of numerous articles on Cartesianism in Portugal and to Dr Francisco Contente Domingues for his bringing to my attention the work of Teodoro de Almeida.

I am grateful to the Presses Universitaires de France for permission to present in Chapter 8 material originally published as 'Le ciel chez les jésuites espagnols et portugais (1590–1651)', in Luce Giard (ed.), *Les jésuites à la Renaissance. Système éducatif et production du savoir*, Paris, 1995, pp.129–44.

Introduction

The foundations of the medieval Christian cosmos[1] linking the Creation in Genesis to the astronomical system of Antiquity were laid in the early Christian centuries and slowly consolidated during the Early Middle Ages. Three interrelated features dominate the medieval Christian cosmos: first the Empyrean, a theological concept; second the Firmament, a Biblical one (assimilated to the sphere of the fixed stars); and third the physical nature of the space in which revolved the seven planets. The prime intention of this work is to analyse the changing perceptions of these features over the long medieval period and their slow transformation in the Counter-Reformation Tridentine culture of the seventeenth century, which is here defined as the Baroque age.

With the recovery of the works of Aristotle from the late twelfth century onward, scholastic theologians set themselves the task of integrating the Stagyrite's natural philosophy with Christian doctrine, the result of which became the monumental philosophical construction of the Later Middle Ages. During the Renaissance, the reinterpretation by theologians of Hebrew meanings in the text of Genesis, coupled with the resuscitation of Neoplatonic and Stoic doctrines, led to a re-ordering of the medieval cosmos in which the Aristotelian adjunction was significantly reduced and the matter of the heavens, previously held to be solid, was admitted to be fluid in nature. On their own account, Reformation Protestants in northern Europe set about pruning the medieval heritage of parts of the Aristotelian component. In the late sixteenth century, again in a challenge to Aristotelian doctrine, astronomers in northern Europe adduced evidence for the fluid nature of the heavens from the observation of the refraction of light rays from stars. Throughout Europe generally, other astronomers claimed to offer similar proof from their observations of the behaviour of comets and *novae*.

---

[1] For the medieval period it has seemed more appropriate to translate the Latin *mundus* by 'cosmos', rather than by 'universe' or 'world'. In the Renaissance, the two latter terms become current and will be used from Chapter 5 on.

Although met with an obstinate rearguard resistance from certain traditionalist natural philosophers, the conclusions of these important figures were to lend convergent support to ancient Greek doctrines of an infinite cosmos resuscitated by Italian philosophers in defiance of medieval Christian tradition, doctrines in which the corporeal and the incorporeal were allowed to interpenetrate. During the same period in southern Catholic Europe, while significantly modified by a partial recognition of the astronomers' claims, a revival of the Aristotelian paradigm in the 'Second Scholasticism' of the Counter-Reformation found its place in the seventeenth century in the flowering of the Baroque spirit, a development which further accentuated the cleavage between the religious culture of the Protestant north and that of the Catholic south. With the close of the seventeenth century, the spread of Cartesianism across Catholic Europe from the Netherlands and France, allied to an ever-widening consensus in favour of the Copernican system, finally sealed the fate of the medieval cosmos.

Although the irreconcilability of the two sources of spiritual and intellectual energy drawn on for the construction of the medieval cosmos – the message of the Bible and the understanding of nature accomplished in Greek Antiquity – is the principal assumption of this book, it is in no way meant to confer a judgement implying failure. Rather it was the clever balancing of the irreducible nature of their respective discourses by generations of scholars that enabled the Christian cosmos to survive for so many centuries.

If a programme of scientific rationalism has, from the eighteenth century onward, directed the course of European civilization with allegedly salutary consequences, it was the revealed truth of the Bible that, for the previous fifteen centuries, provided it with a life-giving myth without which no society can survive in the long run. Since the eighteenth century the rôle of religion has gradually ceased to provide European society with a minimal common sense of identity, being relegated to serve, according to individual choice, as a guide to private behaviour only. The failure in this century of the scientific method to guarantee collective harmony, or to provide meaning and direction to the inner life of the individual, suggests that a long-span overview of the relations between religion and science, in the context of cosmology over the centuries during which European civilization was moulded to receive its distinctive characteristics, might help to bring out new questions on how belief and reason can be brought to coincide, if only for a time.

This work seeks to trace the historical relations of religion and science in the wider context of European culture, treating each of the major components of the medieval cosmos – Biblical myth, astronomy and natural philosophy – in its own right, respecting the legitimate discourse of each. These three have been placed as much as possible on an equal footing, reflecting the way in which they were generally received, even if in certain institutions and in certain periods they were accorded unequal emphasis. Anything like the construction of the linear development of a single idea has been avoided. Rather than a history of the discipline of astronomy or of theoretical cosmology, it is the history of the idea of the heavens in Europe that has been attempted, especially that of Catholic Europe, less well known than that of the Protestant countries. It is an account of the way in which a certain aspect of a culture evolved that has been aimed at, rather than the disembodied history of the origins and development of a method of representing nature. In order to bring the reader as close as possible to penetrating the minds of the authors studied, where it has been deemed necessary, extensive quotations are given together with crucial phrases added in the original Latin. Thus it is hoped that their often unfamiliar cultural make-up can be more directly appreciated than if their thought were merely paraphrased or interpreted. Seemingly awkward authors or those whose work appears dated for the time at which they wrote, often frequently reprinted, have been given a place as, without the background they provide, those who are later seen to have been leading the way cannot be evaluated for what they represented in their time.

Deliberately avoided has been the approach which consists of seeing the history of European cosmology as the history of the 'scientific revolution', a story of the progressive triumph, from the sixteenth century on, of the heliocentric doctrine of Copernicus against the conservative opposition of the Catholic Church. Instead of the classic theme of experimental science calling into question theological dogma, emphasis has rather been given to alternative theological and philosophical doctrines regarding the nature of the heavens that were invoked to legitimize the evidence of new astronomical observations. For the wider public, the Copernican system was only to achieve general acceptance in the eighteenth century. The crucial test of observed stellar parallax had still to wait for Friedrich Wilhelm Bessel (1784–1846) to measure it in 1838.[2]

The first two chapters study theologians and their changing views on the heavens. The third concentrates on practical astronomers and their inputs of new evidence on the nature of the heavens. The fourth analyses the reactions of natural philosophers, theologians and other astronomers to the new astronomical evidence. The fifth recounts the clash of non-Christian philosophies with the traditional scholastic view of the heavens. The sixth discusses representations of the spiritual Empyrean heaven in the seventeenth century. The last two chapters deal with the changing views on the heavens as taught in the universities and as reflected in works destined for the general lettered public.

---

[2] John North, *The Fontana History of Astronomy and Cosmology* (London, 1994), pp.415–420.

Chapter 1 focuses on two themes fundamental to the understanding of the crisis of the medieval cosmos that began in the Renaissance. The first defines three basic models of the cosmos found in writers of the early Christian centuries, a theological one, a Neoplatonic one and an astronomical one. These models, though mutually contradictory, were alternatively turned to or in later periods separate features chosen from them were combined to form new models. The second theme focuses on Aristotelian influence in the treatment by medieval theologians of the hexaëmeral tradition from the twelfth century onward. The medieval Aristotelianization of the cosmos is reviewed in detail for in it lay the roots of the future cosmological crisis of the Renaissance. Analysed in particular are the identification of Aristotle's fifth essence with the supposedly solid Supercelestial Waters of Genesis and the transformation of the Neoplatonic concept of an outer Empyrean spiritual heaven into a solid Aristotelian 'place' housing the Blessed, with all the problems it raised. The parallel Franciscan tradition of Neoplatonic light metaphysics is not touched on since there was no significant continuation of it beyond the Renaissance. Nor are the rôles of Ptolemaic kinematic astronomy or Arabic philosophy discussed, since they are not germane to the main theme considered.

Chapter 2 shows how Reformation and Renaissance theologians, dissatisfied with a now ossified Aristotelianism, turned to a fresh philological exegesis of the Creation story and, incorporating with it revived Stoic and Neoplatonic ideas, replaced the scholastic doctrine of solid heavens with one asserting them to be fluid. While Protestants and Catholics are together seen to recognize the fluid nature of the planetary heavens, the reality of the Empyrean heaven, rejected by the majority of Protestants, is maintained by Catholics far into the Baroque age. The onset of the abandonment of solid planetary heavens, a major turning point in the progressive dismantlement of the medieval scholastic cosmos, is thus shown to be attributable rather to theologians than to astronomers.

Chapter 3 examines the claim by the optician Jean Pena that medieval optical theory contradicted the scholastic doctrine of solid heavens and shows how the astronomers Tycho Brahe and Christoph Rothmann proved with their unique instruments that the heavens were fluid, thus corroborating the views of the Renaissance theologians. From the results of their observations Kepler is shown to have developed his concept of a fluid æther.

Chapter 4 examines the contrasting reception of the new ideas on the heavens during the acute crisis over the nature of the heavens that divided natural philosophers, theologians and astronomers across Europe in the early seventeenth century. A deliberately wide range of authors is presented running from the extreme of those blindly refusing the evidence of astronomers in their obdurate attachment to Aristotelian scholasticism, to those whose committed *a priori* anti-Aristotelianism led them to see in the evidence of astronomers no obstacle to an infinite cosmos. Trapped in this crisis, the Jesuits, divided among themselves, are seen to have opted for a solution of limited credibility.

Chapter 5 deals with the destructive impact on the Aristotelian foundations of the medieval cosmos delivered by the heterodox philosophies of infinity resuscitated from Antiquity by Renaissance philosophers. While offering simultaneous comparisons with minor figures as well as opposing ones, the chapter focuses essentially on the five major figures of Bruno, Patrizzi, Descartes, Gassendi and Newton and how they defined the nature of the space in which the planetary system lay. While the Catholic Church silenced only the first two, a continuity is shown linking Bruno to Descartes, Patrizzi to Gassendi and finally through More to Newton.

Chapter 6 first reviews comments by Protestant Copernican astronomers on the incompatibility of the doctrine of heliocentrism with the concept of the Empyrean and, second, describes the evolving image of the Empyrean in the writings of Catholic theologians of the Baroque age.

Chapter 7 examines the textbooks of natural philosophy used in universities in the Baroque age to teach the lettered élite of Catholic Europe. Examples of textbooks from the beginning, middle and late seventeenth century show the tardy manner in which the new evidence of astronomers was slowly incorporated. As the fluidity of the heavens became gradually accepted, there remained as the sole guarantee of a finite universe the Empyrean, a theological concept.

Chapter 8 examines examples of university textbooks of natural philosophy and general works on science published in the Latin Catholic countries from the late seventeenth century to the middle of the eighteenth, showing how, in spite of the Church's resolute opposition, the challenges of Descartes' indefinitely extended universe and Copernicus' heliocentric system were together regarded with increasing favour across the whole of Europe. Only after the middle of the eighteenth century are the authorities in Rome finally seen to lift the ban on the teaching of heliocentrism and the postulate of an infinite universe, thus bringing the medieval cosmos to a formal end. The Empyrean as a reality had already disappeared.

In the case of the last two chapters it is obvious that the criterion of what was officially taught in the universities may not necessarily reflect the culture of what might be termed the common reader, but a distinction can certainly be made between the public culture transmitted by recognized institutions and the contestatory culture of informal academies and networks of scholars, of a necessarily restricted reach, however lively and annunciative of the future they proved to be.

Though disciplines in the Middle Ages, whether theology, astronomy or natural philosophy, were recognizably distinct (and much effort has been spent in presenting them as separate subjects), there can always be found a constant concern running through the entire period to pull them together into a coherent framework to represent the culture as a whole. Identification of the latter has been our constant aim. Consideration of the polemics surrounding the reception and cultural consequences of the invention of the telescope, a subject already carefully studied, has been passed over, the crucial astronomical revision in the conception of the nature of the heavens having been accomplished by Tycho Brahe and Christoph Rothmann using traditional instruments of great size, constructed well before the invention of the telescope. Galileo's telescopic observations served essentially to confirm and publicize in a spectacular manner the breakthrough already achieved by Tycho and Rothmann. The fluid nature of the heavens having been demonstrated by the latter, Galileo's principal contribution was to furnish evidence that they were corruptible.

1

The medieval foundations of the Christian cosmos

> In principio creavit Deus cælum et terram. [...]
> Et Spiritus Dei ferebatur super aquas [...]
> Et fecit Deus firmamentum, divisitque aquas quae erant sub firmamento, ab his quæ erant super firmamentum [...]
> Vocavitque Deus firmamentum Cælum.
> Gen. 1: 1–8.

In the early Christian era any aim of achieving a rational compatibility between the revealed truth of the Bible and the principles of Greek science was held by some to be unthinkable. 'What', asked Tertullian (150/160–c.222), 'can there be in common between Athens and Jerusalem, between the Academy and the Church, between heretics and Christians?'[1] Yet throughout the whole long period of the Middle Ages, theologians and scholars were to apply intense effort to working out a plausible and coherent synthesis of the historical account of the Creation in the Book of Genesis and the structure of ancient Greek astronomy and physics. Within it lay the interface between the visible motions of the stars and planets and the invisible reality of the origins of the Creation according to Christian belief together with the place of man in the latter, both in life and after death. This construction proved to be the greatest triumph of medieval culture. By the end of the Renaissance, Tertullian's exclusionary conviction had come to be proved largely prophetic. Italian philosophers, Protestants, astronomers, and Cartesians had, in different directions but always in a claimed pursuit of truth, already gone far in unravelling the whole elaborately woven synthesis.

---

[1] Tertullian, 'De Præscriptionibus hæreticorum', VII 9, in *Tertulliani Opera*, Corpus Christianorum, Series Latina I (Turnhout, Belgium, 1954), p.193. On Tertullian see Johannes Quasten, *Initiation aux Pères de l'Eglise* (Paris, 1956), vol. II, pp.293–295: personality; pp.380–381: impossibility of reconciling faith and philosophy. Justo L. González, in defending Tertullian from the charge of being an anti-rationalist, sees 'Athens' in Tertullian's thought as referring to 'dialectical reason', 'Jerusalem' to 'historical reason'. See Justo L. Gonzáles, 'Athens and Jerusalem Revisited: Reason and Authority in Tertullian', *Church History* 43 (1974), pp.17–25, esp. p.22.

In southern, Tridentine Catholic, Europe, Baroque culture set itself to hold together the heritage of many centuries, but was eventually to be subverted by the new pre-Enlightenment philosophies spread from France.

The three early Christian models

This chapter focuses first on three models of the heavens aiming at a synthesis of Greek cosmology and the story of the Creation that emerged in the early Christian period: a theological one, a Neoplatonic one and an astronomical one. The three models are those of the author of the pseudo-Clementine *Recognitiones* (325–380), of Saint Basil (329–379) and of Isidore of Seville (c.570–636). The respective fortunes of these models fluctuated according to the favour accorded them by different groups or to the affinity of one or another with changing focuses of interest in different periods. The main body of the chapter concentrates on how, from the thirteenth century on, the influence of Aristotle's philosophy determined the way the heavens were represented mainly in works by Dominicans, but also in those of certain other theologians. The difficulties in accommodating Aristotelian principles with theological doctrine, particularly in relation to the spiritual heaven, are examined in the writings of the major figures of Robert Grosseteste, William of Auvergne, Albert the Great, Saint Thomas Aquinas, Giles of Rome and Alphonso de Tostado.[2]

The prime difficulty faced by the early Christian commentators on the Book of Genesis was in positioning the second heaven or Firmament created by God on the Second Day (*Et fecit Deus firmamentum [...] Vocavit Deus firmamentum Cælum*) in relation to the First Heaven of the First Day (*In principio creavit Deus cælum et terram*). To this was added the further problem of defining the material nature of the barrier formed by the Firmament to 'divide the waters which were below it from those that were above it' (*divisitque [Deus] aquas quae erant sub firmamento, ab his quæ erant super firmamentum*).

The first of the three models appears in the pseudo-Clementine *Recognitiones*, a mid-fourth-century work which reached the West in Rufinus' Latin translation from the Greek, of the late fourth century.[3] In it we find the Firmament of 'solid ice made hard as crystal' (*gelu concreta et crystallo*

---

[2] The medieval encyclopedia of the Dominican Vincent of Beauvais (1190–1264) has been left aside, as on the heavens the author merely compiles material taken from earlier theologians. The Franciscan theologians Alexander Hales (1170/80–1245) and Saint Bonaventure (1217–74) are not touched on as in their commentaries on the *Sentences* of Peter Lombard they do not discuss in detail the problems raised by the Aristotelianization of the medieval cosmos as do their fellow Dominicans.

[3] [Pseudo-Clement], *Die Pseudoklementinen, II Rekognitionen in Rufins Übersetzung*, ed. Bernhard Rehm (Berlin, 1965).

solidata), taking up all the space between the First Heaven and the earth (*in medio primi illius cæli terræque spatio*). Although the whole cosmos was a single dwelling, the Creator had divided it into two regions, an upper one for the angels and a lower one for men. Pseudo-Clement's justification for putting the planets as well as the fixed stars in the Firmament was that in Genesis on the Fourth Day of the Creation, God placed both the sun and the moon in the Firmament (*Dixit Deus fiant luminaria in firmamento cæli*).[4] Pseudo-Clement's text was taken up by the Venerable Bede (c.673–735) in his *Hexaëmeron*. Bede declared that '... the heaven of the celestial bodies (*sidereum coelum*) was made firm (*firmatum*) in the midst of the waters and nothing prevents us from believing that it was also made of water, for we know that it has as much firmness as crystalline stone (*cristallini lapidis*) ...'.[5] Bede ignored, just as pseudo-Clement had, the problem of how the celestial bodies were able to move freely in a solid Firmament. It was the pseudo-Clementine model as we shall see, integrated with Aristotle's concept of the heavens consisting of a fifth essence, that later provided the basis for the long-lived conviction that the spheres of the planets and fixed stars were hard and solid. When Renaissance astronomers were to demonstrate the untenability of this conviction, the cultural consequences in Europe were to prove immense.

The second of the early Christian models, that expounded by Saint Basil (329–379), was very different from the others and as regards the First Heaven was much influenced by Neoplatonism.[6] According to Saint Basil, the First Heaven (which in the Middle Ages came to be called the Empyrean), had existed already before the Creation in the form of incorporeal light. There

---

[4] *Ibid. Rec.* I 27, pp.23–24.

[5] Venerable Bede, 'Liber quatuor in principium Genesis ... I i 6–8,' in *Bedae Venerabilis Opera*, Corpus Christianorum, Series Latina, CXVIIIA, Pars II I (Turnhout, Belgium, 1967), p.10. Raban Maur (776–856), following Bede, considered the Firmament to be made of rock crystal. See Raban Maur, 'Commentaria in Genesim', in Migne, *Pat. Lat.* vol.111, col.449. Saint Jerome (340/2–420) had previously declared that the Firmament was of a crystalline material originating from the waters; (Saint Jerome, *Commentariorum in Ezechielem prophetam libri quatuordecim* I 1 20, in Migne, *Pat. Lat.* vol.25 col.29), cf. Ezek., 1: 22: 'The likeness of the Firmament above the heads of the living creatures was like the colour of an awesome crystal stretched out over their heads'. Theodoretus (393–466) had spoken of the Firmament as *condensata et consolidata* (Theodoretus, *Beati Theodoreti in loca difficili Scripturæ Sacræ quæstiones selectæ*, in Migne, *Pat. Grec.* vol.80 col.91) and Procopius of Gaza (c.460–c.530) had written of the waters above the heavens that they were of *crystallum vel aqua congelatam* (Procopius of Gaza, *Commentaria in Genesim*, I 6, in Migne, *Pat. Grec.* vol.87 I col.67). According to the sixteenth-century Italian theologian Agostino Steuco, the solidity of the heavens is a concept traceable as far back as Homer. See Agostino Steuco, *Cosmopoeia* (Lyons, 1535), p.70. Cf. Homer, *Iliad*, 5. 504; *Odyssey*, 3. 2.

[6] On Saint Basil's classical sources, Plato, Plotinus and the Stoics as well as Aristotle, see the Introduction by Stanislas Giet to the French edition of his Hexaëmeron, Basile de Césarée, *Homélies sur l'Hexaéméron*, Sources chrétiennes 26bis (Paris, 1968), pp.56–63.

was, declared Saint Basil, '... a certain condition, older than the birth of the world and proper to the supramundane powers, one beyond time, everlasting, without beginning or end. In it the Creator and Producer of all things perfected the works of His art, a spiritual light befitting the blessedness of those who love the Lord ...'.[7]

The postulation of an uncreated entity, existing before God's Creation and which was not God himself, was something very difficult for any Christian theologian to accept. Some, as we shall see, did accept it though they were to run into fierce opposition.

In the spiritual light of the First Heaven, Basil placed the souls of the Blessed: 'If, indeed, the damned are sent into the darkness outside,[8] certainly those who have performed acts deserving of approbation have their rest in the supramundane light'.[9] Basil is thus the first Christian writer to assign different localizations in the cosmos in after-life according to the merits of individuals, but his localization of the Blessed is not clearly identified with the First Heaven of the Creation, as would occur later.

Basil's other divergence from his contemporaries was on the subject of the Firmament, whose solid nature he rejected. 'And surely,' he wrote, 'we need not believe because [the Firmament] seems to have had its origin, according to the general understanding, from water, that it is like either frozen water or some such material which takes its origin from the percolation of moisture, such as is the crystalline rock which men say is remade from the excessive coagulation of the water. [...] Now we compare the Firmament to none of these things'.[10]

Declaring that the Firmament was simply the humid air of clouds, Basil conveniently reduced the physical heavens in Genesis to the hydrological cycle. 'Now, imagine some place [i.e. the Firmament] which tends to separate moisture, and lets the rare and filtered part pass through into the higher regions, but lets the coarse and earthy part drop below ...'.[11] For Saint Basil the Supercelestial Waters were no more than a part of this cycle. 'When Scripture says that the dew and the rain are brought from the heavens, we understand that they are from the waters which are appointed to occupy the region above'.[12]

---

[7] Saint Basil, *Exegetic Homilies*, Homily 1, 5, trans. by Sister Agnes Clare Way CDP (The Catholic University of America, Washington, DC, 1963), p.9. Greek text and French trans. in Basile de Césarée, *Homélies sur l'Hexaéméron*, *ed. cit.* pp.104–105.

[8] Cf. Matt. 22: 13.

[9] Saint Basil, Homily 2, 5, *ed. cit.* p.30. Gr. text and Fr. trans., *ed. cit.* pp.164–165. The Biblical reference later used to justify this Neoplatonic notion was 1 Tim. 6: 16, 'God inhabits an inaccessible light' (*lucem inhabitat inaccessibilem*).

[10] Idem. Homily 3, 4, p.43. Gr. text and Fr. trans., *ed. cit.* pp.208–211.

[11] Idem. Homily 3, 7, p.47. Gr. text and Fr. trans., *ed. cit.* pp.222–223.

[12] Idem. Homily 3, 8, p.50. Gr. text and Fr. trans., *ed. cit.* pp.232–233.

Saint Augustine (354–430), often quoted on this question of the waters above the heavens, merely reviewed Basil's opinion, cautiously avoiding committing himself on whether the Supercelestial Waters had a hard or an airy nature.[13]

Rejecting Aristotle's fifth essence allowing 'even and unforced motion',[14] Basil sidestepped the problem of friction retarding the motion of celestial bodies in his Firmament of air by simply aligning himself with Plato in noting of the seven planets that '... when they cleave through the ether [sic], [they] give out such a melodious and harmonious sound that it surpasses the sweetest of singing'.[15] Aristotle, by contrast, had said that, if the planets 'moved in either air or fire', the friction would 'create a noise that would inevitably be tremendous, [...] shattering things on earth'.[16] The exact nature of celestial matter, the properties attributed to it by natural philosophers and those required of it for different reasons by theologians and astronomers, became a continually debated problem throughout the period dealt with here.

The Basilian model of the nature of the Firmament was followed by few medieval scholars and then only in the twelfth century; thereafter it disappears until revived in the Renaissance under the influence of the renewal of Neoplatonism. Among those few scholars who did adopt the Basilian model of the Firmament were Rupert of Deutz (c.1070–1129/1130) in his work on the Trinity,[17] Thierry of Chartres (?–c.1156)[18] and William of Conches (1080–c.1154),[19] in their commentaries on Genesis. None of them, however, followed Basil's definition of the First Heaven as incorporeal light.

---

[13] Saint Augustine, 'De Genesi ad litteram libri duodecim. La Genèse au sens littéral (Livres 1–VII)', Latin text and Fr. trans., by P. Agaësse and A. Solignac, *Œuvres de Saint Augustin*, 48 7ᵉ Série: Exégèse, Bibliothèque Augustinienne (Paris, 1972), Liber Secundus, IV, 7–V, 9, pp.156–161 and note p.596. Basil is not explicitly named in Augustine's text, but is referred to as a *quidam*.

[14] Saint Basil, Homily 1, 11, *ed. cit.* pp.18–19. Gr. text and Fr. trans., *ed. cit.* pp.133–135.

[15] Idem. Homily 3, 3, *ed. cit.* p.41. Gr. text and Fr. trans., *ed. cit.* pp.200–201. On Plato's concept of celestial music see Pierre Duhem, *Le système du monde* (Paris, 1913–58), vol. II, pp.8–9.

[16] Aristotle, *On the Heavens [De Cælo]*, II X 291a, ed. Guthrie, p.197.

[17] Rupert of Deutz, 'In Genesim', in *De Trinitate et operibus eius*, Corpus Christianorum Continuatio Medievalis, ed. H. Haacke, XXI (1971), I 22, p.151 (*Firmamentum non solidum quid, aut durum, ut vulgo putatur, sed aer est extensus*).

[18] Thierry of Chartres, 'Magister Theodorici Carnotensis Tractatus', in N. Haring, 'The Creation and Creator of the World according to Thierry of Chartres and Clarenbaldus of Arras', *Archives d'histoire doctrinale et littéraire du Moyen Age* 30 (1955), p.187. See also N. Haring in *art. cit.* p.148.

[19] William of Conches, *De philosophia mundi*, II 6, in Migne, *Pat. Lat.* vol.172, col.59. Mistakenly attributed to Honorius Augustodunensis by Migne. See P. Duhem, *Le système du monde*, vol.III, p.90.

The third model appears in the *De rerum natura* of Isidore of Seville. For Isidore, during the first two days of the Creation, three major operations took place: the creation, on the First Day, of the First Heaven at the same time as that of the Earth; then on the Second Day, the second heaven of the Firmament created in order to separate the Waters of below from the Waters of above; finally the Supercelestial Waters above the Firmament. These three operations became three heavens placed one above the other over the spheres of the seven planets of the classic geocentric cosmos.[20] Isidore of Seville is the first Christian writer to relate the account of the Creation in Genesis to the planetary system of Antiquity in clear terms.[21] In the First Heaven, added Isidore, God 'placed the Virtues of the spiritual creatures (*virtutes spiritalium creaturarum*)'.[22] In this expression can be found in outline what later became in the Latin West the Empyrean of the Saints and of the Blessed. The second heaven, the Firmament was, according to Isidore, 'consolidated' by God who also gave to the Supercelestial Waters the 'solidity of ice'.[23] In saying that the spheres of the planets were 'fitted together and encased into one another and carried in a reverse direction from the other stars' (*sibi innexos et velut insertos versari retro et e contrario ceteris*), Isidore implied that the planets were carried by their spheres, though he added nothing specific about the physical nature of the latter.[24]

Later astronomers, such as Michael Scot (1175?–1234?)[25] and Campanus of Novara (c.1205–96),[26] identified the Firmament with the eighth sphere of

---

[20] Isidore of Seville, *De rerum natura*, ed. Jean Fontaine with Fr. trans. (Bordeaux, 1960), #XIII, p.225.

[21] Saint Ambrose (c.340–397) does refer to the stars, the sun and the moon in his Hexaëmeron, but he does not relate them to the Genesis story as specifically as Isidore does. Cf. Saint Ambrose, *Hexameron*, in Migne, *Pat. Lat.* vol.14, col.147b '... *philosophi quinque stellarum et solis et lunae globorum consonum motum introduxerunt* '.

[22] Isidore of Seville, *op. cit.* #XIII, p.225. Isidore borrowed this idea, though without the astronomical context he was to give it, from Hilary of Poitiers (c.315–c.367) (*Tractatum super psalmos*, in Migne, *Pat. Lat.* vol.9, col.773a), who in turn drew on Saint Basil. On Isidore's sources and the implicit continuity between the material and spiritual worlds in this passage, see Jacques Fontaine, *Isidore de Séville et la culture classique dans l'Espagne wisigothique*, Etudes Augustiniennes (Paris, 1983), vol.II, pp.543–549.

[23] Isidore of Seville, op. cit. #XIII and #XIV, pp.225–227.

[24] *Ibid.* #XIII, p.223.

[25] Michael Scot, 'Super auctore spere cum questionibus', in John of Holywood (Johannes de Sacrobosco), ed. Lynn Thorndike, *The Sphere of Sacrobosco and its commentators* (Chicago, 1949), p.283. ('The first heaven is called by the theologians the Empyrean. [...] The second heaven is called the ninth sphere and by the theologians the Crystalline. [...] The third heaven is the eighth sphere [...] The fourth is equivalent to the seven heavens of the seven planets'.)

[26] Campanus of Novara, *Tractatus de sphera*, ed., (Florence, 1518), cap. XII, ff.153^v–154^r. ('The rigour of scholarly reasoning and the truth of Divine Scripture oblige us to say that there

the fixed stars and the 'Crystalline Sphere' of the Supercelestial Waters above it with a ninth astronomical sphere, called by the English astronomer John of Holywood (Johannes de Sacrobosco) (c.1190–c.1236) the *Primum Mobile*.[27] These, together with the First Heaven of the First Day of the Creation above and the seven planets below, produced, according to the first two writers, the often-quoted total of the ten spheres of the medieval cosmos of astronomers. In contrast to the Isidorian model adopted by astronomers, medieval natural philosophers, especially after the recovery of Aristotle's works in the West from the later twelfth century onward, tended to follow the pseudo-Clementine model.

The Empyrean in medieval thought

The first to use the word *Empyrean* (a term nowhere to be found in the Bible) to describe the place of the Blessed in the Christian cosmos[28] was the author of the *Glossa ordinaria*. For long attributed to Walafrid Strabon (ninth cent.), the work has been shown to have been actually compiled by Anselm of Laon (c.1050–1117).[29] 'In the beginning', wrote Anselm, 'God created Heaven and Earth. Heaven is not the visible Firmament, but the Empyrean.'[30] Anselm of Laon borrowed the word *Empyrean* from the fifth-century pagan Neoplatonic writer Martianus Capella, who had written of 'an empyrean realm of pure understanding' lying 'beyond the sphere which bounds (*coercet*) the farthest perimeter (*ambitum ultimum*)'.[31] Peter Lombard (died

---

are at least ten celestial spheres, that is to say the Empyrean heaven, the Crystalline, the Firmament and the seven spheres of the planets. If one adds the four elements, there are in the whole of the universe fourteen spheres.')

[27] John of Holywood (Johannes de Sacrobosco), *Tractatus de spera*, ed. Lynn Thorndike, *op. cit.*, p.119. The origin of this ninth sphere goes back to Ptolemy's *Planetary Hypotheses*. Cf. Michel-Pierre Lerner, *Le monde des sphères*, vol.I, *Genèse et triomphe d'une représentation cosmique* (Paris, 1996), p.205.

[28] The absence of the term in the Bible was remarked on by Cardinal Cajetan (Thomas de Vio) (1469–1534) in his commentary on Saint Paul's second Epistle to the Corinthians, 'In posteriorem Pauli Epistolam ad Corinthios commentarii', in idem, *Opera Omnia* (Lyons, 1639), vol.V, p.195. On Cajetan's approach to Biblical criticism see Guy Bedouelle, in Guy Bedouelle and Bernard Roussel, eds, *Le temps des Reformes et la Bible* (Bible de tous les temps), (Paris, 1989), vol.V, pp.111–114 and pp.335–336. Certain writers found justification in the Bible for representing the Empyrean as a place by quoting Christ's words in John 14: 2 : 'I go to prepare a place for you' (*Vado parare vobis locum*).

[29] Cf. Gregor Maurach, 'Coelum Empyreum, Versuch einer Begriffsgeschichte', in *Boethius* VIII (Wiesbaden, 1968), p.14.

[30] [Anselm of Laon], 'Glossa ordinaria', in Migne, *Pat. Lat.* vol.113, col.68.

[31] Martianus Capella, *De Nuptiis Philologiae et Mercurii*, ed. A. Dick (Leipzig, 1925), II, 200–203, p.76; Cf. also Eng. trans., 'The Marriage of Philology and Mercury', in W.H. Stahl and Richard Johnston, *Martianus Capella and the Seven Liberal Arts*, vol.II (New York, 1977), pp.60–61.

1164), in his widely read work of *Sentences*, helped to spread the concept of the Empyrean throughout the culture of the Latin West where it became a recognized feature of the medieval cosmos.[32]

Although the Empyrean had thus come to be identified with the First Heaven created on the First Day of the Creation, one finds up to this point no specific opinions concerning its material nature. But towards the end of the twelfth century the recovery in the Latin West of the works of Aristotle had a crucial impact on this question, as well as on medieval cosmology as a whole, displacing the previous Neoplatonic approach.

Aristotle, in his work *On the Heavens [De Cælo]*, had affirmed the closed nature of the world which for him contained all existing matter. Outside his heaven there could be 'neither place, nor void, nor time'.[33] Thus through the influence of Aristotle's thought, the Empyrean came to be generally accorded by scholars the rôle of constituting the limit separating the medieval cosmos from that which was not part of it. The interior of the cosmos between the earth and the moon was occupied by the four elements (earth, water, air and fire). From and including the moon, the cosmos was filled with a fifth element, which Aristotle only defined in negative terms: 'ungenerated and indestructible, [...] ageless, inalterable and impassive'.[34] Its properties were so conceived that it enabled the motion of the celestial bodies to take place in it without any friction. Medieval scholars were to allow themselves the temptation to identify not only the Supercelestial Waters of the Creation, but also the physical interior of the Empyrean heaven itself with this incorruptible fifth element, an adventure that led to endless problems. With Aristotle's encyclopædia came the terms *corpus* (body) and *locus* (place), together with his complicated theory of their mutual relationship,[35] as well as that of the *Primum Mobile* or First Mover giving motion to the stars and planets.[36]

Robert Grosseteste

Robert Grosseteste (1175–1253), an English Franciscan who became Bishop of Lincoln in 1235, sought to reconcile his attachment to the waning fortunes of Saint Basil with the growing vogue for Aristotle's doctrines. In his *Hexaëmeron*, written between 1228 and 1235, he evoked two alternative

---

[32] Peter Lombard (Magistri Petri Lombardi), *Sententiae in IV libris distinctae*, lib.II, dist.II, cap.4, Spicilegium Bonaventurianum, ed. PP. Collegii S. Bonaventurae Ad Claras Aquas, Grottaferrata (Rome, 1971), vol.I, pars II, pp.339–340.

[33] Aristotle, *On the Heavens [De Cælo]*, I IX 278a–279a, *ed. cit.* p.91.

[34] *Ibid.* I III 270a–270b, *ed. cit.* p.23.

[35] Cf. P. Duhem, *Le système du monde*, vol.I, pp.198–205.

[36] *Ibid.* pp.174–177.

interpretations of the nature of the First Heaven of the First Day of the Creation. In the first interpretation, he identified the First Heaven with Saint Basil's supramundane light 'in which [...] is the dwelling of the Blessed (*beatorum habitacio*)'. In this identification he saw no apparent contradiction with Aristotle's doctrine of a finite cosmos whose definition he quoted in the same breath.[37] For his second interpretation of the heaven of the First Day, he made it, on the basis of quotations from Josephus and Gregory of Nyssa, the equivalent of the pseudo-Clementine model by which the First Heaven and the Firmament were held to be the same. Declaring that it was not for him to decide the controversy between these authors, Grosseteste nevertheless noted of the first interpretation that, if the heaven of the First Day were different from the Firmament, it would appear to be immobile, an immobility that made it fitting to be the place and dwelling of the Saints (*locus et habitacio Sanctorum*).[38] His calling it thus a place (*locus*) suggests that he leaned more to an intramundane concept of the Empyrean rather than to a Basilian one.

Regarding the nature of the Firmament, Grosseteste showed a similar hesitation. He first quoted the Basilian interpretation of it, declaring that some believed it to be cloudlike vapour, while others held it to be of an icy solidity. 'Philosophers', he said, 'wrote things contrary to one another on this subject. Some said the Firmament consisted of fire, others that it consisted of the fifth essence (*quintum corpus*)'. Either because he felt unable to settle for one or another of these solutions or because the subject did not greatly interest him, Grosseteste concluded that 'dealing with these controversies and arguments would be lengthy and tedious for our readers and for the present purpose it does not seem to be very necessary'.[39]

William of Auvergne

Aristotle's influence appears much more pronouncedly in the work of William of Auvergne (Guilielmus Alvernus) (1180–1248).[40] Born at Aurillac in the Auvergne, he was also known as William of Paris (Guilielmus Parisiensis), having become Bishop of Paris in 1228. In his work *De Universo* (written

---

[37] According to J.T. Muckle, Grosseteste used Eustathius' Latin translation of Saint Basil's *Hexaëmeron* and his translation of the passage in Aristotle's *De Caelo* on the finite nature of the cosmos is so far removed from the original Greek that it would appear to have been taken from a Latin trans. of an Arabic version. Cf. J.T. Muckle, 'Robert Grosseteste's use of Greek sources in his Hexaëmeron', *Medievalia et Humanistica* 3 (1945), pp.35–38.

[38] Robert Grosseteste, *Hexaëmeron*, particula prima, caps XVI–XVII, ed. Richard C. Dales and Servus Gieben O.F.M. Cap., Auctores Britannici Medii Aevi VI (Oxford, 1990), pp.74–77.

[39] *Ibid.* particula tertia, caps I–VI, pp.102–106.

[40] On William of Auvergne's knowledge of Aristotle's works, see P. Duhem, *op. cit.* vol.V, pp.270–271.

between 1231 and 1236) he refuted the Basilian interpretation of the nature of the Firmament as consisting of air and fire,[41] adopting in its place the pseudo-Clementine one, according to which the Firmament consisted of the 'abyss' or the waters of the deep in Genesis, stretching from the earth up to the Empyrean. Into it, he said, were inserted the nine mobile heavens. The waters comprising the Firmament, continued William, deferring to Aristotle, were 'made firm (*firmentur*)' by the 'firmness and stability (*firmitate ac stabilitate*) of the shape of the heaven (*cœlestis formae*), so that they were not subject to the change and corruption (*mutabilitate ac corruptioni*) which ordinary water and the lower bodies are subjected to'. 'Some', he added, 'have understood this firmness to be frozenness and a crystal-like hardness; others have called it simply coagulation.'[42]

'The First Heaven, called the Empyrean, was', said William, following Aristotelian doctrine, 'the highest place (*locus*) in the universe to be destined for a body (*corpus*).'[43] He then raised the 'difficult question' that 'if the Empyrean is a place of a corporeal nature (*locus corporalis*), it can only be filled with substantive bodies (*corporeis substantiis*). Spiritual substances (*spirituales substantiae*), since they have no corporeal magnitude (*magnitudinem corporalem*), cannot thus fill a place (*locum*)'. William of Auvergne was unable to find a better solution than that of a paradox: 'Since we know nothing about bodies in a spiritual habitat, likewise we know nothing about spiritual substances in a corporeal habitat.'[44] Promising that he would deal with the matter and provide his solution in a later chapter, he left the subject.

Rather than placing the Blessed inside the Empyrean where, because of its solidity, they could not breathe, or above it where there was no place (*locus*) for them to live, William propounded the very unusual idea of placing the Blessed in the Supercelestial Waters above the nine heavens. 'The waters which are above the nine heavens', he said, 'are not there in the form of the waters that lie here around us, but from them, the region covered by the Empyrean is made in such a manner that it is pleasant and salubrious and in every way suitable as a dwelling place for the Blessed.' Addressing his reader, he remarked: 'You are not unaware that fish live in water and cannot live in air, but in water is their life and that which keeps them alive. The contrary occurs in the case of men, who cannot live in water but only in air. So it is necessary for the region above the waters to be prepared and accommodated so that it acquires the salubrity of immortality and future uncorruptedness following the resurrection of the dead. It would thus seem

---

[41] William of Auvergne, 'De Universo Pars I', in idem. *Opera Omnia*, edn (Paris, 1704), vol.I, pars I, cap. XXXIV, p.629, col.1 and cap. XXXIX, p.634, col.1.
[42] *Ibid.* cap. XXXIV, p.629, col.1.
[43] *Ibid. loc. cit.* col.2.
[44] *Ibid.* p.630, col. 1.

more fitting for this region to be the dwelling place of the Blessed than the substance of the Empyrean heaven as some no doubt believe. For the solidity of the Empyrean heaven would not enable breathing. If men are to breathe in this life of beatitude, only a dwelling place between the ninth heaven and the Empyrean seems suitable for the status of the Blessed. Furthermore, the beauty and splendour of the Empyrean heaven makes it more worthy to be contemplated (*conspici*) than to be walked upon (*calcari*). Above the Empyrean heaven there is no place (*locus*) and thus no dwelling place (*habitatio*). Further, since this heaven is the roof of the whole universe (*tectum totius mundi*), it is not fitting for it to support the feet of the inhabitants, rather it should reach to their faces (*patere aspectibus*) and emerge above their heads (*supereminere capitibus*)'.[45]

William at this point gave no explanation on how breathing in water could be made any easier than in the solidity of the Empyrean. In a later chapter he said that out of the Supercelestial Waters was made an 'æthereal region (*regio ætherea*)' consisting of 'æther (*æther*)' for the Blessed to dwell in.[46] Having noted the solidity (*soliditas*), of the heavens,[47] and the opinion of the 'philosophers' that they were 'uncuttable and indivisible (*insecabiles et indivisibiles*)',[48] he now said of this æthereal dwelling place of the Blessed that '... the waters out of which its æther had been formed had necessarily passed successively through the stages of vapour, then air, to be finally 'transformed (*transivisse*) into fire or into a subtler and nobler body (*vel in ignem, vel in corpus subtilius, atque nobilius*)'.[49] William gave no explicit indication about the fluid or solid nature of this æther of his chosen dwelling-place for the Blessed. It could hardly have been solid, since the solidity of the Empyrean was his reason for placing them there. Nor did he say anything specific about the breathable nature of his æther.

In placing the Blessed in the region of the Supercelestial Waters, an idea ultimately traceable to Origen (c.185–c.254),[50] William was not alone. That he was obliged to abandon it becomes evident from a document dated 13 January 1241 in which he, together with the Chancellor of the University of Paris and the Masters of the Faculty of Theology, are found condemning ten errors attributed to a certain Friar Stephen, contrary to theological truth, one of which claimed that the glorified souls are not in the Empyrean heaven with the angels and the Blessed Virgin, but in the aqueous or crystalline

---

[45] *Ibid.* cap. XXXIX, p.634, col.1.
[46] *Ibid.* cap. XLII, p.642, col.2–p.643, col.1.
[47] *Ibid.* cap. XXXIX, p.633, col.2.
[48] *Ibid.* cap. XLIV, p.650, col.1.
[49] *Ibid.* cap. XLII, p.644, col.2.
[50] Cf. Origène, *Homélies sur la Genèse*, I,2, texte latin, trad. fr. et notes de Louis Doutreleau, S.J., Sources chrétiennes, No.7bis (Paris, 1976), p.31. (*Illius ergo aquae supernae participio, quae supra caelos esse dicitur, unusquisque fidelium caelestis efficitur*).

heaven. 'This error we firmly condemn for we believe that the Empyrean heaven is the corporeal place of the angels and the souls of the Blessed.'[51] William of Auvergne's entangled attempt to reconcile Aristotle's physics with the doctrine of the Resurrection may seem naive, but, as we shall see later, the problem was to exercise the minds of theologians-cum-natural philosophers continually over the centuries ahead.

Albert the Great

Albert the Great (Albertus Magnus) (c.1200–80) followed William of Auvergne as a purveyor of Aristotelianism in the West. Born in Lauingen in Bavaria, he studied in Padua and entered the Dominican Order in 1223.[52] The convoluted arguments in his numerous works show what Aristotelian doctrines were capable of engendering in the scholastic mind.[53] Seeking, like others, to achieve a synthesis of Genesis and Aristotle, he identified in his *Summa* the Crystalline sphere of the Supercelestial Waters with *Primum Mobile*.[54] Later scholars, it should be remembered, were to keep the two apart as separate heavens, thus increasing the number of spheres to eleven, such as are found in the diagrams published by Juan de Celaya (1518)[55] and by Petrus Apian (1524).[56] The Firmament, said Albert ambivalently, can be represented in two ways (*firmamentum dicitur duobus modis*): either the whole body of the fifth essence above the moon in which lay the ten heavens, of each of the seven planets, of the fixed stars, of the Crystalline Heaven, and of the Empyrean – and here he leaned to Aristotle and Isidore – or the whole solidified space lying between the waters above and the waters below (*firmamentum a firmitati standi et distinguendi inter aquas superiores et inferiores*) – and here he leaned to Genesis, pseudo-Clement and Bede.[57]

---

[51] H. Denifle and A. Chatelain, *Chartularium Universitatis Parisiensis*, vol.I (Paris, 1889), pp.171–172.

[52] See James A. Weisheipl O.P., 'The Life and Works of Saint Albert the Great', in idem, ed., *Albertus Magnus and the Sciences, Commemorative Essays, 1980*, Pontifical Institute of Medieval Studies (Toronto, 1980), pp.13–51.

[53] Of Roger Bacon's judgement of Albert's work that it was '... the confusion and destruction of wisdom, [...] filled with falsehoods and infinite vanities', Duhem observed that the comment was, 'in its violence not without insight' and that 'the study of his works hardly produced a better impression'. See P. Duhem, *Le système du monde*, vol.V, pp.413–414. See also more recently J.M.G. Hackett, 'The Attitude of Roger Bacon to the *Scientia* of Albertus Magnus', in J.A. Weisheipl O.P., ed., *Albertus Magnus and the Sciences, ed. cit.* pp.53–72.

[54] Albert the Great (Albertus Magnus), 'Summæ Theologiæ Pars secunda', tract. XI, qu. 52, mem. II, in idem., *Opera Omnia*, ed. A. Borgnet (Paris, 1895), vol. 32, p.555.

[55] Juan de Celaya, *Expositio magistri ioannis de Celaya Valentini in quattuor libros de celo & mundo Aristotelis cum questionibus eiusdem* (Paris, 1518), lib.II, f.xlii^r [=f.xxxviii^r].

[56] Petrus Apian, *Cosmographicus Liber* (Landshut, 1524), f.6.

[57] Albert the Great, *op. cit.* qu. 53, mem. I, art. I, *ed. cit.* p.559.

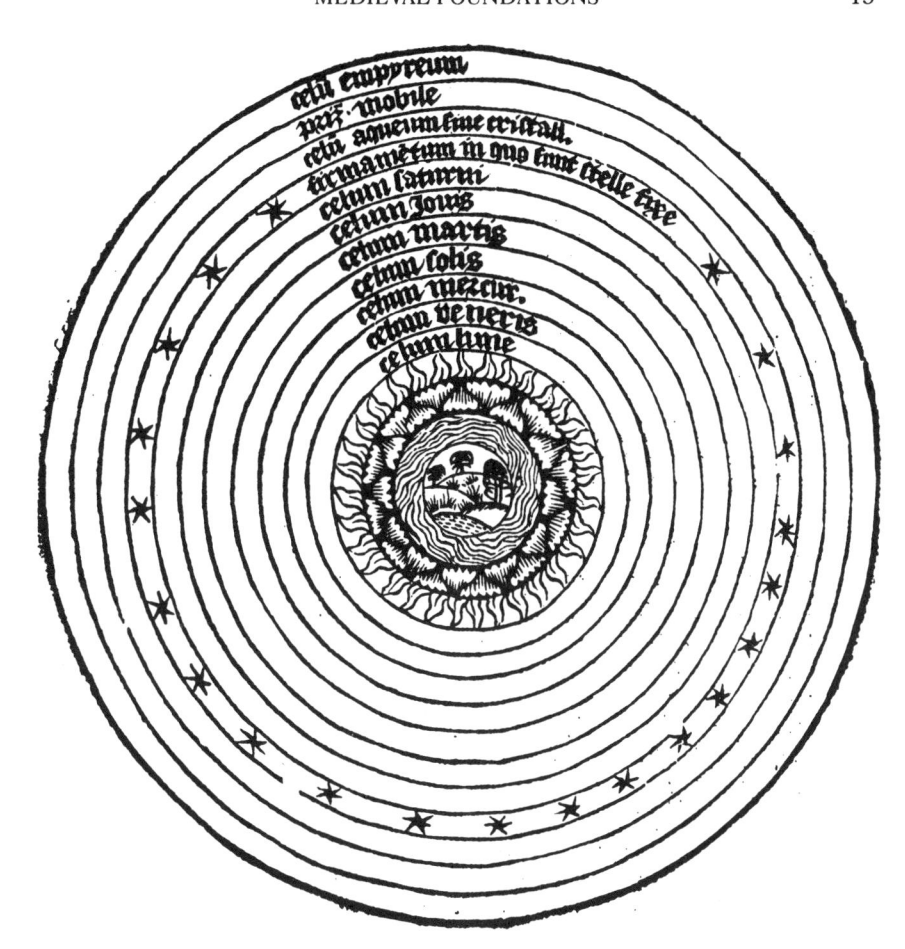

1   The medieval Ptolemaic universe in Juan de Celaya (c.1490–1558), *Expositio magistri ioannis de Celaya Valentini in quattuor libros de celo & mundi Aristotelis cum questionibus eiusdem* (Paris, 1518), f.xlii[r] [=f.xxxviii[r]]. Photo: Bibliothèque Mazarine, Paris.

The Empyrean heaven is shown followed by the *Primum Mobile*, by the Aqueous or Crystalline heaven, by the Firmament of the Fixed Starts, by the heavens of Saturn, of Jupiter, of Mars, of the Sun, of Mercury, of Venus and of the Moon. Thereafter: the elementary spheres of the fire, the air, the water and the earth.

Having at this point thus juxtaposed Christian belief and Greek science, Albert next proceeded to try, through scholastic argument, to conflate consolidated Biblical water with the Aristotelian fifth essence, by eliminating the elementary qualities of the former excepting its hardness (when reduced to crystal), though adding in at the same time some of the qualities of Neoplatonic light. 'It must be said then', he wrote, 'as it has been said before, that the heaven is not as Saint Augustine says of the nature of fluid water that flows downward [i.e. subject to gravity], but that it is made of a water, which because of the nature of its purity regarding its substance and because of the nature of its transparency regarding its material disposition and because of the nature of its luminosity regarding its depth, has, through this difference, been placed above the heavens, so that celestial things can exist as has been said already. And in this water there is nothing of an element, and the humid and the cold in it are not brought together in the making up of an element, but they are thrown together in a disorderly way as are all the other qualities. For this matter is not defined according to the shape of the heaven, but according to the purity, transparence and luminosity of its substance'.[58] The ambiguities created in this obscurely presented thinking were to be perpetuated by certain scholars far into the Baroque period.

Recalling the words of Saint Anselm (1033–1109) concerning the immensity of God ('God is that in relation to which it is not possible to imagine something greater'),[59] Albert realized, in his Commentary on the Sentences, that the Almighty could not be contained within the Empyrean, since it had now become an Aristotelian 'body (*corpus*)'.[60] He therefore added an eleventh heaven, the Heaven of the Trinity, in which he placed the Father, the Son and the Holy Ghost.[61] This notion he took from Anselm of Laon, who in turn gave Saint Jerome as his source,[62] but for Albert, though the Heaven of the Trinity (unlike the Empyrean) was not a body (*corpus*), it did contain itself and everything within it.[63] The majority of later writers, seeking simplification, tended to regard the Empyrean as the outermost heaven in the cosmos. Beyond it, from the time of Thomas Bradwardine (c.1290–1349) in

---

[58] *Ibid.* qu. 53, mem. I, art. II, p.563.
[59] Saint Anselm, 'Proslogion', in Migne, *Pat. Lat.* vol.158, col.227 (*Deus est id quo majus cogitari non potest*).
[60] Albert the Great, 'Commentaria in II Sententiarum', Dist.II H art. 7–8, in *ed. cit.* vol. 27, p. 57. (*Dicit Anselmus quod Deus est majus quam cogitari possit: ergo non ponitur aliquid ambiens ipsum: ergo nec cœlum corporeum.*) Cf. also the Biblical caution: 1 Kgs 8: 27, '*Behold, the heaven and the heaven of the heavens cannot contain you [God]*'.
[61] *Ibid.* pp.57–58.
[62] Anselm of Laon, 'Glossa ordinaria', in Migne, *Pat. Lat.* vol.113, col.69.
[63] Albert the Great, *op. cit. loc. cit.*

the fourteenth century, God alone was held to occupy an infinite imaginary space.[64]

Albert was nevertheless left with the insurmountable problem of the dual nature of Christ and here he resorted again to casuistry for an answer. 'It should be said', he wrote, 'that the person of Christ the man is in the Heaven of the Trinity, not according to his Human nature, but above all in relation to His most excellent qualities.'[65]

In a section of his Commentary on the Fourth Book of Peter Lombard's *Sentences*, Albert discussed how the Blessed could continue inside the Empyrean to enjoy the five senses of vision, hearing, smell, taste and touch.[66]

Vision

Beginning with the problem of vision, Albert responded to the argument that, since bodies in a state of glory will shine as brightly as the brightest part of the sun and that the eyes of these bodies will shine in the same way, so they will not be able to see visible objects, just as it is impossible for objects reflected in a mirror to be seen when the latter faces the sun.[67] Albert discussed an argument drawn from Euclid's *Perspectiva* [sic] [= *Optica*] that the distance at which an object is seen is proportionate to the size of the angle of vision and that beyond a given distance it is no longer visible on account of the decrease in the size of the angle.[68] From this Albert drew the conclusion that the eye of a body in the state of glory will thus be able to see no further than an eye not in the state of glory. This to him was absurd. Albert proposed two possible solutions, neither of which he regarded as being fully satisfactory. The first was the extramission theory according to which vision did not take place by the reception of light, but by the transmission of a *sensibilium species*, 'a species of things sensible'.[69] This raised three difficulties for natural philosophers: the first was that the sense of

---

[64] Cf. A. Koyré, 'Le vide et l'espace infini au XIVe siècle', *Archives d'histoire doctrinale et littéraire du Moyen Age* 24 (1949), pp.45–91, esp. p.51 and pp.82–83. See also Edward Grant, *Much Ado About Nothing* (Cambridge, 1981), chap. 6, §3.

[65] Albert the Great, *op. cit.* p.58. (*Ad aliud dicendum, quod persona Christi hominis in cælo Trinitatis est, sed non natura humana, sed potius in potioribus bonis.*)

[66] Idem. 'De sensibus corporis gloriosi', ed. F.M. Henquinet, 'Une pièce inédite du commentaire d'Albert le Grand sur le IVe livre des Sentences', *Recherches de théologie ancienne et médiévale* 7 (1935), pp.273–293.

[67] *Ibid.* p.279.

[68] Cf. Euclide, *L'Optique et la catoptrique*, Fr. trans. by Paul Ver Eecke (Paris, 1959), Propositions III and V, pp.3–4. As noted by Paul Ver Eecke, p. xvii, although physiologically true, the geometrical proof of Proposition III was illusory.

[69] On the complexity of the concepts covered by the term '*species*' in the Middle Ages, see Pierre Michaud-Quantin, *Etudes sur le vocabulaire philosophique du Moyen Age* (Rome, 1970), pp.113–150.

vision could take place equally well in a vacuum as in a plenum;[70] the second was that it could take place equally well along curved and circular lines as along straight ones; the third was that vision would occur equally well with the eyes shut as with them open. Because of these irrational consequences the extramission theory was an opinion to be refuted.[71] Albert concluded by defending the intromission theory which he said tied in better with what he called the *perspectiva naturalis*, the Aristotelian theory of vision.[72] He further asserted that in the Empyrean every visible object coming into sight will be brightened and will appear with greater clarity as a consequence of the brightness of the pupils of the eyes of the Blessed and that the latter will have an extremely clear vision for picking out visible objects. He did not think that the angle at which a thing was seen had anything to do with light, nor would it affect vision whatever the light might be.[73]

Voice and Hearing

Quoting Psalm 83: 5: *Beati qui habitant in domo tua, Domine, in sæcula sæculorum laudabunt te* ('The Blessed in your house, O Lord, shall praise you for ever and ever'), Albert took up the problem of how voiced praise of God could occur in the Empyrean where, given that voice cannot be produced without what Albert called in Aristotelian terms 'the breaking of air (*fractu aeris*)',[74] there would be no air capable of being divided. The air in the Empyrean, being 'glorified', will be 'indivisible and impassible' and 'not susceptible to being struck by force'. Thus there will be 'neither voice nor sound'. One solution, claimed by some, was that praise in the Empyrean would 'take place in the mind and not be vocal (*mentalis et non vocalis*)'. Another was that voice would be formed by the air already in the chests, throats and lungs of the Blessed. This was rejected by Albert on the grounds that either the air would have to leave the speaker to reach the hearer, or it would have to strike something else until, by continued percussion, it reached the hearer, or else it would remain inside the speaker. Given that the air did not return

---

[70] For Aristotle, light required a medium for its transmission. Cf. David Lindberg, *Theories of Vision from Al-Kindi to Kepler* (Chicago and London, 1976), pp.6–9 and Aristotle, *On the Soul [De Anima]*, II VII 419a, ed. Hett, p.107 ('... some medium must exist; in fact, if the intervening space were void, not merely would accurate vision be impossible, but nothing would be seen at all').

[71] Albert the Great, *op. cit. ed. cit.* p.281.

[72] *Ibid.* p.282. On Albert the Great and the establishment of the Aristotelian tradition on vision, see David C. Lindberg, *op. cit.* pp.104–107.

[73] Albert the Great, *op. cit. ed. cit.* p.283.

[74] Cf. Aristotle, *op. cit.* II VIII 420b, *ed. cit.* p.117. ('Since sound only occurs when something strikes something else in a certain medium, and this medium is the air, it is natural that only those things should have voice which admit the air'.)

to where it came from, the first of these hypotheses implied a vacuum in the heaven, which was false; the second implied that the whole space between the speaker and the hearer would be filled with the expelled air and this could not happen in the heaven; the third would mean that the speaker's utterance did not reach the hearer and that the latter did not hear it, which was false, for then there would be no point in the speaker having spoken.[75]

Asserting that there would indeed be speech and hearing in the Empyrean, Albert proposed two alternative solutions. The first he borrowed from the Arab astronomer Thabit ibn Qurra, in a work that has not come down to us: *Liber de excentricitate orbium*. Thabit, as quoted by Albert, had stated that 'the nature of the whole orb was threefold': one part, not capable of division or alteration, was that of which the celestial bodies were made, another, also not capable of division or alteration, was that of which the spheres were made, while a third part of it, 'filling the space between the spheres', was 'rarefied and transparent', 'capable of division, but not of alteration'.[76] Thus, suggested Albert, 'voices will be formed in this third nature of the fifth essence'.[77] His other solution envisaged the transmission of voice not by 'natural means' but by means of 'a spiritual species (*species spiritualis*)'. While the first solution seemed to him the right one, he left the choice open: 'Let anyone choose that which pleases more, as long as he defends it.'[78]

Smell

Church tradition, said Albert, held that the bodies of the Saints would give forth a most sweet smell, those of the damned a foul one. Against odour and the sense of smell existing in the Empyrean, Aristotelian theory held that these can only occur when there is corruption and since the bodies of the Saints are incorruptible, they would give forth no smell. The argument that odour was carried by a 'smoky vapour (*evaporatione fumali*)' was rejected by Albert on the grounds that vultures can detect carrion at a distance of fifty leagues or more and no sort of vapour could remain extended over such a distance.[79] Albert thus opted for the theory that odour was a 'spiritual species' and that in the Empyrean *sensibilia*, i.e. things capable of being perceived, would be generated in the spiritual bodies there.[80]

---

[75] Albert the Great, *op. cit. ed. cit.* pp. 283–285.

[76] Thabit's theory of a divisible intervening matter was also mentioned by Albert the Great in his Commentary on the *De Cælo*, lib.I, tract.I, cap.XI. Cf. P. Duhem, *Le système du monde*, vol.III, p.334.

[77] Albert the Great, *op. cit. ed. cit.* pp.285–286.

[78] *Ibid.* p.286.

[79] The example of vultures was taken from Averroës (Ibn Rushd) (1126–98), Cf. Aristotle, *Libri tres de anima [...] cum Averroes Cordubensis fidiss. interprete ac apostillis. Ant. Zimara philosophi consummatiss.[...]* (Lyons, 1530), f.lxviii^r.

[80] Albert the Great, *op. cit. ed. cit.* pp.286–288.

Taste

Albert quoted Luke 23 and Acts 1[81] in which Christ is described as eating and drinking with his disciples and he also noted that Saint Augustine in the *City of God*, XIII, had written that it was 'not the power of eating and drinking that would be taken from the Blessed, but the need for it'. On the other hand it could be argued that taste implied the ingestion of something but bodies in that state of glory ingest nothing, therefore they would not be able to taste anything. Following Saint Augustine, Albert answered that there were two kinds of taste: one was the power to taste and the other the need for it. Christ, when with his disciples, showed that he had the power to taste, but the other Saints, for whom such proof of faith was not necessary, would not enjoy the reality of taste. Although there would be nothing to taste in the Empyrean, the Blessed would keep the power of having it.[82]

Touch

Regarding touch, Albert quoted Gregory of Nyssa (actually Nemesius)[83] on the Aristotelian conditions required for touch to be possible: hot and cold, wet and dry, viscosity, hard and soft, rough and smooth and so on.[84] Since these qualities would not be present in a body in the state of glory, it would not therefore feel touch for there would be nothing touchable. On the basis of the verses in 2 Cor. 15, that at the Resurrection our bodies will be spiritual ones,[85] Albert affirmed that whatever they perceive will be perceived in a spiritual way and not in a material one.[86] He repeated the example given by Isidore of Seville of Adam's incorruptible body before the Fall.[87] Had Adam not sinned, said Albert, '... fire would not burn his body, nor a sword cleave it, nor a thorn prick it, nor water choke it. Yet Adam would, without any doubt, have felt all these things through his sense of touch. Hence it follows that a species from them would have been generated in his sense of touch without a quality impairing and wounding his body'.[88]

---

[81] The correct reference is Luke 24: 42–43. There is no specific mention of Christ eating and drinking in Acts I.

[82] Albert the Great, *op. cit. ed. cit.* pp.289–290.

[83] The reference is in reality to Nemesius, 'De natura hominis', in Migne, *Pat. Grec.* vol.40, 651. See F.M. Henquinet, *art. cit.* p.290 n. The work formerly attributed to Gregory is today recognized as being by Nemesius. Cf. Etienne Gilson, *La philosophie au Moyen Age* (Paris,1952), p.72.

[84] Cf. Aristotle, *op. cit.* II XI 422b, *ed. cit.* p.129.

[85] In reality 1 Cor. 15: 44: 'It is sown a natural body, it is raised a spiritual body'.

[86] Albert the Great, *op. cit. ed. cit.* pp.291–292.

[87] Isidore of Seville, 'De Ordine creaturarum', cap.10 no. 8 in Migne, *Pat. Lat.* vol.83, col.940 ('..*dum ignis non ureret, non aqua mergeret, non bestiarum fortitudo macteret, non spinarum vel cujuscunque rei aculei vulnerarent, non absentia aeris suffocaret ...*').

[88] Albert the Great, *op. cit. ed. cit.* p.293.

Thomas Aquinas

Albert's disciple Saint Thomas Aquinas (c.1224/25–1274) was born in Italy at Roccaseca near Naples. After entering the Dominican Order in 1245, he studied in Italy and then later at Paris and Cologne. He taught in Paris, Rome and finally in Naples.[89] Less obscure in his thought than his master, he was no less a scholastic in his involved methods of reasoning.[90] His views on the Empyrean, which, to quote a modern author, he placed in '*une sorte de perspective fuyante et vaporeuse*',[91] showed a mix, as did Albert, of Aristotelian and vestiges of Neoplatonic concepts: '... *empyreum lucidum, immobile et incorruptibile esse* ...'.[92] These were characteristics which certain Jesuits retained right into the seventeenth century. The Neoplatonism in *lucidum* clashed, however, with the Aristotelian notion of the Empyrean having to be in a place (*locus*). The Empyrean therefore, said Saint Thomas, in typical scholastic vein, is not in a *locus per se, sed per accidens*.[93]

In his Commentary on the Sentences (written 1252–56), Saint Thomas separated the ninth Crystalline sphere from the *Primum Mobile*, thus making the latter a tenth sphere followed by the Empyrean,[94] but in his *Summa Prima Pars* (written later, in 1265–68), he simply adopted the ten spheres of the Isidorian cosmos.[95] Regarding the Empyrean, the Crystalline Heaven and the Firmament, he firmly aligned himself with Aristotle in his Commentary on the Sentences, alleging them to be of a fifth essence (*quinta essentia*), only 'resembling [sic] water (*habentes similitudinem cum hac aqua*)'.[96] 'The heaven', he insisted, 'is not of the nature of the four elements, but is a *quintum corpus*'.[97] In his *Summa Prima Pars*, he astutely avoided committing himself to any definite position on the nature of the heavens.[98] As a result many later scholars tended to follow the Aristotelianism of his Commentary on the Sentences.

---

[89] On the life and works of Saint Thomas, see J.P. Torrell, *Initiation à Saint Thomas d'Aquin* (Fribourg and Paris, 1993).

[90] Saint Thomas' work is described by Duhem as 'less of a synthesis, than a desire to reach a synthesis', 'a desire so great that it blinded his ability to make a critical judgement', see P. Duhem, *Le système du monde*, vol.V, pp.569–570.

[91] See the article *Ciel* by P. Bernard, in *Dictionnaire de théologie catholique*; see also on the astronomical aspects of St Thomas' thought, Thomas Litt, *Les corps célestes dans l'univers de Saint Thomas d'Aquin* (Louvain–Paris, 1963).

[92] Saint Thomas Aquinas, *Summa Theologiæ*, I^a 66 3, ed. William Wallace, Latin text and Eng. trans., vol.10 (London and New York, 1967), pp.41–51.

[93] Idem. *Scriptum super libros sententiarum*, lib.II dist. II qu.II art.I, ed. R.P. Mandonnet, vol.II (Paris, 1929), pp.71–75.

[94] *Ibid.*, lib.II dist. XIV qu.I art.I, vol.II, p.348.

[95] Idem. *Summa Theologiæ*, I^a 68 4, *ed. cit.* p.89.

[96] Idem. *Scriptum super libros sententiarum*, lib.II dist.XIV qu.I art.I, *ed. cit.*, vol.II, p.347.

[97] *Ibid.* p.350.

[98] Idem. *Summa Theologiæ*, 1^a 68 I, *ed cit.* p.73 and p.75.

The Aristotelianized concept of the Empyrean as a place (*locus*) (since it was a *corpus* created by God, it had to have a *locus*) suited natural philosophers, as well as astronomers, concerned with giving an integrated account of the whole of the cosmos, because it made Aristotle's explanation of the problem of the 'place of the cosmos (*locus mundi*)', which many had felt to be unsatisfactory, appear more acceptable.[99]

Campanus of Novara (1205–96), an astronomer and contemporary of Saint Thomas, wrote in his *Theorica Planetarum* (1261–64) that:

> Whether there is anything, such as another sphere, beyond the convex surface of the ninth sphere, we cannot know by the compulsion of rational argument [alone]. However we are informed by faith, and in agreement with the holy teachers of the Church we reverently confess that, beyond it, is the Empyrean heaven in which is the dwelling place of good spirits (*bonorum spirituum mansio*) [...]. The Empyrean's convex surface has nothing beyond it. For it is the highest of all bodily things, and the farthest removed from the common centre of the earth; hence it is the common and most general 'place' for all things which have position in that it contains everything and is itself contained by nothing.[100]

In the fifteenth century, Cardinal Pierre d'Ailly (1350–1420) repeated exactly this description of Campanus.[101]

If the concept of the Empyrean as a 'place' for the world suited a certain number of natural philosophers, as well as astronomers, it raised theological problems which Saint Thomas discussed and which his successors were to return to in later centuries, as we shall see. When Christ rose to Heaven – that is to the Empyrean – did He, as Saint Paul had written (Eph. 4: 10) 'rise above all the heavens (*ascendit super omnes coelos*)'? According to Aristotelian doctrine, above the heavens there would be no place for His body, since every body (*corpus*) had to have a place (*locus*) and furthermore Christ could not remain in Heaven forever since his movement upwards would, in Aristotelian terms, be a violent one and violence, according to Aristotle, cannot endure. In his Commentary on the Sentences, Saint Thomas stated, in deference to Aristotle, that Christ did not rise above all the heavens because He would thus be outside the Empyrean (*extra cælum empyreum*). He only rose to its 'highest part (*in altissimam partem*)'.[102] He here left unanswered the problem that, if Christ is both God and man, He cannot be contained in a 'place'. By contrast, in his

---

[99] See P. Duhem, *Le système du monde*, vol.I, pp.202–205; vol.VII, pp.197–202.

[100] Campanus of Novara, *Theorica Planetarum*, Eng. trans. in F.S. Benjamin and G.J. Toomer, *Campanus of Novara and Medieval Planetary Theory* (Madison, Wisconsin, 1971), p.183.

[101] Pierre d'Ailly, 'Quatuordecim questiones in spheram' qu.V, in *Sphera noviter recognita* (Florence, 1518), f.118^r. Cf. P. Duhem, *op. cit.* vol.VII, p.202.

[102] Saint Thomas Aquinas, *Scriptum super libros sententiarum*, lib.III dist.22 qu.3. art.3. *ed.* Maria Fabianus Moos, vol.III (Paris, 1933), p.688.

Summa Tertia Pars (written 1271–73) Saint Thomas placed Christ's body above all the heavens (*supra omnia corpora*) and added that, being a body in a state of glory (*corpus gloriosum*), the motion of Christ's body upwards was not violent, nor was its coming to rest violent, so nothing could prevent it from remaining in or above the heavens for ever.[103] His solution is here seen necessarily to turn upon the physical definition of a body in a state of glory which could strictly only be a matter for theologians to define.

Durandus of Saint-Pourçain (Durandus de Sancto Porciano) (c.1275–1334), a Dominican, who experienced difficulties with his Order because of divergence from the Thomist line, wrote a Commentary on the Sentences, rewritten three times with a final version completed between 1317 and 1327.[104] It was later reprinted eight times in the sixteenth century. In it he took up the question of the Empyrean, raising a further Aristotelian objection that, if Christ rose above the convex surface of the Empyrean, he could not be seen, since light in Aristotelian terms required a medium for it to be transmitted, and outside the world there would be no such medium. This would greatly detract from Christ's beatitude. Durandus' solution was nevertheless the same as that of Saint Thomas in the latter's Commentary on the Sentences: Christ did not rise above the convex surface of the Empyrean, but only to its 'highest part'.[105] He thus again kept Him within it as a 'place' where He could both see and be seen.

Like Albert the Great, Saint Thomas also dealt with the problems of the functioning of the senses inside the fifth essence, of which the Empyrean was held to consist.

Touch

Bodies in the state of glory, said Saint Thomas in his Commentary on the Sentences, will lack a real sense of touch (*actu sensus tactus*).[106] In his *Summa Tertia Pars*, he declared that 'the body of the heaven (*corpus cæleste*) is intangible (*non potest dici palpabile*)'.[107] Cardinal Cajetan (1468–1534), in his commentary on Saint Thomas' *Summa*, was later to assent to this opinion and, perhaps thinking of Dante's voyage with Beatrice through the moon in

---

[103] Idem. *Summa Theologiæ. The Resurrection of the Lord*, 3ᵃ qu.57 art.4, Latin text, Eng. trans., Notes and Glossary by C.Thomas Moore, O.P. (London and New York, 1976), vol.55, p.93.

[104] On Durandus of Saint-Pourçain see Etienne Gilson, *La Philosophie au Moyen Age* (Paris, 1952), pp.623–626.

[105] Durandus of Saint-Pourçain, *In Sententias theologicas Pet. Lombardi commentariorum libri quatuor*, lib.III dist.23 qu.8 (Lyons, 1587), pp.563–564. (1st edn, Lyons, 1540, reprint Ridgewood, NJ, 1964).

[106] Saint Thomas Aquinas, *Commentum in quatuor libros sententiarum*, lib.IV dist.XLIV qu.II art.I, edn (Parma, 1858), vol.II, pars altera, p.1084.

[107] Saint Thomas Aquinas, *Summa Theologiæ, The Resurrection of the Lord*, 3ᵃ qu.54 art.3, *ed. cit.* pp.26–27.

the *Divine Comedy*,[108] declared that, 'if someone on the moon wanted to travel through it, he would not feel its density by touch'.[109] In his Commentary on the Sentences, Saint Thomas declared, following Albert, that 'tangible qualities' in the Empyrean would only be 'spiritual'. He repeated from his master the example of Adam's body.[110] Much later Galileo, in his *Dialogue Concerning the Two Chief World Systems* (1632), mocked the absurdities (as he saw them) of these scholastic arguments over the functioning of the sense of touch in Aristotle's fifth essence.[111]

Taste

Taste, declared Saint Thomas, would not normally exist in the Empyrean, though it might do so if the tongue were wetted.[112] Aristotle had said that '... there must be a liquification of the organ of taste [...] ... the tongue is as insensitive when too wet as when quite dry'.[113]

Smell

Smell would not normally exist as such in the Empyrean.[114] Quoting Albert's evidence on the behaviour of vultures, Saint Thomas declared that smell could not be, as some philosophers had called it, a 'smoky vapour'. Smell, he said, must also be transmitted by a spiritual effect without vaporization. Vaporization requires that the odour from bodies contain humidity, but in bodies in a state of glory, odour would be of the highest perfection in no way altered by humidity. Odour would thus indeed be sensed by them in a spiritual manner.[115]

---

[108] Dante, *Divina Commedia, Paradiso*, ll.31–33 (Dante himself makes no mention of palpability).

[109] Cardinal Cajetan (Thomas de Vio), *Tertia Pars Summæ Totius Theologiæ Sancti Thomæ Aquinatis [...]* qu.54 art.III (Lyons, 1581), vol.III, p.253.

[110] Saint Thomas Aquinas, *Commentum* ..., lib.IV dist.XLIV qu.II art.I, *ed. cit.*, vol.II, pars altera, p.1087.

[111] The *Dialogue* is between Salviati (Galileo) and Sagredo, an honest interlocutor. *Sagredo:* 'What excellent material, the matter of the heaven, for building palaces, if it could be obtained! So hard, and yet so transparent!' *Salviati:* 'Rather what terrible material, since being completely invisible because of its extreme transparency, one could not move about the rooms without grave danger of running into the door posts and breaking one's head!' *Sagredo:* 'There would be no danger if, as some of the Peripatetics say, it is intangible; it cannot even be touched, let alone bumped into'. *Salviati:* 'That would be no comfort, inasmuch as celestial matter, though indeed it cannot be touched (on account of lacking the tangible quality), it may very well touch elemental bodies; and by striking upon us it would injure us as much, and more, as it would if we had run against it'. Galileo Galilei, *Dialogo sopra i due Massimi Sistemi del Mondo* (Florence,1632), 3rd edn (Turin, 1979), *Giornata Prima*, p.87.

[112] Saint Thomas Aquinas, *op. cit. loc. cit.*

[113] Aristotle, *op. cit.* II X 422a, *ed. cit.* p.127.

[114] Saint Thomas Aquinas, *op. cit*, p.1084.

[115] *Ibid.* p.1087.

Voice and hearing

On the transmission of sound in the Empyrean, where there would be no breathing and without breathing there can be no voice, Saint Thomas noted, following Albert, that some had said that praise of God there might be only 'in the mind (*mentalem*)'. The solution that the Blessed would use the air already in their lungs seemed likely enough, since Aristotle had said that vocalization did not require the expulsion and intake of air.[116] Yet, said Saint Thomas, such air might not be sufficient, for voice not only requires air inside but also outside the body, by the 'breaking (*confractione*)' and movement of which, sound would be carried. Or, he suggested, borrowing from medieval optical theory, praise of God might be emitted in a manner similar to a 'species', as in the colours of light (*species colorum*). Or, he added finally, turning to Albert's solution borrowed from Thabit ibn Qurra of a divisible body filling the space between the spheres, a 'breaking (*confractio*)' of the latter could also occur, enabling it to carry the speech of the Blessed and their divine praise. This would not mean that the heaven was generable or corruptible, but rather that rarity and density are said to be equally in this body (i.e. a divisible form of the fifth essence) as in other bodies.[117] Saint Thomas, however, gave no hint as to which solution he regarded as the most plausible.

Vision

On vision in the Empyrean, Saint Thomas repeated the two difficulties raised by Albert, one that the brightness of the pupils of the eyes of the Blessed, shining like their bodies, would be such that they would not be able to receive the species propagated by visible objects, just as a mirror placed directly in the sun's rays does not reflect the species propagated by a body opposite it.[118] The other was Albert's argument from Euclid that everything that is seen, is seen under an angle, but that the further away it is seen, the less it is seen and at a smaller angle. At a very small angle no part of the thing would be seen. Thus, said Saint Thomas, if the eye of one of the Blessed sees at an angle, beyond a given distance the eye would not be able to see further than we are able to, which is absurd.[119]

---

[116] Aristotle, *op. cit.* II VIII 421a, *ed. cit.* p.119, 'It is impossible to speak either when inhaling or exhaling, but only when holding the breath'.

[117] Saint Thomas Aquinas, *Scriptum super libros sententiarum*, lib.II dist.II qu.I art.II, ed. R.P. Mandonnet, vol.II, pp.74–75.

[118] On the propagation of species in medieval vision theory, see David Lindberg, *op. cit.* p.98 *et seq.*

[119] Saint Thomas Aquinas, *Commentum* ..., lib.IV dist.XLIV qu.II art.I, *ed. cit.* vol.II, pars altera, p.1084.

To these objections Saint Thomas responded that the intensity of light does not prevent the spiritual reception of a coloured species as long as the light stays in the nature of a transparency (*dummodo maneat in natura diaphani*).[120] That, if in a mirror placed to receive the rays of the sun directly, the coloured species of objects opposite it does not appear, it is not because of that by which reception is hindered but because of that by which reflection is hindered. The brightness of a body in the state of glory does not adversely affect the transparency of the pupil of the eye because the state of glory does not abolish nature. Hence the great brightness in the pupil of the eye increases the acuity of vision rather than weakening it. Concerning the decrease of vision in relation to a smaller angle of vision, Saint Thomas declared that, since the vision of a body in a state of glory will be absolutely perfect, it will be able to see very easily and hence at a much smaller angle than ordinarily and as a result much more readily at a distance.[121] Saint Thomas' successors, incapable of measuring up to the degree of subtle reasoning achieved by the Angelic Doctor, were to show less of the latter's prudent evasiveness in their handling of Aristotle.

Giles of Rome

The Aristotelianism in Saint Thomas' thought thus appears in bolder strokes and more forthrightly in the work of his disciple Giles of Rome (Aegidius Romanus) (c.1247–1316). Giles of Rome was born in Rome and entered the Augustinian order in Paris where he studied at the University under Saint Thomas Aquinas from whom he imbibed more of Aristotle than the authorities judged suitable. As a result he ran into conflict with Etienne Tempier, the author of the famous condemnations of 1277, and was required to leave the University.[122] Eight years later, having retracted what had been found controversial in his views, and with the strong encouragement of his superiors, he followed a brilliant career, becoming first head of his order in 1292 and finally in 1294 Bishop of Bourges in France.[123]

Giles of Rome's cosmological views on the nature of the heavens appear chiefly at the end of his career in two works, his *Hexaëmeron* and his *Commentaries on the Sentences of Peter Lombard* written at the same time, about the beginning of the fourteenth century. In his *Hexaëmeron*, notable

---

[120] Cf. Aristotle, *op. cit.* II VII 418b, *ed. cit.* pp.105–107.

[121] Saint Thomas Aquinas, *Commentum* …, lib.IV dist.XLIV qu.II art.I, *ed. cit.* vol.II, pars altera, pp.1087–1088.

[122] On Giles of Rome and the 1277 condemnations, see Pierre Duhem, *Le système du monde*, vol.VI, pp.69–72.

[123] On Giles of Rome's life and career see Pierre Duhem, *op.cit.* vol.IV, pp.106–19 and *Dictionary of Scientific Biography* 2, pp.402–403.

for a laborious meandering repetitiveness, he discussed the pseudo-Clementine, Isidorian and Basilian models.[124] The latter he refuted.[125] Into the pseudo-Clementine model, in which the whole of the space from the sphere of the moon up to the Empyrean made up a single heaven consisting of the Firmament, he introduced the Isidorian concept of ten heavens: the Empyrean, the Crystalline Heaven, the heaven of the fixed stars and the heavens of the seven planets. The *Primum Mobile* he identified with the Crystalline Heaven.[126] Perceiving the universe as composed of three parts, 'spiritual substances, celestial corporeal substances and elemental substances', Giles was ready to accept the Aristotelian definition of the nature of the heavens as consisting of an incorruptible fifth essence,[127] but he then ran into the problem of the Supercelestial Waters. Here his equivocal response, in imitation of Albert the Great, was hardly any more convincing than the latter's had been. 'There were', he said, 'two opinions, or two ways of speaking of the Supercelestial Waters', '... one was true *simpliciter* (straight off) in that they belonged to the fifth essence like the other heavens; the other could be true *per expositionem* (through argumentation), that they were of the same nature as the waters below on earth. The nature of the waters on earth could be understood in three ways: first through their great coldness, by which they produced ice, secondly through their weight by which they flowed across the earth and thirdly through their subtlety by which they rose as vapour above a certain part of the air and produced rain. In the same way the Supercelestial Waters could be understood in three ways: first since they are said by some to be icy, by others flowing, and by still others rarefied and subtle'.[128] Giles finally concluded that for him they were of a fifth essence '... though they could', he felt, reasoning in a helplessly circular manner, '... be said, on account of a certain similarity, to be of an icy nature by reason of their solidity because water when turned into ice acquires solidity'.[129]

Aware that his synthesis of the pseudo-Clementine and Isidorian models would require facing the problem of how the planets could move in a supposedly solid fifth essence, Giles, drawing indirectly on Ptolemy's *Planetary Hypotheses* (knowledge of which reached the Latin Middle Ages via Ibn al-Haytham (Alhazen) and through him to Roger Bacon), followed what the latter had termed the *Ymaginatio modernorum*, an attempt to reconcile the

---

[124] Giles of Rome (Aegidius Romanus), *Hexaëmeron*, edn (Rome, 1555), pt I, cap. XVI, f.14^v, col.1–f.15^r col.2.
[125] *Ibid.* cap.XVI, f.15^v, cols1&2.
[126] *Ibid.* cap.XVI, f.15^r, col.2.
[127] *Ibid.* pt I, cap. XIII and XIV, f.12^v, cols1&2.
[128] *Ibid.* pt II, cap. XIV, f.36^r, col.1.
[129] *Ibid.* pt II, cap. XIV, f.36^r, col.2.

astronomy of Ptolemy's *Almagest* with Aristotelian physics.[130] To enable Ptolemy's eccentrics and deferents to carry the planets and move them through the Firmament, the *Ymaginatio modernorum* imagined areas or cavities filled with a fluid substance (which he did not define). They were discontinuous though contiguous with the rest of the heaven. The planetary heaven, Giles declared, '... was like the body of a living being in which there are many veins through which blood runs in different forms, and many bones in which there are different marrows'. Though he admitted that his scarcely illuminating biological image lacked mathematical rigour: '... the veins and bones of a living being do not have a circular form because a living being does not have a circular shape', he nevertheless stuck to it, concluding that, '... there are likewise in the heaven many deferents which move circularly in such a body like marrow in a bone'.[131]

In his Commentary on the Sentences, Giles dealt with the functioning of the physical senses of the Blessed in the Empyrean. In Book II he only treated the possibility of speech, leaving, so he declared, the other senses for Book IV.[132] Sound, he said, is sometimes only in a real form (*realiter*), sometimes only in an intentional form (*intentionaliter*) and sometimes in both. The Blessed would, he said, produce sound in a real form from air that was naturally inside them (*connaturalem*) and innate (*complantatum*) in their throats. Once outside in the fifth essence the sound would be transmitted only intentionally (*intentionaliter*).[133] Giles' handling of Aristotle in his analysis of the heavens showed more a capacity for plodding application than any originality or subtlety.

Alphonso Tostado

From Giles of Rome we turn now to the last great medieval commentator on the Bible, the Spanish Franciscan theologian Alphonso de Tostado de Rivera Madrigal (1401–54/55), sometimes known as Abulensis since he became Bishop of Avila, but more often simply as El Tostado. Born at Madrigal in Old Castile, he studied at the University of Salamanca. A writer of immense capacities, his name among Spaniards came to be a byword for prolixity –

---

[130] On the source of Giles of Rome's representation, later to become known as the '*Theorica* compromise', see Michel-Pierre Lerner, *Le monde des sphères*, vol.I, *Genèse et triomphe d'une représentation cosmique* (Paris, 1996), pp.74–81, pp. 115–121 and Edward Grant, *Planets, Stars and Orbs* (Cambridge, 1994), chap.13 I 5, pp.279–86.

[131] Giles of Rome, *op. cit.* pt II, cap. XXXII, f.49ᵛ, col.1. Cf. also Edward Grant, *op. cit.* pp.304–305.

[132] It has not been possible to locate a printed edition of Bk IV of Giles' manuscript Commentary on the Sentences.

[133] Giles of Rome, *In Secundum Librum Sententiarum Quæstiones*, dist.II, qu.II. edn (Venice, 1581), p.146.

escribir más que el Tostado. His tomb at Avila carries the following epitaph: *Hic stupor est mundi qui scibile discutit omne* – 'Here lies he who astounded the world discussing all things knowable'.[134] His thirteen volume in-folio commentary on the Bible begun before 1436, to which he appended 'Five Paradoxes (*Paradoxa quinque*)', was first printed in Venice in 1507–30 and later followed by four other editions: Venice, 1547, 1596, Cologne, 1613 and Venice, 1615. The work was well known throughout Europe and retained its authority over nearly two centuries. Galileo, in his letter to the Grand Duchess of Tuscany, Christina of Lorraine (1615), referred to a theological position in it in terms of approval.[135] Though still medieval and Aristotelian in his approach, Tostado shows glimmerings of the coming humanist preoccupation with the philological problems raised by the study of Biblical texts in their original languages, instead of persisting with the laborious procedures of scholastic method.

In his Commentary on Genesis (1436), Tostado adopted the pseudo-Clementine model of the Firmament, which he said consists of the '… whole mass of the heaven containing the eight orbs […] And this whole heaven is called the Firmament because of its solidity (*firmitate*) because the substance of the heaven is firm and hard (*firma & durans* [sic]) as is said in Job, XXXVII,18: *Tu forsitan cum eo fabricatus es coelos qui solidi sunt quasi aere fundati?* (With Him, have you spread out the skies, strong as a cast metal mirror?)'.[136] 'In Hebrew', stated Tostado, 'this whole celestial body is called *rakiah* which means "a spread-outness" and not "solidity", as is said in Psalm 103 [= 104: 2]: *extendens coelum sicut pellem*,[137] and it is called a spread-outness because it is spread out over the whole orb and it covers everything.'[138] Tostado then suggested that the latter interpretation of the Firmament, according to the meaning of the word *rakiah*, might be said to correspond to the Basilian synthesis, which he does not name as such but describes correctly, though attributing it to Rabbi

---

[134] See E. Mangenot in *Dictionnaire de théologie catholique*, vol.I (Paris, 1930), cols.921–923; cf. also Tomas Carreras y Artau and Joaquin Carreras y Artau, *Historia de la Filosofía Española, Filosofía Cristiana de los siglos XIII al XIV* (Madrid, 1943), vol.II, pp.542–558; Otto Zöckler, *Geschichte der Beziehungen zwischen Theologie und Naturwissenschaft mit besonderer Rücksicht auf Schöpfungsgeschichte* (Gütersloh, 1877–79), vol.I, pp.467–68 and J. de Viera y Clavijo, 'Elogio de D. Tostado', *Memorias de la Academia Española* (Madrid, 1870), vol.II, pp.602–628.

[135] Galileo Galilei, 'Letter to the Grand Duchess Christina', in *Discoveries and Opinions of Galileo*, trans. Stillman Drake (New York, 1957), p.204.

[136] The Vulgate has *Tu forsitan cum eo fabricatus es coelos qui solidissimi quasi aere fusi sunt?* The New King James version has 'With him have you spread out the skies, strong as a cast metal mirror?'

[137] The Vulgate has *Extendens caelum sicut pellem*. The New King James version has 'Who stretch out the heaven like a curtain'.

[138] Alphonso de Tostado de Rivera Madrigal, 'Genesis', in *Opera Omnia*, edn (Cologne, 1613), vol.I, p.72.

Avenezra [= Ibn Ezra] (1119–75).[139] Tostado, however, rejected the Basilian theory of the Firmament being humid air on the grounds that the Sun and the Moon are, according to Genesis, in the Firmament and they are not in the air. Returning to the traditional medieval view, Tostado declared that the heaven is in fact crystalline, consisting of 'frozen and condensed waters', though not (and here he echoes Saint Thomas) of an 'elementary' nature for they are 'incorruptible and made of subtle matter' resembling (*assimilata*) transparent crystal or frozen water.[140]

Of the Empyrean, Tostado wrote in his Commentary on the Book of Exodus that although it was a body (*corpus*) and thus not entirely spiritual, '... yet it was almost spiritual, because it was not of the [same] matter as the other heavens. It was', he declared, no doubt in an attempt to avoid having to choose between Aristotle's fifth essence and the water of Genesis, 'of a sixth essence (*sexta essentia*)',[141] a definition which the Spanish Jesuit theologian Francisco Suarez (1548–1617) was later to criticize from a more orthodox Aristotelian point of view as being 'obscure'.[142]

In his Commentary on Genesis, Tostado, deferring to the influence of Neoplatonism, said of the Empyrean that it was of a substance that is 'more luminous and denser than the other heavens and for that reason it is visible'. It is the 'ultimate surface of visible things'.[143] However, in his Fifth Paradox (*Paradoxon quintum*), while expanding on the Isidorian model of ten superposed spheres, it appears that Tostado had revised his claim that the Empyrean is visible, for he adopted a more strictly Aristotelian position, stating that '... it remains unknown to [natural] philosophers and astronomers since it has no natural function that can be investigated'.[144]

'Paradise', Tostado declared, 'is a place in the widest sense of the word inside the denseness of the orb of the Empyrean and it is neither vacuous, nor full of air, but it is the heavenly body itself in the dense mass (*spissitudinem*) of which are the souls of the Blessed.'[145] 'After the Resurrection', Tostado continued, 'the Blessed, having recovered their bodies, will be inside the Empyrean

---

[139] Abraham Ibn Ezra was born at Toledo. His commentary on the Bible was printed in Hebrew at Venice, 1524–25. Professor Bernard Goldstein has examined the copy in the Bibliothèque Nationale, Paris and asserts that it does not contain the interpretation attributed to him by Tostado.

[140] Alphonso de Tostado de Rivera Madrigal, 'Genesis', in *ed. cit. loc. cit.*

[141] Idem. 'Commentaria in Exodum', cap.XXIV qu.53, in *Opera Omnia, ed. cit.* vol.II p.455. Albert of Saxony (c.1316–90) had entertained the possible existence of a sixth element for astronomical reasons, only to reject it. Cf. Albert of Saxony, *De celo et Mundo*, lib.I, qu.3, in *Questiones et decisiões physicales ...*, edn (Paris, 1518), ff.87v–88v.

[142] Francisco Suarez, S.J., *De Opere Sex Dierum* (Lyons, 1621), p.21.

[143] Alphonso de Tostado de Rivera Madrigal, 'Genesis', in *ed. cit. loc. cit.*

[144] Idem. 'Paradoxon quintum', cap. CLXVI, in *ed. cit.*, vol.XII, p.201.

[145] *Ibid.* cap. CLXC, p.212.

[...] within the mass of the substance of the heavenly orb, exactly as a man would be inside a stone or inside a wall.' Yet the privilege of bodies in a state of glory is that 'they can easily pass through stones, wood or walls or any other thing without any breaks or fissures in such solid bodies'.[146]

Tostado's conception of the Empyrean as a sixth essence, only made habitable for the Blessed by miracle, was the most extreme materialization attempted of the spiritual part of the Christian cosmos.

In his Commentary on the Gospel according to Saint Matthew, Tostado dealt with the functioning of the five senses in the Empyrean.

Touch

> No sense is better than touch [wrote Tostado] and no sense undergoes change better than touch, because touch never undergoes change without a natural alteration and the more perfect in [*sic*] act change is, that is to say the greater the enjoyment (*delectatio*), the greater will be the natural alteration, as occurs in the sexual act (*actu venereorum*), and, in as much as touch here concerns procreation, it cannot continue to exist in the Empyrean, for the sense of touch in living beings is to maintain life. [...] Life consists in the harmony of hot, wet, cold and dry. If we do not directly feel these qualities, for we can avoid them, they, carried to the extreme, destroy this harmony. Any living being placed in fire or in great cold and being unable to get out of them, will perish immediately, if it feels no pain. Therefore nothing is so necessary as touch, which is common to all living beings, but not to the [Blessed] in as much as the sensation of touch will not continue to exist for the above purpose in the Empyrean, because there is there nothing that can hurt the bodies of the Blessed, removing the harmony in which life consists.[147]

Touch, said Tostado following Albert and Saint Thomas, will occur by means of a non-material, spiritual species. Just as the eye receives the colours of white, black, red and green, so the sense of touch in the Empyrean will receive the species of hot, cold, wet and dry, soft and hard, smooth and rough, but not in a way that will cause alteration. Fire placed near a body in the state of glory will be felt as warmth, but will not heat it nor harm it.[148]

Taste

The sense of taste, said Tostado, will be unnecessary in the Empyrean, since there will be no intake of food or drink. He rejected, as not being an urgent matter to settle, Saint Thomas' suggestion that the Blessed could perhaps enjoy the sense of taste if their tongues were wetted.[149]

---

[146] *Ibid.* cap. CLXCI, p.212.
[147] Alphonso de Tostado de Rivera Madrigal, 'Commentaria in IV. part. Matthæi', cap. XVII, qu.CXVI, in *ed. cit.* vol.X, pars altera, pp.413–414.
[148] *Ibid. loc. cit.*
[149] *Ibid.* p.414.

Smell

On the sense of smell in the Empyrean, Tostado, following Albert and Saint Thomas, repeated their evidence from the behaviour of vultures. Odour, said Tostado, will not only be carried by smoky vapour, but also by a spiritual species as in the case of vision.[150]

Voice and hearing

On the transmission of sound in the Empyrean, Tostado examined the possible solutions and the difficulties in accepting them. Among the various theories he reviewed, some claimed that the Blessed will have no need of voice to understand each other's thoughts, others that voice will be transmitted 'intentionally' (*intentionaliter*) by a species, and others, not identified by him, that at the time of the Creation, God had set aside incorruptible air in the Empyrean to enable voice to be formed in it. The Blessed will thus not be in the Empyrean heaven as such, but 'in a certain kind of air in a sort of cavity within the Empyrean, or above the whole heaven of the Empyrean [sic!]'. This required putting air outside its natural place, and although Tostado was disposed to consider the advantages of such a solution, he concluded against it, saying that since the matter was so uncertain it was not worth lingering over. Tostado gave no indication of the origin of the theory of there being air in or above the Empyrean. He also quoted from Albert Magnus, via Saint Thomas, Thabit ibn Qurra's theory of a body which was not air, but which was rarefied and divisible and which allowed the formation of voices just as in air. This notion that the Empyrean could contain a fluid body enabling breathing and speech was later taken up at the end of the sixteenth century by the Archbishop of Milan, Daniel Maloni, and came to be adopted by the Jesuits, as will be seen later. Tostado next considered the idea that voices would be formed by the air in the lungs and throats of the Blessed. As with odour, voices would be carried partly materially and partly spiritually, first by the air inside the bodies of the Blessed and then outside the speakers 'only spiritually' by a species to the sense of hearing. The latter solution appeared to satisfy Tostado most as it tied in with the theory that there would be no vocalized speech in the Empyrean 'since there does not exist anything for which voice is necessary'.[151]

Vision

Vision in the Empyrean appeared at first to present no problems since the fifth essence was a medium able to carry a visible species. Tostado took up from Albert and Saint Thomas the objection that because of the brightness

---

[150] *Ibid.* pp.414–415.
[151] *Ibid.* pp.415–416.

of the pupils of the eyes of the Blessed, their resulting lack of transparency would prevent them from being able to receive a species. Vision is prevented by strong light, he said, citing the example of night birds such as owls able to see at night but not during the day. Likewise in a mirror on which the sun's rays fall, the species of objects are not seen. To these objections Tostado responded, following Albert and Saint Thomas, that the pupils of the eyes of the Blessed would retain both brightness as well as transparency and that in spite of the brightness, they would receive a species in their pupils and thus be able to see all objects. Again following Albert and Saint Thomas, Tostado asserted that the eyes of the Blessed would see under an angle as we do, though they would not see in the same way as we do. 'Not everyone', he said, 'sees the same thing at the same distance. Those with sharper eyesight see further under a smaller angle. [...] Those with weaker eyesight do not see a thing placed at a distance as they see things placed close up. [...] The Blessed have a keener eyesight, [...] so they will see a thing under an angle however small, and thus, however small the thing is and however far away it is placed, they will see it. Hence there will remain no imperfection in them as there is in us.'[152]

The laborious arguments invented by the scholastics in confronting the Christian doctrine of the Resurrection with the principles of Aristotle's physics and Euclid's optics may appear otiose to us today, yet it is arguable that they may have still served a useful purpose. When faced, in the Christian context of the Empyrean, with incompatibilities between sections of Aristotle's encyclopedia, for example between the properties attributed by him to the fifth essence and his rules for the functioning of the five senses, they found themselves compelled to redefine the properties or the rules or seek solutions drawn from other disciplines. Though the proposed solutions often appear to us, in retrospect, scientifically implausible, the theological pressures to modify certain Aristotelian categories may very well have helped medieval scholars, over the course of time, to overcome the paralysing constraints of the most redoubtable thought system ever encountered by the West.

---

[152] *Ibid.* p.416.

2

Renaissance and Reformation challenges to the medieval cosmos and the response of the Counter-Reformation

The Renaissance brought with it a revival of Neoplatonic and Stoic concepts which clashed with the traditional Aristotelian reasonings of the scholastics. It brought also the humanists' demand that Biblical texts be studied in their original languages. The Hebrew word *rakiah* for 'firmament' in Gen. 1: 6, *Dixitque Deus fiat firmamentum in medio aquarum et dividat aquas ab aquis*,[1] was claimed to have the meaning of 'stretched-outness' or of 'spread-outness'[2] and not of something solid and hard.

This chapter deals principally with Catholic and Protestant theologians of the sixteenth century who both turned to philological analysis of Biblical texts, together with revived Neoplatonic and Stoic themes, in their revolt against an exhausted scholasticism. As a result they set forth a claim that the heavens were fluid rather than solid. To begin with, not all Protestants or Catholics interpreted the fluidity of the heavens as implying the non-existence of rigid spheres carrying the planets. These were only later finally abandoned by both groups in the early seventeenth century in spite of a parenthetic attempt by Spanish Counter-Reformation Jesuits at a full re-Aristotelianization of the heavens. The Empyrean, rejected by the majority of Protestants, remained an important feature of Catholic theology, serving not only to house the Blessed, but also as a solid wall enclosing the cosmos.

Francesco Giorgio

In 1525, a Venetian Franciscan monk, Francesco Giorgio (or Zorzi) (1466–1540), influenced by the Neoplatonism and Hermeticism of Pico della Mirandola and Marsilio Ficino, published in Venice a massive volume enti-

---

[1] Then God said, 'Let there be a firmament in the midst of the waters and let it divide the waters from the waters' (The New King James version).

[2] This is the modern etymological meaning of the word *rakiah*. See the article 'Firmament' by H. Lesêtre in *Dictionnaire de la Bible*, ed. F. Vigouroux, vol.II, 2e partie (Paris, 1926), cols 2279–2281.

tled *De Harmonia mundi totius cantica tria*.³ On the Creation Giorgio wrote as follows:

> In the beginning God created Heaven and Earth, or the matter of each which only later received its form. To one of them He gave form the Second Day, when He said, *Let the rakiah be in the middle of the waters*, that is a stretched-outness or a spread-outness (*extensum vel expansum*) of all the heavens. Hence it follows that He called the heaven *rakiah*, for *rakiah* is not the Firmament, as our translation has it, but it is the globe and the mass of all the heavens (*globus & massa omnium cœlorum*). This is confirmed by that which follows: *God made two great lights* [i.e. the sun and the moon] *and the stars and put them in the rakiah*. These lights were not placed in the Firmament, that is in the heaven of the stars, but each of them in its own orb. Hence one concludes that this *rakiah* means a rounded mass (*glomeratum*) formed out of all the orbs.⁴

If, in this text, Giorgio holds to the pseudo-Clementine theory of the Firmament, he does so with an important difference. The pseudo-Clementine Firmament, stretching from the outer limit of the cosmos down to the earth, instead of being seen to consist of an icy solidity, here appears to take on some of the characteristics of the Basilian model in accordance with the meaning Giorgio gives to the word *rakiah* : 'stretched-outness' or 'spread-outness'.

In a later work, *In Scripturam Sacram Problemata* (1536), Giorgio repeated his words given above, adding only that the Firmament was 'something spread out, stretched out and filled out (*expansum, extensum & ampliatum*)' 'like a piece of gold or silver carefully beaten with a hammer. Hence we can easily understand', he concluded, 'that the whole globe and mass of the heavens was stretched out and round (*circumductam*) with the separation of each of its orbs closed into its place, to be adorned later with the stars [and planets]'.⁵

Giorgio appears to be the first to make the Firmament appear as a globe-shaped plenum (*globus & massa omnium cœlorum*), an image possibly showing the influence of Ptolemy's *Geography*, the Greek text of which had been obtained from Constantinople by the Florentine patron of letters Palla Strozzi and which he had had translated into Latin in 1406.⁶ In neither of his works did Giorgio make any mention of the Empyrean as such. While widely read

---

³ There were three further editions printed in Paris, followed by a French translation in 1579. See C. Vasoli, 'Francesco Giorgio Veneto', in E. Garin *et al*, *Testi umanistici su l'ermetismo* (Rome, 1955), pp.81–90; Lynn Thorndike, *History of Magic and Experimental Science*, VI, pp.450–451.

⁴ Francesco Giorgio, *De Harmonia mundi totius cantica tria* (Venice, 1525), f.39ʳ.

⁵ Idem. *In Scripturam sacram problemata* (Venice, 1536), f.2ᵛ. There were four other editions printed in Paris in 1574, 1575, 1622 and 1624.

⁶ Vespasiano da Bisticci, *Vite di Uomini illustri* (composed in the 15th century), edn (Bologna, 1893), vol.III, pp.9–10 and pp.216–217.

34   THE MEDIEVAL CHRISTIAN COSMOS

throughout Europe, both of them came to be placed on the Index of prohibited books in the early seventeenth century by both the Italian and the Spanish authorities, in spite of their recognition of the difficulties involved.[7]

Martin Luther

It is unlikely that Martin Luther (1483–1546) was influenced by a direct reading of Giorgio; there is no doubt some unidentified common source. But like Giorgio, Luther in his *Lectures on Genesis*, written between 1535 and 1545,[8] adopted the pseudo-Clementine model of the Firmament significantly modified by a definition of its matter as originally humid air in accordance with the Basilian model. Like Giorgio, Luther represented the Firmament in spherical form.

> This unformed mass of mist, which was created on the first day out of nothing, God seizes with the Word and gives the command that it should extend itself outward in the manner of a sphere. The Hebrew word (*rakiah*) denotes 'something spread out' (*extensum*), from the verb (*raka*) which means 'to expand' (*expandere*) or 'fold out' (*explicare*). The heaven was made in this manner, so that the unformed mass extended itself outward as the bladder of a pig (*vesica*) extends itself outward in circular form when it is inflated …[9]

Seeking to reconcile the meaning of *rakiah* in Gen. 1: 6, as 'spread-outness', with the definition of the heavens given in Job 37: 18: *Tu forsitan cum eo fabricatus est coelos qui solidi sunt quasi aere fundata* ('With Him, have

---

[7] On these difficulties see A. Rotondò, 'Cultura umanistica e difficoltà di censori. Censura ecclesiastica e discussioni cinquecentesche sul platonismo', in *Le pouvoir et la plume. Incitation, contrôle et répression dans l'Italie du XVIe siècle*, Centre interuniversitaire de recherche sur la Renaissance italienne, vol.10 (Paris, 1992), pp.20–33.

[8] See Richard Stauffer, 'L'exégèse de Genèse 1, 1–3, chez Luther et Calvin', in [Paul Vignaux, ed.] *In Principio. Interprétations des premiers versets de la Genèse*, Etudes Augustiniennes (Paris, 1973), pp.245–247. The first eleven chapters of Luther's *Lectures* were printed in 1544.

[9] Martin Luther, *In primum librum Mose enarrationes* (Nuremberg, 1544), edn (Nuremberg, 1550), f.vii^v; Eng. trans. in Martin Luther, 'Lectures on Genesis', chaps 1–5, trans. by George V. Schick in Jaroslav Pelican, ed., *Luther's Works* (Saint Louis, 1958), vol.I, p.24. Luther's concept of 'the Word of God' comes from John 1: 1: 'In the beginning was the Word and the Word was with God and the Word was God' (*In principio erat Verbum et Verbum erat apud Deum et Deus erat Verbum*). On Luther's concept of the Word, see D. Bellucci, 'Luther et le défi de la Théologie de la Parole à la science contemporaine du ciel', in O. Fatio, ed., *Les Eglises face aux sciences du Moyen Age au XXe siècle* (Actes du colloque de la commission internationale d'histoire ecclésiastique comparée tenu à Genève en Août 1989), (Geneva, 1991), pp.53–63. Although Calvin (1509–64) translated the term *rakiah* by *extensio* and *expansio*, he made no reference to the rôle of the Word of God in determining the nature of the Firmament. See John Calvin, *In quinque libros Mosis commentarii* (Geneva, 1595), pp.3–4 (1st edn Geneva, 1551). Eng. trans. by Rev. John King M.A., in John Calvin, *Commentaries on the First Book of Moses called Genesis* (Edinburgh, 1847), vol.I, chap.I, p.78.

you spread out the skies, strong as a cast metal mirror?'), Luther claimed that through the 'Word', '... that which was very soft by nature' was 'made very strong'. Job's words referred to 'the tenuousness yet unchanging permanence' of the heaven.[10] Luther added:

> This marvellous expansion of that thick mist, Moses [the presumed author of Genesis] calls a Firmament in which the sun, together with the remaining planets, has its motion around the earth in that most tenuous matter. What maker gives such solidity to this fluid and instable material? Nature certainly does not do so; even in easier circumstances it is incapable of this achievement. Therefore it is the work of Him who says to heaven and to that slippery material: 'Be a Firmament', who through His Word gives strength to all of them and preserves them through His omnipotence. This Word brings it about that the most tenuous air is harder than any steel and has its own limit, and that, on the other hand, steel is softer than water (*Hoc verbum facit, ut tenuissimus aer, sit durior omni Adamante, utque terminum proprium habeat, Econtra ut Adamas sit mollior aqua*).[11]

Although this definition of the Firmament may appear paradoxical, it remains evident that Luther had no use for the rigid crystalline spheres of medieval astronomy. 'The sun', said Luther, 'maintains its course in the most tenuous atmosphere without any support by solid masses.'[12] 'It is the Word', he wrote a few lines further on, 'that brings it about that [...] like fish in the middle of the ocean or a bird in the open sky, the stars move in their place, but with a most definite and truly miraculous motion (*Sicut enim pisces in medio mari, volucris in aperto coelo: Ita stellæ in suo loco moventur*).'[13]

Throughout the Middle Ages Aristotle's hypothesis of the existence of rigid spheres, carrying the planets and the fixed stars along their regular orbits,[14] was recalled by the constantly recurring metaphors that the celestial bodies were fixed 'like nails in a wheel or like knots in wood' and did *not* move freely 'like fish in the sea or like birds in the air'.[15] Luther seems to

---

[10] Martin Luther, *op. cit.* f.vii^v, Eng. trans., p.25.

[11] *Ibid.* f.viii^r; Eng. trans. p.25. It should be noted that Luther's text was partially changed by the editors to bring it in line with the views of Melanchthon. See John Dillenberger, *Protestant Thought and Natural Science* (New York, 1960), reprint (Westport, Connecticut, 1977), p.33.

[12] Martin Luther, *op. cit.* f.viii^r, Eng. trans., p.25.

[13] *Ibid.* f.ix^r; Eng. trans. p.30.

[14] Aristotle, *On the Heavens [De Cælo]* II viii 289b, ed. Guthrie, p.187.

[15] Cf. William of Auvergne (1180–1248), *De Universo, Pars I, ed. cit.* vol.I, p.650; Jean Buridan (1300–58), *Questiones super Libris Quattuor De Caelo et Mundo*, lib.II, qu.18, ed. E.A. Moody (Cambridge, Mass., 1942), reprint (New York, 1970), pp.210–211; Pierre d'Ailly (1350–1420), 'Quatuordecim Questiones in Spheram', in *Sphera mundi noviter recognita*, edn (Florence, 1518), f.117^v; Juan de Celaya (c.1490–1558), *Expositio magistri ioannis de Celaya Valentini in quattuor libros de celo & mundo Aristotelis cum questionibus eiusdem* (Paris, 1511), lib.II, f.xli^v. The origin of these metaphors at present remains untraced.

have been one of the first to reverse this medieval tradition. His reversal of the application of these metaphors marked a crucial turning point to be adopted by others in the perception of the nature of the heavens.

Jacob Ziegler

In the wake of Luther, the Bavarian Protestant Jacob Ziegler (c.1470–1549) made use of the bird and fish metaphor in defending the fluidity of the heavens. He also held to the inexistence of rigid spheres, adducing as evidence Stoic concepts taken from Pliny. Ziegler published two works, the first a commentary on Pliny (1531), the second a commentary on Genesis (1548).[16] In the first, published at Basle, he discussed whether the matter of heaven was '… liquid like water, air and fire, or solid like crystal. […] I affirm', he wrote, 'that the region of the seven planets is liquid (*liquidam*) according to the opinion of Pliny'. Ziegler claimed Pliny as saying that '… the seven planets are held in suspension at given distances from one another in the same *spiritus*', which, according to Pliny as quoted by Ziegler, was an 'incorporeal substance similar to the fire and the air in the upper region (*incorporalem substantiam & qualem priore loco ignem & aërem*)'.[17] Pliny's term *spiritus* corresponds to the Stoic concept of *pneuma*, which occupies the whole of the universe as well as the space normally occupied by the air with which it was also identified.[18] Pliny's actual words were: 'The elements are accepted as being four in number: the topmost the element of fire, source of yonder eyes of all those blazing stars; next the vapour [sic] (*spiritus*) which the Greeks and our nation call by the same name, air – this is the principle of life, and penetrates all the universe and is intertwined with the whole'.[19] Ziegler, as we shall see, was not to be alone in his wielding of Stoicism as a weapon against Aristotle.

There was no reason, Ziegler felt, to think that, if the orbs were not solid, the stars would follow disordered tracks. 'Like fish in water and like birds in

---

[16] Ziegler, a humanist and theologian, became a Protestant in 1521; in 1541 he was Professor of Theology in Vienna. See S. Günther, 'Jacob Ziegler, ein bayerischer Geograph und Mathematiker', *Forschungen zur Kultur und Lit. Gesell. Bayerns*, IV (1896), pp.1–61; V (1897), pp.116–128; also K. Schottenloher, *Jakob Ziegler aus Landau an der Isar*, Reformationsgeschichtliche Studien und Texte, Hefte 8–10 (Münster, 1910) (not seen).

[17] Jacob Ziegler, *In C. Plinii de Naturali Historia librum secundum commentarius*, Pars III, Cap. XI (Basle, 1531), p.27.

[18] Sambursky describes the Stoic cosmos '… as filled with an all pervading substratum called *pneuma*, a term often used synonymously with *air*. A basic function of the *pneuma* is the generation and cohesion of matter and generally of the contact between all parts of the cosmos'. See Samuel Sambursky, *Physics of the Stoics* (London, 1959), p.1.

[19] Pliny, *Natural History*, Book II, IV, Latin text with Eng. trans. ed. Rackham, pp.176–177. The translator translates *spiritus* by 'vapour'. *Pneuma* would seem to be more apposite.

the air, the very earth itself hangs in this liquid element and there is no reason to fear that it might fall.'[20] But he offered no further explanation of how the celestial bodies were held and directed in their orbits. The orbs were not solid, he concluded, but were of a 'very fine æther (*æthram* [sic] *tenuissimum*)'.[21]

In dealing, in his Commentary on Genesis, with the Second Day of the Creation, Ziegler asked how, if the Firmament was of crystalline solidity, the sun, the moon and the stars created in it maintained their various movements back and forth through solidity. For him the Firmament was respirable air (*aerem spiritalem* or *aerem spirabilem*). There was nothing solid about the Firmament, he said, citing his own commentary on Pliny. He had found nothing in Genesis about it. In asserting that '... united opinions had given way to conjectures and sacred evidence to authority', he may have been alluding to the translation by the Septuagint[22] of the word *rakiah* by *stereoma*.[23]

As a Protestant, Ziegler contested the existence of both the Empyrean and the Supercelestial Waters. 'Above the Firmament is the empty void of the outer darkness that Christ spoke of,[24] which after judgement the damned are thrown into away from the joy of being with God.' 'The waters above the Firmament', he declared, 'are not the Angels,[25] but the shades, the void, the emptiness, the abyss, and there is nothing of God's works to be sought beyond the Firmament.'[26]

Philipp Melanchthon

In undertaking to rationalize Lutheran theology to facilitate its being taught in the universities, Luther's close associate, Philipp Melanchthon (1497–1560), the *Præceptor Germaniæ*, reintroduced into it certain scholastic features. In his *Initia doctrinae physicae* (1549), while following Luther in agreeing that

---

[20] Jacob Ziegler, *op. cit.* p.30.

[21] *Ibid.* p.31.

[22] The Septuagint is the Greek translation of the Old Testament from the Hebrew; Saint Jerome translated it from Greek into Latin.

[23] Jacob Ziegler, *Conceptionum in Genesim Mundi & Exodum, Commentarii* (Basle, 1548), pp.15–16.

[24] Cf. Matt. 22: 13.

[25] Rupert of Deutz noted that certain authors whom he refuted had, on the basis of Psalm 148: 4: *Laudate eum, caeli caelorum; et aquae omnes quae super caelos sunt* (*Praise him, you heavens of heavens, and you waters above the heavens*), understood the waters above the heavens as representing multitudes of angels. See Rupert of Deutz, 'In Genesim', in *De Trinitate et Operibus eius, ed. cit.* I, 23, pp.151–152. The source of this notion is traceable to Origen (c.185–c.254), See Origène, *Homélies sur la Genèse*, I, 2, texte latin, trad. fr. et notes de Louis Doutreleau, S.J., Sources chrétiennes, No.7bis (Paris, 1976), p.31.

[26] Jacob Ziegler, *op. cit.* pp.16–17.

the matter of the heaven (*materiam coeli*) was '... of an airy nature' (*naturae aereae*),[27] he however parted with him in insisting on rigid spheres to carry the fixed stars and the planets. 'Under the orb in which are fixed the multitude of the stars that do not wander are seven orbs each of which carry one of the stars called the wandering stars or planets.'[28] The heavenly bodies, he added, were 'carried by the motion of their orbs' and it was 'absurd', for 'the heaven to be cleaved by them as water is by swimming fish'.[29] For Melanchthon, the cosmos contained only ten astronomical heavens; he made no mention of the Empyrean.[30] If Lutheran theology was on the whole to remain marked by Melanchthon's retraditionalization, Ziegler's innovations seem very probably to have inspired others, as will be suggested below.

Protestant rejection of the Empyrean

In his *Lectures on Genesis*, Luther had shown a veiled scepticism for the whole Isidorian synthesis, including the Crystalline Supercelestial Waters and the Empyrean, which latter Isidore had not named as such. Luther's main criticism of the Empyrean was of it as a real place occupied by the Blessed, but in this he was probably influenced by the Catholic theologian Gabriel Biel (c.1418–95), who had attacked the Aristotelianization of the concept. The souls of the Blessed, said Biel, are *illocabiles quia non circonscribunt locum nec commensurantur loco, sed definiunt locum.*[31] ('They cannot be put in a place, because they do not occupy a place nor are they subordinated to a place by their measurements, but it is they who bring into being the existence of a place.')

Luther expressed his sarcasm regarding the Empyrean in his Commentary on 2 Pet. 3: 13. His opinion was given on the following text concerning the Resurrection: *Novos vero cælos et novam terram secundum promissa ipsius expectamus, in quibus justitia habitat.* ('Nevertheless we, according to his promise, look for new heavens and a new earth in which righteousness dwells.') Luther commented: 'Let he who wishes, seek to know whether the Blessed

---

[27] Philipp Melanchthon, *Initia doctrinae physicae* (Wittenberg, 1549); edn (Lyons 1552), = *Doctrinae physicae elementa, sive initia*, p.66. On this work see Sachiko Kusukawa, *The Transformation of Natural Philosophy. The Case of Philip Melanchthon* (Cambridge, 1995), pp.144–160. On Melanchthon's contribution to science see Wilhelm Bernhardt, *Philipp Melanchthon als Mathematiker und Physiker* (Wittenberg, 1865). Reprint (Sändig Reprints, 1973) and John Dillenberger, *op. cit.* pp.39–41.

[28] Idem, *Doctrinae physicae elementa, sive initia*, edn (Lyons, 1552), p.73.

[29] *Ibid.* p.72.

[30] *Ibid.* pp.66–67.

[31] Gabriel Biel, *Commentaria in quartum librum sententiarum*, edn (Brescia, 1574), vol.II, p.523 (1st edn Tübingen, 1501).

will be flitting about (*volataturi*) in the heavens or on earth. This text proves with certainty that they will be living on earth and that both heaven and earth will be one Paradise in which God will dwell, For He is not accustomed to live only in Heaven, and wherever He is, the Blessed will be with Him everywhere'.[32]

Many Protestants were to follow Luther's opinion that Heaven would then be everywhere. Followers of this belief came to be known as *ubiquistæ*.[33] In this they showed themselves vigorously united in their rejection of any such real Aristotelianized place, as the Empyrean had become in the Middle Ages. 'Where then', wrote the Württemberg *ubiquista* Johann Brenz (1498–1570) in 1563, 'does Holy Scripture say that, in His true Heavenly and Divine Majesty, Christ occupies in Heaven a physical place, where he stands bodily and walks about? This is all dreams'.[34]

The majority of Catholic theologians understandably treated these views as erroneous and dangerous. They were soon to react with equal violence to the ideas of one of their own, one of the most original minds of the Renaissance.

Agostino Steuco

Agostino Steuco (1497–1548) was born in Gubbio (Italy), for which reason he is sometimes known as Eugubinus. He began his career as Luther did by entering the Augustinian order. Steuco entered the convent of the order at Gubbio in 1512 or 1513, remaining there till 1517. He spent the years 1518 to 1525 at the University of Bologna where, as well as taking courses in Greek, Latin and Hebrew, he learnt Aramaic, Syriac, Arabic and Amharic. From 1525 to 1529 he was librarian to Cardinal Grimani in Venice; in 1538 he became the Librarian of the Vatican Library. In 1546 he attended the Council of Trent where he took up a strong anti-Lutheran position. He returned to Bologna in 1547 and died the following year.[35]

---

[32] Martin Luther, 'Enarrationes Martini Lutheri in Epistolas, Petri duas ... (1525)', in idem D. *Opera* (Wittenberg, 1554), vol.V, f. 500ʳ.

[33] See Jacob Gretzer, S.J., *Disputatio de variis coelis Lutheranis, Zwinglerianis, Ubiquetariis, Calvinianis &c. Sanctorum vel veris vel fictiis receptaculis et habitaculis* (Ingolstadt, 1621), in idem, *Opera Omnia* (Ratisbon, 1734), vol.V, cap.XIV, pp.245–247.

[34] Johann Brenz, *De Majestate Domini nostri Iesu Christi ad dextram Dei patris et de vera praesentia corporis et sanguinis ejus in Coena*, (Frankfurt, 1562), edn (Frankfurt, 1563), p.44. On Brenz see H.M. Maurer and K. Ulshöfer, *Johannes Brenz und die Reformation im Herzogtum Württemberg* (Stuttgart, 1975).

[35] On Steuco see Theobald Freudenberger, *Augustinus Steuco aus Gubbio*, Reformationsgeschichtliche Studien und Texte, Heft 64/65 (Münster, 1935) and Otto Zöckler, *Geschichte der Beziehungen zwischen Theologie und Naturwissenschaft mit besonderer Rücksicht auf Schöpfungsgeschichte* (Gütersloh, 1877–79), Vol. I, pp.634–639.

Steuco is well known for his Neoplatonism,[36] but in the texts here quoted he had not forgotten his Aristotle. In his early works, Steuco follows a medieval orthodoxy regarding his treatment of the cosmos, although at the same time being fully aware of the semantic problem involved in the word *rakiah*.

In his first little book *Recognitio veteris testamenti ad hebraicam veritatem* (Venice, 1529), he notes that the word 'firmament' does not correctly render the Hebrew *rakiah*.

> FIRMAMENTUM: On this word we have followed the translators of the Septuagint who translate the Greek *stereoma* by *firmamentum*, but the Hebrew word *rakiah*, has the meaning of 'spread-outness' or of something which is extended and spread out, like a sail or like curtains. The word comes from the verb *raka* 'to beat out' as in Exod. 39: 3 'They beat out sheets of gold' [...]. Thus the whole stretched-outness and spread-outness of the heaven is called *rakiah* in Hebrew and does not have the meaning of 'firmament' [firmness]. That is why it may be asked why the translators of the Septuagint and Saint Jerome after them, translated the Hebrew word by a term with such a different meaning, since they seem to have been the inventors of the word and we do not find among any people that the heaven is called *stereoma* i.e. *firmamentum*. We shall here state what we have found on this subject; the translators of the Septuagint called the heaven *stereoma* seeking to show the solidity and hardness or stability which it had received from God in the place where it is situated. [...] Thus the Hebrews looked to the stretched-out nature (*porrectionem ac diffusionem*) of the heaven and the translators of the *Septuagint* looked to its stability (*stabilitatem*). The heaven is thus both stretched out and firm (*porrectionem ac firmatum*) [...] Or what is indeed better, the translators of the Septuagint called it 'firmament' to emphasize its hardness and solidity.[37]

Of the Empyrean Steuco wrote that it was both *firmamentum* and *æthereum* and that it was *materiale*.[38]

Though Steuco proposed to resolve the contradiction between the Hebrew word *rakiah* for heaven and its Greek translation in terms of a differing emphasis, he ended by following the Greek rendering. He did the same in a later work on the Psalms, *Enarrationum in Psalmos pars prima* (Lyons, 1533), in which he wrote in his commentary on Psalm 18: 2 [= 19: 1][39] that the solidity of the heaven was 'greater than that of a diamond'.[40]

---

[36] Cf. Agostino Steuco, *De Perenni Philosophia* (Lyons, 1540); (Basle, 1542); reprint (New York, 1972). On this work see Charles B. Schmitt, 'Perennial philosophy from A. Steuco to Leibnitz', *Journal of the History of Ideas* XXVII (1966), pp.505–532.

[37] Agostino Steuco, *Recognitio veteris testamenti ad hebraicam veritatem* (Venice, 1529), f.12ᵛ.

[38] *Ibid.* f.13ʳ.

[39] (*Caeli enarrant gloriam Dei, et opera manuum eius annuntiat firmamentum*. 'The heavens declare the glory of God and the Firmament shows his handiwork'.)

[40] Idem, *Enarrationum in Psalmos pars prima* (Lyons, 1533); edn (Lyons, 1548), pp.169–170.

In his next work, *Cosmopoeia*, Steuco undertook a much deeper and very different analysis of what he had set out in his earlier writings. Composed in the traditional style of a Hexaëmeron, or commentary on the six days of the Creation, his *Cosmopoeia*, published in 1535 at Lyons, resuscitated Saint Basil's interpretation of Genesis, including the latter's contention that the Empyrean existed from before the Creation.[41]

Disagreeing with '... the Hebrews, the Latins and the Greeks' of whom many believed that the Empyrean is the heaven mentioned on the First Day of the Creation, Steuco maintained that it is '... unlikely that Moses [the presumed author of Genesis] would, in describing the origin of corruptible and visible things, start his account with that of invisible things, and, as the rest of his description deals entirely with the natural and physical order, there is no reason why the beginning should be theological ...'.[42]

Although primarily defending Saint Basil's interpretation, Steuco also brought in the authority of Aristotle and in this he may well have received inspiration, directly or indirectly, from Grosseteste's Hexaëmeron. 'The Empyrean Heaven', wrote Steuco, 'appears to be none other than that which Aristotle describes as the dwelling place of God, where there is neither place, nor time, nor any corruptible thing.'[43]

Aristotle, in the *De Cælo*, had made no explicit reference to the 'dwelling place' of God; he had merely written that, 'It is obvious that there is neither place, nor void, nor time outside the heaven, since it has been demonstrated that there neither is, nor can be body there. Wherefore neither are the things there born in place, nor does time cause them to age, nor does change work in any way upon any of the beings whose allotted place is beyond the outermost motion: changeless and impassive, they have uninterrupted enjoyment of the best and most independent life for the whole aeon of their existence'.[44]

'The Empyrean', Steuco continued, returning to his major source, Basil, 'can be nothing other than the brightness that emanates from God, surrounding Him, beyond the world and beyond the realm of created and corruptible things.' He concluded, therefore, 'that the Empyrean would be the uncreated heaven and it does not seem to be mentioned by Moses'.[45]

For asserting the existence of something that was not God but which was as eternal and as uncreated as God himself, Steuco was later violently taken

---

[41] In his *Enarrationum* ..., Steuco, in commenting on Psalm 67, had already in passing spoken of the Empyrean as uncreated (... *coelo empyreo nunquam creato*) but it was only really in the *Cosmopoeia* that he developed the idea fully. See *Enarrationum* ..., *ed. cit.* p.441.
[42] Agostino Steuco, *Cosmopoeia* (Lyons, 1535), p.29.
[43] *Ibid. loc. cit.*
[44] Aristotle, *On the Heavens [De Caelo]* I 9 179a, ed. Guthrie, pp.91–93.
[45] Agostino Steuco, *loc. cit.*

to task by his fellow Catholic theologians as we shall shortly see. His *Cosmopoeia* was placed on the Index of prohibited books in 1583 and again in 1596.[46] The work was also attacked for the same reasons by Calvin.[47]

Turning to Steuco's analysis of the rest of the cosmos, we find him conceiving an original synthesis of both the pseudo-Clementine and Basilian interpretations of Genesis, into which he introduced his own interpretation of the heaven of the astronomers. On the First Day of the Creation, according to Steuco, the immensity of the waters reached to fill the whole of the heaven:

> Out of the purified waters was formed an æthereal substance both luminous and transparent which cannot be held to have been just stretched over the waters [a refusal here of the Isidorian interpretation]. Rather, when the mass of the heavens was created, there was extracted out of the waters enough to create the æthereal orbs whose watery nature was reduced to a minimum, while the rest became air and sea. If then Nature in an admirable manner, can condense water to become a very pure crystal, and if in the same manner Nature can produce out of water very pure little stones which shine in the darkness, what cannot God do, the Creator of all natural things?[48]

Steuco had previously defined his æther as a very liquid substance of the consistency of fire resulting from the violent agitation of, and friction between, the waters when the Spirit of God moved upon them,[49] immediately becoming the crystalline material of the 'orbs' which carried the sun and the stars, themselves of the same substance.[50] Never mentioning Aristotle's fifth essence, Steuco astutely pushed the whole problem of the rigid orbs of the traditional heaven of the astronomers back into the very beginnings of the Creation.[51]

Steuco next proceeded to reinterpret the meaning of *rakiah* which had so perplexed him.

> The word *rakiah* has two meanings, referring sometimes to the solid heaven itself and sometimes to the air, the first meaning emphasizing the solidity of the heaven, the second evoking the air. The term [*rakiah*] signifies spread-outness (*diffusionem*), a spread-outness that concerns [both] the starry heaven itself and the air. The term *stereoma* used by the Septuagint in their translation does not

---

[46] See Heinrich Reusch, *Die Indices Librorum Prohibitorum des Sechzehnten Jahrhunderts* (Tübingen, 1886), reprint (Nieuwkoop, 1961), p.400 and p.540.

[47] Cf. John Calvin, *op. cit. ed. cit.* p.2.

[48] Agostino Steuco, *op. cit.* p.46.

[49] *Ibid.* pp.35–37. This idea is hinted at by Saint Basil, *Exegetic Homilies*, Homily 2, 6, *ed. cit.* p.31. Gr. text and Fr. trans. *ed. cit.* pp.168–169.

[50] Agostino Steuco, *op.cit.* p.69.

[51] On this point Steuco was no doubt here drawing on Saint Augustine and his doctrine of simultaneous creation. See Jules Chaix-Ruy, 'La création du monde d'après Saint Augustin', *Revue d'Etudes Augustiniennes*, II (1965), pp.85–88.

render the second meaning of the word *rakiah*, but it does render that of the first. The [second meaning] is normally used of the clouds and the regions of the air which appear spread in all directions. Since this word [*rakiah*] comes from *raka* to 'spread', to 'stretch', it is correctly used of the air which is spread out and rarefied. Just as a hammer spreads out gold into sheets, and this is the sense of the word in Hebrew, so the sun rarefies the waters into air, for air is nothing other than very finely rarefied water. Since what we have said of this heaven fits in with Nature and is quite the opposite of what certain Hebrews lacking in philosophical knowledge have said, it is evident that their opinion should be rejected. For they have said that on the Second Day the matter of the heavens, which had been created at the beginning, was then spread everywhere and called the *rakiah*. How can this be? Why should not we believe that the heaven was [both] created and spread out at the same time?[52]

While making the term *rakiah* refer to the entire extent of the heavens in the First Day of the Creation as defined in the pseudo-Clementine model, Steuco, instead of adopting the Septuagint's translation *stereoma* for the whole of it as he had in his previous works, allowed the Greek meaning to relate to the astronomical orbs carrying the heavenly bodies and the Hebrew one to relate to the air. Steuco thus proposed a heaven that was 'spread out and stretched out' in which he was able to preserve the rigid orbs of traditional astronomy. In his use of the term *rakiah* he denied a complete separation of the celestial region from the elementary one as set down by Aristotle.

Denying the existence of the Supercelestial Waters as such, Steuco declared that these so-called waters, *shamaim* in Hebrew, occupied that part of the *rakiah* corresponding to the air (air that had been transformed by the evaporation of water by the sun). Claiming a parallel between the latter interpretation of *Shamaim* in Genesis and Aristotle's account of the hydrological cycle in his *Meteorology*, Steuco asserted that the second Hebrew meaning of *rakiah* designates both Aristotle's upper and lower regions of the air (the upper region being that of comets, according to Aristotle's theory of the latter). *Shamaim*, on the other hand, refers to the lower region only, which Steuco, quoting Aristotle, defined as '... the joint province of water and air', where, as he (Aristotle) says, 'one should think of a river with a circular course, which rises and falls and is composed of a mixture of water and air'.[53] 'Who', concluded Steuco, 'could interpret Moses [=Genesis] better than Aristotle? Behold Aristotle and Moses marvellously in agreement and what is more, Aristotle is here an interpreter of Moses' philosophy.'[54] But Steuco was of course here expounding, though in a more rationalized manner, Saint Basil's interpretation of the Supercelestial Waters.

---

[52] Agostino Steuco, *op. cit.* p.70.
[53] Cf. Aristotle, *Meteorologica*, I IX 346b–347a, ed. Lee, p.71.
[54] Agostino Steuco, *op. cit.* p.66.

Robert Bellarmine

In his Lectures at Louvain in 1570–72, *Lectiones Lovanienses* (unpublished), Robert Bellarmine, S.J. (1542–1621), who was later, as a Cardinal, to become deeply involved in the Church's censure of Galileo's defence of the doctrine of heliocentrism,[55] showed an unexpected sympathy for the Basilian interpretation of the Firmament in Genesis, as opposed to the Isidorian or the traditional pseudo-Clementine one. Though his exposition lacks the clarity of Steuco, he took the startling step of abandoning the rigid orbs carrying the planets and the fixed stars and of making the entire heavens conform to the Basilian model (the uncreated Empyrean excepted), without any Aristotelian separation of the celestial and elementary regions. Although aware of the differences of meaning between the Hebrew text and the translation by the Septuagint, Bellarmine made no mention of the problem raised by the word *rakiah* and there is nothing that could tell us if the debate on the meanings attached to it influenced him in his adoption of the Basilian model.

Bellarmine's cosmos consists of three heavens in accordance with Saint John of Damascus (died c.749),[56] an *Aereum*, a *Sidereum* and the *Empireum*. He said nothing about the physical nature of the Empyrean as he did in a later work published in 1616.[57] 'The thesis of Saint Basil', he wrote, 'that the Firmament touches upon and is contiguous with the air we breathe [...] appears very probable. [...] ... the Firmament was not made out of nothing but rather with the matter created the first day; and in fact God formed the Firmament through the rarefaction of water. [...] ... every day we see the air being crossed by water, that going up in the form of vapors and that coming down in the form of rain.'[58]

Bellarmine recognized the *sidereum* heaven as fluid but he remained ambiguous about its exact physical nature. 'If we wish to hold', he said, 'that the heaven of the stars is one only and formed of an igneous or airy substance, an hypothesis which we have declared more than once to be more in accord with the Scriptures [i.e. in accordance with Saint Basil's interpretation of them], we must then of necessity say that the stars are not transported

---

[55] See Richard J. Blackwell, *Galileo, Bellarmine, and the Bible* (Notre Dame and London, 1991), esp. chap.5.

[56] Saint John of Damascus, 'De Fide Orthodoxa', lib.II cap.VI, in Migne, *Pat. Grec.* vol.94 col.883.

[57] Robert Bellarmine, S.J., *De Æterna Felicitate Sanctorum, Libri quinque;* see below, Chapter 6.

[58] Idem, 'The Louvain Lectures (Lectiones Lovanienses) of Bellarmine and the autograph copy of his 1616 Declaration to Galileo', texts [extracts] in the original Latin (Italian) with English translation, introduction, commentary and notes by Ugo Baldini and George V. Coyne, S.J., Vatican Observatory Publications, Studi Galileiani, Vol.1, No.2 (Città del Vaticano, 1984), p.14.

2   Engraving of Robert Bellarmine, S.J. (1542–1621). Photo Bibliothèque Nationale, Paris.

with the movements of the heaven but they move themselves like the birds of the air and the fish of the sea.'[59]

While offering no explanation as to how the planets were directed or held in their orbits, Bellarmine nevertheless stands out as the only Catholic scholar in this period to take the step, as Luther had done, of reversing the bird and fish metaphor.[60] He did so only as far as the planets were concerned, for he maintained the sphere of the fixed stars as solid.[61]

Michael Neander and Valentin Nabod

Two astronomers of the second half of the sixteenth century were to define the heavens in non-Aristotelian terms. Michael Neander (1529–81), a professor of mathematics and Greek, taught at the Hohe Schule at Jena which became Protestant in 1558. In a work published in 1561, he was able to write, thus freed from the constraints of scholasticism, 'of a most liquid æther (*æther*)' lying '… from the moon upwards as far as the limit of the heaven'. In his assertion 'that it holds and hugs everything in its embrace (*suo circumflexu capiat & foveat omnia*)' and in describing it as being 'a force penetrating all bodies (*vis penetrandi per alia corpora*)', his definitions are essentially Stoic ones, though he makes no specific reference to his sources.[62]

Valentin Nabod (?–1593), a professor of mathematics at Cologne, wrote, in 1573, of the heaven extending from the moon to the 'outer walls of the universe (*ultima universitatis moenia*)' as consisting of an æther (*æthera*) which was 'burning and bright (*flagro & splendido*)' and 'shining (*res lucida*)'. He found confirmation of these definitions in Genesis; the words 'And there was light' referred to this 'æthereal and light-filled celestial part of the universe'.[63] Nabod's sources, which he does not identify, appear to be Neoplatonic.

If such theoretical astronomers and most Protestant theologians found no difficulty in admitting the fluid nature of the Firmament or of the heavens,

---

[59] *Ibid.* pp.18–20.

[60] Steuco by contrast had referred to the stars being like knots in the [wood] of a tree. See Agostino Steuco, *Cosmopoeia*, ed. cit. p.69.

[61] See Ugo Baldini, 'La scuola di Clavio e la crisi della teoria astronomica', in idem, *Legem Imponere Subactis, Studi su filosofia e scienza dei Gesuiti in Italia 1540–1632* (Rome, 1992), p.233 and idem, 'La astronomia del Cardinale', in *op. cit.* p.294.

[62] Michael Neander, *Elementa sphæricae doctrinae seu de primo motu* (Basle, 1561), pp.22–23. The colophon is dated 1555. On the tensional function of the *pneuma* of the Stoics, a continuous field of force interpenetrating matter and spreading through space, see David E. Hahm, *The Origins of Stoic Cosmology* (Columbus, Ohio, 1977), pp.165–167 and S. Sambursky, *op. cit.* p.36. On Neander see the succinct note in *Dictionary of Scientific Biography*, X (1974), pp.7–8.

[63] Valentin Nabod, *Primarum de Coelo et Terra Institutionum [...] libri tres* (Venice, 1573), f.27ᵛ. On Nabod see Lynn Thorndike, *op. cit.* vol.V, p.155 and vol.VI, p. 40.

Tridentine Catholic theologians wedded anew to Aristotelianism in the second half of the sixteenth century (Bellarmine excepted) were, on the whole, to admit only certain aspects of the Basilian model while of course unanimously refuting as anathema Steuco's concept of an uncreated Empyrean.

Benito Pereyra

Steuco's cosmology, his theory of the Empyrean excepted, was nevertheless to have a marked influence on the Jesuits and in particular on the Spanish Jesuit Benito Pereyra (c.1535–1610). Born at Rusafa near Valencia, Pereyra became professor at the Collegio Romano at the Vatican, where he wrote a voluminous commentary on Genesis (1590), which went into ten editions by 1685.[64] On the Empyrean, Pereyra violently attacked Steuco. 'This doctrine, I consider should be not only refuted, but should be utterly condemned and execrated and if possible consigned to eternal oblivion. What mind would not feel horror at hearing that there exists something which is not God, but which is as eternal and uncreated as God himself?'[65]

In spite of his attack on Steuco's Empyrean, Pereyra was nevertheless to draw heavily on the *Cosmopoeia* in his analysis of the Creation in Genesis, though, at the same time, a certain withdrawal back to Aristotelian principles can be detected in it. In the very beginning, said Pereyra, the Empyrean was created the First Day 'impassible and immutable', not to be in any way renewed or changed when the world came to an end. At the same time God created '... the whole body of the heaven together with its encircling orbs (*universum corpus coeleste cunctos orbes complectens*)', and with 'the substance and number of all the heavens (*substantiam & numerum omnium coelorum*), though without light or movement or separation of the stars (*sine luce tamen, motu, & distinctione syderum*)', these being added later.[66]

Concerning the Firmament, Pereyra refuted the Isidorian model.[67] Forging in the wake of Steuco his own synthesis of the Basilian and the pseudo-Clementine interpretations, he declared that on the First Day the whole space lying between the earth and the Empyrean contained '... a humid watery or nebulous matter, not uniformly dense or rare, but which could be compressed into the element of water and out of which, hardened in a wonderful fashion (*ex qua mirabili ratione concreta*), the celestial orbs were made'.[68]

---

[64] On Pereyra's life and career see Marcial Solana, *Historia de la Filosofía Española, Epoca del Renascimiento (siglo XVI)* (Madrid, 1941), vol.III, pp.373–400.

[65] Benito Pereyra, *Prior tomus Commentariorum et Disputationum in Genesim* (Lyons, 1594), vol.I, p.46 (1st edn Lyons, 1590).

[66] *Ibid.* p.53. As with Steuco there appears here again a recourse to Saint Augustine's doctrine of simultaneous creation.

[67] *Ibid.* pp.103–104.

[68] *Ibid.* p.61 and p.93.

Pereyra followed Steuco's interpretation of the word *rakiah* (Firmament) as signifying 'stretched-outness' or 'spread-outness'.[69] Again in the wake of Steuco, he defined the Firmament as occupying all the space between the earth and the highest stars as far as the sharpest vision can reach, containing water progressively rarefied into vapour, then into air and finally into fire.[70] The celestial bodies moved in the upper part of this space separated (*separatum*) from the air and fire,[71] where their orbs, he said, deferring on this final point to Aristotle, though never explicitly mentioning his fifth essence, were 'incorruptible'.[72]

Pereyra, like Steuco, thus remained ambiguous as to whether the celestial region was of a purely aqueous nature, or whether it became partly transformed into Aristotle's fifth essence. If, following Steuco, his rigid orbs moved in a fluid heaven, his account in no way rises to equal the latter's directness, clarity and subtlety. To settle what he called the *litigiosam et perplexam* question of the Supercelestial Waters, Pereyra adopted, after much discussion and hesitation, Steuco's Basilian interpretation, identifying them with the clouds formed in the upper air from vapours rising from the earth and its waters.[73]

Luis de Molina and Francisco Suarez

Pereyra's celebrated Spanish Jesuit contemporaries, Luis de Molina, S.J. (1536–1600)[74] and Francisco Suarez, S.J. (1548–1617),[75] both joined Pereyra in their Hexaëmerons in denouncing Steuco's view of the Empyrean. Neither Suarez nor Molina had been able to read Steuco's text directly; Suarez observed that his words on the Empyrean had been obliterated by a pious hand in the copy of the *Cosmopoeia* he consulted. He only knew Steuco's opinion at second hand through Pereyra.[76]

Both Molina and Suarez sought to complete, as far as they could, a re-Aristotelianization of the heavens begun by Pereyra. The Empyrean, said Molina, quoting Pseudo-Clement,[77] was 'eternal and perpetual', created the

---

[69] *Ibid.* p.94.
[70] *Ibid.* p.94.
[71] *Ibid.* p.97.
[72] *Ibid.* p.102.
[73] *Ibid.* p.97 and p.105.
[74] On Molina's life and work, though without reference to his Hexaëmeron, see Marcial Solana, *op. cit.* pp.401–424.
[75] On Suarez cf. idem, *op. cit.* pp.453–513.
[76] Luis de Molina, S.J., 'Tractatus de Opere sex dierum', in *In primam D.Thomae partem, in duos tomos divisa*, disp.III (Lyons, 1593), edn (Lyons, 1622), p.662. (Molina also attacks the views of Cardinal Cajetan on the Empyrean. Cf. disp.III, p.659); Francisco Suarez, S.J., *De Opere sex dierum*, lib.I, cap.4 (Lyons, 1621), p.18.
[77] Cf. Pseudo-Clement, *Die Pseudoklementinen, II Recognitionen in Rufinus Übersetzung*, ed. cit.

First Day of the Creation, 'after it and not before it' (*à parte post: non vero à parte ante*). He contrasted it with the Firmament which, although 'incorruptible by nature, will be dissolved and corrupted supernaturally when the world shall be destroyed by fire'.[78] Refuting the Basilian model of the Firmament identified as clouds, Molina followed the medieval tradition of a solid Firmament, in which he saw the aqueous Firmament of the First Day in the pseudo-Clementine model transformed to become, with its celestial orbs, 'incorruptible and ungenerable' by the 'divine power' of 'supernatural generation'.[79] This divinely ordered Aristotelianization of the Firmament still left unresolved the problem of the nature of the Supercelestial Waters. Here Molina, parting company with Saint Thomas and Aristotle, settled to return to Saint Augustine and Genesis by acknowledging that they could not be other than 'real elementary waters' (*veras aquas elementares*).[80]

In contrast to Molina, Suarez, who had taught in Paris, Salamanca, Rome and Coimbra, handled the influence of Pereyra and through him of Steuco more subtly. Into Pereyra's version of the Basilian model of the Firmament, Suarez introduced a further stronger Aristotelian emphasis. Whereas Pereyra had restricted himself to noting that the 'orbs' of the celestial bodies were 'incorruptible', Suarez declared in Book One of his work that '... in the first instant of the Creation were created all the celestial bodies from the *Primum Mobile* to the sphere of the moon'. This occurred in the same instant in which the Empyrean was created. Dividing the heavens into three parts, after Saint John of Damascus – the *Cælum Empyreum*, the *Cælum æthereum* and the *Cælum aëreum* – he defined the *Cælum æthereum* containing the celestial bodies as 'incorruptible and inalterable'. 'The claim that the heavens are incorruptible cannot', he said, 'be either proven rationally or convincingly shown from Scripture. Nevertheless scholastics and philosophers, both pagan and Christian, habitually and readily accept it.' After quoting Job 27: 18 on the nature of the heavens (*Solidissimi, & quasi ære fusi sunt*), together with other similar references in Scripture, Suarez concluded that Bible commentators (among whom he included Saint Thomas) 'almost all interpret [these references] as describing the incorruptible solidity of the heavens'. He then paradoxically added that he would show that, in the phrase *In principio creavit Deus cælum*, the word *cælum* could also be understood as 'air'.[81]

In a long discussion in Book Two of the problem of the Supercelestial Waters, he recognized that if these waters were, as the Bible stated, of an

---

Rec.II, 68, 2, p.92 (*caelos autem, [...] quorum unum caelum sit superius, [...] illud esse perpetuum et aeternum cum his qui habitant ibi ...*).

[78] Luis de Molina, *op. cit.* disp.III, p.659.
[79] *Ibid.* disp.II, p.658 and disp.V, p.664.
[80] *Ibid.* disp.X, pp.676–677.
[81] Francisco Suarez, *op. cit.* lib.1, cap.3, pp.15–16.

elementary nature, it would follow that below them the *cælum æthereum*, created in the first instant of the Creation, in which the celestial bodies move, would likewise have to be of a corruptible nature. This would be in contradiction with what had been expounded in Book One. To resolve this problem he proposed his modified version of Steuco's and Pereyra's interpretations: '... there is', he said, 'a final opinion, with which I agree, which states that given that the waters above the heavens are real and elementary, they do not however lie above the *cælos æthereos*, but above the *cælum aëreum*, that is in a certain upper region of the latter heaven and that those waters are no other than the waters of clouds ...'.[82]

Where Steuco, and to a lesser extent Pereyra, had proposed a progressive transformation of the waters to become the matter of the heavens of the celestial bodies, Suarez placed an Aristotelian heaven over the Basilian one. While Steuco had sought to establish a continuity between the terrestrial and celestial components of the cosmos, Suarez was by contrast to restore the separation of the elementary region from Aristotle's celestial one of a fifth essence. Though appearing to partially adopt the Basilian interpretation of Renaissance exegetists, in actual fact he neutralized it.

Girolamo Zanchi

The Jesuits were not alone in their indignation regarding Steuco's theory of the Empyrean. An Italian Protestant Girolamo Zanchi (1516–90) argued in more measured terms than the Jesuits against its uncreated nature. Zanchi, a near contemporary of Steuco, was born in Bergamo. After becoming a regular canon at the Cathedral of St John Lateran in Rome, he converted to Protestantism and fled Italy to teach at Basle, Nîmes and Strasbourg, before becoming in 1567 a professor of theology at Heidelberg University until his death. It has been said that he was neither Lutheran, nor Calvinist, nor Zwinglian, perhaps a Zwinglero-Calvinist.[83]

In his Hexaëmeron published at Neustadt in the Palatinate in 1591 and which went into six editions by 1619, Zanchi began by taking issue with the *ubiquistæ*, '... those who claim that above the ninth sphere, there is no other heaven [i.e. the Empyrean] in which there is already the body of Christ and where in the future will be our own bodies and those of all the Blessed'.

---

[82] *Ibid.* lib.2, cap.4, p.84. Although Suarez appears to have written his *De Opere sex dierum* after his *Metaphysicarum Disputationum* (1597), his opinions given here follow the same line of reasoning as those expounded in the latter work. Cf. idem, *Metaphysicarum Disputationum*, disput.XIII, sect.XI (Salamanca, 1597), edn (Paris, 1605), vol.II, pp.302–311.

[83] On Zanchi see C. Schmidt, 'G. Zanchi' in *Theologische Studien und Kritiken* XXV (1859), pp.625–708 (pp.697–699 on his Hexaëmeron), and Christopher J. Burchill, 'Girolamo Zanchi: Portrait of a Reformed Theologian and his Work', *Sixteenth Century Journal* XV No.2 (1984), pp.185–207.

'The heaven of the Blessed', said Zanchi, '... is according to them, God himself, since according to I Cor.15, God is in everything.[84] Since God is everywhere, the heaven of the Blessed is also everywhere, that is to say on earth as well as in the air and in the celestial orbs.' To this claim Zanchi opposed a more orthodox view that, 'God is not the heaven of the Blessed; the latter is something very different, created and prepared by God. One thing is the Father's house and another thing is the Father Himself.'[85]

Zanchi then proceeded to refute Steuco's position on the Empyrean. 'It is certain', he wrote, 'that Steuco himself knew that his opinion of an uncreated Empyrean had not been accepted by the Church.' 'If Steuco had examined carefully what he said and if he had read the Bible more closely than the profane writers with which he surrounded himself [...] he would have written the opposite and followed Sacred Scripture.'[86]

Zanchi's solution to the problem of the Empyrean as a 'place' appears in a section paradoxically entitled *De loco non physico*.

> The term 'place' has another meaning when one speaks of 'a non-physical place'. Any space of whatever kind, in which a body can be placed is called a 'place' in Sacred Scripture. Thus the Heaven of the Blessed is indeed a place, since it really contains bodies, such as already the body of Christ and later our own bodies when we shall be risen again from the dead. And Christ said that in His Father's house, there are many mansions and that He would go before us to prepare us a place.[87] Why should we be surprised that there is no air filling this place? As if God had only one way in which to make a place. Just as we are here surrounded by air, sometimes bright, sometimes dark, we will be there surrounded by a celestial light which passes our understanding. It is certain that Christ's physical body is there. It is thus a place, since any true body must be in a place. Deprive bodies of their place and they will be nowhere. And if they are nowhere, they will not exist, so says Saint Augustine.[88]

This Protestant's very ambiguous text shows that although he was determined to refute the extreme views of both the *ubiquistæ* and of Steuco and that although he strained himself to break with Aristotle, infusing Neoplatonic light in exchange, he was nevertheless still left with a very material and traditional Empyrean. His recourse to Neoplatonic light was, as we shall see, later to be likewise taken up by the Jesuit Riccioli in an attempt to get free from the fetters of Aristotelianism.

---

[84] The New King James Version has 1 Cor. 15: 28: '... that God may be all in all'.

[85] Girolamo Zanchi, 'De operibus Dei intra spacium sex dierum creatis', lib.I, cap.IV, in idem, *Operum theologicum*, edn (Geneva, 1613), vol.III, col.47.

[86] *Ibid.* col.50.

[87] Cf. John 14: 2.

[88] G. Zanchi, *op cit.* pt II, lib.I, cap.VIII, col.274.

In Zanchi's interpretation of the rest of Creation and of the nature of the heavens, Steuco's influence appears once more, though with none of the latter's subtlety. Both the heavens and the celestial orbs as well as the air and the æther were formed from the *materia prima* of the 'waters of the deep' in Genesis,[89] 'probably also of a fiery nature'.[90] Aristotle's fifth essence he unceremoniously rejected.[91] His division of the cosmos was tripartite, following Saint John of Damascus. The First Heaven is the *rakiah* or 'spread-outness' extending from the earth up to the moon, embracing both air and æther; the second heaven contains both the planets and the stars, and the third the Empyrean.[92] The second heaven is 'neither fluid nor solid', but solid enough for its component parts to maintain a constant relationship between each other, while at the same time fluid enough so that the orbs do not touch one another causing friction or preventing the ascension of Christ through them.[93] Such unscientific ambiguity is not one of the most convincing aspects of Zanchi's thought.

Conrad Aslachus

Zanchi's work, and through it Steuco's also, became known to Cort Aslaksen (1564–1624), or Conrad Aslachus as he is usually called. A Norwegian Protestant, born in Bergen, he was for a time one of Tycho Brahe's assistants. His ideas on the physical nature of the heavens reflect those of his master except that his universe is infinite,[94] though containing three finite parts.[95] His *De Natura cæli triplici libelli tres*, published in 1597, is divided, after Zanchi in imitation of Saint John of Damascus, into three sections: *De cælo aereo, de cælo sidereo, de cælo perpetuo*. The third part, on the Empyrean, was published in English in London in 1623 under the title of *The Description of Heaven*. Aslachus began in this latter section by following Zanchi in refuting Steuco's doctrine of an uncreated Empyrean.

The Empyrean, he declared, was created by God, is corporeal and is a place. 'If the bodies of the Blessed are spiritual and in a state of glory, they

---

[89] *Ibid.* lib.II, cap.II, thesis IV, col.282.
[90] *Ibid.* col.285.
[91] *Ibid.* lib.II, cap.III, thesis II, col.284.
[92] *Ibid.* lib.II, cap.III, thesis I, col.284. (*Triplex enim Cœlum tradit Scriptura. Primum est tota haec Rachiah, seu expansio, Aëris atque Aetheris ab Aquis & Terra, ad Luna usque orbem. Alterum omnes cœlestes sphæras continet. Tertium est illud in quod raptus fuisse Paulus dicitur: quod Beatorum cœlum appelatur ...*)
[93] *Ibid.* lib.II, cap.III, thesis V, col.285.
[94] Conrad Aslachus, *De Natura cæli triplici libelli tres* (Sigenae Nassoviorum [Siegen], 1597), p.7 (*... spatii ab hoc terræ globo sursum est in infinitum ...*) and p.92 (*Cælum, quod extima, esse infinitum*).
[95] *Ibid.* p.89.

do not cease to be physical and natural, but they cease to be mortal and corruptible, this is to say they retain their natural and essential properties.'[96] Aslachus then refuted the position of the *ubiquistæ*.

> These sacrilegious people do not fear to confound the Creator with his Creation. God is infinite and uncircumscribable. Heaven is finite and is circumscribable, since it is a place, the seat and throne of God. [...] How can the Heaven of the Elect, since it is situated and set by God above all the other visible heavens in a most excellent place, exist simultaneously in all other places, in Heaven, in the air, in the water and on earth etc? [...] No natural body can be simultaneously in several places. He who claims that the Heaven of the Elect is everywhere is compelled to admit these things and others even more absurd.[97]

Aslachus showed himself, as regards the Empyrean, just as attached to the Aristotelian concept of place as was his predecessor Zanchi. Neither of them made any reference to the faculties of the senses enjoyed by the Blessed.

Helisæus Roslin

The Hexaëmeron as a genre became progressively rarer after the early decades of the seventeenth century. One of the last Protestant ones was written by Helisæus Roslin (1544–1616). Born in Pleiningen, in Württemburg, he studied at the University of Tübingen and practised as a physician. His *De Opere Dei Creationis* went into two editions, the first published in Frankfurt in 1597 and the second in Geneva in 1619.[98]

Roslin described a cosmos with an Empyrean resembling Steuco's. It is divided like Zanchi's into three parts after Saint John of Damascus. His universe, as created by God, is closed and finite with an infinite uncreated Empyrean beyond it.[99] The matter of the heavens is 'æthereal' and fluid in which the heavenly bodies move, not as birds in the air, but led by a certain inner Divine knowledge (*insita divinitus scientia*), or alternatively, he added, they are moved by orbs which assure their regular motion.[100] Roslin hesitated between the rigid orbs of traditional astronomy and their abandonment proposed by Tycho Brahe, as will be described later. The rest of the tradi-

---

[96] *Ibid.* pp.191–193.
[97] *Ibid.* pp.200–202.
[98] On Roslin's life and work see Miguel A. Granada, *El debate cosmológico en 1588. Bruno, Brahe, Rothmann, Ursus, Roslin*, Istituto Italiano per gli studi filosofici, Lezioni della Scuola di Studi Superiori in Napoli, 18 (Naples, 1996), pp.109–161; also the succinct though documented remarks of C. Doris Hellmann, *The Comet of 1577: its Place in the History of Astronomy* (New York, 1944), reprint (New York, 1971), pp.159–161.
[99] Helisæus Roslin, *De Opere Dei Creationis seu de Mundo Hypotheses* (Frankfurt, 1597), p.13.
[100] *Ibid.* p.15.

tional medieval cosmos he rejected in its entirety. 'That which the Ancients have written of the ninth sphere, the tenth called the *Primum Mobile*, the eleventh or Empyrean sphere and the crystalline or aqueous sphere is', wrote Roslin, 'nothing but fictions and dreams lacking in sound sense.'[101] If Roslin thus dissociated the realm of the Blessed from the order of traditional astronomy, he did not deny to the former what he called a 'space (*spatium*)'.[102] 'Reason itself and Holy Scripture teach us', he wrote, 'that the world of the angels, which is reserved for pure spirits and God's elect, occupies a space very far removed from the centre of the earth and that it lies above all else and that is why it is called Supercelestial. The Supercelestial world is infinite, immutable and eternal.'[103]

Agostino Oreggi

By the first quarter of the seventeenth century the re-Aristotelianization of the heavens expounded by the Spanish Jesuits came to be finally abandoned by Catholic theologians. Agostino Oreggi (1577–1643), a Canon of the Vatican, adviser to the Holy Inquisition and private secretary to Pope Urban VIII, composed a sumptuously produced Hexaëmeron published at Rome in 1625 in which he gave a succinct account of the order of the heavens.[104] Taking them to be, in accordance with Genesis, of a purely elementary nature, Oreggi abandoned all reference to Aristotle's incorruptible fifth essence. Following the pseudo-Clementine model modified by the Basilian interpretation of the nature of the Firmament, he described 'the whole mass of the body extending from the earth to the Empyrean' as 'transparent, rarefied and fluid', consisting of water progressively rarefied into air, then into fire and finally into 'æther', a term 'now used for the whole celestial body within the Firmament'. Oreggi, however, unlike Saint Basil, insisted on retaining the Supercelestial Waters above the Firmament. In answer to the question as to what purpose these waters served, he replied that '... some said that they were to provide the varied colours of light that the Blessed would have to look at for their enjoyment'.[105] Oreggi did not identify those who held that the light of the Empyrean when refracted through the Supercelestial Waters produced different colours. The idea,

---

[101] *Ibid.* p.16.

[102] In this he may have been influenced by the ideas of Francesco Patrizi. Cf. Chapter 5 below.

[103] Helisäeus Roslin, *op. cit.* p.20.

[104] Agostino Oreggi (Augustinus Oregius), *De Opere sex dierum tractatus quattuor* (Rome, 1625). On Oreggi's work see Lynn Thorndike, *A History of Magic and Experimental Science*, vol.VII, pp.58–59.

[105] Agostino Oreggi, *op. cit.* edn (Rome, 1632), pp.10–14.

however, was later taken up by the astronomer Riccioli as we shall see. Oreggi divided his heavens into three: the first containing '... the planetary orbs or the fluid æther in which the planets moved like fish in water or like birds in the air'. Oreggi's second heaven was the Firmament, the third the Empyrean.[106] He added nothing further about the condition of the Blessed in the Empyrean.

Denis Petau

A more traditional view of the heavens, loaded with a great wealth of scholarship, appeared in the De sex prinorum mundi dierum Opificio' of the French Jesuit Denis Petau (1583–1652). As a Hexaëmeron, it was the last of the traditional kind. Published in Paris in 1644 in Petau's collected works, *Theologica dogmata*, it was published again in 1700 in Antwerp in his *Opus de theologicis dogmatibus*. After having taught at the Jesuit College at La Flèche, Petau taught rhetoric and then theology at the Clermont College in Paris between 1621 and 1643. His thorough knowledge of Greek and Hebrew earned him the tribute of Pierre Bayle who, in emphasizing his 'vast and profound scholarship', wrote of him that he was 'one of the most learned persons in Europe'.[107] In astronomy, however, his competence reached nowhere near a comparable standard. Ignoring medieval scholastic writers, he presented his views, buttressing them with extensive quotations culled from the Bible, early Christian writers or Christian and Jewish Bible commentators.

Petau divided the cosmos into three heavens, in one of which was placed 'the system of the orbs placed inside one another', one above 'in which was the place of the souls of the Blessed'; below was 'the third heaven containing the fire and the air', 'although philosophers', he said, 'doubted the existence of the former'.[108] *Empyreum*, he declared, was a 'barbarous word meaning nothing' (*vox nihil est ac barbara*) and nowhere mentioned in Scripture.[109] He said nothing about the condition of the Blessed.

The whole of nature, said Petau, was created from either one of two things, earth or water. This included both Heaven and the Stars.[110] Petau nowhere makes any reference to Aristotle's fifth essence. Among ancient and modern opinions he had found 'two which were very common and

---

[106] *Ibid.* p.14.

[107] Pierre Bayle, *Dictionnaire historique et critique*, edn (Paris, 1820), vol.11, p.661. On Petau see also the article by Fr Galtier in *Dictionnaire de théologie catholique*, vol.XII (1933), pp.1313–1337.

[108] Denis Petau, S.J.,'De sex primorum mundi dierum Opificio', lib.I, cap.X, in idem, *Opus de theologicis dogmatibus* (Antwerp, 1700), vol.III, p.139.

[109] *Ibid.* cap.II, p.125.

[110] *Ibid.* cap.IV, p.128.

seemed probable'. The first stated that on the First Day, together with Earth, was created the Heaven which, 'later through custom', came to be called the *Empyrean*. On the Second Day were created the lower celestial orbs from the waters 'hardened and compacted' and this was called the Firmament, although the word *Firmament* usually referred to the heaven of the fixed stars called the eighth sphere. The second opinion held that 'the term Heaven reached to cover the outermost part of the whole world containing the splendid round orbs which we can observe with our eyes extending throughout the immense spaces of physical phenomena'. All these, called by the one word Heaven, were, together with the Earth, created at the same time.[111]

The two opinions can be recognized as respectively the Isidorian and the pseudo-Clementine models. Declaring that he preferred an intermediate opinion between the two, Petau then proceeded to argue in favour of the Basilian model of the Firmament. 'At the beginning of the six days of the Creation there were only the Earth and the Water', he wrote. The latter, '... in the form of fine mist and vapour, occupied the whole of the space above and round the earth. From part of it God made, the Second Day, the celestial bodies and from part of it the air and the fire, if such there is near the heaven.' Petau's concept of the fire may be a half-doubted concession to Aristotle. 'The name *Firmament* was given to the whole region extending from the Earth and the Waters as far as the edge and limit of the world.' Petau's one difference with Saint Basil was that the latter separated this heaven from the highest one (Petau's term for the conventional Empyrean) making it, together with the air, a single one named the Firmament. The highest heaven, said Petau, was already in existence the Second Day, having been created at the same time as the earth.[112]

After much hesitant discussion of contrary opinions, Petau declared that he considered the Supercelestial Waters to be no more than clouds and vapours, a view he attributed to Pereyra.[113]

Petau's deployment of an uncommon erudition with long and often superfluous quotations from obscure early Christian authorities was not enough to cover up his limited grasp of the principles of natural philosophy. Lacking the drive to analyse in depth the problems he was faced with, he bears witness to a distinct falling off of the inventiveness and mental vigour shown by his predecessors.

By the early seventeenth century the fluid nature of the heavens of the planets and the stars became largely accepted throughout Europe by authoritative Protestant and Catholic theologians. If the majority of Protestants

---

[111] *Ibid.* cap.X, p.140.
[112] *Ibid.* p.141.
[113] *Ibid.* cap.XI, p.143.

in northern Europe had long ceased to be concerned with the Empyrean as occupying a definite closed place in the cosmos, its nature as such became preserved in Catholic Europe up until the later part of the century and a great amount of detailed attention was given to discussing the physical conditions of the Blessed within its confines.

3

The challenge of applied optics

The fluid nature of the heavens, expounded by Renaissance theologians and theoretical astronomers, was now to be corroborated by practical astronomers for whom the results of applied optical theory appeared to prove the untenability of the traditional scholastic opinion that the heavens were hard and solid.

This chapter deals first with the claim by the optician Jean Pena that optical theory contradicted Aristotle's doctrine of the material nature of the heavens. It then describes how the astronomers Tycho Brahe and Christoph Rothmann successfully tested his claim, although they differed on the precise lessons to be drawn from their observations. The chapter ends by showing how, from their conclusions, Johann Kepler developed his concept of a fluid æther replacing Aristotle's fifth essence.

During the Middle Ages, no particular incompatibility had been discerned between, on the one hand, Aristotle's doctrine of the concentric arrangement of the spheres of the four elements (earth, water, air and fire) together with that of his fifth essence,[1] and, on the other hand, the principles of optics as laid down in both the *Optica* of Euclid (fl. 300 BC)[2] and in the *Optica* of Claudius Ptolemy (90 AD–168 AD).[3] Both these texts were translated into Latin in the twelfth century.[4]

Jean Pena

In 1557, a young Frenchman, Jean Pena (c.1528–58) published the first edition of the Greek text of Euclid's *Optica* together with a Latin translation.[5]

---

[1] Aristotle, *On the Heavens [De Cælo]*, II 4 287a, ed. Guthrie, p.161.

[2] Euclide, *L'Optique et la catoptrique*, Fr. trans. by Paul Ver Eecke (Paris, 1959).

[3] Claudius Ptolemy, *L'Optique de Claude Ptolémée dans la version latine d'après l'arabe de l'Emir Eugène de Sicile*, ed. Albert Lejeune, critical edition with Latin text (Louvain, 1956).

[4] See David Lindberg, *op. cit.* pp.210–211.

[5] Although Pena was a good Greek scholar his Greek text is not absolutely reliable and his Latin translation is not without faults. See Paul Ver Eecke in *op. cit*, pp.xxxviii–xxxix.

In his preface he made the startling declaration, later to be taken up by numerous scholars across Europe, that if, in accordance with the optical theories of Euclid and Ptolemy, light rays passing from one medium to another undergo refraction (the degree of refraction being greater, the greater the angle of their incidence),[6] the variation in the refraction of light rays from different stars as they pass through Aristotle's fifth essence to the sphere of fire, and from the latter to the sphere of the air, would be such that no two stars (except those perpendicular to the observer) would be seen in their right places and nothing in astronomy could be relied upon to be certain. But astronomy as practised by many great men over many centuries could not be wrong; it must be Aristotle. The heavens, concluded Pena, consisted of nothing but ordinary air.[7]

Little is known of Jean Pena. Born at Moustiers (Provence), he came from an old Provençal family and went to study at Paris where he moved in the circle around Peter Ramus (1515–72). He died young of tuberculosis at the age of thirty, but not before becoming a professor of mathematics at the Collège Royal.[8] Nicolas Nancel (1539–1610), in his biography of Peter Ramus, wrote in praise of Pena that he was '... a lonely and solitary person [...] always hiding himself away in the library, content with poor clothes and food, a small, thin, graceful man, and somewhat consumptive as the manner of his death was to prove, but remarkably studious and diligent [...] I never heard of any student in the city at the time who was more learned or more earnestly engaged in the study of every art, language and other useful subject.'[9]

Pena's argument against Aristotle's fifth essence is set out as follows:

> Though on the subject of the matter of the heavens, (that is of the whole body lying between the convex [i.e. lower surface of the sphere] of the moon and that of the most distant stars), there are many opinions, that which should be followed is clearly set down by the authorities on Optics (*Optici*). Let Empedocles [c.493–433 BC] say that the heaven is solid and consists of air

---

[6] The sine law governing the refraction of light was only found much later in 1621 by Willebrord Snell (1580–1626) and derived by Descartes (1596–1650) in his *Dioptrique* (1637). See *Dictionary of the History of Science*, ed. W.F. Bynum, E.J. Brown and Roy Porter (London, 1982), p.235.

[7] Jean Pena, *De Usu optices Præfatio*, in idem, *Euclidis Optica et Catoptrica* (Paris, 1557), sign.aa.ij^v–sign.aa.iij^r. A second edition of Pena's preface was printed in Peter Ramus, *Collectaneæ, Præfationes, Epistolæ, Orationes* (Marburg, 1599), pp.140–157. See Miguel A. Granada, 'Petrus Ramus y Jean Pena: crítica de la cosmología aristotélica y de las hipótesis astronómicas a mediados del siglo XVI', *ER Revista de Filosofía*, Seville, No. 12/13 (1991), p.14.

[8] On Pena, besides Granada, see Lynn Thorndike, *History of Magic and Experimental Science*, VI, pp.19–20 and Peter Barker, 'Jean Pena (1528–1558) and Stoic Physics in the sixteenth century', *The Southern Journal of Philosophy* XXIII (1985), Supplement, pp.93–107.

[9] Nicolaus Nancelius, *Petri Rami Vita* (Paris, 1595), ed. with Eng. trans. by Peter Sharrat, *Humanistica Lovaniensis*, XXIV (1975), p.198.

hardened into crystal. Let Anaxagoras [500 (?)–428 BC (?)] believe that fire is the matter of heaven. Let others imagine that the fifth essence is more subtle and purer than the base mass of the elements and yet call it solid (*solidam*) so that it can carry the solid bodies of the stars and, for this solidity not to collapse, let them sustain it with the majesty of their authority.

But holding these opinions in contempt and despising the arrogance of their overbearing authority, let Optics freely declare that the whole of this space, in which the planets move in a most regular and unerring way, is this life-giving spirit (*animabilem spiritum*) spread throughout the whole of nature, which we breathe and which differs in nothing from air.

If indeed this body (*corpus*) which we call heaven is different from air and has as many orbs contiguous to one another as there are planets, and though solid and hard (*solidum et durum*), is more subtle (*rarius*) and more limpid (*limpidius*) than air, Great God, what monstrosities Optics will have here brought together? and how many deceits will it have practised? Fixed stars and even others, if they are observed at places other than vertically above the observer and if they are seen through so many media, so widely spread and separated from one another by so many surfaces, will never have been seen in their right places; those that are very far away will appear near and almost touching each other and some of them distant from each other by one or two degrees will appear as one star, because [their light rays] will be refracted from the perpendicular on account of the difference between the media, as Optics teaches us. On the other hand, when they have reached the pole of the horizon, those which had seemed elsewhere to be joined together, will appear separated and even distant from each other as they are in reality, because through all these media [their light rays] will fall perpendicularly. If this be indeed so, then Good-bye to astronomy, Good-bye to Hipparchus' observations; the works of Ptolemy, of Mohammed [=Albattani], of Copernicus and of other excellent astronomers can be torn up. What then will be certain in astronomy? But the movements of the stars are most certain and nothing of the sort has ever been seen in the course of centuries by the many illustrious men who have carefully observed the stars. When all this has been examined with care, the art of Optics concludes that this space which lies between the moon and the fixed stars (for of the limits of the heavens I shall not speak here) is full of this life-giving air (*aeris anima*), which I declare is no different from air itself.

For I am not moved by the credulity of the common herd, nor do I fear the opinion of Witelo,[10] an optician of authority, who states that the splendour of celestial matter is more subtle and more limpid than the transparency of air, from whence it follows that air is distinct from the matter of the heaven. Witelo tries to show this by [claiming] that the distance observed between two stars emerging above the horizon appears different from that which the

---

[10] Witelo (fl.1250-75), a Pole born in Polish Silesia, was educated in Paris (c.1253), Padua (c.1262–68) and Viterbo (1269). His *Perspectiva* [=*Opticæ libri decem*] was printed by Friedrich Risner, *Opticæ thesaurus Alhazeni Arabis libri septem [...] Item Vitellionis [...]* (Basle, 1572), reprint (New York,1972).

same two stars have when they pass the vertical.[11] This is something that I would readily agree to, were it not that Gemma Frisius [1508–55] in the explanation in his *De Radio Astronomico* [1545], states that the distances as observed with an instrument between stars situated at any altitude appear always the same.[12] Thus the art of optics teaches us that everything that lies between us and the fixed stars is just air. By this sole and unique truth, of which Optics has made us aware, from how many inveterate errors shall we now be able to free those around us?[13]

Although he was not the first to do so, Pena declared Aristotle's fourth element of fire to be non-existent for the same reasons given above regarding Aristotle's fifth element. 'Optics teaches us', he wrote, 'that everything that the natural philosophers maintain about the sphere of fire, is imagination (*somnium*)'.[14] Hieronymus Cardanus (1501–76) had already in 1550 denied the existence of the sphere of fire, though he gave no explanation to justify his view.[15]

Pena's exuberant attack on the nature of the Aristotelian celestial matter came to be widely discussed and integrated into the rising challenge to the whole Aristotelian paradigm. It made its mark throughout Europe, though largely outside the universities since the latter still remained strongholds of scholastic conservatism. The origins of Pena's thrust can be traced to three sources: to his close association with Peter Ramus who was violently anti-Aristotelian, to the influence of Stoicism, and to his attentiveness to Gemma Frisius' attempt to quantify astronomical observations. Gemma Frisius' conclusions were shortly to be proved wrong, though Kepler was later to excuse '… the keen-sighted Gemma Frisius, working alone with a rough instrument'.[16]

That Pena had espoused Stoicism as an alternative to Aristotelianism is claimed by Peter Barker who, in a recent article,[17] shows that Pena's expression *animabilem spiritum* is an extremely rare form of *animalis*, of which only a single occurrence is known in Cicero's *De Natura Deorum*, one of the sources of Stoic physics. The expression is there employed by Cicero's

---

[11] Cf. Witelo, *Opticæ libri decem*, lib.10 §51, in Risner, *op.cit*. pp.445–446. Witelo copies Ibn al-Haytham (Alhazen), lib.VII §52, in Risner, *op. cit*. pp.278–279.

[12] Gemma Frisius had written that '… the distances between stars near the horizon appear much greater, but when they are observed with the 'radius' [i.e. Jacob's staff] they do not differ from those which one observes when they are at the vertical'. Cf. Reiner Gemma Frisius, *De Radio Astronomico* (Antwerp, 1545), cap.XVI, f.29^v.

[13] Jean Pena, *De Usu optices Præfatio*, in idem, *op. cit*. sign. aa.ij^v–sign. aa.iij^r.

[14] *Ibid*. sign. bb.ij^r.

[15] Hieronymus Cardanus, *De subtilitate libri XXI* (Nuremberg, 1550), lib.II, p.23. (*Sed certe sub coelo Lunae nullus est ignis*. 'But it is certain that below the sphere of the moon there is no fire.')

[16] Johannes Kepler, *Dioptrice* (Augsburg, 1611), edn (London, 1653), p.61; *GW*, IV, p.335.

[17] Peter Barker, *art. cit*. p.99.

spokesman Lucilius Balbus. But Cicero through Balbus did not actually say that the planets and fixed stars move in the air as Pena has it. When Cicero wrote that '... the earth, which is situated in the centre of the world, is surrounded on all sides by the living and respirable substance named the air (*animabili spirabilique natura cui nomen est aer*)' he further added that '... the air in turn is embraced by the immeasurable æther which consists of the most elevated portions of fire'.[18] Cicero in fact follows the succession of air–fire–æther, though his æther is evidently fluid and not then the same as Aristotle's fifth essence. As noted by Sambursky, with Cicero there had begun a confusion between æther and the Stoic *pneuma*.[19] It is thus not directly obvious that Pena's sole Stoic source was Cicero. Ziegler's commentaries on Pliny and on Genesis are more likely to have been influential.

The phenomenon of refraction had been recognized by Claudius Ptolemy (c.90–168 AD) in his *Optics*, but he thought it would be impossible to measure it as such and he showed no concern that it might distort the quantitative values of his observations.

> It is possible for us to see from the phenomena which I am about to discuss, that at the boundary between air and æther there is a bending of the visual ray because of a difference between these bodies. We find that the stars which rise and set seem to incline more to the north when they are near the horizon and are measured by an instrument used for such a measurement. For the circles parallel to the equator, described upon these stars when they are rising or setting are nearer to the north than the circles described upon them when they are in the middle of the heaven. As they draw nearer to the horizon they have a greater inclination toward the north [...] This is due to the bending of the visual ray at the surface which divides the air from the æther, a spherical surface of necessity, whose center is the common center of all the elements and of the earth.[20]

The Arab astronomer and optician Abu 'Ali al-Hasan ibn al-Hasan ibn al-Haytham (known in medieval Europe as Alhazen) (c.965–1039) described refraction in similar terms to those of Ptolemy. For both of them refraction only occurred at the interface between air and æther. Fire they associated with air, there being a gradual transition from one to the other and for this

---

[18] Cicero, *De Natura Deorum*, lib.2, cap.36, ed. Rackham, pp.210–211. (*Principio enim terra sita in media parte mundi cicumfusa undique est hac animabili spirabilique natura cui nomen est aer [...] Hunc rursus amplectitur inmensus aether, qui constat ex altissimis ignibus* ...) Modern editions have the form *animalis*, which was brought in in the twentieth century instead of *animabilis* in earlier editions.

[19] S. Sambursky, *The Physics of the Stoics* (London, 1959), p.34.

[20] Claudius Ptolemy, *Optics*, V, Eng. trans. in M.R. Cohen and I.E. Drabkin, *A Source Book in Greek Science* (Cambridge, Mass., 1958), p.281. Latin text in Claudius Ptolemy, *L'Optique de Claude Ptolémée dans la version latine d'après l'arabe de l'Emir Eugène de Sicile*, ed. Albert Lejeune (Louvain, 1956), pp.237–238.

reason no refraction was believed to occur between them. 'The further air reaches [up] to heaven', wrote Ibn al-Haytham, 'the more it is purified, until it turns into fire. Therefore its subtlety increases gradually and not in discrete steps. The forms of celestial bodies, when they come into sight, are not refracted at the concave [surface] of the sphere of fire, since there is no [clean] concave surface there. Therefore there is no body more subtle than air in which visible forms reach [us] and at the surface of which they are refracted, except the æther.'[21]

Both Ptolemy and Ibn al-Haytham understood as the cause of refraction the difference in transparency between air and æther, which they saw as separated by a clean spherical interface. They had however no empirical proof of the existence of the æther, only the authority of Aristotle. Ibn al-Haytham, followed in identical terms by Witelo, both using an armillary sphere as an instrument, described in more precise detail than Ptolemy had given a method for measuring the distance from the pole of a rising star observed first at the horizon and then at the vertical. The change in distance they only noted as a proof of the existence of a body different from the air causing refraction of light rays proceeding from the star, and they paid no attention to the errors in astronomical theory which might result from this effect.[22]

Tycho Brahe and Christoph Rothmann

Pena's call upon astronomical optics to challenge Aristotelian physics was taken up and tested in what was designed to be a rigorous quantitative investigation by two of the most remarkable astronomers of the late sixteenth century, the Danish nobleman Tycho Brahe (1546–1601) and the astronomer to the Landgrave Wilhelm IV of Hesse-Cassel, Christoph Rothmann (c.1550–between 1597 and 1608).[23] The letters exchanged

---

[21] Ibn al-Haytham (Alhazen), *De Aspectibus*, lib.VII §51 in *Opticae thesaurus Alhazeni Arabis libri septem*, ed. Friedrich Risner (Basle, 1572), reprint with introduction by David C. Lindberg (New York, 1972), p.278. (… *quanto magis appropinquat aer coelo, tanto magis purificatur, donec fiat ignis. Subtilitas ergo eius fit ordinate secundum successionem, non in differentia terminata. Forme ergo eorum, quae sunt in coelo, quando extenduntur ad visum, non refringuntur apud concavitatem sphaerae ignis, cum non sit ibi superficies concava determinata. Nullum ergo invenitur corpus subtilius aere, in quo extenduntur formae visibilium & refringantur apud superficiem eius, nisi corpus coeleste* …) Witelo follows Alhazen on this point, declaring that the spheres of fire and air 'are almost one' (*medias sphaeras ignis & aeris […] sunt sphaera quasi una* …) Witelo in *Opticæ thesaurus, ed. cit.* lib.X §50, p.445.

[22] Ibn al-Haytham, *De Aspectibus*, lib.VII §15, in Risner, *Opticæ thesaurus, ed. cit.* pp.251–252; Witelo, *Opticæ libri decem*, lib.10 §49, in Risner, *op. cit.* p.444.

[23] On Tycho Brahe's life and work see the article by C. Doris Hellman in *Dictionary of Scientific Biography*, II (1970), pp.401–416. On Rothmann see *ibid.* vol. XI (1975), pp.561–562. On Tycho Brahe cf. also Alain Segonds, 'Tycho Brahe (1546–1601)', in Colette Nativel, ed., *Centuriæ Latinæ. Cent figures humanistes de la Renaissance aux Lumières offertes à Jacques Chomarat* (Geneva, 1997), pp.175–182.

between them and later published by Tycho provide a unique insight into the procedures of the time for approaching a scientific truth.[24] Furthermore these two men were in touch with a network of like-minded figures across the whole of Europe.

There is no evidence that either Tycho or Rothmann had in their hands, or had read directly or indirectly, Jean Pena's preface to his edition of Euclid, though it is highly likely, since Tycho often refers to him by name,[25] and certain expressions of Rothmann's recall those used by Pena, as will be seen below. Both astronomers were almost unique in being able to use instruments of very large size and consequently of great precision.[26] Neither used the telescope, only invented later after them. Rothmann had access to observational instruments at Cassel constructed by two exceptionally talented artisans, Eberhardt Baldwein (1525–92) and Jost Bürgi (1552–1632).[27] Technical innovations were exchanged between Cassel and Denmark and certain of Tycho's were brought to Cassel in 1584 by Paul Wittich (1550–87).[28]

On the island of Hveen in the sound between Denmark and Sweden, given to him by the King of Denmark, Tycho Brahe had built for him, with the rents granted him by the King, a Gothic Renaissance palace. He named this palace Uraniborg; it was flanked by an observatory which he called Stjerneborg, in which the instruments were placed in underground rooms to protect them from the weather.[29] His books were printed on his own private

---

[24] Tycho Brahe, *Epistolarum astronomicarum libri* (Uraniborg, 1596) hereafter abbreviated as *Epist.*

[25] Tycho Brahe, *Astronomiæ Instauratæ Progymnasmata* (Prague, 1602); *TBOO*, II, p.77; idem, *Epist.* p.107; *TBOO*, VI, p.135 (Tycho to Rothmann, 17/8/1588); also *Epist.* p.157; *TBOO*, VI, p.187 (Tycho to Rothmann, 24/11/1589).

[26] On Tycho's instruments, see Victor Thoren, 'New Light on Tycho's Instruments', *Journal of the History of Astronomy* 4 (1973), pp.25–45. On their precision cf. Walter G. Wesley, 'The Accuracy of Tycho Brahe's Instruments', *Journal of the History of Astronomy* IX (1978), pp.42–53.

[27] On Bürgi and Baldwein, see Bernhard Sticker, 'Landgraf Wilhelm IV und die Anfänge der modernen astronomischen Messkunst', *Sudhoffs Archiv* 40 (1956), pp.15–25 and Bruce T. Moran, 'Princes, Machines and the Valuation of Precision in the 16th Century', *Sudhoffs Archiv* 61 (1977), pp.209–228; idem, 'Wilhelm IV of Hesse-Kassel: Informal Communication and the Aristocratic Context of Discovery', in T. Nickles ed., *Scientific Discovery: Case Studies*, Boston Studies in the Philosophy of Science, (Dordrecht and London, 1980), p.79. Cf. also the article in *Dictionary of Scientific Biography*, II (1970), pp.602–603.

[28] Bruce T. Moran, 'Christopher Rothmann, the Copernican Theory and Institutional and Technical Influences in the Criticism of Aristotelian Cosmology', *Sixteenth Century Journal* XIII, No.3 (1982), pp.85–108. On Wittich see the article in *Dictionary of Scientific Biography*, XIV (1976), pp.470–471.

[29] John Christianson,'The Celestial Palace of Tycho Brahe', *Scientific American* 204 No. 2 (1961), pp.118–128. The instruments (quadrants and armillary spheres) are described and illustrated in Tycho's work *Astronomiæ Instauratæ Mechanica* (Wandesburg, [Wandsbeck], 1598). Partial English translation with reproductions of the engravings of the instruments by Hans Raeder, Elis Strömgren and Bengt Strömgren, *Tycho Brahe's Description of his Instruments and Scientific Work* (Copenhagen, 1946).

3   Tycho Brahe (1546–1601). Engraving in Tycho Brahe, *Epistolarum astronomicarum libri*, edn (Frankfurt, 1610), frontispiece. Photo: Bibliothèque Nationale, Paris.

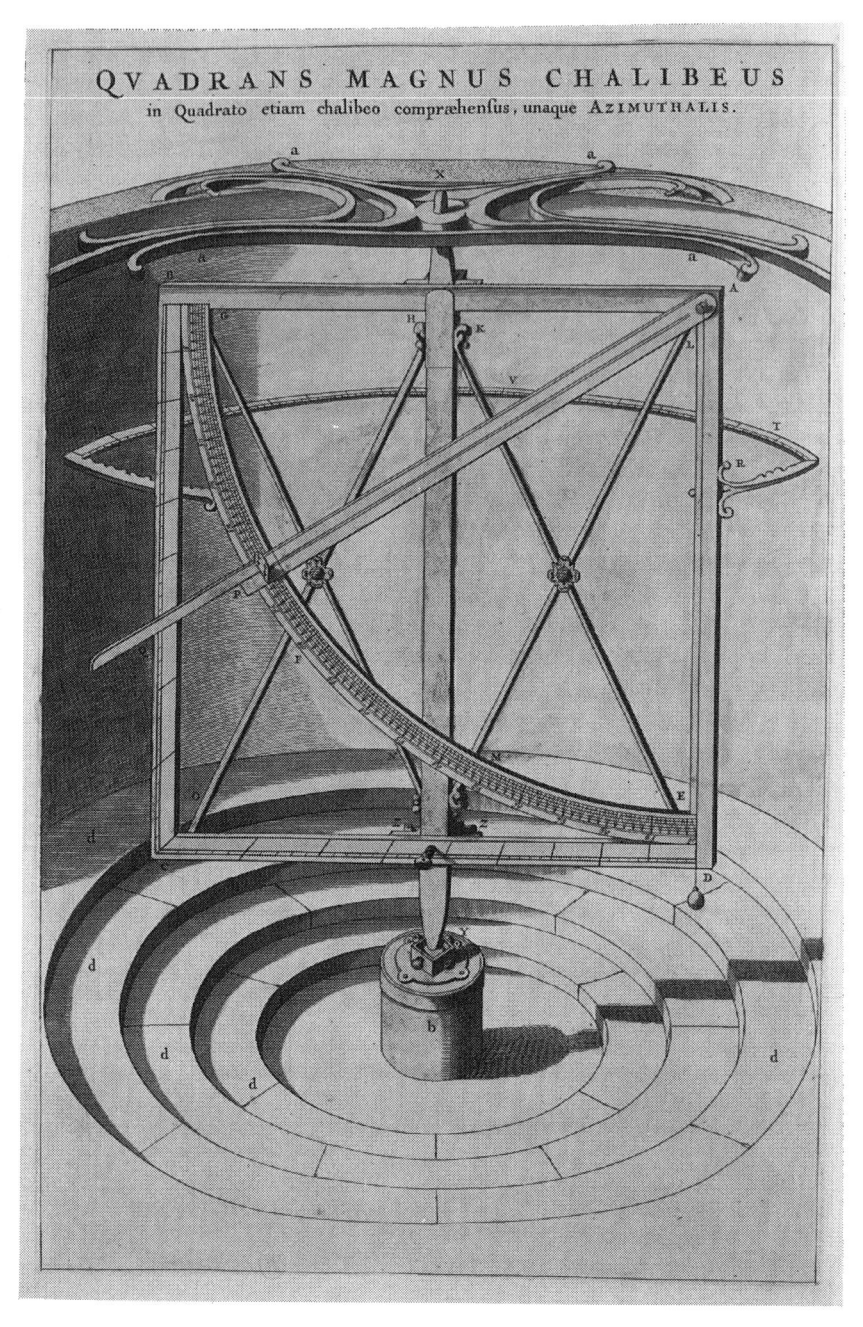

4   The type of instrument used by Tycho Brahe to measure solar and stellar refraction. Engraving in Joan Blaeu, *Le Grand Atlas ou Cosmographie Blaviane* (Amsterdam, 1663), vol.I. Photo: Bibliothèque Nationale, Paris.

press and circulated by him to scholars with whom he had already corresponded. Uraniborg, where Tycho worked for more than twenty years, became Europe's first private scientific research centre and was visited by students, scholars and noblemen from all over the Continent as well as from the British Isles.[30]

As part of their other astronomical observations, Tycho and Rothmann proceeded with their instruments to make a series of systematic observations of solar and stellar refraction at different altitudes to obtain the most exact values possible, something which neither Ibn al-Haytham nor Witelo had undertaken.[31] But as regards the nature of the matter of the heavens, upon which their at first not dissimilar results had an important bearing, they came to very different conclusions, which each defended in his letters to the other with persistent conviction and to us intriguing arguments.

Tycho's method for measuring solar refraction, undertaken during the years 1585 to 1598, consisted of choosing a day near the solstice when the sun's declination changed very slowly, and of measuring the altitude and azimuth of the sun at frequent intervals. Then from the latitude of the observatory, the azimuth and declination, he computed the altitude, which, deducted from the observed altitude, gave the amount of refraction.[32] The method, as Victor Thoren has noted, was vitiated by circular reasoning since the computed values depended on observed (and refracted) positions and Tycho further assumed an excessive ancient value of three minutes for the parallax of the sun, a value it never occurred to him to check empirically.[33]

Tycho, in a letter to Rothmann of 20 January 1587,[34] found that both solar and stellar refraction faded out above an angle of 30° (he was later to give a value of 45°).[35] Rothmann had previously written to Tycho in a letter of 18 May 1586 asserting that he also had found a value of 30° for both the sun and the stars[36] (he was later to maintain one of only 20° for stellar refraction).[37]

---

[30] On Tycho's life and scientific achievements, J.L.E. Dreyer's lively book has not aged and is more readable than Victor Thoren's recent tedious biography. Cf. J.L.E. Dreyer, *Tycho Brahe: A Picture of Scientific Life and Work in the Sixteenth Century* (London, 1890), reprint (Gloucester, Mass., 1977). Victor Thoren, *The Lord of Uraniborg. A Biography of Tycho Brahe* (Cambridge, 1990).

[31] They followed the method described by Ibn al-Haytham (Alhazen), (lib.VII §15) and by Witelo (lib.10 §49 & §50). Tycho cast doubt upon their claimed success, since their instruments, he said, would not have been big enough to provide the necessary precision. Cf. Tycho Brahe, *Astronomiæ Instauratæ Progymnasmata*, in idem, *TBOO* I, p.76.

[32] J.L.E. Dreyer, *Tycho Brahe*, p.334.

[33] Victor Thoren, *op. cit.* pp.227–234.

[34] Tycho Brahe to Christoph Rothmann, 20/1/1587, in Tycho Brahe, *Epist.* p.64; *TBOO*, VI, p.93.

[35] Tycho Brahe, *Astronomiæ Instauratæ Progymnasmata* (Prague, 1602); *TBOO*, II, p.76.

[36] Christoph Rothmann to Tycho, 18/5/1586, in Tycho Brahe. *Epist.* p.29; *TBOO*, VI, p.57.

[37] Christoph Rothmann, 'Descriptio accurata cometæ anni 1585', in Willebrord Snell, *Descriptio cometæ qui anno 1618 mense Novembri effulsit* (Leiden,1619), cap.V, p.104.

In his letter of 18 May 1586, Rothmann wrote that he was sending Tycho his treatise on the comet of 1585, which contained a chapter on stellar refraction.[38] Rothmann's treatise, *Descriptio accurata cometae anni 1585*, was later to be published in 1611 by Willebrord Snell (1580–1626). In it Rothmann declares that he will show that belief in the existence of solid spheres to carry the planets is absolutely unfounded and that, through astronomical optics, he will show that, between the fixed stars and the earth, besides the seven planets, there is nothing but air.

'Though this belief in celestial spheres [i.e. that they are solid] is held', he wrote, 'by the greatest writers, and commonly possesses the authority of a general axiom, yet, out of the love of truth, we shall show that it is absolutely false and while others maintain it with futile conjectures, we shall, in calling upon the most solid proofs of optics and of astronomy, refute it and we shall show that, between the sphere of the fixed stars and the earth, there is nothing other than life-giving air (*animalem hunc aërem*) and the seven planets suspended in it'.[39] The use by Rothmann of the expression *animalem aërem* suggests the influence of Stoicism in his thought, but is no direct proof that he had himself read Pena's work.

Rothmann then proceeded to describe the phenomenon of the refraction of light passing from one medium to another, citing as examples air and water. Following this analogy, the celestial spheres are different from air and all stars seen away from the vertical will, because of refraction, never be seen in their right places. 'But', he continued, 'in the course of many centuries nothing of the sort has ever been seen by the very many illustrious men who have assiduously worked to observe the stars.'[40] Such refraction as Rothmann had observed and which he had found to reach no further than 20° above the horizon was due, he said, to vapours lying above it. If refraction was caused by the celestial orbs, it would not stop at 15° or at 20° above the horizon, but would continue up to the vertical, but no one had ever encountered this. 'This refraction', Rothmann insisted, 'is not caused by the difference in transparency between air and æther, but by the difference in transparency between the vapours and the air …'.[41] In conclusion Rothmann took the very contestable step of asserting that, 'It would be a great error to agree that these two media [air and æther] have the same transparency and the same subtlety and nevertheless claim that they are different in sub-

---

[38] Christoph Rothmann to Tycho, 18/5/1586, in Tycho Brahe, *Epist.* p.27; *TBOO*, VI, p.54.

[39] Christoph Rothmann, 'Descriptio accurata cometae anni 1585', in *ed. cit.* cap.V, pp.102–103. Although Rothmann stated further on (p.117) that 'the very motion of the comet was the strongest argument that the spheres of the planets cannot be solid bodies', the main thrust of his chapter from its beginning was based on proof from the refraction of light that the matter of the heavens was no different from air.

[40] *Ibid.* p.103.

[41] *Ibid.* p.105.

stance (*essentiam*)'.[42] For this rash inference Rothmann was hotly taken to task by Tycho; it was later to be the subject of debate all over Europe.

In his letter to Rothmann of 20 January 1587, Tycho acknowledged receipt of some chapters of Rothmann's treatise and wrote back, 'I would readily agree with you, as you assert in the part that you have sent me, that the heaven is all air and does not consist of solid matter, indeed is nothing but air and even that the air above the moon is much more subtle than the air which you understand as elementary air, to the extent that it rather deserves the name of a most liquid and subtle æther [sic], than that of the element air'.[43]

Tycho's answer is reminiscent, *mutatis mutandis*, of Ibn al-Haytham's concept quoted above of air being transformed progressively into fire. It in no way satisfied Rothmann, for he replied carefully, repeating what he had said in his treatise.

> You indeed rightly declare with me that the celestial spheres are not hard and impenetrable, but liquid and subtle, easily allowing the movement of the planets. But I disagree when you say that because of refraction, the transparencies of æther and air are different and that there is no element of air contained in the celestial spheres, but rather a most liquid æther different from the element of air. Yet the argument concerning refraction which you think serves you, rebuts and refutes your opinion. For if, by this refraction, which we discover through observations, the transparency of æther is different from that of the element of air, such could only be so if it [the refraction] continues [to be observed] up to the vertical.[44]

In a letter of 17 August 1588, Tycho still only appeared to have understood half of Rothmann's point; far from convinced, he returned to the issue at length. 'You claim', he wrote to Rothmann, 'that the matter of the celestial spheres consists of nothing but the element of air and that there is no refraction caused by the difference in transparency between æther and air and you attribute the causes of refraction to vapours alone which lie just above the horizon. But I have learnt, either from what is believed up to now by the principal [natural] philosophers, or from the tracks of comets, that the heaven is not made of hard and impenetrable material which is spread out in

---

[42] *Ibid.* p.151.

[43] Tycho Brahe to Christoph Rothmann, 20/1/1587, in Tycho Brahe, *Epist.* pp.59–60; *TBOO*, VI, p.88 (*Quod autem in portione eius mihi transmissa Caelum totum aëreum, nec e solida materia constare, imo nil aliud quàm Aërem ipsum esse asseveras, id facile tibi concesserim, modo aërem qui supra Lunam sit, multo subtiliorem quam hunc Elementarem intelligas, adeo ut Ætheris potius liquidissimi & subtilissimi, quam Aëris elementaris nomen mereatur*). Edward Rosen, in quoting these words, omitted an important part of the sentence which changed the whole meaning that he sought to give it: '... to the extent that it rather deserves the name [...] of aether' (*adeo ut Ætheris potius [...] nomen mereatur*). Cf. Edward Rosen, 'The Dissolution of the Solid Celestial Spheres', *Journal of the History of Ideas* XLVI (1985), p.27.

[44] Christoph Rothmann to Tycho, 11/10/1587, in Tycho Brahe, *Epist.* p.83;*TBOO*, VI, p.111.

the form of diaphanous membranes. Nevertheless, I shall never agree that the airy heaven (*cœlum aëreum*) has any elementary material in it'.[45]

Taking his cue from Aristotle's remark that the friction of the planets and stars moving in air or fire would create tremendous noise,[46] Tycho argued back to Rothmann that, '… if there were air in the celestial region, the rapid movement of the celestial bodies would produce an enormous noise which we would hear. Air would also be detrimental to the perpetual motion in the revolutions of celestial bodies and as a result of wear over a long period of time, would diminish their purity and even further, through friction, distort their constant harmony'.[47]

Tycho saw the air gradually turning into æther without there being a clean interface, much as Ptolemy and Ibn al-Haytham had seen air turning into fire without there being an interface separating them. 'The air', wrote Tycho, 'in fact combines as one with the æther (*cum Æthere quasi in unum coalescit*) and is progressively imbued with a celestial nature and that is why no observable refraction occurs. For there is no definite point (*locus*) at a given distance from the earth at which such refraction takes place, but little by little the transparency of air is transformed into that of æther'.[48]

Declaring that the matter of the heavens was inscrutable (*imperscrutabilis*) and that it had nothing in common with the nature of the elements, Tycho nevertheless concluded to Rothmann that,

> … It suffices that we agree between us that the heaven is not made up of real orbs, hard and impenetrable, to which the stars are fixed and with which they revolve, but that it consists of a very liquid, very rare and very subtle substance which allows the seven planets to move freely and without hindrance in whatever direction their natural impetus and innate knowledge (*naturalis impetus et congenita scientia*) carry them.[49]

This crucial statement of Tycho's shows that while he had come to abandon the rigid spheres carrying the planets and to accept the fluid nature of the heaven, he still held to the Aristotelian difference between celestial and elementary matter, which Rothmann, under the very probable influence of Pena, had stood to abolish. If Tycho's expression 'natural impetus' can be traced to its fourteenth-century origins in the Frenchman Jean Buridan (c.1300–58),[50] his other expression 'innate knowledge' seems to be his own.

---

[45] Tycho Brahe to Christophe Rothmann, 17/8/1588, in Tycho Brahe, *Epist.* p.106; *TBOO*, VI, pp.134–135.

[46] Cf. above Chapter 1, p.5.

[47] Tycho Brahe to Christoph Rothmann, 17/8/1588, in idem, *Epist.* p.106; *TBOO*, VI, p.135.

[48] Idem, *Epist.* p.108; *TBOO*, VI, p.136.

[49] Idem, *Epist.* p.111; *TBOO*, VI, p.140.

[50] On Buridan's concept of impetus, see Edward Grant, *A Source Book in Medieval Science* (Cambridge, Mass., 1974), pp.275–280.

As we have seen above, it was taken over by Roslin, who entertained the notion as a possible explanation to replace that provided by rigid orbs.[51]

In his letter of 13 October 1588, Rothmann replied to Tycho's letter of 17 August 1588, refuting his argument that air combined gradually with æther. There would have to be, Rothmann contended, a clean optical interface or 'point' between the two at which refraction would take place. His insistence on the existence of a 'point of refraction' can in part be explained by the fact that he could not imagine a curved ray of refraction, not having the mathematics to treat it. For Rothmann, it was impossible to maintain that

> ... these two different media [air and æther] assimilate into each other by a mutual association (*mutua connexione*) [...] and be changed progressively from one into the other. There will nevertheless be, in such a mutual combination and assimilation, a point at which the image of the stars will be, as it were, slowed down and this point is the point of refraction (*punctum refractionis*).[52]

Rothmann then sought to consolidate his argument with a comparison from his own experience, which though clever, lacked validity:

> I have often noted in winter [he wrote to Tycho] when I was in the middle of the observatory with the window open, surrounded by warm air, that the thing looked at in the cold air appeared refracted. Certainly neither the identity [of the two media – hot air and cold air], nor their gradual combination and assimiliation eliminated the refraction.[53] If indeed these media are in themselves so similar that there is no difference between them, why do you call them different? Why do you not call this pure sublunary air, æther, or, as Pliny calls it, æthereal spirit (*Æthereum spiritum*)?[54] I do not wish to fight with you over it. For I merely claim this, that the pure media of æther and air are not different, since no refraction is produced by them. But I fail to understand how you can remain firmly attached to your opinion, which you hold against all experience, that the refraction [at the interface] of æther and air goes on up to the vertical, whereas you will never perceive such with instruments.[55]

Rothmann then addressed Tycho's contention that if the matter of the heaven was air, friction would alter the regularity of the motion of the planets, producing audible noise. Pure air as opposed to damp air, asserted

---

[51] See above, Chapter 2, p.53.

[52] Christoph Rothmann to Tycho, 13/10/1588, in Tycho Brahe, *Epist.* p.122; *TBOO*, VI, pp.151–152. Rothmann seems to have taken the expression *punctum refractionis* from Witelo, lib.10 §52, in Risner, *op cit.* p.447.

[53] Professor Costabel has emphasized to me that Rothmann's argument is vitiated by the fact that the change in density between hot and cold air would be very great, that between æther and air very small.

[54] Rothmann's reference to 'æthereal spirit' may have been drawn from Ziegler's commentary on Pliny. It would seem to be an allusion to the *pneuma* of the Stoics.

[55] Christoph Rothmann to Tycho, 13/10/1588, in Tycho Brahe, *Epist.* pp.122–123; *TBOO*, VI, p.152.

Rothmann, produces no friction, and if pure air were indeed capable of such, storms would, in our damp air, have long ago worn and eroded away the whole earth through their friction. 'I can remember', he wrote, 'in a place situated five miles from here, there blew a wind so violent that it overturned houses and brought down trees and yet I heard nothing of the noise it made. And so when things are true [i.e. known by experience] they cannot be controverted by conjecture.'[56] Rothmann's reasoning may seem to us naive. But was it so untypical of that of his contemporaries of the sixteenth century in similar contexts?

In his letter of 21 February 1589, Tycho returned to the main epistemological point of their polemic, that for him the identity of optical characteristics did not guarantee a corresponding identity of material substance:

> I will only make one objection to your main argument, by which you try to show that the heaven and the element of air are absolutely one and the same on the basis of the fact that the refractions do not go up to the vertical, but fade out to become insensible beyond 45°. Although this may prove that the transparency of air and æther are not different, and as a result, that they both have the same matter and substance, you seem to me to be inferring more than this assumption can bear, for even if one grants that there is no observed refraction of the [rays of] the sun and the stars at a given altitude, this may indeed suffice for it to follow that there is no difference between the transparent media (*diaphana*) or at least no perceptible difference, but it is not necessarily to be inferred from this that both transparent media have the same quality and substance.[57]

Tycho then proceeded, just as Rothmann had done, to give an example taken from the elementary world: the comparison between water and wine. If both are freed from impurities and made crystal clear so that the transparency of the one does not differ from that of the other, and as a result, that there be no difference in the refraction caused by either, the substance and the nature of the liquor and body of each, he argued, will still be found to be different.[58]

Tycho's one-time assistant, Conrad Aslachus, produced in his work *De Natura caeli triplicis* (1597) a further example to defend his master's point of view. Given two windows, one of crystal and the other of ordinary glass, having both the same density and transparency, they will refract light in the same way, but this does not prove that they are of the same substance.[59]

---

[56] Idem, in Tycho Brahe, *Epist.* p.121; *TBOO*, VI, p.150.
[57] Tycho to Christoph Rothmann, 21/2/1589, in Tycho Brahe, *Epist.* pp.138–139; *TBOO*, VI, p.168.
[58] Idem, *loci citati*.
[59] Conrad Aslachus, *De Natura caeli triplicis libelli tres* (Sigenæ Nassoviorum [=Siegen], 1597), pp.68–69.

In his letter of 24 November 1589, Tycho wrote querulously that Rothmann was drawing conclusions that went far beyond what he felt to be scientifically legitimate and was attributing to him positions that he had never held:

> Why then, I ask you, do you boast that you have got out of me, what I have said in clear words has not yet been sufficiently proved? Why do you unjustly twist my thought and why do you rush so thoughtlessly into passing judgement on these points on which there was agreement? If truth, which is the daughter of time, is to inform me better, I shall not hesitate to accept it and that on any occasion that may be given me. I do not however see how I can agree with those of your opinions on which we have differed.[60]

Tycho's prudent caution undoubtedly showed better judgement than Rothmann's one sided anti-Aristotelian commitment.

In 1596 on his own private press Tycho printed his correspondence with Rothmann, as well as that with other scholars. In 1602 he then published his *Astronomiæ Instauratæ Progymnasmata* in which he recapitulated his position on the material substance of the heaven and his differences with Rothmann, mentioning Jean Pena as the source of the latter's ideas.

> For if [he wrote, summing up] the difference between the degree of transparency of the æther and of the air were as obvious as they [Ibn al-Haytham (Alhazen) and Witelo] claim, the refractions of the [light of the] stars would be evident at least almost up to the vertical, something which in no way corresponds to what is revealed from experience. For the value of these refractions diminishes [as one lifts the line of sight above the horizon] until, at an altitude of about 45° they are almost imperceptible, even in the case of the sun. The principal and certain cause of these refractions lies in the vapours which hang continually over the surface of the earth and which make the air around us slightly thicker and less transparent than the part which lies higher up. Hence it happens that near the horizon the refractions are more noticeable and that they diminish progressively as the [line of sight is raised]. And though, in order to prove that the nature and the matter of the heaven itself is absolutely identical with that of the air, certain modern scholars have claimed that it is in this [=the vapours] that lies the sole cause of the refractions, nevertheless, I have no doubt whatever that the heaven itself in which the heavenly bodies revolve perpetually, is different from the life-giving element of air, however freed it may be from terrestrial vapours. And that is why, on this point, I have sound reasons never to concur with their opinions, as I shall explain more fully elsewhere. For although the heaven is very fluid and very subtle (*liquidissimum & rarissimum*) and that it is in no way packed (*compactum*) with real spheres (*orbibus realibus*) (a notion which a large number of [natural] philosophers have, over many centuries, mistakenly put into the minds of the credulous) – I shall give adequate proof of this at the end of this book from

---

[60] Tycho Brahe to Christoph Rothmann, 24/11/1589, in *Epist.* pp.164–165; *TBOO*, VI, pp.194–195.

[the behaviour of] comets which run their entire courses in the heaven – I would not however readily agree that, because of this, the nature of the heaven and its substance is the same as that of the element air, [...] even given that the difference which comes from the difference in transparency between æther and air is very small and in no way as big as the opticians have thought, but on the contrary so small that it is hardly perceptible. It follows then that as the air gets closer and closer to [the sphere of] the moon, it becomes, because it has greater purity, more subtle, so that its transparency in no way differs, or hardly differs, from that of the æther.

Furthermore, even if the transparency were the same and no refractions [were seen to] occur because of the difference between the transparencies of æther and air, it would not however be enough to infer, on account of this, that the matter of the heaven is everywhere the same as the sublunary element of air, as Jean Pena was, as far as I know, the first to claim and as certain modern scholars still do not hesitate to assert. Among them is that most erudite man of solid learning in astronomical matters, Christopher Rothmann, the mathematician to Prince Wilhelm, Landgraf of Hesse, with whom I have exchanged letters on the subject. However, because the refractions diminish so rapidly and that they are [not seen] to go up to the vertical, this scholar, persisting in his hasty opinion, will not bear being parted from it.

Indeed, because the transparency of the air, especially of the upper air, is practically identical with that of the heaven, so that the refractions due to the difference in transparency between the æther and the air are hardly sensible and that they are never seen to reach up to the vertical, this argument is not however valid, even if the very great distance of the heaven makes the smallest refractions escape being observed. For it does not sufficiently follow that two bodies having the same transparency also have exactly the same substance and matter.[61]

Although more an astronomer than a natural philosopher, Tycho remained adamant that evidence from the science of optics could not be used to invalidate Aristotle's distinction between celestial and elementary matter. However the 1572 Nova, or Supernova as it would be called today, had, as a result of Tycho's observations that it revealed no parallax, been placed by him above the moon in the sphere of the fixed stars.[62] Its situation there clashed with Aristotle's doctrine concerning comets.[63] In his *De Mundi Ætherei*

---

[61] Tycho Brahe, *Astronomiæ Instauratæ Progymnasmata* (Prague, 1602), in *TBOO*, II, pp.76–77.

[62] Tycho Brahe, *De Nova et nullius ævi memoria prius visa stella iam pridem anno a nato Christo 1572 mense Novembri primum conspecta contemplatio mathematica* (Copenhagen, 1573), sign. A^{4v}. Parallax in the case of the geocentric astronomical system defines the apparent change (measured angularly) in the position of a heavenly body when viewed from different points on the earth's surface.

[63] Comets, according to Aristotle, were objects which only appeared in the elementary region below the moon, since for him no transitory phenomena, including *novae*, could exist in the celestial region above the moon where all movement was necessarily perfectly circular and perpetual. Cf. Aristotle, *Meteorologica*, I 6–7 342b–345a, ed. Lee, pp.39–57.

Recentioribus Phænomenis (1588), Tycho had already announced his promise to show from his observations of comets that the heaven was fluid and that real spheres carrying the planets and stars were non-existent: 'I shall add at the end of this work and there it will be shown, first of all from the motions of comets and then clearly proved, that the machine of Heaven is not a hard impervious body stuffed full of real spheres. [...] It will be proved that it extends everywhere most fluid and simple ...'.[64] Yet Tycho never afterwards furnished the proof he promised, in spite of Kepler's claim in Book IV of his *Epitome* that he had done so. 'Tycho Brahe', wrote Kepler, 'disproved the solidity of the spheres with three reasons: the first from the movement of comets; the second from the fact that light is not refracted; the third from the proportions of their orbits. For if the spheres were solid, comets would not be seen to cross from one sphere into another, for they would be prevented by the solidity; but they do go through from one orbit to another, as Brahe showed'.[65] As has been noted by J.V. Field, Kepler's account is an oversimplification of what really occurred, Kepler in fact 'ascribing to Tycho Brahe what really originated in his own mind'.[66] Michel-Pierre Lerner has since carefully shown that Tycho's abandoning of solid spheres was the result of a number of converging factors in his mind, astronomical, optical, physical, scriptural and philosophical in nature.[67]

Scholars all over Europe were to take sides in Tycho's argument with Rothmann concerning the lessons to be drawn from refractions. The Protestants, with no more evidence than that which had failed to satisfy Tycho, tended to side with Rothmann. Catholics from the 1620s onwards tended by and large (with certain notable exceptions) to side with Tycho.

Among Tycho's correspondents was Caspar Peucer (1525–1602), Rector of the Protestant University of Wittenberg.[68] In a letter of 10 May 1589, Peucer

---

[64] Tycho Brahe, *De Mundi Ætherei Recentioribus Phænomenis* (Uraniborg, 1588); *TBOO*, IV, p.159. Partial Eng. trans. in Marie Boas and A. Rupert Hall, 'Tycho Brahe's System of the World', *Occasional Notes of the Royal Astronomical Society*, 3 No. 21 (1959) pp.259–260.

[65] Johannes Kepler, *Epitome Astronomiæ Copernicanæ* (Linz, 1620), lib.IV, pars 1, edn (Linz, 1622), p.442 and in *GW*, VII, pp.260–261.

[66] J.V. Field, 'Kepler's rejection of solid celestial spheres', *Vistas in Astronomy* 23 (1979), pp.207–211.

[67] See Michel-Pierre Lerner, *Le monde des sphères*, vol.II, *La fin du cosmos classique* (Paris, 1997), pp.39–66 and idem, 'Le Scoperte celesti a partire dal 1572 e la loro assimilazione teorica', in idem, *Tre Saggi sulla cosmologia alla fine del Cinquecento*, Istituto Italiano per gli studi filosofici, Lezioni della Scuola di Studi Superiori in Napoli, Naples, 14 (1992), pp.73–104. Cf. also Miguel A. Granada, *El debate cosmológico en 1588. Bruno, Brahe, Rothmann, Ursus, Roslin*, Istituto Italiano per gli studi filosofici, Lezioni della Scuola di Studi Superiori in Napoli, Naples, 18 (1996), pp.47–52.

[68] Peucer was later cruelly persecuted by his fellow Protestants and imprisoned for twelve years for his unorthodox views on the Eucharist. His prison experience is described in his *Historia carcerum et liberationis divinae* (Zurich, 1605), esp. pp.363–364.

wrote to Tycho that he had found evidence in Holy Scripture that the Heaven consisted of a '... very subtle and very pure æthereal substance through which light rays can pass and which is liquid and fluid'.[69] For this interpretation of Genesis, Peucer may have been partly influenced by Ziegler's Commentaries on Pliny and on Genesis, though he further added that '... the heaven is something spread out (*expansum*) expressed by the word *rakiah*',[70] a term not however used by Ziegler.

On 24 November 1589 Tycho wrote to Rothmann how pleased he had been to learn that confirmation could be found in Holy Scripture of the fluidity of the heaven. 'The most illustrious Caspar Peucer himself', wrote Tycho, 'a man whose publicly expressed doctrine reveals his exceptional merit, has written me letters treating in particular of this question, letters in which, having brought together with exemplary erudition a great many quotations from Holy Scripture which abound in this sense, he has supported my opinion concerning the extreme rarefiedness and limpidity of the matter of the heaven [...] What is very important is that he has thereby also recognized that the conclusions I have reached are in no way absurd'.[71]

If the Basilian interpretation of the nature of the Firmament, together with the original Hebrew meaning of the term *rakiah*, lent theological support to Tycho's concept of a fluid heaven in which the planets were guided by their 'innate knowledge' (*congenita scientia*), there yet remained an unanswered question. How did the fixed stars maintain constant distances between each other in the fluid heaven?

Jean-Baptiste Morin (1593–1656), an Aristotelian traditionalist and professor at the Sorbonne, later put this question to one of Tycho's assistants, Christian Severinus Longomontanus (1562–1647).[72] Longomontanus answered that he had himself asked this question of Tycho, who had replied that it was not absolutely impossible that '... the *rakiah* in which the stars are located and which, although it is similar to something immaterial, [...] nevertheless possessed a very powerful force capable of penetrating and invading the bodies of the world and of maintaining each fixed star in the place destined for it'.[73] Tycho thus seems to have conveniently attributed to the *rakiah* the 'holding' or tensional function of the *pneuma* of Stoic physics.[74]

---

[69] Caspar Peucer to Tycho Brahe, 10/5/1589, in Tycho Brahe, *TBOO*, VII, p.185.

[70] *Ibid. loc cit.*

[71] Tycho Brahe to Christoph Rothmann, 24/11/1589, in Tycho Brahe, *Epist.* p.157; *TBOO*, VI, p.187.

[72] Longomontanus was Tycho's assistant from 1589 to 1597 and again at Prague c.1600. He became Professor of Astronomy at Copenhagen University from 1605 to his death in 1647.

[73] Jean Baptiste Morin, *Responsio pro telluris quiete ad I. Lansbergi Apologiam pro telluris motu* (Paris, 1634), pp.47-48.

[74] Cf. David E. Hahm, *op. cit.* pp.165–167.

Longomontanus later wrote in his *Astronomia Danica*, published in 1622, that the *rakiah* was '... a very fine and very subtle spread-outness (*expansum*) resembling something incorporeal and imperceptible to the senses'.[75] It was also, he said, the support that carried light. 'Some', he added in an Appendix where he appears to be alluding to Patrizi, 'claimed that the heaven consisted of *fluor*'.[76] This, for Longmontanus, was nothing other than '... the spread-outnesses (*expansi*) or the *Rhachias* [sic] penetrating the whole of nature'.[77] In his work *De natura caeli triplici* (1597), Conrad Aslachus denied that the fixed stars were attached to a solid orb. He claimed that the constancy of their positions in relation to each other in the very rarefied expanse of the heaven (*tenuissimo caeli expansio*) was, as in the case of the planets, ordained by God.[78] But such simplistic providentialism accomplished little as an explanation.

Johannes Kepler

Of the many scholars in Europe who discussed the controversy between Tycho Brahe and Christoph Rothmann over the lesson to be drawn from refractions, the first to resume and analyse it in depth was Johannes Kepler (1571–1639), in his work on light, *Ad Vitellionem Paralipomena* (1604).[79] Declaring that the argument became so confused that it was difficult for him to explain it, Kepler levelled his criticism at both the protagonists. 'If they had applied the true [method] of measuring refractions', he stated, 'Tycho would not have had to allege a double cause of refraction, the one due to the air and the other due to vapours, and Rothmann would not have been able to deny that light is refracted, even insensibly, at the vertical'.[80]

---

[75] Christian Severinus Longomontanus, *Astronomia Danica, Pars Altera* (Amsterdam, 1622), p.35.

[76] Francesco Patrizi's Neoplatonic concept of *fluor*, a fluid both corporeal and incorporeal, is expounded by him in his work, *Nova de Universis Philosophia libris quinquaginta comprehensa*, lib.XIV (Venice, 1593), p.95 (1st edn Ferrara, 1591). See John Henry, 'Francesco Patrizi da Cherso's Concept of Space and its Later Influence', *Annals of Science* 36 (1979), p.556.

[77] Christian Severinus Longomontanus, *op. cit. Pars Altera*, Appendix, pp.7–8.

[78] Conrad Aslachus, *De natura caeli triplici libelli tres* (Sigenae Nassoviorum [=Siegen], 1597), p.156.

[79] On Kepler's life and work Max Caspar's very thorough detailed biography (1948) still remains unsurpassed. See Max Caspar, *Kepler*, Eng. trans. ed. C. Doris Hellman, London 1959. New edn with introduction, references and bibliographical citations by Owen Gingerich and Alain Segonds, Dover Publications (New York, 1993). Cf. also Alain Segonds, 'Kepler (Johannes) (1571–1630)', in Colette Nativel, ed., *Centuriæ Latinæ. Cent figures humanistes de la Renaissance aux Lumières offertes à Jacques Chomarat* (Geneva, 1997), pp.457–472.

[80] Johannes Kepler, *Ad Vitellionem Paralipomena* (Frankfurt, 1604), cap.IV, p.79. Cf. partial Fr. trans. by Catherine Chevalley, *Les fondements de l'optique moderne: Paralipomènes à Vitellion* (Paris, 1980), p.204.

Where did Kepler himself stand in all this? 'I hold to a middle [position]', he said. 'First, what they call vapour, I say that it is air and I limit it to the tops of mountains. Above are the smoky exhalations (*fumosae exhalationes*), which are seen in the glow of twilight (*crepusculorum lampades*) and the æther follows immediately after (*statim æther succedit*).'[81] Kepler brought his fluid æther down to within half a German mile (or two and a half English miles) above the earth,[82] a height which he calculated to be the height of the air or the 'atmosphere', as the German Jesuit Christoph Scheiner (1575–1650) later named it, in 1617.[83] Kepler defined the æther not very helpfully as having '... its own substance (*Est enim & ætheri sua materia*)'.[84] 'The æthereal substance', he stated, '... is not entirely nothing, but has its own proportion of density (*ætherea substantia quae non est omnino nihil sed suam quoque densitatis rationem habet*)'.[85] Later in Book I of his *Epitome* (1618), Kepler took a different view:

> The distance between us and the fixed stars is incalculable and yet the æthereal air (*aura ætherea*) which lies over a very great depth between us and the fixed stars carries to us, in all their purity, little gleams of light from very tiny stars while respecting the difference in their colours. This could not occur if the æther (*æther*) had the slightest density or colour. For the rays of the sun when they shine through a red liquid, take on a red colour in passing. If physics allows it, the astronomer can take it that the whole of the space of the æther can entirely be held to be a void.

---

[81] Idem, *op.cit.* cap.IV prop.XI, p.129 (Fr trans. p.265). Kepler's reference to 'smoky exhalations' derives from Aristotle's *Meteorologica*, I 4 341b; that to the 'glow of twilight' is found in the description of one of the two methods he used for measuring the height of the atmosphere from the solar depression angles for twilight. The method in question is that of the medieval astronomer Ibn Mucadh (2nd half of the 11th century), often identified incorrectly with Ibn al-Haytham. Cf. Bernard Goldstein, 'Refraction, Twilight and the Height of the Atmosphere', in idem, *Theory and Observation in Ancient and Medieval Astronomy* (London, 1985), ch.IX, pp.105–107; Variorum Reprints, idem, 'Ibn Mucadh's Treatise on Twilight and the Height of the Atmosphere', ch.X, pp.97–118, in *ibid.*; also A.I. Sabra, 'The authorship of the *Liber de Crepusculis*', *Isis* LVIII (1967), pp.77–85.

[82] Johannes Kepler, *op. cit.*, cap.IV prop.XI, p.129 (Fr. trans., p.265); idem, *Epitome Astronomiæ Copernicanæ*, lib.I, pars tertia (Linz, 1618), in *GW*, VII, pp.59. and B. Goldstein, *art. cit. loc. cit.*

[83] Christoph Scheiner, S.J., *Refractiones coelestes, [...]* (Ingolstadt, 1617), p.13. (*Cum vero in nostro proposito corpus diaphanum refringens sit vaporum regio terrae homocentrica, ipsa non incommode Atmosphera videbitur indiganda.* 'Since the refracting transparent body, with which we are concerned, is the region occupied by the vapours concentric to the earth, it would seem that it could usefully be designated by the word "Atmosphere".') Before Scheiner, the Dutchman Simon Stevin had, in 1605, used the word 'Atmosphere', a Latinization of the Dutch *Damphoogde*, but his context related to the Portuguese mathematician Pedro Nunes' work, *De Crepusculis* (1542), not to Kepler's *Paralipomena*. See Simon Stevin, *Hypomnemata*, Latin trans. by Willebrord Snell (Leyden, 1605–1608), parsII, lib.3, pp.70–71.

[84] Johannes Kepler, *Ad Vitellionem Paralipomena, ed. cit.* p.259.

[85] *Ibid.* p.301.

Tycho, he added, had '... rightly doubted whether he could agree that the æther was of a material nature (... *nec immerito dubitavit Tycho Brahe, an ætherem agnosceret materiatum*)'.[86] Yet in his letter to Rothmann of 21 February 1589, while making no mention of a void, Tycho had remained thoroughly ambiguous, describing the æther as '... a kind of matter [...], or a kind of fifth essence (*quandam materiam [...] velut quintam quandam Essentiam*)', then adding that he would 'agree' that it '... was rather fire than air, as Paracelsus has said (... *ego potius illud Igneum, quam Aëreum esse concederem, prout a Paracelso traditum est*)'.[87] In Book IV of his *Epitome* (1620), Kepler defined the *aura ætherea* as frictionless, saying that it '... allowed the passage of mobile objects no less easily than it did of the light from the sun and the stars'.[88]

In Kepler's term *aura ætherea* for his fluid æther, replacing the solid heavens of the scholastics, there emerged a definition that combined the optical evidence concerning the matter of the heavens with the Basilian interpretation of its nature. The definition further incorporated notions derived from Neoplatonism and Stoicism. The concept of an *aura ætherea*, later adopted by both Protestants and Catholics, introduced a major fracture line in the representation of the medieval cosmos. For Kepler the Protestant, there still remained, as will be shown below, the Biblical grounding of the Supercelestial Waters to sustain his conviction of a finite cosmos. For Catholics, a remnant of Aristotelian doctrine continued to assure the solidity of the sphere of the fixed stars and the theological dogma of the Empyrean guaranteed for them the finite nature of the cosmos. If the concept of a fluid æther became universally recognized, its exact material nature has continued to perplex scientists right up the present day.[89]

---

[86] Johannes Kepler, *Epitome Astronomiæ Copernicanæ Liber I* (Linz, 1618), pp.53–54; *GW*, VII, p.52. It should be noted that for Kepler, light was immaterial and incorporeal. Cf. David C. Lindberg, 'The Genesis of Kepler's Theory of Light: Light Metaphysics from Plotinus to Kepler', *Osiris*, 2nd series 2 (1986), p.36.

[87] Tycho Brahe to Christoph Rothmann, 21/2/1589, in Tycho Brahe, *Epist.* p.137; *TBOO*, VI, p.167. Paracelsus (c.1490–1541) had described the heaven not as compact (*compactum*) or hard (*durum*), but as soft (*molle*), rarefied (*tenue*), penetrable (*penetrabile*) and as having the corporeality of fire (*ignis corporalitatem*). Cf. Theophrastus Philippus Aureolus Bombastus von Hohenheim Paracelsus, *De Meteoris liber unus* (Basle, 1569), pp.5–6.

[88] Johannes Kepler, *Epitome Astronomiæ Copernicanæ. Liber Quartus, Pars I* (Linz, 1620), edn (Linz, 1622), p.443; in *GW*, VII, p.261.

[89] On modern conceptions of the aether, see G.N. Cantor, 'Introduction', in G.N. Cantor and M.J.S. Hodge, eds, *Conceptions of the Ether: Studies in the History of Ether Theories* (Cambridge, 1981), pp.53–54.

4

The reception of new astronomical evidence

In the early decades of the seventeenth century, the clash between the traditional scholastic doctrine of the heavens and the astronomers' evidence of their nature brought on a crisis throughout Europe involving natural philosophers, theologians and astronomers. In this chapter a wide range of figures from the period will be examined running from die-hard Aristotelians to astronomers ready to admit that the cosmos might not be finite. An evolving trend can be discerned as the centre of gravity of opinion moved from one extreme to the other, though at different rates for scholars of different religious beliefs and of different disciplines. A number of scholars, particularly Protestants, sought to tie the astronomical evidence in with their own adopted theological views of the nature of the heavens. Plunged into the midst of this crisis, the Jesuits, ill-prepared and divided among themselves, emerged ingloriously, accepting the compromise solution of a Lutheran astronomer, Tycho Brahe.

The Protestants

Among those Protestants who took up the question of the matter of the heavens, all referred to the Tycho/Rothmann correspondence, though most ignored Kepler's criticism of the controversy between the two astronomers.

One of the few in England to show interest in the subject was Thomas Lydyat (1575–1646) a graduate of New College, Oxford, who taught briefly at Trinity College, Dublin, before giving up university teaching to take a living in Oxfordshire.[1] In his *Praelectio astronomica de natura cœli*, published in London in 1605, Lydyat briefly discussed the physical nature of the heavens, bringing in Holy Writ together with Stoicism drawn from Pliny and

---

[1] On Lydyat see the article in *Dictionary of National Biography*, XXXIV, pp.316–318; William H. Donahue, *The Dissolution of the Celestial Spheres 1595–1650* (New York, 1981), pp.81–87 and Mordecai Feingold, *The Mathematicians' Apprenticeship. Science, Universities and Society in England, 1560–1640* (Cambridge, 1984), p.48, p.72 and pp.148–150.

Cicero to sustain a vigorous anti-Aristotelianism. 'The whole of the region from the sphere of the fixed stars down to the earth', he declared, citing Pena, 'is no different in nature from the air.'[2] This air, he said, is 'subtler and lighter and hotter the further it reaches upward'.[3] While aware of the controversy between Tycho and Rothmann over refraction, Lydyat said that he sought 'something better and clearer' in the form of the 'very solid evidence of astronomers showing that comets appeared in the celestial region above the moon'.[4] Here was proof, he said, that the heaven was not of a fifth essence as held by Aristotle.[5]

Contrary to what Lydyat claimed, the 'very solid evidence of astronomers' was far from generally corroborated by astronomers of the period and there emerged no widely held consensus of opinion on the lesson to be drawn from the behaviour of comets until the later part of the seventeenth century, following the very accurate observations of Hevelius (1665) and Dörfel (1681).[6] The celestial spheres, Lydyat nevertheless insisted, were not 'distinct, solid and hard'. 'The æthereal body is rarefied, subtle and fluid'.[7] The orbs of the celestial bodies invented by the scholastics and the commoner astronomers should be removed from the heaven.[8] How did the celestial bodies maintain their regular positions in the fluid æther and by what were they moved? 'Certain recent scholars rightly spoke of a certain divinely implanted force.'[9] Insisting on the existence of the Supercelestial Waters, Lydyat asserted that, since they were heavier than air, 'they had to be supported by some kind of rigid sphere (*necessum est ut sustentetur firmo aliquo orbe*)'.[10] He implicitly assumed a finite cosmos; he made no mention of the Empyrean. Lydyat appears to have been a relatively isolated scholar without influence.

In Holland Nicolaus Müler (Mulerius) (1544-1630), a professor of medicine and mathematics at the University of Groningen, published there his *Institutionum astronomicarum libri duo* (1616). Though Pena had been the first to claim that the heaven and air were of one and the same matter, it was Tycho, wrote Müler, resuming the question with careful exactitude, '...

---

[2] Thomas Lydyat, *Prælectio astronomica de natura cœli & conditionibus elementorum* (London, 1605), cap.3, pp.23-24.

[3] *Ibid.* p.32.

[4] *Ibid.* p.24.

[5] *Ibid.* p.25.

[6] Cf. J.L.E. Dreyer, *A History of Planetary Systems from Thales to Kepler* (London, 1906), new edition with title of *A History of Astronomy from Thales to Kepler*, revised with foreword by W.H. Stahl (New York, 1953), pp.415-416.

[7] Thomas Lydyat, *op. cit.* p.29.

[8] *Ibid.* p.30.

[9] *Ibid.* p.33 and p.55.

[10] *Ibid.* p.50.

who, through his very precise observations, had shown that the heaven was very liquid and very subtle and that it contained no real orbs. Nevertheless it had not seemed to Tycho to be of the same nature and substance as the elementary air'. Müler then asked the same question as that which Morin was later to ask of Longomontanus: What had been Tycho's position on the nature of the Firmament or sphere of the fixed stars? In Tycho's writings he had found nothing clear about this, yet reason, he wrote, convinces us of the solidity of this heaven, since how otherwise could '... the armies of stars in it be carried by a very rapid movement in the form of a continuous battle front without its ranks being broken in disorder'.[11] Though Müler's proposed explanation for the existence of a solid sphere of the fixed stars, drawing on a military metaphor, was less paradoxical than Tycho's, the question continued to cause difficulties that were both physico-astronomical as well as theological, as we shall come to. Müler, it should be noted, held to a finite cosmos.[12]

Another Dutchman, David van Goorle (Gorlaeus) (1591–1612?), in his work *Exercitationes Philosophicae*, published posthumously at Leyden in 1620, took sides with Pena and Rothmann over the nature of the heaven, ignoring, in his anti-Aristotelian commitment, Tycho's prudent objection that, from the identity of the transparency of two bodies, it could not be inferred that they were of the same matter and substance. Van Goorle first brought forward as evidence of the airy nature of the heaven the Basilian interpretation of Genesis. 'Heaven', he wrote, 'is the air, and it is therefore not the fifth essence. [...] We shall prove this first from the Holy Scriptures and then by natural reasonings.[...] That the stars are situated in the air is explained by Moses in Genesis I. For the "spread-outness" created on the Second Day [of the Creation] is air. The stars were placed in this "stretched-outness" of the heaven, which was created the Second Day.'[13]

Van Goorle continued:

> Thus Holy Scripture is on our side. Let us now come to the [natural] philosophical arguments. It is a dogma among the opticians, that different transparent bodies produce a refraction of visible rays. The rays of light from the stars reach us both through the heaven and the air because [although the stars] are situated in the heaven yet we [can] observe them. Because if the transparency

---

[11] Nicolaus Müler, *Institutionum astronomicarum libri duo* (Groningen, 1616), cap.IX, pp.46–47. The metaphor of the ranks of an army comes from Patrizi. Cf. Francesco Patrizi, *Nova de Universis Philosophia*, lib.XII (Venice, 1593), f.90^v, (1st edn 1587).

[12] Nicolaus Müler, *op. cit.* cap. II, p.22 (*Talis est totius Mundi [...] forma cuius extima superficies caelum vocatur, complexu suo concludens quicquid in rerum natura esse voluit opifex*).

[13] David Gorlaeus, *Exercitationes Philosophicae*, n.p.n.d. [=Leyden,1620], pp.293–94. On this author see Lynn Thorndike, *History of Magic and Experimental Science*, vol.VII, p.379 and William H. Donahue, *The Dissolution of the Celestial Spheres 1595–1650* (New York, 1981), pp.171–175.

of the air were different from that of the heaven, the [light] rays from the stars would be refracted and the stars would not be seen in their [right] place. [...] But the opposite is shown from the observations of mathematicians who have proved that there are no refractions, except occasionally in the lower region of the air on account of vapours and exhalations [...]. Thus the heaven and the air have the same transparency. Because they have the same qualities, who will say that they are not of the same essence? They must then have the same.[14]

Van Goorle did not discuss Tycho's arguments to the contrary. He ignored the Empyrean and the Supercelestial Waters. Of the latter he wrote sarcastically, 'And what, I ask, would be their purpose? Perhaps for the angels and the Blessed to swim in!'[15] Van Goorle's remarks nevertheless reveal how much in this period persistent effort was maintained to reconcile the evidence of Holy Writ with that of experimental observation.

Marc Friedrich Wendelin (1584–1652) taught at the Heidelberg Collegium Sapientiae, a Calvinist institution. Though written in a scholastic style, his anti-Aristotelianism led him, in his *Contemplationum Physicarum Sectiones Tres* (1628), to take sides with Pena and Rothmann against Tycho and in terms which he carefully justified. Wendelin first quoted Pena at length and then followed with the Basilian interpretation of the Firmament in Genesis, the *rakiah*, as he called it. For this he drew on Benito Pereyra, though he otherwise criticized the Jesuit for asserting that '... the whole system of the heavens' had been created the First Day of the Creation. The Creation, for Wendelin, had taken place in successive stages over six days.[16] The *rakiah*, or diffusion, he claimed, consisted of nothing other than air. Recalling Tycho's assertion that the air combines as one with æther (*cum æthere quasi in unum coalescit*), Wendelin resumed the conclusion of Tycho's argument in the form of two statements, which he presented as contradictory: (1) the image carried from heaven into the air is not refracted as a result of the difference between the media, in particular at the point where air and æther touch one another; (2) there is no definite point of refraction such as Rothmann maintained, since the air changes gradually into æther. Wendelin then showed the logical absurdity of Tycho's position:

> If the affinity of air and æther is so great that air can be transformed into æther by simple contact (*per solum contactum*), what was the point, I ask, of fighting so stubbornly [in favour of] the fifth essence? Would it not have been possible to simply say that the æther does not differ from air in purity and subtlety, such as was Rothmann's opinion as well as is our own? For it would

---

[14] David Gorlaeus, *op. cit.* pp.297–298.
[15] *Ibid.* p.306.
[16] Marc Friedrich Wendelin, *Contemplationum Physicarum Sectiones Tres*, 3 vols (Hannover, 1625–28); edn (Cambridge, 1648), vol.III, pp.407–409.

be no more absurd to say that æther and air do not differ in essence, but merely in purity and subtlety, than to say that air and æther, different bodies in substance, are transformed into each other by mutual contact.[17]

In the wake of Aslachus,[18] Wendelin wrote that the heaven was '... a fluid body which cannot be contained by its limits, but which takes up its shape from what it contains' (*corpus fluidum, quod terminis suis contineri nequeat sed continentis figuram assumat*). There was no such thing as a void, he said, 'unless one may call a void that imaginary and immense space which some claim lies outside the world'. Naturally Wendelin said that he had found no proof of the existence of the Empyrean.[19]

For these Protestants the Aristotelian doctrine of the heaven had ceased to be an obstacle as far as the planets were concerned. That the cosmos must necessarily have a solid outer shell, whether of the fixed stars or one derived from theological authority, was maintained by some, especially by Kepler, whom we shall return to. Others were, as we shall see, to accept, without difficulty, an infinite cosmos.

The Catholics

For Catholic cosmologists guided by the doctrine laid down by the Council of Trent, Aristotelianism remained a force that was still very much alive and, being widely cultivated in the universities, it continued to retain a firmer hold on the minds of the élite in southern Europe.

Among such was a doctor of medicine, Joannes Heckius (Joannes van Heeck) (1579–1620?), a Catholic refugee from Deventer in the Netherlands who settled for a time in Rome. His principal work, *De nova stella disputatio*, actually written in Prague, was published in Rome in 1605 by Prince Federico Cesi (1585–1630), the founder of the Accademia dei Lincei, a learned society created in 1603 for the study of philosophy and science, of which Heckius was a member.[20] Using what he claimed were Tycho Brahe's methods of measurement, Heckius analysed the *nova* of 1604 to show no evidence of parallax, thus situating it in or above the Firmament. But he nevertheless remained a determined defender of the Aristotelian doctrine of the nature of celestial matter. After detailing and refuting twelve different theories put forward by various scholars, both ancient and modern, to explain the appearance of *novae*, he concluded with his own opinion that the *nova* of 1604 together with those of 1572 and 1600 were permanent stars located above

---

[17] *Ibid.* p.414.
[18] For Aslachus see below pp. 114–15.
[19] Marc Friedrich Wendelin, *op. cit.* pp.468–469.
[20] On Heckius and Cesi, see Saverio Ricci, *'Una Filosofica Milizia' Tre Studi sull'Accademia dei Lincei* (Udine, 1994), pp.7–31.

the Firmament, becoming occasionally visible through the less dense parts of the Milky Way. In seeking to defend Aristotle's doctrine of the heavens against Tycho Brahe (whom he branded as a Calvinist) and Rothmann (whom he did not mention by name), he conflated the positions of both, mistakenly attributing to the former the claim that the heavens were elementary and corruptible.[21] In publishing the manuscript of Heckius' work, Cesi, whose ideas on the nature of the heavens were evolving in a quite different direction, undertook to tone down the violence of his attack on those who defended the doctrine of fluid heavens. In his manuscript Heckius had written that fluid heavens were contrary to Holy Writ and that Tycho's error on this score was bound up with his religious belief.[22]

In the reception of Tycho's theory of the heavens, one may ponder which carried greater weight: the authority conferred upon him by his noble birth for those who accepted it, or his Protestant religion for those who rejected it.

Turning to Galileo (1564–1642), also a member of the Accademia dei Lincei, what was his position as regards the hard or fluid nature of the heavens?[23] The theological implications of the problem do not seem to have been a major preoccupation for Galileo, as they were to be for Prince Federico Cesi, whom we shall come to. Galileo's position evolved as the views of those around him changed. In 1584, the heaven, he said, was *solidissimum et densissimum*.[24] In 1613, in his work on sunspots, he declared it 'hardly necessary' to believe in '… that farrago of spheres and orbs thought up by the astronomers …' (*quella faragine di sfere ed orbi figurati da gl'astronomi*).[25] In 1614 he wrote to Monsignor Dini rejecting the existence of 'solid, material and distinct orbs'.[26] In 1623, in the *Assayer*, he wrote, '… we would not suppose the multiplicity of solid orbs formerly believed in, but we suppose a very subtle æthereal material to be diffused through the vast reaches of the universe, through which the solid bodies of the world go wandering with their own movements'.[27] But in the same work, he unfortunately compromised any astronomical originality he might have laid claim to in this definition, for he there applied himself to refuting Pena's argument (though without mentioning his name) that, be-

---

[21] Joannes Heckius, *De nova stella disputatio* (Rome, 1605), p.19.

[22] Saverio Ricci, *op. cit.* pp.15–17.

[23] On Galileo's life and work see the short concise note by Isabelle Pantin, 'Galileo Galilei (1564–1642)', in Colette Nativel, ed., *Centuriæ Latinæ. Cent figures humanistes de la Renaissance aux Lumières offertes à Jacques Chomarat* (Geneva, 1997), pp.385–389.

[24] Galileo Galilei, in *OG* I (*Iuvenalia*), p.66.

[25] Idem, *Istoria e dimostrazioni intorno alle macchie solari e loro accidenti, cumprese in tre lettere scritte al […] Marco Velseri Linceo* (Rome, 1613), *Prima lettera*, p.18; *OG* V, p.102.

[26] Idem, Lettera a Monsignor Dini, 23 Marzo 1614, *OG* V, p.299.

[27] Idem, *Il Saggiatore* (Rome, 1623), para 37; Eng. trans. by Stillman Drake, *The Assayer*, in Stillman Drake and C.D. O'Malley, eds, *The Controversy on the Comets of 1618* (Philadelphia, 1960), p.276.

cause of refractions, none of the stars would be seen in their right places. Such reasoning, he asserted, was idle, since the celestial spheres were so great that there would be no refraction, the observer being to all intents and purposes situated at their centre and the rays striking the spheres perpendicularly.[28] For this piece of faulty reasoning, he was taken to task by Kepler, who pointed out that if they were indeed orbs, they would necessarily be eccentric and that therefore none of the light rays would reach the earth striking the orbs at the perpendicular, except at apogee and at perigee.[29]

Signs of the tensions building up in the intellectual atmosphere in Rome preparatory to the later crisis over Galileo appear in the correspondence of Prince Federico Cesi. In 1618 Cesi, who had become a thorough convert to the idea of fluid heavens, set forth in a letter to Robert Bellarmine, S.J., now a Cardinal and an eminent pillar of the Church, an elaborate defence of the doctrine. The letter was later printed by Christopher Scheiner in his *Rosa Ursina* (1630).[30] Marshalling numerous references culled from early Fathers of the Church, some of whom he interpreted very freely, Cesi endeavoured to prove that the heavens were not only fluid, but even devoid of a spherical shape. His argument, he said, could be seen to be corroborated by Galileo's astronomical observations; he made no mention of either Tycho or Rothmann.

Referring to previous correspondence with Bellarmine, he wrote as follows: 'You have accepted to listen to my opinion and have not only approved my idea of a single heaven, tenuous, and penetrable, and of the banishing from the purity of nature of the many entangled masses of orbs and epicycles, but you have also willingly assented to it and that it is thoroughly in agreement with the pages of Holy Writ'.[31] The heaven, said Cesi, in evident contradiction to Aristotle, was one, though he admitted to a tripartite division: the two *aëream* and *sydeream* regions and a third, the *Empyreum* heaven. The word *rakiah* for the Firmament signified a 'spread-outness and a stretched-outness' and 'hence an adamantine solidity of the orbs can in no way be implied'. No mention of such orbs was to be found in Scripture.[32]

Cesi then proceeded to make his surprising claim regarding the extent of the cosmos. That the '... heaven [...] does not appear to be embraced by

---

[28] *Ibid.* para 22; Eng. trans. p.249.

[29] Johannes Kepler, 'Appendix Hyperaspistis seu Spicilegium ex Trutinatore Galilei', in Tycho Brahe, *Hyperaspistes*, ed. Johannes Kepler (Frankfurt, 1625), p.196. Eng. trans. by C.D. O'Malley in Stillman Drake and C.D. O'Malley, eds, *op. cit.* p.350.

[30] Federico Cesi, 'De Caeli unitate, tenuitate fusaque et pervia stellarum motibus natura ex sacris litteris epistola (1618)', in Christoph Scheiner, S.J., *Rosa Ursina sive Sol* (Bracciano, 1630), pp.775–784. Mod. edn of Cesi's Latin text with introduction, Italian trans. and notes by Maria Luisa Altieri Biagi and Bruno Basile, eds, in *Scienziati del Seicento* (Milan–Naples, 1980), pp.1–38.

[31] *Ibid.* pp.10–11.

[32] *Ibid.* p.15.

any exact limit' was, he said, to be seen in 'the innumerable plainly visible stars, the many indistinctly visible, and the evidence we have of a vast number of hidden ones [i.e. to the naked eye]'. Cesi saw this confirmed by 'a great number of experimental observations', by which he meant those made by Galileo with a telescope.[33] However the indifference of contemporary scholars to them led Cesi to

> ... despair of the sickmindedness (*aegritudinem*) of many philosophizers of our time who not only avoid experiments (*experimentis*) and observations, but shun them altogether. There are indeed not a few of them who not only curse the telescope which has extended man's vision more deeply, as well as Galileo himself who has revealed to us so many celestial phenomena unknown to the ancients – new planets, new fixed stars and new aspects of the faces of stars – but they, without even simple naked eye vision, prefer to proceed blindly and wander in an ancient forest enthralled by the opinions of old writers, rather than, led by sense and reason, set themselves ever so slightly apart from them and change or add anything to established principles or rules.[34]

'Furthermore,' contended Cesi, 'from all these facts, such as the unity, the immobility and the spread-out nature of the heaven, not enclosed by any solid limit to its a shape (*figurae*), yet fluid and penetrable to the different movements of the stars, those visible to us and those invisible to us, each one serving to prove this in mutual corroboration, I believe that it is possible to gather [evidence] in great abundance out of Holy Writ that the heaven is not like a hard stone and is not divided into orbs different in kind, in motion and in other characteristics, and that it does not, by its regular rotation, carry round the stars fixed in it, as has been held by many with general approval, but that it is fluid and rarefied and is like the air itself to which is also given the name "heaven"'.[35]

In asserting that '... the heaven was not enclosed by any solid limit', Cesi left his reader without any clue as to where he situated the Empyrean, although he twice mentioned the latter in his text. To the question relating to how the heavenly bodies were carried, Cesi answered that angels resided in them, and that as movers they were also acknowledged by the Aristotelians, though the latter 'wrongly made them drive the orbs as in a mill'.[36]

In Bellarmine's reply to Cesi, also printed by Scheiner,[37] the Cardinal wrote that he had found Cesi's text, '... indeed very scholarly and very new

---

[33] In his *Sidereus Nuncius* Galileo had drawn no specific conclusion about the limits of the universe from the vast number of previously unobserved fixed stars revealed by the telescope. Cf. Galileo Galilei, *Sidereus Nuncius*, edn (Frankfurt, 1610), p.31.
[34] Federico Cesi, *op. cit.* pp.20–22.
[35] *Ibid.* p.22.
[36] *Ibid.* p.32.
[37] Cardinal Bellarmine to Federic Cesi, Rome, 1618, in mod. edn of Cesi *ed. cit.* pp.36–38.

and for the most part in agreement with what I hold to be true. There is only one thing that does not in the end satisfy me and that is the shape (*figura*) of the heaven, which you deny to be round'. Bellarmine was here quick to react to Cesi's defence of a cosmos without a definite limit. But Bellarmine appeared to show as much concern over kinematic astronomy as over the heterodox idea of an infinite creation. 'What I would like to know from you', he asked Cesi, 'is not whether Holy Writ or the Holy Fathers hold the heaven to be immobile and that the stars move and also that the Heaven is not hard and impenetrable like iron, but soft and easily penetrable like the air, which are things which we know already, but I want to learn from you how you work out the motions of the sun and the stars and especially of the fixed stars which always keep together'.[38]

When he had been young, Bellarmine confided, he had tried to work out the motions of the planets, but his conclusions had not satisfied him for all the planets, nor for the stars of the Firmament. Such and similar things were what he would like Cesi to tell him. In the resigned tone of the ending to his letter: 'Let us seek to live in the holy awe of God so that we may reach Heaven and there in one instant all will be clear',[39] Bellarmine reveals something of the unease of this high prelate faced with the deepening conflict between the claims of theology and the pressures for a reform of astronomy.

During the early decades of the seventeenth century in the Catholic *milieux* of northern Europe, the work of Tycho Brahe and Rothmann met much the same contrasted reception as it had in Rome. The influential French Minorite Friar, Marin Mersenne (1588–1648),[40] though contributing little of enduring originality to his field of study, maintained an active correspondence with a wide variety of scholars all over Europe. In his voluminous Hexaëmeron, *Quæstiones celeberrimæ in Genesim*, published in 1623, he discussed at length the nature of the heavens on the basis of the evidence from refractions. He wrote that he '... did not think that it could be rightly concluded that the heavens and the air were identical [...] or, on the basis of these refractions, that they were liquid'.[41] Mersenne then criticized Kepler, putting his finger on one of Kepler's weakest points. 'It was quite obvious', he stated, 'how unsure Kepler had been on the subject of refractions, especially when he sought the origins of their values, hence we should not

---

[38] *Ibid.* pp.36–37. In his Louvain Lectures of 1570–72 Bellarmine had previously expressed his concern about how to reconcileastronomical hypotheses with the truth of Holy Writ. Cf. Robert Bellarmine, 'The Louvain Lectures (Lectiones Lovanienses) of Bellarmine and the autograph copy of his 1616 Declaration to Galileo', ed. cit. pp.20–21.

[39] Cardinal Bellarmine to Federic Cesi in *op. cit. ed. cit.* p.38.

[40] See William L. Hine, 'Mersenne and Copernicanism', *Isis* 64 (1973), pp.21–22.

[41] Marin Mersenne, *Quæstiones celeberrimæ in Genesim* (Paris, 1623), cap.I, versiculus VIII, problema XLV, quæstio VII, art.II, cols 819–820.

reject outright the solidity of the heavens on the basis of one little optical reason (*ob unicam ratiunculam opticam*).'[42] Though rejecting the evidence of refractions, Mersenne hesitantly concluded that the heavens of the planets were 'not improbably liquid like air', that it was 'more probable that the sphere of the fixed stars, the Firmament, was solid', then added paradoxically a few lines further down that it was also 'not absurd to believe in the solidity of the planetary heavens'.[43]

In marked contrast to the evasiveness of Mersenne stands the forthrightness of Libert Froidmont (Fromondus) (1587–1653), a professor of philosophy at the University of Louvain who wrote a commentary on Aristotle's *Meteorologica*, published at Antwerp in 1627, later to go into six further editions. Influenced by experimental evidence, he inclined more to Rothmann's conclusions rather than to Tycho's. 'It is probable that the upper region of the air stretches up to the fixed stars and as far as the vault of the Firmament.' He made no mention of the Empyrean. Furthermore, he added, the trajectories of comets, as shown by the physician Thomas Fyens in his work on the comet of 1618, had proved that the heavens below the Firmament were fluid and not solid.[44] Froidmont's reliance on such 'proof' was far from universally shared in the period, as been noted above.

> It is probable that the whole of the space from here [i.e. the earth] up to the fixed stars is filled with air (unless the upper part of the air is rather called æther). Tycho believes that that which flows between (*interfluit*) the planets is a certain *aura* of a celestial nature. But [in this] he has not so far persuaded me, for he has not been able to infer more from the refractions of the [light] of the stars than that the æthereal part [of the heaven] is more rarefied than our air, which would be true even if they were made of the same substance. For the most widely spread, rarefied exhalations of the earth sometimes rise above the Moon, while a part of this celestial tychonic æther descends into the sublunary world, so that mortal things become mixed with the divine and incorporeal ones, and this [added Froidmont in deference to Catholic doctrine] cannot be admitted.[45]

---

[42] *Ibid.* col.820.

[43] *Ibid.* art.IX, cols 843–845. Hine seeks to excuse Mersenne's equivocation on this point by claiming that Mersenne considered fluid spheres as 'probable' and solid ones as 'possible'. Cf. William L. Hine, *art. cit. loc. cit.*

[44] Cf. Thomas Fyens in Thomas Fyens and Libert Froidmont, *De cometa anni MDCXVIII, Dissertationes Thomae Fieni [...] et Libert Fromondi* (Antwerp, 1619), pp.21–22. (*Si cometas essent in coelo [...] sequeretur quod caelum esset liquidum & quod Cometa deferretur per coelum, sicut pisces per aquam. [...] Denique sequeretur [...] esset unum continuum liquidum corpus à terra usque ad inania spacia per quod sidera vaguerentur.* 'If there are comets in the heaven it will follow that it is liquid and that the comet is carried through the heaven as fish are in water. [...] Hence it will follow that [the heaven] is one continuous liquid body from the earth as far as the empty spaces through which the stars move.') Fyens made no mention of the Empyrean.

[45] Libert Froidmont, *Meteorologicorum libri sex* (Antwerp, 1627), cap.II, art.I, p.3.

Although he uses Kepler's term *aura* to designate the latter's fluid æther, it is unlikely that Froidmont had read Kepler's work *Ad Vitellionem Paralipomena*. It was Longmontanus, and not Tycho, whose æther, defined as 'a very rarefied and very subtle spread-outness resembling something incorporeal and imperceptible to the senses' (*expansum tenuissimum & subtilissimum quippe incorporeo & insensibili similimum*), penetrated to the 'inmost part of the earth' (*in intimam tellurem*), so that 'it necessarily follows that the sublunary region is not entirely different in kind from the æthereal one (*sequi necesse est sublunarem regionem non toto genere [...] ab ætherea esse distinctam*)'.[46] Tycho, as we have already seen, rejected any interpenetration of the 'incorporeal' with the elementary world.

The Jesuits

The optical evidence brought forward by Tycho and Rothmann produced among the scholars of the Jesuit Order a crisis, the severity of which is only now slowly being brought to light.[47] It is often held that Jesuit scholars were obliged to maintain a disciplined uniformity of doctrine in their works (*uniformitas et soliditas doctrinae*), but close examination of their writings reveals considerable variety in their positions on issues of astronomy and physics having theological implications. This variety can be seen first of all to evolve in time, then to distinguish different provinces of the order from each other (Spain from Portugal for example), and finally to distinguish individual scholars of the same province.[48]

Faced with the evidence brought forward by astronomers at the end of the sixteenth century on the physical nature of the heavens, the scholars of the Jesuit Order were, on the whole, to show themselves more concerned by the existence or absence of parallax in new stars and comets, in particular relating to the *nova* of 1572, than by measurements of the refraction of light rays.

The great German Jesuit mathematician Christoph Clavius (1538–1612), who taught at the Collegio Romano from 1563 until his death, does not seem to have touched upon the issue of refractions, but he did examine the problem of the 1572 *nova* in the 1585 edition of his commentary on the *Sphæra* of Sacrobosco.[49] He recognized that the *nova* was in the Firmament

---

[46] Christian Severinus Longomontanus, *Astronomia Danica* (Amsterdam, 1622), *Pars Altera*, pp.35–37.

[47] Cf. Richard J. Blackwell, *op. cit.* chap. 6.

[48] Cf. Ugo Baldini, '*Uniformitas et Soliditas doctrinae. Le censure Librorum e Opinionum*', in idem, *Legem Impone Subactis. Studi su filosofia e scienza dei Gesuiti in Italia* (Rome, 1992), pp.75–119.

[49] Of the seven editions and sixteen printings of this work, this is the earliest we have been able to consult. There were three previous editions, one in 1581 (augmented) and two earlier

5   Engraving of Christoph Clavius, S.J. (1538–1612). Photo Bibliothèque Nationale, Paris.

of the fixed stars and that it had no observed parallax. 'Since this is so', he wrote, 'I am persuaded that this star is either created by God in the eighth sphere [...] or that it could have been born in that sphere as comets are in the air, although this occurs very rarely.'[50] Half taking refuge in providentialism and half indulging in gratuitous speculation, Clavius was nevertheless forced to admit, in a conclusion that committed him much further, that, 'If this is true, the Aristotelians will have to see how they can defend Aristotle's opinion concerning the matter of the heaven. For perhaps it will have to be said that the heaven is not a fifth essence, but a changeable body, though less corruptible than the lower [elementary] bodies'.[51] But Clavius added no more.

In 1592 a group of Jesuit scholars of the University of Coimbra, headed by the Portuguese Jesuit Pedro Fonseca, S.J. (1528–99), had conceived the idea of publishing for students a series of commentaries on Aristotle's works. These commentaries were reprinted many times in Portugal, Italy, France and Germany and repeatedly quoted all over Europe. The commentary on Aristotle's *De Cælo* was prepared by Manuel de Góis, S.J. (1542–97) and published at Lisbon in 1593.[52] In it the 'Conimbricenses', as they came to be called, discussed at length the question that had much occupied medieval scholars: whether the matter of the heavens was a fifth essence according to Aristotle or originally of water according to the pseudo-Clementine interpretation of Genesis, which they followed in preference to the two other interpretations. Declaring that they were '... compelled by an ambiguity of opinion to accommodate themselves to both points of view',[53] they thus showed that they had even less success than Albert the Great in attempting a synthesis of Greek science and Biblical truth. Unaware of Tycho's published works and therefore of the controversy over the lessons to be drawn from his measurement of refractions or of his observations of the 1572 *Nova*, the Conimbricenses maintained the traditional view of the solid nature of the heavens, which they described, quoting Alexander of Aphrodisias' Commentary on Aristotle's *Meteorologica*, as *consistentis et solidae*.[54] Examination of

---

ones in 1570 and 1575. On Clavius' life and writings see James M. Lattis, *Between Copernicus and Galileo, Christoph Clavius and the Collapse of Ptolemaic Cosmology* (Chicago and London, 1994), chapter I.

[50] Christoph Clavius, *In Sphæram Ioannis de Sacrobosco* (Rome, 1585), p.193.

[51] *Ibid. loc. cit.*

[52] Cf. J.S. da Silva Dias, 'O Cânone Filosófico Conimbricense (1592-1606)', *Cultura História e Filosofía* IV (1985), p.257; António Alberto de Andrade, *Curso Conimbricense I*, Instituto de Alta Cultura (Lisbon, 1957), Introduction, pp. xiv and xxvi and Marcial Solana, *Historia de la Filosofía Española* (Madrid, 1941), vol.III, pp.366-371.

[53] [Manuel de Góis], *Commentarii Collegii Conimbricensis Societatis Iesu in quatuor libros De Coelo*, lib.I, cap.II, qu.VI, art.III, edn (Lyons, 1598), p.52 (*cogamur ambiguitate sententiae nos ad utramque partem accomodare*).

[54] *Ibid.* lib.I, cap.III, qu.I, art.IV, p.69.

this work of Alexander of Aphrodisias (2nd–3rd cent.) has however revealed nothing to support this reference and it remains unexplained.[55]

In their passing reference to the 1572 *nova*, the Conimbricenses did no more than copy Clavius' opinion. Although they mentioned Clavius' name among the several references cited in the margin of the page of their work where they dealt with the 1572 *nova*, his opinion, which they quoted, failed to shake the orthodoxy of their Aristotelian convictions. 'The heavens', they asserted, 'are not fluid.'[56]

Clavius' unwillingness to commit himself further to defining the nature of the heaven in clear terms was confirmed by a fellow Jesuit Fr. Christoph Grienberger (1564–1636), who noted that he knew, and that those close to him knew, that, '... until his death, Clavius had had a horror of liquid heavens and that he had often sought ways to enable the phenomena to be saved in the ordinary way. He was simply less attached to the incorruptibility of the heavens.'[57] Clavius the astronomer thus appeared to cling more to rigid spheres than had Bellarmine the theologian, both members of the same order.

Clavius' fellow German Jesuit, Adam Tanner (1571–1632), expounded, in his *Dissertatio peripatetico-theologica de cœlis* (1621), his Aristotelian conviction that the heavenly spheres were all solid – the Firmament definitely so on 'the grounds of Scripture'; the planetary heavens 'very probably so'.[58] He proceeded, using in his preface Tycho's own words from his letter to Rothmann of 17 August 1588, to mount a systematic attack on Tycho's opinions and method. Tycho was here quoted as saying that '... the question of the matter of the heavens is not properly for astronomers to decide', their business being to investigate from observations how the heavenly bodies moved; the rest to be left to theology and natural philosophers (*Theologia & Physicis reliquere*).[59] To Jean Pena's argument that the multiple spheres of the Aristotelian fifth essence would render impossible any accurate astronomical observations with light from stars thus refracted by it, Tanner replied with an imagined cleverness that, as when light is refracted through two

---

[55] Alexander of Aphrodisias, *Commentary on the Meteorologica of Aristotle*, Lat. trans. by William of Moerbeke, ed. A.J. Smet (*Commentaire sur les Météores d'Aristote*), (Louvain, 1968).

[56] [Manuel de Góis], *op. cit.* lib.I, cap.III, art.IV, *ed. cit.* pp.69–70.

[57] Note by Fr. Christoph Grienberger, S.J., Fondo gesuitico 655, f.109^r, Archivum Romanum, Societatis Iesu, printed by Ugo Baldini, in 'Dal geocentrismo alfonsino al modello di Brahe. La discussione Grienberger-Biancani', in idem, *Legem impone subactis, Studi su filosofia e scienza dei Gesuiti in Italia 1540–1632* (Rome, 1992), pp.237–238.

[58] Adam Tanner, *Dissertatio peripatetico-theologica de cœlis* (Ingolstadt), 1621, p.104 and p.110. Born at Innsbruck, Tanner taught theology at Munich, Ingolstadt and Vienna and became Chancellor of the University of Prague.

[59] Idem. *op cit.* Ad Lectorem, sign. A$_4^v$. Cf. Tycho to Rothmann, 17/8/1588 in *Epist.* p.111; *TBOO* VI, pp.139–140.

lenses placed together, one plane convex and the other plane concave, with the resulting refraction being, so he said, no more than that when it passes through a piece of flat glass, so the same occurs in the body of the heaven which behaves as if it were a continuum.[60] Here he fell into a trap of faulty reasoning similar to that which Galileo was accused of by Kepler, as will be seen below. He failed to see that the spheres of the planets would be eccentric to one another and that the angle of incidence of a refracted ray would be different from one sphere to another.

Tanner refuted at considerable length, often with plausible arguments, Tycho Brahe's claims that the heavens were fluid on the evidence of his observations of the behaviour of comets. At the same time he set out equally extended refutations of Galileo's claims made with the telescope that the matter of the heavens was of a corruptible nature.[61] Galileo's claims had been based on the apparent unevenness of the moon's surface (valleys and mountains), of sunspots, the phases of Venus, Jupiter's satellites and Saturn's protuberances (rings), all phenomena held to be incompatible with Aristotelian doctrine.[62]

Although Tanner was followed by some other Jesuits, as will be seen, his only significant contribution to the history of astronomy was in reporting that Clavius, whose opinion of Tycho was certainly worth more than his, had said just before he died that, 'Tycho's observations seemed to him suspect (*suspectas sibi videri Tychonis observationes*), especially in points on which they differed from experience and from opinions held over many centuries.'[63]

In the last (1611) edition of his Commentary on Sacrobosco's *Sphæra*, Clavius had quoted a list of the newly observed phenomena in the heavens revealed by Galileo's telescope. The evidence of these phenomena had led Clavius to admit that astronomers would now have to work out a new theory of planetary motions. 'Since this is so, astronomers will have to see how the celestial orbs may be arranged so that the phenomena can be saved. (*Quae cum ita sint videant astronomi quo pacto orbes coelestes constituendi sint, ut haec phaenomena possint salvari*).'[64] From this remark Tanner drew the following

---

[60] Adam Tanner, *op. cit.* p.167.

[61] *Ibid*. qu.VII, pp.115–167.

[62] Cf. Galileo Galilei, *Sidereus Nuncius*, ed. cit. pp.12–29 (unevennness of the moon's surface); pp.33–55 (Jupiter's satellites); idem, *Istoria e dimostrazioni intorno alle macchie solari ...*, ed. cit. pp.10–13 (sunspots); pp.14 (phases of Venus); p.25 (Saturn's protuberances or rings). Partial English translations from the above works are given in *The Discoveries and Opinions of Galileo*, trans. and introduction by Stillman Drake (New York, 1957). Both the errors as well as the justness of Galileo's conclusions are critically analysed by William R. Shea, *Galileo's Intellectual Revolution* (New York, 1972), chap. 3.

[63] Adam Tanner, *op. cit.* p.159.

[64] Christoph Clavius, *In Sphæram Ioannis de Sacrobosco commentarius*, in idem, *Opera omnia* (Mainz, 1611), vol.III, p.75. Clavius was here using the term 'phenomena' as relating to the motions of planets and not just to Galileo's observations. On Clavius' slow half-admitted

conclusion: 'So Clavius, as you can see, never doubted the solidity of the heavens, for he acknowledged the [existence of the] celestial orbs, but he judged that another system of these orbs should be constructed.'[65]

If, in spite of his avowed hesitations, Clavius' immense authority was thus invoked and 'interpreted' by Tanner to justify his committed Aristotelian orthodoxy, such was not to be the case with the great mathematician's pupil, Giuseppe Biancani, S.J. (1566–1624), who later taught at the College of S. Rocco at Parma.[66] In his work *Aristotelis loca mathematica*, published at Bologna in 1615, Biancani, after encountering some difficulty in getting past the censorship of his order,[67] 'interpreted' his master's carefully chosen remarks in a quite opposite manner. 'The observations of the ancient astronomers', he wrote, 'though consistent with Aristotle [sic!] clash with those of our time, especially the ones concerning the planets.' Biancani made no mention of refractions. 'The planetary heaven', he now asserted outright in conformity with Bellarmine's view, 'is liquid and the planets move through it by their own movement as fish move in water.'[68] Of the nature of the sphere of the fixed stars Biancani said nothing, but in a later work, *Sphæra Mundi* (1620), he stated that it was a *corpus solidum ac constans*, since the fixed stars in it kept a constant order and maintained their distances between each other.[69]

The Empyrean had been described by Biancani's master in conventional medieval terms as the final outer sphere beyond which there was no body but, '… an infinite space (if it is possible to speak of such) in which God exists in essence'.[70] Biancani, who became the first Jesuit astronomer to resign himself to adopting Tycho Brahe's ungainly geo-heliocentric system,[71] adjoined to it the Empyrean, which he defined in his *Sphæra Mundi*,

---

capitulation, see Michel-Pierre Lerner, 'L'entrée de Tycho Brahe chez les jésuites ou le chant du cygne de Clavius', in Luce Giard, ed., *Les jésuites à la Renaissance* (Paris, 1995), pp.145–185.

[65] Adam Tanner, *op. cit*, p.233.

[66] On Biancani's life see the art. by E. Grillo in *Dizionario Biografico degli Italiani*, X (1967), pp.33–35.

[67] Biancani was accused by the censorship of his order of quoting heretics such as Tycho Brahe, Rothmann and Kepler with approval as well as of declaring that the heavens were fluid and that, contrary to the opinion of Aristotle, the planets moved in them like fish in water. See the document printed by Ugo Baldini, in *art. cit. op. cit.* pp.230–231.

[68] Giuseppe Biancani, S.J., *Aristotelis loca mathematica* (Bologna, 1615), p.79.

[69] Idem, *Sphæra Mundi seu Cosmographia* (Bologna, 1620), p.132. There were three other editions (Modena, 1630, 1635 and 1653).

[70] Christoph Clavius, *In Sphæram Ioannis de Sacrobosco commentarius* (Rome, 1585), p.72.

[71] The system conceived by Tycho Brahe sought to retain the astronomical advantages of the Copernican system while respecting the physical and theological constraints of an immobile earth. The earth remained immobile in the centre of the universe; round it revolved the sun and round the sun the other planets. See Christine Jones Schofield, *Tychonic and Semi-Tychonic Systems* (New York, 1981), pp.50–107.

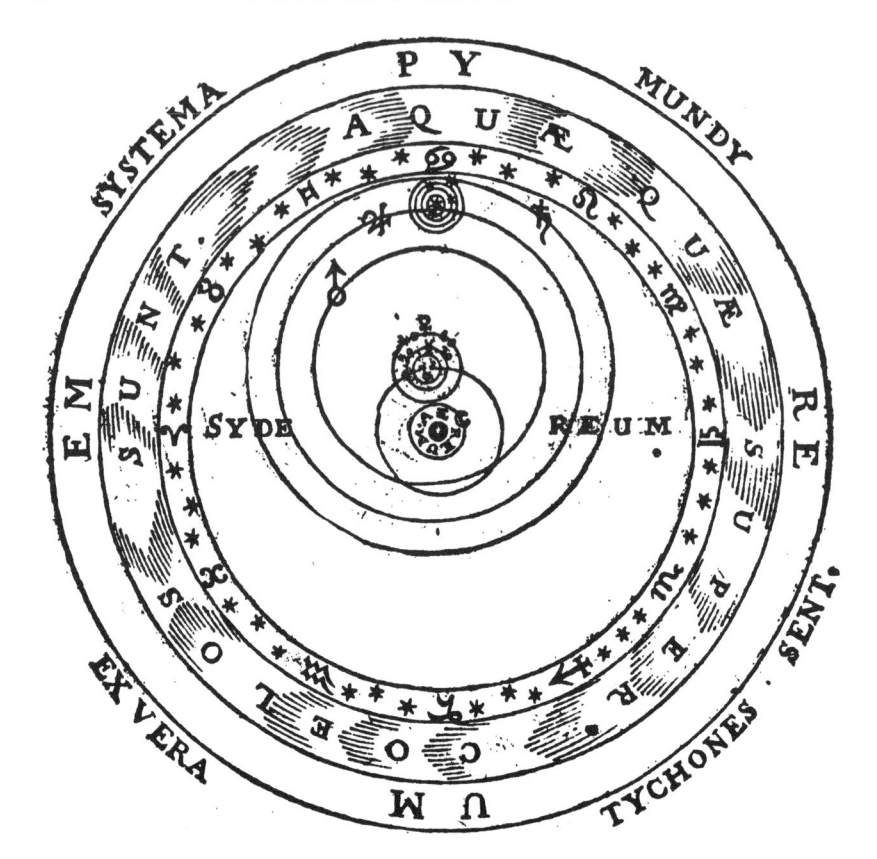

6   The Tychonic geo-heliocentric astronomical system first expounded by
Tycho Brahe, *De Mundi Ætherei Recentioribus Phænomenis liber secundus*, Uraniborg,
1588. The Supercelestial Waters and the Empyrean were dropped by Tycho, but
were later restored by the Jesuits. Diagram in Melchior Cornäus, S.J., *Curriculum
philosophiæ peripateticæ*, Herbipoli, [Würzburg], 1657, p.528. Bibliothèque
Municipale de Bordeaux, S 1012; Photo P. Canal.

The earth is shown in the centre of the universe with the sphere of the fixed
stars concentric to it. Above them are the Supercelestial Waters and above them the
Empyrean. The planets revolve round the sun which itself revolves round the
earth. Jupiter is shown with its satellites.

in traditional scholastic terms as '... the seat of the Blessed', enclosing the 'whole fabric of the world'.[72] He said nothing about any infinite space beyond it. Clavius had made no explicit mention of the Blessed.

During the last two decades of the sixteenth century and the first two of the seventeenth, the Isidorian model of eleven spheres, to which Clavius had, through the influence of Copernicus via Magini, added in 1593 a further sphere making twelve,[73] was abandoned by the majority of the Jesuits. The now generally recognized fluid nature of the heavens had rendered it untenable. Included in this abandonment was the Crystalline heaven first eliminated by Benito Pereyra when he dropped the Isidorian model,[74] together with the *Primum Mobile* eliminated by Biancani.[75] In its place appeared a tripartite division of the heavens in which they were henceforth divided into the heaven of the Empyrean (*coelum empyreum*), the heaven of the æther (*cœlum æthereum*) and the heaven of the air (*cœlum aëreum*). The model was first expounded in these terms by Bellarmine,[76] who drew on Patristic authority for it from Saint John of Damascus.[77] The latter in turn had drawn on Scriptural authority for it from Saint Paul's story of a man being carried up to 'the third heaven' (2 Cor. 12: 2).[78] Claiming authority for it in Aristotle, Agostino Steuco had, previously to Bellarmine, set forth a tripartite division of the heavens, but without using the latter's exact terms.[79] Francesco Patrizi, on the basis of Neoplatonic authority, also divided the heavens into three parts.[80] The tripartite division was likewise adopted by the very conserva-

---

[72] Giuseppe Biancani, *op. cit.* pp.56–57.

[73] Christoph Clavius, S.J., *In Sphæram Ioannis de Sacrobosco commentarius*, edn (Rome, 1593), cap.I, pp. 67–69. Magini, shortly before Clavius, had adopted in 1589 an astronomical model (without the Empyrean) of eleven spheres. Cf. G.A. Magini, *Novæ Cælestium Orbium Theorica congruentes cum observationes Copernici* (Venice, 1589), preface and pp.1–5.

[74] Benito Pereyra, *Commentariorum et Disputationum in Genesim*, *ed. cit.* vol.I, p.104. Cf. above, Chapter 2, p.47.

[75] Giuseppe Biancani, *Sphæra Mundi seu Cosmographia* (Bologna, 1620), p.352.

[76] Robert Bellarmine, 'The Louvain Lectures', *ed. cit.* p.16.

[77] Saint John of Damascus, *op. cit. loc. cit.*

[78] A tripartite division of the heavens based on Saint Paul's story had been proposed in the Renaissance by Cardinal Cajetan (1469–1534), but he had replaced the Empyrean, which he denied on the grounds that it was not mentioned in Scripture, by the Supercelestial Waters. See Cardinal Cajetan (Thomas de Vio), 'In posteriorem D. Pauli Epistolam ad Corinthios Commentarii', in idem, *Opera Omnia* (Lyons, 1639), vol.V, cap.XII, p.195.

[79] Agostino Steuco, *Cosmopoeia*, *ed cit.* p.29. 'Aristotle conceives the heaven in a tripartite manner; first there is the habitat of the gods beyond the celestial movements, where there is neither place, nor void, nor time but only things of supreme beatitude. Secondly there is the substance of the celestial orbs, the orbs of the sun and of the moon. Thirdly there is the heaven, that is outside the earth and above the earth to which air and aether are adjoined.' Cf. Aristotle, *On the Heavens [De Cælo]*, I ix 278b, ed. Guthrie, p.89.

[80] Francesco Patrizi, *Nova de Universis Philosophia* (Ferrara 1591), edn (Venice, 1593), f.81ʳ (*Sphæras Empyrei, Aetherei, & Hylæi*).

tive Spanish Jesuit theologians Francisco Suarez and Pedro Hurtado de Mendoza.[81]

These two, resolutely turning their backs on Renaissance flirtations with Neoplatonism, formed a conservative movement seeking a return to an orthodox Aristotelian vision of the heavens. They were to be joined in this by Tanner and his followers.[82] Suarez summarily rejected the evidence of astronomers from the behaviour of comets that the heavens were corruptible. 'Aristotle's opinion is to us more likely', he declared. 'All the bodies [from the Empyrean] to the heaven [i.e. sphere] of the moon have an incorruptible nature.'[83]

A second tradition, different from the above, followed the position of Biancani. In it much of the evidence brought forward by Tycho Brahe, Rothmann and Galileo on the material nature of the planetary heavens was accepted and the rigidly conservative Aristotelianism of Tanner and the two Spanish Jesuits was for the most part abandoned. In both of the Jesuit traditions referred to, the planets were held to be moved by angels or intelligences, a hypothesis which Tanner welcomed as 'convenient and not absurd', though on its truth he suspended judgement.[84] In Book IV of his *Epitome* (1620), Kepler examined and rejected this solution, proposing in its stead his concept of magnetic *species*.[85]

After Clavius, the most celebrated Jesuit astronomer was Biancani's student, Giovanni Baptista Riccioli (1598–1671), who taught at Parma and at

---

[81] Francisco Suarez, S.J., *Metaphysicarum Disputationum*, disput.XIII, sec.XI (Salamanca, 1597), edn (Paris, 1605), vol.II, p.307; idem, *De Opere sex dierum*, lib.I, cap.III (Lyons, 1621), p.14 and Pedro Hurtado de Mendoza, *Disputationes de Universa Philosophia*, 'De Substantia corporea incorruptibilitate sive de Coelo', disput.II, sect.I (Lyons, 1617), p.534 (1st edn Valladolid, 1615).

[82] One of these, the Peruvian-born Spanish Jesuit Ildephonso de Peñafiel (born Rio Bamba, 1594, died Guanca-Velica, 1657), closely reproduced in his *Cursus integri Philosophici* (Lyons, 1655), Tanner's rebuttal of Tycho's and Galileo's proofs that the heavens were not solid and incorruptible. See Ildephonso de Peñafiel, *op. cit.* vol.III, pp.262–281. Peñafiel taught philosophy and theology at Cusco and at Lima.

[83] Francisco Suarez, *Metaphysicarum Disputationum, ed. cit.* p.305. There were ten editions in the seventeenth century. On this important work, which made its mark on the period, see the wide-ranging study by Martin Grabmann, 'Die Disputationes Metaphysicae des Franz Suarez in ihrer methodischen Eigenart und Fortwirkung', in *Mittelalterliches Geistesleben*, I (Munich 1926), pp.525–560.

[84] Adam Tanner, S.J., *Dissertatio peripatetico-theologica de cœlis* (Ingolstadt, 1621), pp.216–217 and p.223.

[85] Johannes Kepler, *Epitome astronomiæ copernicanæ*, lib.IV, pars II, cap.III (Linz, 1620), edn (Linz, 1622), pp.516–520; *GW*, VII, p.335. Kepler's concept of magnetic species was inspired by his reading of William Gilbert's work *De Magnete* (London, 1600). Cf. Johannes Kepler, *Astronomia Nova* ([Heidelberg], 1609), Eng. trans. by William H. Donahue: Johannes Kepler, *New Astronomy* (Cambridge, 1992), pt III, chap. 34, pp.390–391.

Bologna.[86] While admitting that '... although it cannot be proved metaphysically, mathematically, and above all physically or morally', Riccioli declared in his *Almagestum Novum* (1651) that 'both sacred and profane authority affirms that the heaven and the stars are moved by intelligences or angels'. He refuted Kepler's theory at length, saying that, 'for me Kepler's argument gets more obtuse, the more penetrating it has seemed to him (*discursus Kepleri, tanto mihi obtusior, quanto ipsi acutior visus est*)'.[87] No more satisfactory solutions to the problem of celestial dynamics were to appear until Newton proposed his laws of gravity. Riccioli asserted that '... though it is scarcely evident mathematically or physically, it is much more probable that the sphere of the fixed stars is solid and that that of the planets is fluid'.[88] His claim for the existence of a solid sphere for the fixed stars appeared to be based rather more on convenience than on any appeal to experimental observation or theoretical deduction. 'If one makes the sphere of the fixed stars solid, a simpler reason why these stars continually keep the same distance between each other is forthcoming and there is no need to multiply countless movers for each of them.'[89] Riccioli restored both the Crystalline Sphere and the *Primum Mobile*.[90] We shall come to his original treatment of the Empyrean in the next chapter.

The Jesuits of the more modern tradition otherwise showed systematic efforts to analyse in depth the new developments in astronomy in an attempt to maintain a coherent synthesis with theological principles. Scholars of other orders, and university professors of philosophy in particular, tended to be slower in abandoning traditional Aristotelianism, while professional astronomers, less shackled by the claims of theology, were more ready to shake themselves free of scholasticism.

Professional astronomers

The Spanish Valencian astronomer Jerónimo Muñoz (c.1520–92) taught Hebrew and mathematics at the University of Valencia. In his work *Libro del Nuevo Cometa* (1573), Muñoz wrote that he had endeavoured to measure the parallax of the 1572 *nova* and had found none. Observations with instruments, he declared, had proved the weakness of Aristotle's arguments

---

[86] On Riccioli see Ugo Baldini, 'La formazione scientifica di Giovanni Battista Riccioli', in Luigi Pepe, ed., *Copernico e la questione copernicana in Italia dal XVI al XIX secolo* (Florence, 1996), pp.123–182, esp. pp.161–164.

[87] Giovanni Baptista Riccioli, *Almagestum Novum* (Bologna, 1651), lib.IX, sect.II, pp.248–249.

[88] *Ibid.* lib.IX, sect.I, cap.VII, p.244.

[89] *Ibid. loc. cit.*

[90] *Ibid.* lib.IX, sect.III, cap.IX, p.289 and lib.X, sect.II, p.550.

claiming that the heaven was an incorruptible fifth essence. 'I have been compelled', wrote Muñoz, '... by natural reasons and geometrical proofs to admit that there are alterations and combustion in the heaven.'[91] Muñoz's anti-Aristotelianism appears especially in his unpublished Commentary on the second Book of Pliny's *Natural History* as of clearly Stoic inspiration.[92] While recognized and appreciated by astronomers elsewhere in Europe for his astronomical work (it was known to Tycho), Muñoz was unable to shake the Aristotelian commitment of the majority of the university teachers in Counter-Reformation Spain. For criticizing Aristotle he had been, as he wrote himself, 'pelted with insults by many theologians, philosophers and courtiers of King Philip [II] (*rociado de injurias por muchos teólogos, filósofos y palaciegos del rey Felipe*)'.[93]

In Portugal, Aristotle's doctrine of the heavens was outrightly criticized by Manuel Bocarro Francês (1588–1662) in a treatise on the comet of 1618, published in 1619 at Lisbon.[94] Bocarro Francês, a physician and astrologer of Jewish extraction who had studied at Montpellier and Alcalà, was later to wander through Europe publishing works in Hamburg and in Florence.[95] Having resumed in his treatise the standard Aristotelian account of the nature of the heavens, he declared, 'I well know that if anyone today wants to go against this opinion he will be completely abandoned and held to be less intelligent. [...] However I shall recount the true doctrine in this matter in order to explain what is here dealt with, leaving, for another occasion, proof thereof, both according to natural and philosophical reasons, as well as

---

[91] Jerónimo Muñoz, *Libro del Nuevo Cometa y del lugar donde se hazen; y como se vera por las Parallaxas quan lexos estan de tierra; y del Prognostico deste* (Valencia, 1573), sign. A₃ᵛ. Modern edition, transcription in mod. Spanish with Eng. trans. by E. Ladd and facsimile of Spanish original with introduction, notes and appendices by Victor Navarro Brotóns, Valencia, 1981, p.116. On Muñoz's career and disciples, see José María López Piñero and Victor Navarro Brotóns, *Història de la Ciència al País Valencià* (Valencia, 1995), pp.105–120.

[92] See Jerónimo Muñoz (Hieronymi Munnos), *Commentaria Plinii libri segundi De Naturali Historia*, in Victor Navarro Brotóns and Enrique Rodriguez Galdeano, *Matemáticas, cosmología y humanismo en la Espāna del siglo XVI. Los Comentarios al segundo libro de la Historia Natural de Plinio de Jerónomo Muñoz*, Latin text with Spanish trans. by Victor Navarro Brotóns and Enrique Rodriguez Galdeano; introduction by Victor Navarro Brotóns, Valencia, 1998, pp.290–292 and pp.384–386. Rejecting the existence of rigid orbs, Muñoz asserted that the heaven consisted of air. As for Pliny, the universe for Muñoz was finite though he admitted to a void placed outside it. See also the introduction by Victor Navarro Brotóns, p.169.

[93] Jerónimo Muñoz, Letter to Bartholomew Reisacher of Vienna, 13/4/1574, in Jerónimo Muñoz, *Libro del Nuevo Cometa, ed. cit.* p.109.

[94] Manuel Bocarro Francês, *Tratado dos cometas que appareceram em Novembro passado de 1618* (Lisbon, 1619). The work was prudently dedicated to the Inquisitor General of Portugal.

[95] On Manuel Bocarro Francês, see Armando Cotarelo Valledor, 'El Padre José de Zaragoza y la astronomia de su tiempo', in *Estudios sobre la ciencia española del siglo XVII* (Madrid, 1935), pp.98–99; pp.204–205 and the notice by Innocêncio Francisco da Silva, *Diccionário Bibliográfico Portuguez*, vol.V (1860), pp. 377–378 and vol.XVI (1893), pp.140–144.

according to mathematical ones and geometrical observations and there, with Divine help, I shall show the falsity of what the Peripateticians say.'[96] Bocarro then quoted the opinions of the pre-Socratics, of the Stoics and of Saint Augustine that the heavens were of elementary matter. There was no *Primum Mobile*, he said: '... the planets and the stars run their courses not in orbs or in spheres but by themselves (*por si só*)'. Eccentrics and epicycles are '... imagined and invented because in reality they do not exist, as many modern astronomers have affirmed. [...] There is only one region of the air from here to the Empyrean and the further it reaches from us, the more it is purified.'[97] Bocarro made no reference to Tycho or to any other modern astronomers by name and his work appears to have been ignored by his contemporaries in Portugal.

In Italy, during the first half of the seventeenth century, there was a wide recognition of the importance of the conclusions of the astronomers of the Protestant north, not only of Tycho and Rothmann, but also of Kepler, even if some continued to maintain resistance to them. Two Italian mathematical astronomers professionally unconstrained by allegiance to Aristotelianism, Giovanni Camillo Gloriosi (1572–1643) and Andrea Argoli (1570–1657), both showed, in their works published during the first third of the seventeenth century in 1624 and 1629, the extent to which they were aware of the new developments in the north.

Gloriosi, who succeeded Galileo in the chair of mathematics at the University of Padua, published his *De Cometis Dissertatio* at Venice in 1624. In it he wrote that Tycho's and Galileo's observations had shown that there was '... nothing hard and solid in the heaven and that all known bodies moved freely through it, fluid and liquid as it happens to be'.[98] He then recapitulated Pena's argument (though without mentioning him by name) that the whole heaven must consist of air, otherwise light rays refracted through more than one medium would render all astronomical observations uncertain, something which no astronomers over many centuries had ever recognized. Tycho, wrote Gloriosi, was wrong to say that vapours were the only cause of refractions. It was the air itself, spread round the earth, which we breathe, as Kepler had claimed, and which Christoph Scheiner had called the Atmosphere.[99] 'The whole universe', he wrote, 'which we say consists of air, [...] is divided by recent scholars into air as such and æther

---

[96] The proof referred to by Bocarro Francês may have been given in his *Vera mundi compositio seu systema contra Aristotelem* (n.p., 1622), a work cited by Cotarelo Valledor, but which it has not been possible to consult. It is not in either the Biblioteca Nacional, Lisbon or in the Biblioteca da Universidade, Coimbra.

[97] Manuel Bocarro Francês, *op. cit.* ff.3^v–5^r.

[98] Giovanni Camillo Gloriosi, *De Cometis Dissertatio Astronomico-Physica* (Venice, 1624) p.163.

[99] *Ibid.* pp.166–167.

which is what they call air.'[100] Æther does not differ from air in substance or essence but in its fineness and in its purity (*tenuitate & puritate*).[101] In the Tycho/Rothmann controversy, Gloriosi was here siding with Rothmann. He then broached the question of the infinity of the universe: 'Whether this space of air (*spacium aereum*) is finite or infinite has not been explained or proven by any mortal.'[102] 'It is not known', continued Gloriosi, 'how the multitude of the fixed stars keep together and are held in place, though it is not necessary for them to maintain the same distances between each other by being fixed to a solid body [=sphere]; they could have been made to do so from the beginning (*ita naturae opifice ab initio*) or they could as Patrizi says,[103] keep the ranks of an army advancing and attacking without abandoning or changing order.'[104] If armies of men, flights of cranes, troops of elephants, herds of deer or shoals of tunny fish can move in concerted order, why should not stars do the same? asked Gloriosi.[105]

Andrea Argoli, who taught mathematics at the Sapienza at Rome from 1622 to 1627, and later at Padua from 1632, showed awareness, in his *Astronomicorum libri tres* published at Rome in 1629, of the work of Tycho and Rothmann. The planets and the fixed stars, he said, moved in a fluid *ætherea aura*, an expression which he borrowed from Kepler without mention of his name. Like Gloriosi, he added that it was uncertain how far the 'aethereal region' extended and whether it had been created by God as finite or infinite. This, he said, was not a matter to be considered by the astronomers, who were limited to the extent of their vision.[106] Philosophers, however, were not to be deterred from asking this crucial question and it was greatly to disturb theologians, as we shall see.

During the first half of the seventeenth century the French astronomer Jean-Baptiste Morin (1593–1656), noted for his rigorous conservatism, became widely known because of his active and acrimonious engagement in university life. Morin, a prolific writer, became in 1630 a professor of Mathematics at the Collège Royal in Paris (now Collège de France).[107] This

---

[100] *Ibid.* p.182.
[101] *Ibid. loc. cit.*
[102] *Ibid.* p.183.
[103] Francisco Patrizi, *Nova de Universis Philosophia libris quinquaginta comprehensa*, Pancosmia (Venice, 1593), lib.XII, f.90ᵛ (1st edn 1587). On Patrizi see below, Chapter 5, pp.112–113.
[104] Giovanni Camillo Gloriosi, *op. cit.* p.184.
[105] *Ibid.* pp.184–185.
[106] Andrea Argoli, *Astronomicorum libri tres* (Rome, 1629), edn (Lyons, 1659), p.10. On Argoli see the article by M. Gliozzi in *Dizionario biografico degli italiani* 4 (1962), pp.132–134.
[107] On Morin's life and work see the notice by Monette Martinet in Jean-Pierre Schobinger, ed., *Die Philosophie des 17. Jahrhunderts*, Bd 2 (*Frankreich und Niederland*) (Basle, 1993), pp.623–631; the article on Morin by Pierre Costabel in *Dictionary of Scientific Biography* and Lynn Thorndike, *A History of Magic and Experimental Science*, VII, chap. XVI.

privileged institutional position enabled him to exercise considerable influence on students and on the society around him. His monumental *Astrologia Gallica*, written by 1631,[108] but only published posthumously in 1661, can be said to reflect his opinions during his teaching years (1630–56). In spite of its title, it dealt also with natural philosophy. Following in the steps of Tycho Brahe and Kepler, Morin asserted that there was no doubt that the region of the planets contained '... an æther that was very rarefied and very fluid (*ætherem tenuissimum atque fluidissimum*)'.[109] Although he quoted Kepler on the subject, the height of the æther above the earth was, he said, 'uncertain and unknown (*incertam & incognitam*)'.[110] Above the æther there were, he declared, two very solid heavens (*duo coeli solidissimi*), the sphere of the fixed stars and that of the *Primum Mobile*. In dealing with the problem of how the fixed stars maintained constant distances between one another, Morin recapitulated Tycho's solution which Longomontanus had described to him in a letter.[111] Above the *Primum Mobile* Morin placed the Empyrean Heaven of the Blessed, giving quotations from Scripture as authority for its existence.[112]

Pierre Gassendi (1592–1655), a contemporary of Morin, by whom he was violently attacked, was a competent astronomer as well as a teacher of philosophy. A native of Digne in south-eastern France, Gassendi became a celebrated figure of French intellectual life in the seventeenth century. He took Holy Orders at Aix and taught philosophy there from 1617 to 1623. He resided in Paris for several periods from 1624 on and was appointed Professor of Mathematics at the Collège Royal from 1645 to 1648, in which year he returned for health reasons to his native south.[113] He was considerably influenced by the ideas of Francesco Patrizi,[114] though also fully aware of the work of Tycho and Kepler. In his monumental, meandering and laboriously written *Syntagma philosophicum* published posthumously in 1658, having once admitted, after involved argument, that the region of the planets was fluid, he came round to agreeing that the fixed stars also lay in a fluid medium. To explain how they maintained their positions in relation to each other, he invoked, following Patrizi, the metaphor of the ranks of an army of

---

[108] Morin states this in his work *De Telluris Motu*, published in 1631, chap.10, p.75.
[109] Jean-Baptiste Morin, *Astrologia Gallica* (The Hague, 1661), p.94.
[110] *Ibid. loc. cit.*
[111] See above, p.76.
[112] Jean-Baptiste Morin, *op. cit.* p.98.
[113] On Gassendi's life and career see Bernard Rochot in *Pierre Gassendi, sa vie et son œuvre, 1592–1655* (Paris, 1955), pp.11–54, and the article by Bernard Rochot in *Dictionary of Scientific Biography*.
[114] On Gassendi's debt to Patrizi, see Pierre Gassendi, *Syntagma Philosophicum*, in idem, *Opera Omnia* (Lyons, 1658), vol.I, pars 2, sect.I, lib.III, cap.III, p.246. There is a facsimile reprint of his *Opera Omnia*, 6 vols (Stuttgart–Bad Canstatt, 1964).

veteran soldiers.[115] Gassendi then considered at length the material nature of the æther as evidenced from the results of observations of the refraction of light rays from stars. However rarefied and pure the æther might be, there still remained for him the problem of how light rays could reach us over such vast distances without being refracted.

> Make the æther ten times, a hundred times, a thousand times or many more times purer than air, [...] these spaces are so vast that it would end up by being far more opaque than air as regards vision and would thus darken the stars and make them to be seen less clearly. (*Nam fac Ætherem aëre puriorem & decies, & centies, & millies, & pluribus adhuc longè vicibus, [...] sunt tamen spatia adeo infanda, ut debeat Æther denique evadere longe aëre ad visum opacior, sicque Stellas obducere, & non tanta hac limpitudine exhibere.*)[116]

Gassendi here made no reference to Kepler's argument, recorded above, that since the colours in light from stars maintained their differences when they reached the observer, the æther must have no density and could even be considered to be a void. Gassendi concluded by refusing to commit himself on the nature of '... this æthereal substance which some call *Auram Ætheream* [a proof that he had read Kepler] and which extends from our upper air as far as the fixed stars'.[117] He preferred to take refuge in scepticism, quoting Philo of Alexandria (c.20 BC–c.45 AD), that the Heaven has 'an incomprehensible nature' and that 'no mortal can ever understand what it is'.[118] Why such a retreat from trying to fathom its nature? Was it that Gassendi was really less interested in the physical substance of the heavens than in the philosophical nature of space? We shall return to Gassendi and his conception of space in the next chapter.

By the first two decades of the seventeenth century the fluid nature of the planetary heavens had, except for a few obdurate figures like Tanner and his followers, come to be recognized throughout Europe by a fair number

---

[115] *Ibid*, vol.I, pars 2, sect.II, lib.I, pp.500–501.

[116] *Ibid*, p.503.

[117] *Ibid. loc cit*.

[118] *Ibid.* pp.503–504. Philo of Alexandria had written in his work *De Somniis*, that '... the heaven has sent us no sure indication of its nature, but keeps it beyond our comprehension. For what can we say? That it is a fixed mass of crystal, as some have thought? Or that it is absolutely pure fire? Or that it is a fifth substance, circular in movement, with no part in the four elements? Or again, we ask, has the fixed and outermost sphere upward-reaching depth, or is it nothing but a superficies, without depth, resembling a plane geometrical figure? [...] Yes, all these and suchlike points pertaining to the heaven, that fourth and best cosmic substance, are obscure and beyond our comprehension, based on guesswork and conjecture, not on the solid reasoning of truth; so much so that one may confidently take one's oath that the day will never come when any mortal shall be competent to arrive at a clear solution of any of these problems.' See Philo of Alexandria, *De Somniis*, I iv, in *Philo V*, Gr. text and Eng. trans. ed. F.H. Colson and G.H. Whitaker (London and Cambridge, Mass., 1949), pp.305–307.

of front-rank scholars convinced by the converging evidence of Renaissance Biblical exegesis and experiential observation of the heavens. The scholars concerned, however, allowed themselves to be persuaded by the optical evidence (both of refractions and the behaviour of comets) without demanding the full and indisputable mathematical proof that only emerged later. The majority of natural philosophers, if not the astronomers, continued, at least until the middle of the century, to hold out for the solidity of the sphere of the fixed stars to explain the constant relationship maintained by the stars between one another as well as in deference to Aristotle's principle of a finite cosmos. The universities, on the other hand, as we shall see, were to take much longer to incorporate the new evidence into their textbooks used for teaching.

5

The challenge of infinity

Of the philosophies of Antiquity recovered and revived during the Renaissance, those proclaiming the infinity of the universe,[1] and those confounding the corporeal and the incorporeal,[2] threatened the coherence of the medieval cosmos and eventually brought on its ruin. Their undermining of its material structure was however only to take wide effect once the astronomical evidence accumulated from the close of the sixteenth century onward had started to be interpreted in support of them. It was mainly from Renaissance Italy that these philosophies reached the rest of Europe and their reception there remained until the end of the seventeenth century largely confined to circles outside the universities. In Catholic countries their spread was retarded by the institutional structure of the universities which were closely allied to the Church.

This chapter will begin with an analysis of the defence of an infinite universe by the two major Italian figures of Giordano Bruno (1548–1600) and Francesco Patrizi (1529–97).[3] The continuation of their ideas will then

---

[1] Of significant impact in the Renaissance was the affirmation of an infinite universe by Lucretius (c.99–c.55 BC) in his *De Natura Rerum*, the manuscript of which was found by Poggio in 1417 in a monastery near Constance. See Lucretius, *On the Nature of Things*, Loeb edition, Latin text and Eng. trans. by W.H.D. Rouse, revised by Martin F. Smith (Cambridge and London,1992). For the date of Poggio's discovery, see Introduction p.lvi and for Lucretius' defence of the infinity of the universe, see text I, pp.958–1020. However, as D.J. Furley has noted, Lucretius distinguished a known finite cosmos from a postulated infinite universe. See D.J. Furley, 'The Greek Theory of the Infinite Universe', in idem, *Cosmic Problems. Essays on Greek and Roman Philosophies of Nature* (Cambridge, 1989), pp.1–13.

[2] For pagan Antiquity see G.S. Kirk and J.E. Raven, *The Pre-Socratic Philosophers* (Cambridge, 1969), pp.246–250. For attempts by early Jewish and Christian writers at spiritualizing the material *pneuma* of the Stoics, see G. Verbeke, *L'évolution de la doctrine du pneuma du stoïcisme à S. Augustin* (Paris–Louvain, 1945), chap.III, pp.257–260, pp.348–349 (Philo); chap.V, pp.508–510 (Christian Writers) and chap.VI, pp.515–517, pp.534–535 (Conclusion). Newton was to be driven to having recourse to a conflation of the corporeal and the incorporeal, as will be seen.

[3] On Bruno's life and work see P.H. Michel, *La cosmologie de Giordano Bruno* (Paris, 1962), Eng. trans. by Dr R.E.W. Madison (Ithaca, NY, 1973). On Patrizi, see John Henry, 'Francesco

be examined in the works of Descartes, Gassendi and Newton. At the same time comparisons will be made with minor figures such as Ursus, Gilbert, Guericke and More, as well as with the resolute opponents of an infinite universe, such as Tycho Brahe and Kepler.

Giordano Bruno and Francesco Patrizi

At the end of the sixteenth century, inspired by revived currents of Neoplatonism and Stoicism, the doctrine of an infinite universe was being proclaimed by the two Italian scholars, both of them violently anti-Aristotelian. Though neither reveals any technical knowledge of astronomy, they were nevertheless to influence, with their doctrines, the speculations of astronomers and cosmologists in northern Protestant Europe concerning the nature of the sphere of the fixed stars and its extent outward.[4]

In southern Catholic Europe and in the native Italy of the two protagonists, their views were regarded by the Church with the greatest hostility. Patrizi's work was put on the Index and Bruno was tried for heresy and burned at the stake in Rome in 1600 after an imprudent return to Italy following his long wanderings in northern Europe.

In the proceedings of his trial, at which he was accused, among other heresies, of defending the doctrine of an infinite universe filled with infinite worlds, Bruno said that he '... had taught nothing contrary to Christian Catholic religion, except indirectly in relation to the way it is interpreted in Paris'.[5] Although Bruno drew principally on currents of Renaissance thought resuscitated from Antiquity, he may have been here seeking to cover himself by invoking a fourteenth-century tradition in theology of logico-metaphysical exercises using imaginary hypothetical examples.[6] He may possibly have been alluding to the *Propositum de infinito* of the Scots theologian, logician and natural philosopher John Major (1467/68–1550), a well-known figure of late medieval scholasticism who had taught at the Collège de Montaigu in Paris in the early decades of the sixteenth century. In his treatise, published in 1506, Major, following the above tradition,

---

Patrizi da Cherso's concept of space and its later influence', *Annals of Science* 36 (1979, pp.549–575. See also Edward Grant, *Much Ado About Nothing* (Cambridge, 1981), pp.183–192 (Bruno) and pp.199–206 (Patrizi). Bernardino Telesio is not here considered among the protagonists of an infinite cosmos since, while admitting fluid space, he still did not reject rigid orbs.

[4] On the different dimensions of the universe proposed by Copernicus and Tycho, see Albert Van Helden, *Measuring the Universe. Cosmic Dimensions from Aristarchus to Halley* (Chicago and London 1985), chap. 5, p.53.

[5] Quoted by V. Spampanato, *Vita di Giordano Bruno* (Messina, 1921), vol.II, p.708.

[6] See A. Koyré, 'God and the Infinite', in idem, *Newtonian Studies* (Chicago, 1968), Appendix L, pp.195–197 and Edward Grant, *Planets, Stars and Orbs, The Medieval Cosmos, 1200–1687* (Cambridge, 1994), pp.106–113.

carried his interpretation of it to the point of affirming the real existence of an actual infinite, stating that '... like Democritus he was of the opinion that there existed an infinity of worlds that were eccentric and perhaps concentric'.[7] This astonishing claim, apparently running counter to received theological orthodoxy, does not seem, at the time it was made, to have been either refuted or commented on. It was related through a long scholastic tradition to the condemnation in 1277 by the theologians of the University of Paris of Aristotle's doctrine that there could be only one world, an affirmation which, it was held, implied a limitation of God's infinite power. The Paris theologians had then only insisted that God *could* create a plurality of worlds, not that he had in fact done so.[8] From this early acknowledgement of the potentiality of God's infinite power, Bruno, building on later involved discussion of the subject, took the step of affirming its actual realization.[9]

At his trial Bruno stated that '... he believed in an infinite universe, being the result of an infinite Divine Power, since he deemed it unworthy of Divine Goodness and Power, that, being able to create beyond this world another and other infinite ones, he had [only] created a finite world'.[10] Such a view was naturally destined to collide with the doctrine of the Empyrean as an enclosed Aristotelian place in the universe.

A thinker known with certainty to have influenced Bruno was Cardinal Nicolas of Cusa (1401–64), a highly original mind astride the late Middle Ages and the Renaissance, who was led through the influence of Neoplatonism to expound ideas that, from a strict Christian point of view, bordered on the heterodox.[11] In his work *De Docta Ignorantia* (1440) he stated that our world '... is not infinite, yet it cannot be conceived as finite, since there are no limits within which it is enclosed'.[12] Bruno, who was not to enjoy, in a post-Tridentine Italy, the tolerance that the Church of the waning Middle Ages had reserved for Major and the Cardinal, transformed their speculative ideas into terms that were much more directly assertive.

---

[7] John Major [Jean Mair], *Le Traité de l'infini [Propositum de infinito]*, nouvelle édition avec traduction et annotations par Hubert Elie (Paris, 1937), p.62. Published in Paris, 1506, the work was followed by four other editions (Lyons, 1508); (Lyons and Toulouse, 1513); (Lyons, 1516) and (Caen, n.d). On John Major [Jean Mair] see Pierre Duhem, *Etudes sur Léonard de Vinci, ceux qu'il a lu et ceux qui l'ont lu* (Paris, 1909), vol.II, pp.92–94 and Edward Grant, *op. cit.* pp.166–167.

[8] See Pierre Duhem, *Le système du monde*, vol.IX, chap. XX; Edward Grant, *op. cit*, pp.150–168.

[9] Bruno could have encountered Major's work in the course of his two sojourns in Paris in 1581–83 and 1585–86. See Dorothy Waley Singer, *Giordano Bruno. His Life and Thought* (New York,1950), reprint (New York, 1968), pp.17–25 and pp.133–139.

[10] See V. Spampanato, *op.cit.* p.709.

[11] See Pierre Duhem, *op cit.*, vol.X, chapter III, §VII, p.342.

[12] Nicolas of Cusa, *Of Learned Ignorance [De Docta Ignorantia]*, trans. by Fr Germain Heron with intr. by Dr D.J.B. Hawkins (New Haven, 1954), lib.II, cap XI, p.107; cf. also Pierre Duhem, *Le système du monde*, vol.X, chap.III, §II, J, pp.278–279.

In his Italian dialogue, *De l'Infinito Universo et Mondi* (1584),[13] the character Philotheo, with whom Bruno identifies himself, speaks: 'We are then at one concerning the incorporeal infinite; but what preventeth the similar acceptability of the good, corporeal and infinite being? And why should not that infinite which is implicit in the utterly simple and individual Prime Origin rather become explicit in his own infinite and boundless image able to contain innumerable worlds, than become explicit within such narrow bounds?'[14] Philotheo continues:

> Why should we imagine that Divine Power were otiose? Divine goodness can indeed be communicated to infinite things and can be infinitely diffused; why then should we wish to assert that it would choose to be scarce and to reduce itself to naught – for every finite thing is as naught in relation to the infinite? [...] Why should infinite amplitude be frustrated and the possibility of an infinity of worlds be defrauded? [...] Why wouldst thou that God should, in power, in act and in effect (which in Him are identical), be determined as the limit of the convexity of a sphere, rather than that he should be, as we may say, the undetermined limit of the boundless?[15]

The Church had already a long-standing experience of this apparently innocent argument which nevertheless contained the seeds of doctrines inevitably destined to clash with traditional orthodoxy.

At the end of his dialogue on infinity Bruno puts into the mouth of Albertino the following piece of florid rhetoric: 'Convince our minds of the infinite universe. Rend in pieces the concave and convex surfaces which would limit and separate so many elements and heavens. Pour ridicule on deferent orbs and on fixed stars. Break and hurl to earth with the resounding whirlwind of lively reasoning those fantasies of the blind and vulgar herd, the adamantine walls of the *Primum Mobile* and the ultimate sphere. Dissolve the notion that our earth is unique and central to the whole. Remove the ignoble belief in that fifth essence'.[16]

Though this iconoclastic outburst contains no evidence of a practical competence in either astronomy or mathematics, we find a very similar tone in the writings of Tycho's arch-enemy Nicolai Reymers Baer (Nicolaus Raimarus Ursus) (1551–1600), a self-taught swineherd from Ditmarshen in Holstein, who later became court mathematician to the Emperor Rudolf II

---

[13] See the 'Introduction' by Miguel Angel Granada to the French edition of *De l'infini, de l'univers et des mondes*, texte italien établi par Giovanni Aquilecchia, notes de Jean Seidengart, traduction française de Jean-Pierre Cavaillé, revue et corrigée par A. Ph Segonds, Y. Hersant, N. Ordine et J. Seidengart, *Œuvres Complètes [de Giordano Bruno] IV* (Paris, 1995), pp.ix–lxxvii.

[14] Giordano Bruno, *De l'Infinito Universo et Mondi* ([London], 1584), Eng. trans. by Dorothy Waley Singer, in idem, *Giordano Bruno: His Life and Thought*, ed. cit. First Dialogue, p.257 (Italian text and Fr. trans. in *ed. cit.* pp.74–75).

[15] *Ibid.* pp.260–261 (Italian text and Fr. trans. in *ed. cit.* pp.82–85).

[16] *Ibid.* Fifth Dialogue, pp.377–78 (Italian text and Fr. trans. in *ed. cit.* pp.370–371).

at Prague.[17] We also find an analogous approach in the work on magnetism of the Colchester doctor William Gilbert (1544–1603). While Gilbert himself explicitly refers to Bruno, there is no direct evidence that Ursus had read his writings.

In his *Fundamentum astronomicum* (1588), Ursus took up the ideas of Pena and Rothmann, to which he added empirically unsupported philosophical speculations akin to Bruno's, though expressed in language that was closer to that of natural philosophy than that of Bruno's. Ursus presented his ideas in the form of 'theses':

> Air is a very rarefied and very subtle essence and the further away from, and the higher it is above, the terrestrial globe, the more immobile, rarefied and subtle it is. Downwards on the other hand, the closer it is to the earth, the more mobile, thicker and denser it is. Whether the air is finite or infinite [in extent] has not so far been explored or proven by any mortal. The nonsense spoken by physicists about the celestial orbs in which they believe the stars are encrusted and about the fire in heaven which they ambiguously say is fire and is not fire, these things I say can be considered empty fictions and delusions. It is conceivable and not at all absurd and even quite in agreement with reason and nature that the air stretches and spreads far beyond the fixed stars and as a result these fixed stars themselves, such as the Cyclades, are scattered through the air, whether it be of infinite extent, or much higher.[18] These stars are not called fixed because, as people wrongly imagine, they are attached to a sort of vaulted or spherical paved surface (*ceu concamerato cuidem vel sphaerico pavimento*), in which they are imprinted or as it were engraved (*vel eidem impressae & quasi insculptae*).[19]

Ursus admitted that he did not know what held the fixed stars together in a constant relationship. 'Whether the fixed stars are placed in the air at the same, or at a different, altitude or distance from the earth cannot possibly be known to us and it cannot be sought out by the sharpness of human ratiocination' (*neque humanae ratiunculae sagacitate excogitari potest*).[20] Allying a philosophical imaginativeness with the properly prudent scepticism of an astronomer, Ursus had no misgivings about entertaining the idea of the infinity of the universe.

---

[17] Ursus, whom Dreyer describes as a 'very skillful mathematician', was court mathematician to Rudolf II from 1591 till his death in 1600, when he was succeeded by Tycho. Tycho, in a violent quarrel continued over years, claimed that Ursus had plagiarized his planetary system. On Ursus' life see J.L.E. Dreyer, *Tycho Brahe; a picture of scientific life and work in the 16th century* (London, 1890), reprint (Gloucester, Mass., 1977), p.183 and p.274. On Ursus' *Fundamentum astronomicum* see Miguel A. Granada, *El debate cosmológico en 1588. Bruno, Brahe, Rothmann, Ursus, Roslin*, Istituto Italiano per gli studi filosofici, Lezioni della Scuola di Studi Superiori in Napoli, 18 (Naples, 1996), pp.77–107.

[18] *Alterius* emended to *altius*, following the opinion of Michel-Pierre Lerner.

[19] Nicolas Reymers Baer (Ursus), *Fundamentum astronomicum* (Strasbourg, 1588), ff.37r–v.

[20] *Ibid.* f.38v.

The English Protestant William Gilbert expressed himself on the immensity of the universe in a language closer to Bruno's than to Ursus'. 'Who', asked Gilbert in his *De Magnete* (1600), 'was the clever expert who ever found on one and the same sphere those stars which we call fixed or ever proved rationally that there were any real, as it were, adamantine spheres? No one has ever proved this, nor is there any doubt that, even as the planets are at different distances from the earth, so too are those very great luminous bodies ranged at various heights and at very remote distances from the earth. They are not set in any spherical framework or firmament (as is imagined) nor in any vaulted structure [...]. What then is this inconceivably great space between us and the fixed stars? How vast is the immeasurable depth of this imaginary sphere? How immensely far away from the earth are those remotest stars beyond the reach of the eye or man's devices of thought.'[21] But Gilbert, unlike Bruno, did not specifically assert the infinity of the universe, only its immensity. He does not show any very close knowledge of the philosophical issues involved and his speculations appear rather more directed against Aristotelians than revelatory of original insight.

Bruno's evolving definitions of the nature of the æther are worthy of attention and bear comparison with those of Tycho and Kepler, though there is nothing to show that he either influenced or was influenced by them. In his work in Italian *De l'Infinito Universo et Mondi* (1584), Bruno defined æther and air less in terms of two separate substances than as two different states of the same substance.

> ... There is, as we have said, [...] the ether which both envelopeth and penetrateth all things. In so far as æther entereth into and formeth part of the mixture of the elements it is commonly named air. [...] In so far as it is pure and entereth not into composition, but formeth the site and the enveloping space through which the compound body moveth on its course, we name it properly ether. [...] Thus the æther is of its own nature without determined quality, but it receiveth all the qualities offered by the neighbouring bodies.[22]

In a prose passage in his poem *De immenso* (1591), his last great work, Bruno made a clear distinction between air and æther. 'Air', he defined, 'as a humid substance which we breathe and which belongs to the earth and moves in its space. [...] Æther is the heaven itself, is void, is absolute space which penetrates bodies and which surrounds all bodies infinitely.' Bruno then proceeded to divide the heaven into three categories: the *Coelum telluris*, the space round our planet or round other planets (*corpora mundana*); the

---

[21] William Gilbert, *De Magnete* (London, 1600), pp.215–216.

[22] Giordano Bruno, *De l'Infinito Universo et Mondi*, trans. cit. ed. cit. Fifth Dialogue, p.372 (Italian text and Fr. trans. in *ed. cit.* pp.356–359).

Coelum coeli, the interplanetary space in which are assembled the planets of our solar system; and the *Coelum coelorum*, the vast and immense space of æther, that is, the interstellar space which separates these assemblages.[23] Since the traditional Empyrean could have no rôle in Bruno's system, the seat of the Blessed, he declared, is in the stars (*Sedes ergo beatorum sunt astra*); that of God 'is everywhere in the whole of this immense heaven, the void space of which is entirely filled' (*Sedes vero Dei est universum ubique totum immensum cælum, vacuum spacium cuius est plenitudo*).[24] It is scarcely surprising that the ecclesiastical authorities felt unable to brook such heterodox definitions.

The second Italian to be considered, Francesco Patrizi, a competent Greek scholar, became Professor of Platonic Philosophy at Ferrara from 1578 to 1592 and thereafter Professor of Platonic Philosophy at the University of Rome where he was called to teach by Pope Clement VIII.[25] Such recognition was not however to prevent his *Nova de Universis Philosophia* (1591) from being censured and put on the Index in 1592, 1594 and 1596.[26] Patrizi attacked in particular the Aristotelian concept of natural place (*locus*), substituting for it his doctrine of 'space' (*spatium*). 'I maintain', wrote Patrizi, 'that the space outside the world is both finite and infinite. It is finite on the side where it touches the outermost surface of the world; finite not with respect to its own natural limit, but with respect to the boundary of the world. But where it recedes from the world and moves away from it, it passes over into the infinite.'[27]

Patrizi's ambiguous definition, to be taken up, as we shall see, by Aslachus, had its origin in the intermingling of the corporeal and the incorporeal in pre-Socratic and Neoplatonic philosophy.[28] It supposed a finite universe lying in something infinite called 'space' of which Patrizi wrote that it '… antedates the world, and of course it is the first of all things in the world. And why not even prior to the world itself? […] Before this world that we inhabit was made by God, there was an empty space, in which either atoms floated hither and

---

[23] This analysis of Bruno's definitions of the aether is largely based on that of P.H. Michel, *op. cit.* pp.260–263.

[24] Giordano Bruno, 'De Immenso et Innumerabilibus', lib.IV, cap.XIV, in idem. *Opera Latine conscripta*, ed. F. Fiorentino (Naples, 1884), vol.I, pt 2, pp.76–80.

[25] See Paul Oscar Kristeller, *Eight Philosophers of the Italian Renaissance* (Stanford, California, 1964), p.113.

[26] L. Firpo, 'Filosofia italiana e controriforma', in *Rivista di filosofia* 41 (1950), pp.159–173, and Tullio Gregory, '*L'Apologia* e la *Declarationes* di Francesco Patrizi', in *Medievo e rinascimento: studi in onore de Bruno Nardi* (Florence, 1955), pp.387–424.

[27] Francesco Patrizi, *Nova de Universis Philosophia*, (*Pancosmia*) (Ferrara,1591); edn (Venice, 1593), (*Pancosmia*), lib.I, 'De Spatio physico', f.64^r. Partial Eng. trans. in Benjamin Brickman, 'On physical space. Francesco Patrizi', *Journal of the History of Ideas* 4 (1943), p.236. Patrizi's two books on space had already been published at Ferrara, 1587 under the title of *De Rerum Natura libri II priores etc.*

[28] Cf. John Henry, *art. cit.*, pp.555–556.

yon, chaos was rolled around, or unformed matter was rolled about in irregular movements. Therefore space was there before the formation of the world.'[29] Although a few lines before Patrizi had admitted (or had felt compelled to admit) that space was created by God and not independent of Him,[30] he quite ignores the Church's doctrine of a Creation *ex nihilo*.

Patrizi divided the universe into three regions, the Empyrean, the æthereal region and the elementary region.[31] His Empyrean, purely Neoplatonic and quite unrelated to the medieval scholastic Empyrean, he identified with the infinite space surrounding the world and filled with nothing but light.[32] He made no reference to it as the abode of the Blessed. The æthereal region, he affirmed, was finite,[33] and fluid in which the stars moved freely.[34] Patrizi's speculative postulation of fluid heavens thus appeared independently of Tycho's claim to have demonstrated their existence from empirical observation.

Tycho Brahe and Johannes Kepler

Tycho's confrontation with Neoplatonic thought and his firm rejection of it appears in an undated letter of c.1590 replying to a letter from the Wittenberg Protestant Caspar Peucer, dated 10 May 1589, on the subject of the outer nature of the universe.[35] Peucer's thought, as Tycho recapitulates it, envisaged a universe in which the Supercelestial Waters were placed to provide a separation between '… on one hand the created world and the light created within it and on the other hand the Heavens of the Heavens (*Cælos Cælorum*),[36] where God resides in an eternal light uncreated and inaccessible to creatures'.[37] Peucer's representation is not the direct expression of the Basilian Neoplatonic interpretation of Genesis as expounded by Steuco, for in the latter's definition the waters above the heavens do not form a separation between the Creation and the uncreated. Tycho had evidently never heard of Steuco's Neoplatonic Empyrean, for he asked of Peucer: 'But what do you mean by eternal and uncreated light and what do you mean by the Heavens of the Heavens?' Addressing the latter notion, which he understood in Aristotelian terms of delimited and finite 'places', Tycho continued:

---

[29] Francesco Patrizi, *op.cit. ed. cit.* f.65ʳ. Eng. trans. in Benjamin Brickman, *art. cit.* p.240.
[30] *Ibid.* f.61ʳ, Eng. trans. p.225.
[31] *Ibid.* (*Pancosmia*), lib. VIII, ff.80ᵛ–81ʳ.
[32] *Ibid.* ff.82ᵛ–83ᵛ.
[33] *Ibid.* lib.IX, f.85ᵛ.
[34] *Ibid.* lib.XIV, f.96ᵛ.
[35] Caspar Peucer to Tycho Brahe, 10/5/1589, in Tycho Brahe, *TBOO*, VII, p.185.
[36] Cf. 1 Kings 8: 27 (*Si enim cælum et cæli cælorum te capere non possunt* …)
[37] Tycho Brahe to Caspar Peucer, s.d. [c.1590], in *TBOO*, VII, p.233. For the allusion to 'eternal light inaccessible to creatures' cf. 1 Tim. 6: 16 (*lucem inhabitat inaccessibilem*).

Do you not think it most unseemly to prescribe finite limits to the infinite and to the immense and to confound eternal things with temporal ones and invisible things with visible ones? Only God is infinite and uncreated and that is why dimension, place (*locus*), space (*spatium*), situation (*situs*) and other similar things which are the attributes of creatures cannot concern Him. And if this light which you call eternal and uncreated is something other than God himself, there will be two eternal and uncreated things and as a result two Gods and two principles.

'But', argued Tycho for whom, as an astronomer, astronomical observations were necessarily related to time,

> ... there is nothing uncreated and eternal except God himself, who is unique. For if there were indeed outside the corporeal world such an eternal light, it would not be perceived by human eyes even if all that lies in between were removed. For in Optics, it is held with great certainty that all things that are seen are apprehended in [terms of] time. Whence it follows that things which are situated beyond time, are eternal and are not visible to the eyes of beings who live in time. According to you, those waters which surround the Heaven are assigned the rôle of limiting and defining the range of our vision lest it stray outside the universe or into the infinite.[38]

To this claim of Peucer's, Tycho retorted that since our eyes are unable to see beyond the world into infinity, the rôle of the Supercelestial Waters as 'a dense and dark barrier', separating created things from 'the most august majesty of uncreated things' in order to prevent their being seen, was based on absurdities. Quoting as authorities Melanchthon, Castellion and Calvin, Tycho accepted the Supercelestial Waters simply in the form of cloudy vapour (*nubes aquosas*) in accordance with the Basilian model.[39] As a professional astronomer concerned only with phenomena visible to human eyes, observed in secular time, he considered the universe to be necessarily finite.

Tycho's assistant Aslachus knew of Tycho's letter to Peucer, since he uses his one-time master's very words in alluding to those who think like Peucer: 'They further insist that it is absolutely necessary that a solid interval separate the created light created in it from the Heaven of the Heavens in which God resides in an eternal light, uncreated and inaccessible to creatures.'[40] To Peucer and to those who expressed themselves in similar fashion, Aslachus responds as follows:

> All the things that exist in this vast universe are either infinite or finite. That which is infinite, as only God is, besides whom there is nothing uncreated, nothing immense, cannot be enclosed by any finite barriers. As for finite

---

[38] *Ibid. loc. cit.*
[39] *Ibid.* pp.233–234.
[40] Conrad Aslachus, *De natura cæli triplici libelli tres* (Sigenæ Nassoviorum [=Siegen], 1597), lib.I, p.37.

things, they do not need any, since they place themselves spontaneously within the limits of their own essence and they enclose themselves easily within their own limits. Why then imagine a solid vault made from the waters spread out above all the stars so that through its interposition as a sort of barrier, created and uncreated things are kept apart and separated from each other? Do you not see on what rocks of error you are going to land in following this course? Thus you prescribe finite limits to the infinite or rather prisons. Thus you seek to enclose the uncreated with created spaces. Thus you measure the immense according to the finite limits in which you have enclosed it.[41]

In his explanation (with its hint of the idea of gravity) of how finite things prevent themselves from dissolving into infinity ('Finite things place themselves spontaneously within the limits of their own essence'), Aslachus seems to have been influenced by Patrizi's remark that 'Space is both finite and infinite; it is finite on the side where it touches the outermost surface of the world; But where it recedes from the world [...] it passes over into the infinite'. If like Tycho, Aslachus had no use for the rôle of the Supercelestial Waters marking off the province of the astronomers, he had, contrary to Tycho (perhaps through reading Patrizi), no qualms about extending the universe into infinity.

The furthest Tycho got to extending the universe outwards was to admit that '... not all the stars were at the same distance from the centre of the universe and that it was probable that some were placed higher and others lower'.[42] In his refusal to entertain the possibility of the universe that was infinite, he was followed by Johannes Kepler whose strong opposition to the notion of an infinite universe appears in his work *De Stella Nova in pede serpentarii* ... (1606). 'The very idea [of an infinite universe] carries with it', he wrote, 'I know not what secret horror when one finds onself wandering in this immensity to which are denied any limits, or centre and thus any determined place.'[43]

Kepler's understanding of the universe was based on the notions of quantity and measurement, both of which were for him incompatible with the concept of infinity.[44] Leaving open the question of the outward extent of

---

[41] *Ibid.* lib.I, pp.37–38.

[42] Tycho Brahe, *Astronomiæ Instauratæ Progymnasmata* (Prague, 1602), p.481 and p.470; *TBOO*, II, p.419 and p.430.

[43] Johannes Kepler, *De Stella Nova in pede serpentarii* ... (Prague, 1606), pp.105–106; *GW*, I, p.253. Kepler's carefully reasoned arguments against an infinite universe have been analysed by A. Koyré, *From the Closed World to the Infinite Universe* (Baltimore and London,1957), chap. III and more recently by Alain Segonds, 'Kepler et l'infini', in F. Monnoyeur, ed., *Infini des philosophes, infini des astronomes* (Paris, 1995), pp.21–40.

[44] Cf. Jürgen Hübner, *Die Theologie Johannes Keplers zwischen Orthodoxie und Naturwissenschaft* (Tübingen, 1975), p.180.

the fixed stars, Kepler criticized Bruno's doctrine of a universe of undifferentiated space. 'First of all I believe that astronomy teaches most exactly that downwards the region of the fixed stars is terminated by an obvious limit and that it is not true what they say of this lower world with its sun not differing in aspect from any of the fixed stars, that is to say that a region or place does not differ from another region or place.'[45]

In the first book of his later work *Epitome Astronomiæ copernicanæ* (1618), Kepler thought fit to reintroduce the Supercelestial Waters placed above the Firmament, in spite of the fact that Tycho had opted for the Basilian model. 'By vision alone', Kepler announced, 'nothing can be deduced in any direction. Therefore we rightly follow the authority [i.e. of the Bible] which teaches us that all the stars are in the spread-outness (*in expanso*) which in Hebrew is called the *rakiah*. The upper part of this spread-outness is covered by the waters above the heavens; that is to say that above the æthereal air (*auram æetheream*) rendered subtle to an extreme degree and above the stars which are in it, the orb is made of water. If anyone claims that this water is solidified into ice and turned into crystal on account of its great distance from the sun, Copernican astronomy allows him to do so as long as he limits himself to the appearance of the stars and does not concern himself with the [physical] nature of this orb'.[46]

'Æthereal air' (*aura ætherea*) had become Kepler's term for the new 'fluid æther'. To define it further, he drew on the Renaissance interpretation of the *rakiah* of Genesis. His term *aura ætherea* had already appeared in his *Mysterium Cosmographicum* (1596) as both *auram coelestem* and *auram ætheream*.[47] If Kepler allowed Biblical myth a rôle in his cosmology for defining the nature of the physical matter in which the planets and the stars moved, he here posited a clear separation of astronomy from myth in putting the waters above the heavens outside the domain of the astronomer. Yet in Book IV of his *Epitome* (1620), where he presented a more developed exposition of the tripartite division of his heliocentric universe modelled on the Trinity which he had already outlined in his *Mysterium Cosmographicum*,[48] Kepler accorded the Supercelestial Waters a completely integrated rôle enclosing his finite universe. The passage starts:

> These three bodies [the sun, the æthereal air and the sphere of the fixed stars] are analogous to the centre, the spherical surface and the interval [between them]. They are symbols of the three persons of the Holy Trinity. It is believable that there is as much matter in one, as there is in any of the other

---

[45] Johannes Kepler, *op. cit. loc. cit.*
[46] Idem, *Epitome Astronomiæ Copernicanæ*, lib.I (Linz, 1618), p.51; *GW*, VII, p.52.
[47] Idem, *Mysterium Cosmographicum. The Secret of the Universe*, Latin text and Eng. trans. by A.M. Duncan (New York, 1981), chap. II, p.95 and chap. XVI, p.167.
[48] *Ibid.* chap. II, *ed. cit.* p.93.

two, so that a third of the whole matter of the universe is concentrated in the body of the sun, although in relation to the vast dimensions of the universe, it is extremely compacted. Another third of the matter is thinned out and spread out throughout the space of the universe so that the sun has in its body enough matter for it to illuminate beyond itself this space with the very powerful virtue of its light and to penetrate it with its rays. Finally the last third of the matter is expanded into an orb and wrapped in the form of a wall round the outside of the world.[49]

Kepler calculated this 'skin' (*cutis*) or 'tunic' (*tunica*) of the world, as he called the orb of the fixed stars, to be two German miles (or 10 English miles) in thickness.[50]

Kepler's representation of the universe as symbolized by the three persons of the Trinity: the centre the Father, the spherical surface the Son, the intervening space the Holy Ghost,[51] shows the influence of the 'Complementum theologicum' (c.1493) of Cardinal Nicolas of Cusa (1401–97).[52] The Cardinal had however related the circumference (*circumferentia*) to the Holy Ghost and the radius (*linea*) to the Son. He had said nothing about the distribution of matter in the universe. This was entirely Kepler's own idea.

Kepler continued his description of the universe stating that by analogy, '... we imagine the body of the sun to be all of gold, the orb of the fixed stars to be aqueous, vitreous or crystalline and the interior space full of air. Hence to a certain extent it is possible to understand what Moses meant by the Firmament (*rakiah* which really means spread-outness (*expansionem*), that is a 'breath' (*insufflationem*) of the *aura ætherea*),[53] as well as what he meant by the waters above the heavens.'[54] Kepler's ingenious tripartite universe was for the most part ignored by his contemporaries, largely because immediately in its wake appeared the very successful, if thoroughly unorthodox, cosmology proposed by René Descartes.

Among the few writers to take up aspects of Kepler's cosmology was the Frenchman Ismael Boulliau (1605–94). Born a Calvinist, he then converted to Catholicism at the age of twenty-one, and became four years later an ordained priest. In his *Astronomia Philolaica* (1645), Boulliau showed great

---

[49] Johannes Kepler, *Epitome astronomiæ copernicanæ*, lib.IV, cap.I (Linz, 1620), (edn Linz, 1622), pp.495–497; *GW*, VII, pp. 287–288. On Kepler's representation of the cosmos symbolized by the Trinity see Jürgen Hübner, *op. cit*, pp.186–192.

[50] Johannes Kepler, *Epitome*, lib.IV, cap.I, *ed. cit. loc. cit.*; *GW*, VII, p.288.

[51] Idem, *Epitome*, lib.IV, cap.I, *ed. cit.* p.438; *GW*, VII, p.258.

[52] Nicolas of Cusa, 'Complementum theologicum' [1453] in idem, *Opera Omnia* (Basle, 1565), chap. VI, pp.1111–1112. Cf. Dietrich Mahnke, *Unendliche Sphäre und Allmittelpunkt* (Halle, 1937), reprint (Stuttgart–Bad Cannstatt, 1966), p.142.

[53] Kepler's notion of 'breath' may be an echo of the Stoic concept of the *pneuma* conceived of as 'the breath of life'. On this aspect of the *pneuma*, see David E. Hahm, *op. cit.* pp.159–163.

[54] Johannes Kepler, *Epitome*, lib.IV, cap.I, *ed. cit.* p.497; *GW*, VII, p.288.

enthusiasm for Kepler (*ingeniossimus Keplerus*), accepting most of the important features of the latter's thought, including a finite universe, and elliptical orbits, but he made not the slightest allusion to Kepler's introduction of Biblical motifs into his cosmology, one of its most original aspects.[55] Another (though he later became a Cartesian), was the Dutchman Johannes Phocylides Holwarda (Johannes Fokkes) (1618–51) a professor of philosophy at the Protestant University of Franeker. However, in his *Physica Vetus-Nova* (1651), Phocylides does no more than resume Kepler's cosmology in coldly prosaic terms from which all biblical themes are eliminated.

> Therefore we believe that heaven is divided into three important regions or, if you prefer, intervals or spaces, of which the first or lowest occupies the centre in which is the Sun, the guide and controller of all the heavenly motions. The second or middle region contains the whole æthereal system in which the primary planets move with their adjoined features. Finally the third or highest æthereal region, placed at the outermost circumference of this circular assemblage of the universe, consists of the huge number of the fixed stars.[56]

René Descartes

The incorporeal had no place in the philosophy of René Descartes (1596–1650) any more than did mathematical astronomy. A product of Jesuit education at the Collège de la Flèche in France, where among the textbooks used were those of the Conimbricenses,[57] his ideas were to become far removed from those his teachers had been trained to transmit. By his identification of matter and extension in his work *Principia Philosophiæ* (1644), later followed by a revised French translation *Principes de la Philosophie* (1647), he proposed a cosmology in which he eliminated both the Aristotelian concept of place and the Stoic one of space. '... We declare', he wrote, 'that the nature of corporeal substance only consists in that it is an extended thing and its extension is no different from that which it is usual to attribute to empty space.'[58]

In Descartes' 'extended substance' (*substance étendue – res extensa*),[59] with which he filled the universe, we can perhaps discern a echo of the Renais-

---

[55] Ismael Boulliau, *Astronomia Philolaica*, lib.I, cap.IV (Paris, 1645), pp.6–21.
[56] Johannes Phocylides Holwarda, *Philosophia Naturalis seu Physica Vetus-Nova* (Franeker, 1651), p.167. On Phocylides, see Paul Dibon, *La philosophie néerlandaise au siècle d'or* (Paris, Amsterdam, London and New York, 1954), vol. I, pp.155–158.
[57] René Descartes to Mersenne, Leiden, 30 Sept. 1640, in Charles Adam and Paul Tannery, eds, *Œuvres de Descartes* (Paris, 1975), vol. III, p.185.
[58] René Descartes, *Principes de la Philosophie*, seconde partie, §19 (1647), in *Œuvres de Descartes, ed. cit.* vol. IX-2, p.73.
[59] *Ibid.* seconde partie, §1, p.64.

sance interpretation of the *Rakiah* in Genesis, but Descartes, in contradistinction to Genesis, placed no boundaries on the universe. If he did distinguish the infiniteness of God from the extent of His Creation by referring to the 'indefinite' extension of matter,[60] this nuance in no way saved his philosophy from being incompatible with the theological doctrine of a finite Creation.[61] 'We recognize moreover', continued Descartes, 'that this world, or the entirety of the corporeal substance, has no limits in its extension. Indeed, whenever we imagine such limits, we always not only imagine beyond them some indefinitely extended spaces but we even perceive them to be truly imaginable, that is real; and therefore to contain in them also the indefinitely extended corporeal substance.[62] This is because, as we have already sufficiently shown, the idea of this extension which we conceive in such a space is obviously identified with that of the corporeal substance itself'.[63]

Besides the absence of any place for the Empyrean in Descartes' universe, there was, as Alexandre Koyré has noted, '… no place for spirits, souls or even God'. 'Descartes' teaching', adds Koyré, 'leads to materialism and, by his exclusion of God from the world, to atheism.'[64] Descartes' works were condemned in 1663 by the Church authorities in Rome *donec corrigantur*, though only one of his works, the 1650 Amsterdam edition of his *Méditations*, was actually placed on the Index of 20 November 1663. University and governmental authorities in France made every endeavour to prevent the teaching of Cartesian physics.[65] In 1685 the Faculty of Arts at Paris received an order from the King forbidding the teaching of the philosophy of both Descartes and Gassendi. This was repeated again in 1691 and in 1704 the Paris university professors signed an undertaking not to teach a list of propositions, certain of which were identified as Cartesian.[66]

His contemporary Jean-Baptiste Morin (1593–1656) immediately denounced the incompatibility of Descartes' philosophy with the structure of the traditional Christian cosmos. 'The Empyrean', wrote Morin, 'does not

---

[60] *Ibid.* première partie, §27, p.37. In all these quotations the French text follows the Latin.

[61] The Bishop of Avranches, Pierre-Daniel Huet (1630–1721), accused Descartes of dissimulating his doctrine of the infinity of the universe by his use of the equivocal term 'indefinite'. Cf. Pierre-Daniel Huet, *Censura philosophiae cartesianae* (Paris, 1689), cap.5, pp.149–151.

[62] The French text gives 'body' (*corps*) instead of 'corporeal substance' (*substantiam corpoream*).

[63] René Descartes, *Principia Philosophiæ*, pars secunda, §21, *ed. cit.* vol.VIII–1, p.52; idem, *Principes*, seconde partie, §21, *ed. cit.* vol. IX–2, p.74. English translation from A. Koyré, *op. cit.* p.104.

[64] A. Koyré, *op. cit.* p.138.

[65] See Paul Mouy, *Le développement de la physique cartésienne 1646–1712* (Paris, 1934), reprint (New York, 1981), pp.169–170.

[66] Charles Jourdain, *Histoire de l'Université de Paris aux XVIIe et XVIIIe siècles* (Paris, 1862–1866), p. 269 and p.138 (second pagination).

extend infinitely; therefore there is above it a space into which probably its light flows. Descartes contradicts this doctrine in his new Physics. For, so he claims, space is something extended in length, breadth and depth, constituting the essence of matter or body. [...] He also states [...] that this world has no limits to its extension. But we answer that [...] he is very far from the truth in saying that extension in length, breadth and depth constitutes the essence of matter and physical body. [...] This world', pronounced Morin, 'is finite and has definite limits to its extension.'[67]

Besides his rejection of the traditional Christian doctrine of the cosmos's finite extent in space, Descartes also turned his back on the entire scholastic tradition of attempts, from Albert the Great and St Thomas Aquinas, through to Steuco, Pereyra and Suarez, to harmonize the six days of the Creation in Genesis with the doctrines of Aristotelian physics. 'Genesis', he wrote in a letter, said probably to have been addressed to Boswell in about 1646, 'can all be explained much better according to my way of thinking (so it appears to me), than by all the ways in which the interpreters have explained it, something which up till now I had never hoped to do. Indeed now, after the explanation of my new philosophy, it is my intention to show clearly that it fits much better with all the things of true faith than the Aristotelian philosophy does.'[68]

In order to sidestep the scholastic hexaëmeral exegesis of the Creation, Descartes had recourse to Saint Augustine's very particular doctrine of a simultaneous Creation, in which the division of the work of the Creation in Genesis into six days was interpreted as having been so represented merely for the purpose of being more readily understood. In Descartes' letter dated 16 April 1648 replying to François Burman, concerning difficulties raised by the latter, he wrote that in his opinion, '... as far as Genesis is concerned, the description contained therein is probably metaphorical and for this reason it should be left to the theologians. And it should not then be understood in terms of six separate days, but should only be understood as divided up thus for us to get a grasp of it, just as Saint Augustine did in his distinguishing of the days according to the understanding of the angels.'[69]

---

[67] Jean-Baptiste Morin, *Astrologia Gallica* (Hagae Comitis [=The Hague], 1661), [published posthumously], p.113.

[68] René Descartes, to [Boswell?], [1646?], in *Œuvres de Descartes, ed. cit.*, vol. IV, *Correspondance*, p.698. On Descartes' attempts to reconcile his philosophy with Genesis, see Vincent Carraud, 'Descartes et l'Ecriture Sainte', in *L'Ecriture Sainte au temps de Spinoza et dans le système spinoziste*, Groupe de recherches spinozistes, Travaux et Documents, No.4 (Paris, 1992), pp.41–70, esp. pp.49–52.

[69] René Descartes, *L'entretien avec Burman*, Latin text with French translation and notes by Jean-Marie Beyssade (Paris, 1981), p.111. *Quantum autem ad Genesim attinet, forsan illa creationis narratio, quae ibi habetur, est metaphorica, ideoque Theologis relinquenda, nec tum sumi debet creatio tanquam sex diebus distincta, sed tantum hoc ob nostrum concipiendi modum ita distingui dici debet,*

In his doctrine of simultaneous Creation, Saint Augustine had seen the Creation as taking place in two phases, not differing temporally, but logically: the first in which everything was created at once and the second in which the parts were set in order and distinguished.[70] If Descartes allowed God a rôle at the very beginning in initiating motion, he made his own imagined formation of the world out of vortices following on from this primordial motion. Although he does not mention him, he may have drawn inspiration from the very similar description by the Greek philosopher Leucippus (c.460 BC–c.370 BC) of the formation of the world out of vortices.[71]

The unusually involved manner in which Descartes wrote of the Creation in his *Principia* is but a reflection of his claim in his earlier unpublished work, *Le Monde* (1633), that his representation of the formation of the world was '... a fable through which I hope that truth will not fail to appear sufficiently'.[72] By his use of the term 'fable' in *Le Monde*, together with his claim in the *Principia* that his account of the formation of the world in no way corresponded to traditionally received truth, he seems to have wanted to avoid the censure of ecclesiastical authorities. The expressions in italics in the following text from the *Principia* were added by him to his revised French translation and are not found in the Latin original.

> And far from wanting *all the things that I shall write to be believed, I shall even claim to lay forth some here which I believe to be absolutely false. For example,* I do not doubt that the world was created in the beginning with all the perfection that it has, to the extent that the sun, the earth, the moon and the stars were from that moment, and that the earth did not only have in it the seeds of plants, but that the plants themselves even *covered a part of it* and that Adam and Eve were not created as children, but as perfect adults. The Christian

---

quemadmodum Augustinus per cogitationes Angelicas illa distinxit. The expression *per angelicam cognitionem* is used by Saint Augustine, Cf. Saint Augustin, *La Genèse au sens littéral (livres I–VII), De Genesi ad litteram libri duodecim*, Latin text with French trans., introduction and notes by P. Agaësse and A. Solignac, *ed. cit.* lib.IV, cap.XXXIV, §53, p.362. François Burman, then aged twenty, was later to become professor of theology at Utrecht from 1662 to 1679. See Paul Dibon, 'Descartes et ses disciples hollandais' in idem, *Regards sur la Hollande du siècle d'or* (Naples, 1990), p.601.

[70] See Aimé Solignac, S.J., 'Exégèse et Métaphysique. Genèse 1 1–3 chez saint Augustin', in [Paul Vignaux ed.], *In Principio. Interprétations des premiers versets de la Genèse*, Etudes Augustiniennes (Paris, 1973), pp.153–171, esp. pp.164–171; also H. Pinard, art. 'Saint Augustin', in *Dictionnaire de théologie catholique*, vol. 1–2, (1937), cols 2349–2350.

[71] Cf. E.J. Aiton, *The Vortex Theory of Planetary Motions* (London and New York, 1972), p.34. Leucippus' description of the formation of the world out of vortices is reported by Diogenes Laertius, *Lives of Eminent Philosophers*, Greek text with Eng. trans. by R.D. Hicks (London and New York, 1925), bk IX, chap. 6, §30–§33, pp.439–443. On Leucippus and the sources of his ideas in Anaximenes and Anaxagoras, see G.S. Kirk and J.E. Raven, *op. cit.* pp.409–414.

[72] René Descartes, *Le Monde*, in *ed. cit.* vol. XI, p.31.

religion wills that we believe thus and natural reason persuades us absolutely of this truth, because considering the all-powerfulness of God, we should judge that all that He has done, has had *from the beginning* all the perfection which it should have. But nevertheless, how much better would we understand what was the nature *of Adam* and of the trees in Paradise, if we had examined *how children are slowly formed in their mothers' womb* and how plants come forth from their seeds, than if we had only considered what they were when God created them. Even so, we will give a better idea of what is generally the nature of all the things which are in the world, if we can imagine a few principles that are very understandable and very simple, from which we can show clearly that the stars and the earth and finally the whole visible world could have been produced thus from only a few seeds, although we know that it was not produced in this way, than if we describe it just as it is, *or as we believe it to have been created*. And because I think I have found such principles, I shall try to explain them here.[73]

Although Descartes here asserts his apparently Christian belief in a simultaneous Creation, his restrictive caveat regarding his account of the formation of 'the whole visible world', that 'we know [...] was not produced in this way', appears simply as another formulation of his representation of the Creation as a 'fable'. It has been alleged that his decision to present his ideas as a fiction was the result of fear of the disapproval of the theologians and especially of the Jesuits. His letters to Mersenne show a constant concern on this point.[74] He had put aside publication of his *Le Monde* when news reached him in 1633 of the Church's condemnation of Galileo's defence of heliocentrism, since he had based his whole philosophy on the assumption of the earth's motion.[75] When he finally published his *Principia*, he sought to avoid ecclesiastical censure by claiming, with a certainly specious argument, that the earth did not itself move in terms of local motion, but that, motionless, it was transported by his imagined vortices.[76] In venturing this ambiguous definition he may have been encouraged by the stance taken up by the Jesuits themselves at the Collège de la Flèche, where on 23 February 1642 a thesis was defended in which it was asserted that: 'Although the opinion of Copernicus is false and ill-considered, it cannot however be definitely disproved by any commonly accepted observations. (*Licet sententia Copernici falsa sit et temeraria, non potest tamen ullis*

---

[73] René Descartes, *Principes de Philosophie*, troisième partie, §45, *ed. cit.* vol.IX–2, pp.123–124.

[74] René Descartes to Mersenne, 30 Juillet 1640, in *Œuvres*, vol.III, pp.126–127 and René Descartes to Mersenne, 11 Nov. 1640, in *Œuvres*, vol.III, p.233.

[75] René Descartes to Mersenne, fin Nov. 1633, in *Œuvres*, vol.I, pp.270–271 & idem, Fév. 1634, in *Œuvres*, vol.I, p.281 & idem, Avril 1634, in *Œuvres*, vol.I, pp.284–288.

[76] René Descartes, *Principes de Philosophie*, troisième partie, §26–§29, *ed. cit.* vol. IX–2, pp.113–115.

popularibus experientiis sufficienter impugnari.)'[77] A thesis in almost identical terms had already been defended by a Jesuit in Rome in 1638.[78] Of his complex character, Bossuet (1627–1704) wrote in 1701, perhaps at that date too far from the event to be able to judge, that '... Descartes always feared the opinion of the Church and one finds him taking precautions to the point of excess'.[79]

By using the artifice of claiming that his cosmology was but a fiction and by limiting the rôle of God to a single gesture in setting the Creation in motion, Descartes sought to by-pass the traditional medieval hexaëmeral exegesis of Genesis and so open the way to expounding the method by which he deduced the formation of the world from *a priori* principles defined by himself.[80]

In 1669 the Dutch Protestant *Predikant* Johannes Amerpoel (?–1671) endeavoured to show, in a short work entitled *Cartesius Mosaizans*, that there was no incompatibility between the philosophy of Descartes and the story of the Creation in the first chapter of Genesis.[81] Alternately confronting relevant passages from Genesis and from Descartes' works, Amerpoel began by citing numerous references from Descartes showing the world to have been created by God '*ab initio*', '*in tempore*' and therefore that it had not existed '*ab æterno*'.[82] Unaware of the discussion with Burman quoted above, Amerpoel ignored Descartes' recourse to the doctrine of a simultaneous creation. Descartes, he declared, '... believed the work of God in the beginning not to have come into being all at once, but to have emerged slowly to its perfection over the period of six days'.[83]

---

[77] Camille de Rochemonteix, *Un Collège des jésuites aux XVIIe et XVIIIe siècles. Le Collège Henri IV de la Flèche* (Le Mans, 1899), vol. IV, p.114.

[78] The terms of the thesis were: '*Systema Copernici, quod de facto terra cum caeteris elementis et stellae moveantur circa solem, reiicimus ut contrarium Fidei principiis et phisicis rationibus, licet non demonstretur impossibile per astronomicas rationes.*' See Benedetto Castelli, letter to Galileo, 30/7/1638, in Galileo Galilei, *OG*, 17, p.363.

[79] Bossuet, *Correspondance* (Paris, 1920), vol. XIII, p.46.

[80] On the threat to theological dogma created by Descartes' abandon of the hexaëmeral ordering of the Creation, see J.A. van Ruler, *The Crisis of Causality. Voetius and Descartes on God, Nature and Change* (Leiden, New York, Köln, 1995), pp.255–258.

[81] Johannes Amerpoel, *Cartesius Mosaizans seu evidens & facilis conciliatio Philosophiæ Cartesii cum historia Creationis primo capite Geneseos per Mosem tradita* (Leovardiæ [=Leeuwarden], 1669). On Amerpoel see Caroline Louise Thijssen-Schoute, *Nederlands Cartesianisme* (Amsterdam, 1954), pp.494–495. Accused of incorrectly quoting Descartes, Amerpoel became involved in a dispute that reflected differences of opinion between Church and academic authorities as much as between him and his adversaries. See J. van Genderen, *Herman Witsius* (Utrecht, 1953), pp.39–40. I am grateful to Dr R. Richard of the Rare Books division of the Amsterdam University Library for kindly providing me with this information on Amerpoel.

[82] Johannes Amerpoel, *op. cit.* pp.6–7.

[83] *Ibid.* p.11.

Following the Renaissance theologians, Amerpoel defined the Firmament as a spread-outness (*expansionem*) or a stretched-outness (*extensionem*). The Supercelestial Waters he saw in Basilian terms as 'vapours and clouds'. The stretched-outness of the Firmament he described in pseudo-Clementine terms with a tripartite division: a lower part consisting of the air, a middle part containing the celestial bodies, and a third, 'the heaven of the Blessed, the Celestial Paradise'. Sidestepping consideration of this designation of the Empyrean, no doubt for reasons connected with his Protestant faith, Amerpoel declared that only the first and second parts were his concern, they alone being mentioned as spread-outness (*expansi*) in Genesis.[84] He noted that Descartes assumed the fluidity of the heavens and that he affirmed celestial matter to be penetrable, allowing the passage of solid bodies. It thus appeared that Descartes and Moses [i.e. Genesis] both defined the spread-outness (*expansum*) as fluid. Descartes, remarked Amerpoel, did not hold that '... the heaven as such, or the heaven of the air, or in a word the whole spread-outness (*expansum*) had been created without space (*sine spatio*) [i.e. *ex nihilo*], for he distinctly maintains that the nature of matter and of space do not differ in reality'.[85]

The created finiteness of the world in time, assented to by Descartes, was inevitably to imply, so charged his adversaries, its finiteness in space.[86] In identifying matter and space, Descartes stated the world to be 'indefinite' in extent. This contradiction with the conclusion implied by his adversaries was ignored by Amerpoel, though not by those whom we shall examine later.

Pierre Gassendi

In France, as well as in the rest of Europe, Pierre Gassendi (1592–1655), though less remembered by later generations than Descartes, exercised a considerable influence over the second half of the seventeenth century, rivalling that of his contemporary. While readily recognizing the advantages of the Copernican system, he, like Descartes, nevertheless bowed to the Church's condemnation of it. It was on the nature of space, however, that he made a spectacular break with the orthodox scholastic doctrine of the cosmos.

In his major work, published posthumously, *Syntagma Philosophicum* (1658), Gassendi discussed in turn the three astronomical systems of Ptolemy, Copernicus and Tycho Brahe. To the Ptolemaic system he attributed twelve spheres, eleven mobile ones and one immobile recognized by the Doctors of Theology (*Sacri Doctores*), of 'almost fiery splendour called the Empyrean, the

---

[84] *Ibid.* pp.27–30.
[85] *Ibid.* pp.30–43.
[86] See below, Chapter 8, p.200. and p.206.

dwelling of the Blessed'. This was his only reference to the Empyrean. His ignoring of it in his description of the other two systems can be accounted an early sign of its coming abandonment. The question of the fluid or solid nature of the region of the planets Gassendi called a 'famous controversy', dividing those for whom it consists of '... a most pure and liquid air or æther [...] in which the planets moved freely like birds through the air [...], and those like Eudoxus, Callipus and Aristotle who have held it to be filled with seven solid spheres'. There was general agreement, however, that the sphere of the fixed stars was solid, they being set in it 'like knots or nails in a board'.

In his account of the Copernican system, without mentioning Galileo's name, Gassendi noted his discoveries of sunspots, Jupiter's satellites and Saturn's rings. Turning to the Tychonic system, he said it seemed to be nothing other than the Copernican one turned inside out (*inversum*). The Ptolemaic system was 'the least probable' for a number of reasons, among which he cited the evidence of the phases of Venus. The Copernican system was 'clearer and more elegant' (*planius et concinnius*), but '... because there are sacred texts which hold that the earth remains immobile and that the sun moves, and because they have given rise to a decree by which these texts must be interpreted to concern, not apparent, but real immobility and motion, it remains that, in accordance with such a decree by the ecclesiastical authorities, it is rather the Tychonic system which should be approved of and upheld'.[87]

Gassendi's approach to evaluating the three astronomical systems was taken up throughout the second half of the seventeenth century in numerous textbooks of natural philosophy. As will be seen below, their authors can be found either falling back on the Tychonic system for the same reason as that given by Gassendi or, in the case of a few, adopting a position of complete scepticism by declaring that there was no way of knowing if any system corresponded to reality.

Influenced by Patrizi, Gassendi declared that the world lay in infinite space,[88] while being finite in extent '... in accordance with the belief of Holy Faith'.[89] However, unlike Patrizi's, his space was void of body, æther and light.[90] Beyond his astronomically finite world,[91] Gassendi placed what he further on defined as the

---

[87] Pierre Gassendi, *Syntagma Philosophicum*, in *Opera Omnia* (Lyons, 1658), vol.I, pars II, sect.I, lib.I, cap.III, pp.145–149. Gassendi returned to the three systems in greater detail at the end of his work, but his conclusions remained the same. Cf. *ibid.* pars II, sect.II, lib.III, cap.IV, p.615 and cap.V, p.630. Gassendi's approach to the Copernican system is discussed by Olivier René Bloch, *La philosophie de Gassendi* (The Hague, 1971), pp.326–332.
[88] Pierre Gassendi, *op. cit.* pars II, sect.I, lib.III, cap.III, p.246.
[89] *Ibid.* pars II, sect.I, lib.I, cap.II, p.139.
[90] Cf. Edward Grant, *Much Ado About Nothing*, p.210.
[91] Pierre Gassendi, *Syntagma, ed. cit.* vol.I, pars II, sect.I, lib.I, cap.IV, p.151 (*Figura mundi [...] admiserimus esse finitum*).

immense spaces existing before God created the world (*spatia immensa fuisse antequam Deus conderet Mundum*) [...] immobile [...] incorporeal [...] uncreated (*improductum*) and independent (*independens*) of God. God [...] would therefore not be the Creator of all things (*Deum igitur non fore Authorem omnium rerum*).

'And so', he continued, seeking to legitimize this extraordinary contention by identifying it with the views of respectable authorities,

... it is evident that by the term space and spatial dimension, we mean nothing other than those spaces commonly called imaginary, which the majority of the Doctors of Theology agree lie beyond the world. And they do not say that these imaginary spaces are just suspended in the imagination like chimeras, but that we imagine them to have the same dimensions as corporeal ones perceptible to the senses. There is nothing inconvenient in calling these spaces uncreated and independent of God, since they are nothing positive (*positivum nihil sunt*), being neither substance nor accident. Indeed they appear to be something far more tolerable (*longè tolerabilior*) than that which the Doctors commonly accept them to be: eternal essences (*Essentias æternas*) of things both uncreated and independent of God.[92]

Was Gassendi implying an 'infinite' space when he used the term 'immense?'[93] Was Gassendi emulating Descartes' prudence in speaking of the indefinite extent of the universe, while privately intending that it was 'infinite', as Edward Grant suggests?[94] But had not Gassendi, already a few lines previously, used the word *infinitum* of space as Grant himself notes?[95] In saying that space was uncreated and independent of God, Gassendi was undoubtedly overstepping the bounds of Christian orthodoxy, further aggravating his case by affirming that God did not appear to be the Creator of all things.[96] His English Protestant contemporary, Isaac Barrow (1630–77), in referring to the terms *improductum* and *independens*, found that the idea of '... something not created by God and not dependent on Him' went '... as much against right reasoning as it is seen to offend Godliness'.[97] Even Steuco had never claimed that his uncreated Empyrean was independent of

---

[92] *Ibid.* vol.I, pars II, sect.I, lib.II, cap.I, pp.183.

[93] Olivier René Bloch unhesitatingly translates *spatia immensa* by 'espaces infinis', without comment or justification. Cf. Olivier René Bloch, *op. cit.* p.177.

[94] Edward Grant, *op. cit.* p.391, n.174.

[95] Pierre Gassendi, *op. cit. loc.cit.*

[96] This is the view of Edward Grant, *op. cit.* pp.211–213. Thomas Lennon formulates three Gassendian counter-arguments to theological objections to Gassendi's ideas on space, but none of them really overcome the difficulty created by his statements as quoted above. Cf. Thomas M. Lennon, *The Battle of the Gods and Giants. The Legacies of Descartes and Gassendi (1655–1715)* (Princeton, New Jersey, 1993), pp.120–122.

[97] Isaac Barrow, *Lectiones Mathematicæ*, lectio II (1665) (London, 1684), p.27 (*tam rectæ rationi discrepare, quam à pietate videtur abhorrere*).

God. The extra-cosmic 'imaginary space' of the 'Doctors of Theology', to which Gassendi sought to assimilate his concept of space in an attempt to legitimize it, had been defined in the Middle Ages as infinite, where God existed before the Creation as well as at present,[98] but it had none of the characteristics of Gassendi's alarming definition.

The 'eternal essences, uncreated and independent of God' would appear to correspond to the 'supramundane powers' mentioned by Saint Basil, 'beyond time, everlasting without beginning or end', 'older than the birth of the world'.[99] But by what 'Doctors of Theology', other than Saint Basil, were they 'commonly admitted'? Gassendi seems to have taken no account of the Church's censure of this aspect of Saint Basil's Neoplatonism as manifested in Steuco's work. Having earlier asserted that his spaces were 'true things and real entities' (*res verae entiave realia*),[100] then later that they were 'nothing positive', his claim that they were 'more tolerable' than the 'eternal essences' with which the Doctors identified them in no way clarified the fundamental ambiguity of his conception.[101] Was Gassendi himself aware of the heterodox nature of his ideas? If he was spared the censures of the Church that his predecessors in Italy had experienced, it was no doubt because he was living in a later age and in a different country.

Otto von Guericke

One of the last to expound the new ideas on space within a scholastic framework was Otto von Guericke (1602–86). Born in Magdeburg, he received a Protestant education at the University of Helmstedt and later trained as a civil engineer at the University of Leyden.[102] His book describing experiments on creating an artificial vacuum, *Experimenta Nova de Vacuo Spatio* (1672), goes far beyond what is suggested in the title and contains a general exposition of his ideas on cosmology.[103]

---

[98] Cf. A. Koyré, 'Le vide et l'espace infini au XIVe siècle', *Archives d'histoire doctrinaire et littéraire du Moyen Age* 24 (1949), pp.45–91 and Edward Grant, *op. cit.* chaps 5 and 6.

[99] See above, Chapter 1, p.4.

[100] Pierre Gassendi, *op. cit.*, p.182.

[101] Cf. Alexandre Koyré in Bernard Rochot, ed., *Pierre Gassendi 1592–1655 sa vie et son œuvre* (Paris,1955), p.110 and Olivier René Bloch, *op. cit.* pp.314–317. In saying that Gassendi's analysis of space merely 'shifts the problem elsewhere', Koyré's criticism appears more apposite than Bloch's attempt to justify it as 'a reflection on the nature of the concepts of science'.

[102] See H. Schimank, *'Nachwort'*, in Ottonis de Guericke, *Experimenta Nova* (*ut vocantur*) *Magdeburgica de Vacuo Spatio* (Amsterdam, 1672), reprint (Aelen, 1962), pp.I–II, and Fritz Krafft, *Otto von Guericke*, in the series 'Erträge der Forschung', 87 (Darmstadt, 1978), pp.5–6.

[103] Besides the facsimile edition mentioned above, there is a German trans., Otto von Guericke, *Neue (sogenannte) Magdeburgica Versuche über den Leeren Raume*, trans. by Hans Schimank (Düsseldorf, 1968); also an Eng. trans. by Margaret G.F. Ames, Otto von Guericke, *The New (so-called) Magdeburg Experiments* (Dordrecht, 1993).

In examining the limits to which the fixed stars extend outwards, Guericke, as a Protestant, was under fewer of the constraints that a Catholic might have felt. Reviewing all the medieval, as well as the recent, opinions on the subject, he wrote that, 'Since nearly all agree that there is a limit to the [outward extent of] the fixed stars, it may be asked what limits them. Regarding this question and its answer there are so many and such different opinions that there is no sound way of reconciling them. Some would have it that they are bounded by the outermost heaven, that which is called the *Primum Mobile;* some say that they are bounded by the Supercelestial Waters; some say that they are bounded by the Empyrean Heaven; some by a plurality of Worlds, some by Imaginary Space; some by Nothing and some by a Void.'[104] Casting aside all these theories, Guericke then proposed his own, a view a little more in line with Christian orthodoxy than Gassendi's, even if, as a Protestant, he saw no reason to justify his ignoring of the Empyrean.

'As far as we are concerned', he wrote, 'we have sufficiently explained that BEING is IMMENSE and that it exists NECESSARILY everywhere and to Infinity in such a way that it cannot, not exist. Indeed this *Universal Container of All Things*, which we shall call by a single word Space, has no bounds to its immensity and there is no limit beyond which it cannot exist, nor have in it more created things and especially better things of which we know nothing. Thus it follows necessarily that this Space always limits the stars wherever they are.'[105]

In his use of the term 'BEING' Guericke implies a reference to God, whose immensity he identified with infinite (though non-dimensional) space and, it would seem, with God himself. Thus, unlike Gassendi, Guericke did not make space independent of God.[106] Both Gassendi and Guericke sought to avoid postulating an infinite three-dimensional space identified with God's immensity, for this would have led them into the doubtful position of making God into an infinite three-dimensional being.[107]

Henry More

Undeterred by such a consequence, the Cambridge Platonist Henry More (1614–87), who had first been an enthusiastic Cartesian before finally reject-

---

[104] Ottonis de Guericke, *Experimenta Nova (ut vocantur) Magdeburgica de Vacuo Spatio* (Amsterdam, 1672), reprint (Aelen, 1962), lib.VII, cap.V, p.242.

[105] *Ibid. loc. cit.*

[106] Fritz Krafft, in his article 'Guericke' in the *Dictionary of Scientific Biography*, states that Guericke *did* make space independent of God, a claim rightly disputed by Edward Grant, who provides quotations from Guericke to prove his point. Cf. Edward Grant, *op. cit.* p.397, n.225.

[107] Edward Grant, *op. cit.* p.178, p.215 and p.223.

ing the Frenchman's philosophy and in particular his identification of matter with extension,[108] went as far as taking this extraordinary step by arguing for a fusion of God and space in his book *Enchiridion Metaphysicum* (1671).

Descartes, said More, 'aims at another goal than I. Indeed [...] he endeavours to conclude that the space that is called void is the very same corporeal substance as that called matter. I, on the contrary, since I have so clearly proved that Space or internal place (*locum internum*) is really distinct from matter, conclude therefrom that it is a certain incorporeal subject or spirit, such as the Pythagoreans once asserted it to be. And so, through that same gate through which the Cartesians want to expel God from the world, I, on the contrary (and I am confident I shall succeed most happily), contend and strive to introduce Him back.'[109]

Declaring that 'this infinite and immobile extension [i.e. space] is not only real, but would appear to be something divine', More added that, 'there are no less than twenty titles by which the Divine Numen is wont to be designated and which perfectly fit this infinite internal place (*infinito loco interno*) [i.e. space] the existence of which in nature we have demonstrated; omitting moreover that the very Divine Numen is called by the Cabalists, MAKOM, that is 'Place (*locum*)'.[110] He concluded by asserting that his arguments had shown that 'this infinite extension, which is commonly considered to be pure space, is in fact a certain substance and that it is incorporeal or spirit'.[111]

Isaac Newton

While there is no direct proof that Isaac Newton (1642-1727) actually read More's work, the latter's mystical conflation of 'substance' and 'spirit' as 'space' was, together with other similar ideas derived from classical sources, to become a key feature of Newton's cosmology. Probably not unaware of the theological difficulties involved, in the *General Scholium* to the second edition of his *Principia* (1713), Newton first wrote that God 'is not duration

---

[108] See More's letter to Descartes 11 Dec. 1648, in R. Descartes, *Œuvres*, vol.V, pp.236–246 (in Latin); partial Eng. trans. in Milic Capek, ed., *The Concepts of Space and Time* (Boston, 1976), pp.85–87. On the stages of More's first enthusiasm for, and his later break with, Cartesianism, see A.R. Hall, *Henry More and the Scientific Revolution* (Cambridge, 1996), chap. 8 and A. Koyré, *From the Closed World to the Infinite Universe*, pp.126–127.

[109] Henry More, *Enchiridion Metaphysicum* (London, 1671), p.69. The English translations are modelled on those in A. Koyré, *op. cit.* chap. VI. On God and Space in this work see A.R. Hall, *op. cit*, pp.188–189 and Edward Grant, *op. cit.* pp.225–228.

[110] Henry More, *op. cit.* pp.68–69. On the Cabalist term MAKOM 'place' and its relation to God in More's thought, see Brian P. Copenhaver, 'Jewish Theologies of Space in the Scientific Revolution', *Annals of Science* 37 No. 5 Sept. (1980), pp.489–548, esp. p.529.

[111] Henry More, *op. cit.* p.73.

or space, but he endures and is present', yet then in the very next line paradoxically asserted that '... by existing always and everywhere, he [God] constitutes duration and space'.[112] The ambiguity of the word 'constitutes' (Latin: *constituit*), creating uncertainty on whether God was prior to space or co-extensive with it, may have been at the root of subsequent divergent interpretations by scholars. But Newton went on to add, in less equivocal terms, that God '... is omnipresent not *virtually* only, but also *substantially* for virtue cannot exist without substance. In him all things are contained and moved'.[113]

Scholars of repute have rejected or been hesitant in accepting that Newton identified space with God. Their expressions range from a 'close connection' (Koyré and Cohen, 1962)[114] to a 'near identification' (McGuire and Rattansi, 1966).[115] However, other more recent scholars, analysing the subject, have understood God as unequivocally 'conceived of as an incorporeal æther' by Newton (Grant, 1981),[116] or that the æther of space was conceived by Newton as 'a ubiquitous God and a ubiquitous active spirit [...] combined' (A.R. Hall, 1990),[117] or as 'a substance intermediary between the incorporeality of God and the full corporeality of body' (Dobbs, 1991).[118]

It was the physical problem of reconciling Kepler's laws governing the motions of the planets with his own concept of the force of gravity keeping them in their orbits that led Newton to adopt what came to be seen by some as a heterodox doctrine of the nature of space. In an earlier unpublished work, *De Gravitatione* (1684/85), Newton had realized that if planetary space was filled with a mechanical æther or subtle fluid, such as Descartes had postulated, it would inevitably offer enough resistance to the movement of heavenly bodies for a deviation to be observed from the mathematical predictions of their orbits worked out by Kepler. Experience showed this not to be the case. 'For it is impossible', wrote Newton, 'that a corporeal fluid [such as Descartes' æther] should not impede the motions of bodies passing through it, assuming that (as I supposed before) it is not disposed to move at the same speed as the

---

[112] Isaac Newton, *Philosophiae Naturalis Principia Mathematica*, 2nd edn (1713), Eng. trans. *Mathematical Principles*, by Andrew Motte, 1729, ed. Florian Cajori (Berkeley and London, 1934), ed. 1962, here cited as *Principia*, vol.II, p.545.

[113] *Ibid. loc. cit.*

[114] A. Koyré and I. Bernard Cohen, 'Newton and the Leibniz–Clarke Correspondence', in *Archives internationales d'histoire des sciences*, 15ᵉ année (1962), p.88.

[115] J.E. McGuire and P.M. Rattansi, 'Newton and the "Pipes of Pan"', *Notes and Records of the Royal Society of London* 21 (1966), p.121.

[116] Edward Grant, *op. cit.* p.247.

[117] A.R. Hall, *op. cit.* p.240.

[118] B.J.T. Dobbs, *The Janus Faces of Genius, the Role of Alchemy in Newton's Thought* (Cambridge, 1991), p.248.

body.'[119] For Newton, on the one hand, Kepler's astronomical laws describing the orbits of celestial bodies required space to be a frictionless void. On the other hand he knew that if he made his gravitational force controlling the movements of celestial bodies act across a void, he would be accused of making gravity an occult quality. His gravity thus required an æthereal medium through which to act, but such a medium, however rarefied, would never be totally frictionless. Newton seemed caught in an impasse.

His way out, besides drawing on the context provided by More's ideas, was to turn to ones he found in pre-Socratic and Stoic philosophy, also confounding the corporeal and the incorporeal. In a draft manuscript for an unimplemented edition of the *Principia* of the 1690s, Newton wrote: '... those ancients who more rightly held unimpaired the mystical philosophy of Thales and the Stoics, taught that a certain infinite spirit pervades all space into infinity, and contains and vivifies the entire world. And this spirit was their supreme divinity, according to the Poet cited by the Apostle. In him we live and move and have our being.'[120] The expression *In him we live and move and have our being* comes from Saint Paul (Acts 17: 27–28), who probably took it from Aratus, a Stoic poet.[121]

In a footnote to the passage quoted from the *General Scholium*, among other Stoic works, Newton cited Philo of Alexandria's (c.20 BC–c.45 AD) *Allegorical Interpretation of Genesis*.[122] In Philo's Platonizing version of Stoicism, the Stoic *pneuma* was, according to Dobbs, made spiritual and incorporeal and all pervasive.[123] Like others before him Philo did not clearly separate the corporeal from the incorporeal. 'World', he said, 'in the case of mind, means all incorporeal things, things discerned by mind alone: in the case of sense perception it denotes things in bodily form and generally whatever sense perceives.'[124] The spiritualizing of the material Stoic Deity is also a tendency that can be found in certain of the early Church Fathers,[125] but Newton might just as well have drawn inspiration from

---

[119] Isaac Newton, *[De Gravitatione et aequipondio fluidorum]*, Ms Add. 4003, s.d., in A. Rupert Hall and Marie Boas Hall, eds and trans., *Unpublished Scientific Papers of Isaac Newton* (Cambridge, 1962), Latin text p.113, Eng. trans. pp.146–147. B.J.T. Dobbs gives substantial reasons for dating the *De Gravitatione* to '1684 or early 1684/5'. Cf. B.J.T. Dobbs, *op. cit.* pp.141–144.

[120] Isaac Newton, Ms. University Library, Cambridge, Ad. 3965.12, f.269, cited by J.E. McGuire and P.M. Rattansi, *art.cit.* p. 120.

[121] B.J.T. Dobbs, *op. cit.* pp.199–200.

[122] Isaac Newton, *Principia, ed. cit.* vol.II, p.545, note.

[123] Cf. B.J.T. Dobbs, *op. cit.* pp.200–209 and idem, 'Stoic and Epicurean doctrines in Newton's system of the world', in Margaret J. Osler, ed., *Atoms, pneuma, and tranquillity. Epicurean and Stoic themes in European thought* (Cambridge, 1991), pp.234–237.

[124] Philo of Alexandria, *Allegorical intepretation of Genesis*, in *Philo, I*, Eng. trans. by F.H. Colson and G.H. Whitaker (London and Cambridge, Mass., 1949), vol.I, p.147.

[125] Michel Spanneut, *Le Stoïcisme des Pères de l'Eglise: de Clément de Rome à Clément d'Alexandrie* (Paris, 1957), pp.288–291; pp.396–397.

Longomontanus' remarks recorded above, though he makes no mention of him.[126] Such a frictionless 'spirit' was precisely what Newton needed as a medium for his gravitational force. In spite of his deliberately involved phrasing, his definition of space was inevitably to imply for certain of his readers an identification with God, a consequence he would certainly have sought to avoid committing himself to outright.

Newton's concept of space, in which he had allowed the Creator to be perceived as merged with His Creation, was seen by the Protestant theologian Bishop George Berkeley (1685–1753) to be as incompatible with Christian doctrine as had been Descartes' by Catholic theologians. In his *Treatise concerning the Principles of Human Knowledge* (1710), Berkeley denounced as 'pernicious and absurd' the ideas of '... not a few divines as well as philosophers of great note' (he was thinking of Newton), who '... imagine themselves reduced, to wit, of thinking either that real space is God, or else that there is something beside God which is eternal, uncreated, infinite, indivisible, immutable'.[127]

Besides Berkeley's objection, Newton's universe, on account of its infinite nature, was also to appear incompatible with a finite Christian Creation. But, strangely enough, explicit criticism of Newtonianism on these grounds does not seem to have emerged much in Catholic Europe. It was indeed precisely the enthusiastic reception of Newtonianism throughout the Continent, even if at a somewhat slower rate in the south, that led the Catholic Church to relax some of the formal opposition it had hitherto maintained to the Copernican system.[128]

By the end of the eighteenth century in northern Europe, if not as yet in southern, the association between absolute space and God came to be seen as superfluous.[129] God no longer appeared related to the world in terms either of traditional philosophy or of the account in Genesis. The universe of the Enlightenment seemed to have no need of Him.[130]

---

[126] See above, Chapter 3, pp.76–7.

[127] George Berkeley, 'A Treatise concerning the Principles of Human Knowledge', §117, in A.A. Luce and T.E. Jessup, eds, *The Works of George Berkeley Bishop of Coyne* (London and New York, 1949), vol.II, p.94. In a note the editors show that Berkeley had Newton in mind.

[128] Cf. Paolo Casini, *Newton e la coscienza europea* (Bologna, 1983), pp.143–155 and p.176.

[129] Edward Grant, *op. cit.* p.262.

[130] Cf. A. Koyré, *Newtonian studies* (Chicago, 1968), p.21.

6

The Empyrean in the late Renaissance and the Baroque age

As has been already noted, the whole concept of the Empyrean heaven had been rejected by the majority of the Protestants by the middle of the sixteenth century, largely as a result of their aversion to scholasticism. Copernicus, a Canon of the Catholic Church, for reasons unexplained by him, paradoxically made no mention whatever of the Empyrean or of any feature of Biblical cosmology in his work on heliocentrism, *De Revolutionibus Orbium Cœlestium*, published in Nuremberg in 1543, confining himself to the analysis of the motions of observable celestial bodies. He went even further with his visibly anti-Aristotelian statement that, '… whether the universe is finite or infinite is for the natural philosophers to argue. […] … its limit is unknown and cannot be known'.[1] For ignoring the Empyrean he was immediately taken to task by the first ecclesiastic to review his work, the Italian Dominican astronomer Giovanni Maria Tolosani (c.1470/71–1549). In about 1546/47 Tolosani wrote in a manuscript, only published recently, that 'Copernicus, in Book I, Chapter 10, falsely supposes that the first and highest of all [the spheres] is the sphere of the fixed stars, which contains itself and everything and is therefore immobile.[2] Copernicus would have spoken correctly', said Tolosani, 'had he agreed with the theologians that above the *Primum Mobile* the highest sphere is immobile, the sphere called by the theologians the Empyrean Heaven.'[3] Contrary to what is

---

[1] Nicolas Copernicus, *De Revolutionibus Orbium Cœlestium Libri VI* (Nuremberg, 1543), lib.I cap.8 f.6ʳ (*Sive igitur finitus sit mundus, sive infinitus, disputationi physiologorum dimittamus […] mundus cuius finis ignoratur scirique nequit*). See Eng. trans. by A.M. Duncan, *Copernicus: On the revolutions of the heavenly spheres*, a new translation from the Latin with introduction and notes (London, Vancouver and New York, 1976), bk I chap.8 p.44. On Copernicus' life and work, see Michel-Pierre Lerner, 'Copernic (Nicolas) (1473–1543)', in Colette Nativel, ed., *Centuriæ Latinæ. Cent figures humanistes de la Renaissance aux Lumières offertes à Jacques Chomarat* (Geneva, 1997), pp.285–292.

[2] Nicolas Copernicus, *op. cit.* lib.I cap.10 f.9ᵛ (*Prima & suprema omnium, est stellarum fixarum sphæra, seipsam & omnia continens: ideoque immobilis*).

[3] Giovanni Maria Tolosani, 'Opusculum quartum de cœlo supremo immobili et terra infima

133

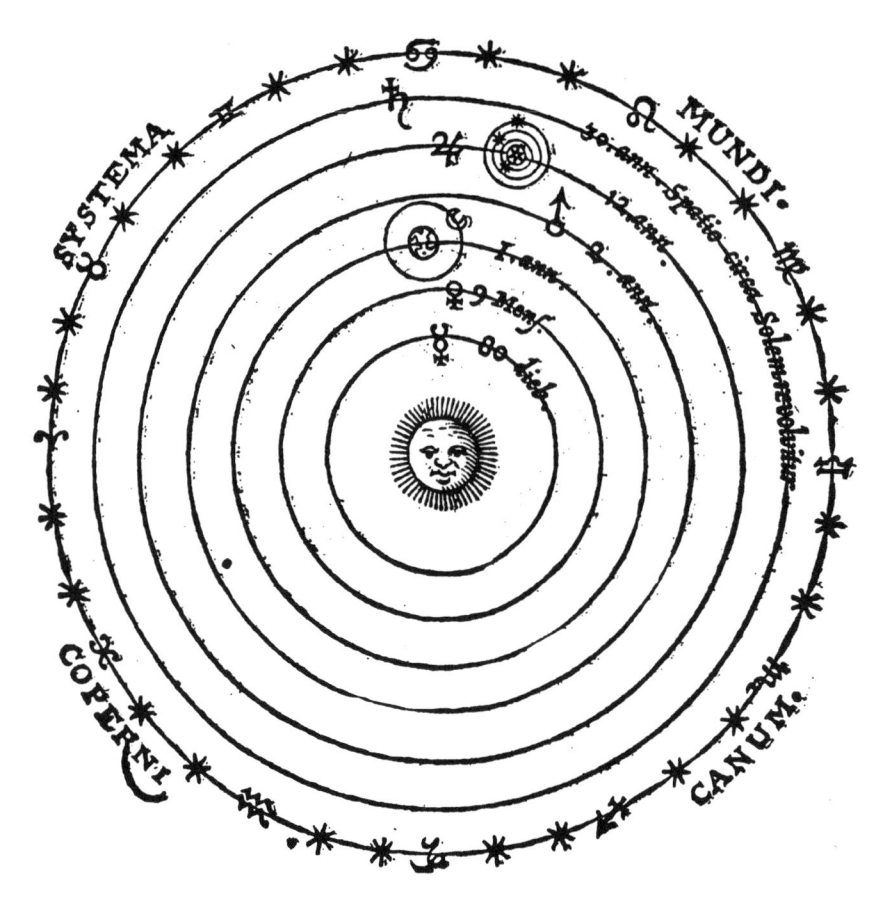

7   The Copernican heliocentric astronomical system first expounded by
Nicolaus Copernicus (1473–1543), *De Revolutionibus Orbium Cœlestium Libri VI*
(Nuremberg, 1543). Diagram in Melchior Cornäus, S.J. (1598–1665), *Curriculum
philosophiæ peripateticæ* (Herbipoli [Würzburg], 1657), p.527, Photo Bibliothèque
Municipale de Bordeaux.

The sun is placed, not as Copernicus had placed it *near* the centre of the universe, but as Kepler had put it, at the centre; the planets are shown with their periodic times of revolution and Jupiter is shown with its satellites. The Empyrean and the Supercelestial Waters were omitted by Copernicus.

often written, the Catholic Church was quick in its opposition to Copernican doctrine.

After noting the comments of Protestant astronomers on the Empyrean, the main body of this chapter will show how the Empyrean continued to remain an important feature of Catholic theology into the middle of the seventeenth century for Flemish, Italian, French, Spanish and Portuguese writers of the Baroque tradition, the majority of them Jesuits.

Protestants

It might be expected that by the close of the sixteenth century, Copernicans such as Rothmann and Kepler would ignore the Empyrean. Their references to it tend to be hardly more than ironic in tone and only appear in manuscripts that remained unprinted. In a text entitled *Observationum stellarum fixarum liber primus* (1586), partially printed recently by Miguel Angel Granada, Rothmann asks, 'If the heavens are not solid, where is the seat of God and of the Blessed?' Concerning God, he answered quoting Isaiah, 'God said: Heaven is my seat and the earth my footstool' [Isa. 66: 1]. As for the Blessed, Rothmann declared, 'we know that they are "in the hand of God" [Wisd. 3: 1], "in Abraham's bosom" [Luke 16: 22], "in Paradise" [Luke 23: 43]. Exactly where the place is, we do not know. That which is alleged concerning the Empyrean is utterly groundless and fabricated. For if one wanted to make a case for it, one could put the seat of the Blessed in the stars.[4] There would be more room for them than in the Empyrean, since the bodies of the stars are round, and such roundness would not seem ill-suited for them as a dwelling-place.'[5] Rejecting any real place for the Blessed, Rothmann as a Protestant restricted himself to quoting Scripture's symbolic locations.

Kepler's only reference to the Empyrean appears in an undated manuscript fragment in the Pulkova Archive, in which, in a somewhat facetious vein, he stated that '... It is in the Sun in which God, if he were to enjoy

---

stabili, ceterisque coelis et elementis intermediis mobilibus', [1546/47], a fourth appendix later added to his *De veritate S. Scriptura* (completed in 1544), Biblioteca Nazionale di Firenze, Ms Conventi Sopressi, J.I.25, f.340^r, printed by Eugenio Garin, 'Alle origini della polemica anticopernicana', *Studia Copernicana*, VI (1973), p.37. (Eng. trans. in Edward Rosen, 'Was Copernicus' *Revolutions* approved by the Pope?', *Journal of the History of Ideas* XXXVI No. 3 (1975), p.538). See also Eugenio Garin, 'A proposito de Copernico', *Rivista critica di storia della filosofia*, Anno XXVI fasc.1 (1971), pp.83–87.

[4] This was the solution proposed by Giordano Bruno; cf. above, Chapter 5, p.112.

[5] Christoph Rothmann, *Observationum stellarum fixarum liber primus*, Murhardsch Bibliothek der Stadt Kassel, 2° Ms Astr. 5 nr 7, f.71^v, in 'Appendice' in Miguel Angel Granada, 'Il problema astronomico-cosmologico e le sacre scritture dopo Copernico: Christoph Rothmann e la "teoria dell'acccomodazione"', *Rivista di storia della filosofia* 51 (1996), p.828.

being in a corporeal residence and if he could be constrained within it, would reside with the Blessed Angels. Since who would banish to outer darkness above the heavens (*exteriores et supercoelestes tenebras extruderet*), He who is said to dwell in an unapproachable light (*lucem inaccessam habitare*) (John 15)?'[6] Kepler's allusions to darkness and light have nothing Aristotelian or Neoplatonic in them, but are purely biblical. The first comes from Matt. 2: 13 (*mitte eum in tenebras exteriores*) and the second from 1 Tim. 6: 16 (*lucem inhabitat inaccessibilem*) and not 'John 15' as Kepler says.

The only writer to take up the idea of putting the Empyrean in the sun, though in more or less the same tone as Kepler's, was the Englishman Jeremiah Horrocks (1618–41) in his posthumous work published in 1673. Horrocks, as an astronomer, insisted that as we cannot see anything above the fixed stars, he did not see why we should believe that anything lay beyond them, unless some had there situated the Empyrean as a place for the Blessed.

'But', he objected, '... they put the seat of the Blessed outside the beautiful assemblage of the world. Why do they not rather put the place of the Blessed at the centre of the universe (that is in the Sun), since, because of the spherical representation of the Trinity, the centre (the Sun) is destined for God the Father who is beatitude itself? The place of the Empyrean will thus be included among all created things.'[7] Horrocks was no theologian and failed to appreciate the historical weight of the problem of the Empyrean.

Catholics

For many Catholic writers from the beginning of the seventeenth century, the fluid nature of the planetary heavens and the non-existence of solid spheres had become an accepted reality. The solidity previously attributed by medieval scholastic doctrine to the two remaining heavens had now, in the case of the fixed stars, only the argument of a certain number of astronomers to defend it and, in the case of the Empyrean, only theological dogma.

The collapse of the doctrine of solid planetary spheres raised even more acutely the problem of the physical conditions of the Blessed inside a solid Empyrean. A proposed solution appeared in the form of a revival of Albert the Great's theory, though abandoned by Tostado, that the interior of the Empyrean was of a divisible nature.[8] It was propounded in 1596 without acknowledgement of its origin by Daniel Maloni (died after 1616), a Hieronymite professor of sacred literature at Bologna and later Archbishop

---

[6] Johannes Kepler, 'Fragmentum Orationis de Motu Terrae', *Collectanea ex codicibus Pulkoviensibus*, in idem, *Opera Omnia*, ed. Ch. Frisch (Frankfurt, 1858–1878), vol.8, p.267.

[7] Jeremiah Horrocks, *Opera posthuma*, disputatio II cap.I (London, 1673), p.54.

[8] See above, Chapter 1, p.17.

of Milan. After refuting the views of Steuco, for the placing of the Empyrean outside the Creation, and of Cajetan for denying its existence altogether,[9] Maloni admitted that it remained uncertain whether the Empyrean was either solid or fluid, while asserting its reality.

> There was nothing in Genesis about this, Christ had taught nothing about it; God had made no revelation on this point. No theologian could say he knew and no philosopher had been able to offer proof. And yet it is extremely probable that it is a fluid body like air to enable the Blessed to move about, especially after the Resurrection, so that they can enjoy the faculty of speech. However these functions are merely probable and likely, but not necessary, because the opposite opinion can [also] be maintained in that the incorruptible bodies of the Blessed have no need of respiration or require cooling of the heart (*cordis refrigeratione*),[10] since, in bodies in a state of glory, the elements function in a highly temperate way. [...] As for moving about, the Blessed have no need of a fluid medium since, on account of their admirable agility, they can pass through everything.

Maloni concluded, though doubtfully, in favour of a fluid interior to the Empyrean: 'Although the latter opinion can be defended, the former', he said, 'seems to me the more probable.'[11]

Conservatively attached to Aristotelianism, Francisco Suarez found it necessary in his Hexaëmeron (1621) to refute Maloni's argument for a fluid Empyrean. The Empyrean, he claimed, even if solid, would still allow movement just as here below. For speech, only 'intentional species' (*intentionales species*) would be emitted to be heard by others without there being any disturbance or movement in the body of the heaven. Respiration would not be necessary as there would be no [Aristotelian] alteration (*alteratio*), nor would the heart suffer heating (*calefactione*) on account of a lack of respiration.[12]

In his earlier Commentary on St Thomas' *Summa* (1594), Suarez had taken up the problem, treated by both Saint Thomas and by Durandus of

---

[9] Daniel Maloni, *Scolasticae Bibliothecae in secundum librum Sententiarium, Tomus Primus*, Sectio I–Sectio III (Venice, 1596), pp.79–84. Maloni sought to excuse Steuco saying that, if he had indeed taught that the Empyrean was uncreated and eternal, he had however stated that the Empyrean is divine light itself, not independent of God, but God himself and that for this he should not be stigmatized with such a bad reputation. Maloni, however, concluded by declaring that the Empyrean was a real heaven distinct from God and not just the light of God. On Steuco see above, Chapter 2, p.41.

[10] The concept comes from Aristotle, 'On Respiration' XVI 478a in his *On Breath [Parva Naturalia]*, ed. Hett, p.469. 'Speaking generally, the nature of animals requires cooling [of the heart] owing to the fierce heat which the soul acquires in the heart. This cooling is achieved by breathing ....'

[11] Daniel Maloni, *op. cit.* sectio V, pp.85–86.

[12] Francisco Suarez, *De Opere sex dierum*, lib.I, cap.5 (Lyons, 1621), pp.22–23.

Saint-Pourçain, of reconciling the statement in Eph. 4: 10 that Christ had risen above all the heavens (*ascendit super omnes coelos*), that is above the Empyrean, with the Aristotelian doctrine that above the heavens there is no 'place'.[13] Criticizing Durandus for his contention that for lack of an Aristotelian medium for the transmission of light, Christ could not see or be seen above the Empyrean, he declared that the Blessed would enjoy the faculty of vision even beyond the convex surface of the heaven. Suarez had either not understood or had ignored Aristotle's conditions for the transmission of light. In seeking to align himself with Saint Thomas' position in the latter's Commentary on the Sentences that Christ had risen only to the 'highest part of the Empyrean' (*in altissima parte coeli Empyrei*), he rashly added the materializing gloss that '... one may conceive that He touches it with his feet and that He walks on the upper side of the Heaven (*suis pedibus tangit & calcat supremam partem coeli*)'.[14] In his Hexameron, Suarez added that the Blessed would not always be inside the Empyrean, but that they could put their feet on its convex surface whenever they wanted and go back again inside whenever they wanted to.[15]

Without directly naming him, the Flemish Jesuit Leonard Lessius (Leys) (1554–1623), a professor of theology at Louvain, took issue with Suarez in his work *De Summo Bono* (1616).

> The Blessed, you say, will be with Christ on the top of the Empyrean heaven so that they can walk with their feet on its convex surface and be with their whole body outside the world. They will thus not be able to see each other, for a visible *species* cannot be emitted in a vacuum. In similar manner it can be proved that there will be no singing, voices or sound, for these require air or a body similar to air which does not exist there and as a result there can be no hearing [...] My answer is that all the above seems hardly credible. First, because according to such an opinion, the place of the Blessed and of the Kingdom and throne of God would not be in Heaven but outside it in the immense void where there is nothing. This is not consistent with the words of Scripture, which everywhere says that the throne of God and his Kingdom made up of the society of the Saints, whether Angels or men, is in heaven and not outside it. [...] Scripture describes the Heaven as a very beautiful city full of light and amenities as is described in Apocalypse, 21 and 22. Above the Heaven there is no light, there are no amenities, no variety of things, nothing good, nothing beautiful. [...]. Hence it would be far better to live in a terrestrial environment (*in terris*) where there are mountains and valleys, springs and rivers, woods and fields, gardens and flowers and a multitude of things to delight the senses, rather than in that horrible vast space where there is

---

[13] See above, Chapter 1, pp.20–21.

[14] Francisco Suarez, S.J., *Commentariorum ac Disputationum in tertiam partem D. Thomæ, Tomus Secundus*, disp. LI, sect.I (Lyons, 1594), p.720.

[15] Idem, *De Opere sex dierum*, lib.I, cap.III, *ed. cit.* p.23.

nothing to delight. [...]. If all the Blessed were outside the world, either the place occupied by some would be above the place occupied by others, or the contrary. If some occupied a higher place, such as Christ, the Blessed Virgin Mary and the most glorious of the Saints, they would not touch the convex surface of the Heaven with their feet, but they would be lifted up and be suspended in that empty space, some higher, others lower and only the most humble would stand on the convex surface of the heaven. If no one had a place higher that the others, but if they all stood on the same surface, then the reason for the localization of their bodies would collapse. Indeed the more anything participates in divine perfection, the more it should, for that reason, be in a higher place.[16]

For Lessius, the hierarchical ordering of the celestial host, a notion inherited from the work of Pseudo-Dionysius (sixth century), *The Celestial Hierarchy*, could only be conceived inside an Aristotelian place.[17]

Lessius adopted Maloni's tentative suggestion of a fluid interior to the Empyrean. He started by attacking the problem of how the Blessed could sing inside an Empyrean of an Aristotelian fifth essence in which there was no air. Its adamantine solidity would make breathing impossible. 'Who could live inside solid marble? (*Quis enim habitet in solido marmore?*),' he asked. 'It is much more likely, that it is a breathable body like air (*corpus spirabile instar aëris*) or some sort of celestial air (*auram quamdam cælestem*).' In Lessius' use of the word *aura* the influence of Kepler seems detectable. 'It is conceivable', he wrote,

> that the Empyrean consists of three parts of which the lowest is solid providing the Blessed, as it were, with a floor they can walk on.[...] The middle part is breathable and spread all about throughout vast spaces just as the air is around the earth. The upper part is solid, containing and confining within it this breathable air (*auram spirabilem*), together with the whole lower world just as the sphere of the Moon contains the air entirely. [...] How great the distance is between the upper and lower parts is quite unknown to us, yet it is conceivable that it is much greater than the distance between the surface of the earth and the sphere of the Moon, calculated by astronomers to be more than a hundred and sixteen thousand miles. Together with the thickness of the eighth sphere, they put this distance [between the upper and lower parts of the Empyrean] at a hundred and eighty million miles at the most.[18]

The fluid nature of the interior of Lessius' Empyrean solved all the problems of the perception of the senses by the Blessed. The Blessed

---

[16] Leonard Lessius, S.J., *De Summo Bono* (Antwerp, 1616), pp.517–521.

[17] See Pseudo-Dionysius (Denys l'Aréopagite), *La hierarchie céleste*, intr. par René Roques, étude et texte critiques par Günther Heil, trad. et notes par Maurice de Gandillac (Paris, 1970), chaps VII–VIII.

[18] Leonard Lessius, *op. cit. loc. cit.*

would enjoy the sense of hearing, for sound would be easily transmitted given the breathable nature of its body. They '... would enjoy the sense of smell, which would give pleasure from sweet odours spread by the bodies of the Blessed and perhaps by the place itself [the Empyrean]. The odours would be spread without any evaporation [...] not as in the case of the scent left in the tracks of animals such as dogs pick up several hours afterwards, because [in the Empyrean] the vapours would be immediately dispersed.' The senses of taste and touch would give pleasure, '... even if some have doubted this, but I see no reason why it should be doubted'. The sense of taste would '... give pleasure not as in the taste of food and drink, but in a kind of very sweet moisture permeating the tongue and the palate.[19] The sense of touch would give pleasure through the touch of the heavenly *aura* or the body of the heaven (*ex aura caelesti, & cælestis corporis attactu*). For if one feels great pleasure at a gentle breeze (*aura suavi*) and at the contact of water, how much more so [in the Empyrean] from the contact of the celestial *aura* and the celestial body.'[20]

Although otherwise conservatively attached to the Aristotelian doctrine of solid planetary spheres, Adam Tanner adopted Lessius' fluid Empyrean, limited above and below by solid surfaces. He identified the lower surface with the Firmament, but the fluid interior he boldly assimilated, following Origen's idea repeated by William of Auvergne,[21] to the waters above the heavens in Genesis, '... understood to be a simple, transparent, liquid and breathable celestial body intended as a habitat for the Blessed'.[22] Quoting Lessius' figures for the dimensions of the Empyrean, Tanner found no difficulty in accepting the existence of such a vast space for this celestial substance.

Unaware of the arguments for a fluid interior to the Empyrean, the Portuguese Jesuit Sebastião Barradas (1543–1615), who taught at the University of Evora, examined, in his Commentaries on the Four Gospels (1599), the physical conditions of the Blessed in the Empyrean, including their use of the five senses, which had so preoccupied medieval scholars from William of Auvergne to Tostado. Numerous editions of his work were published all over Catholic Europe in France, Germany and Italy. Accepting the Empyrean as solid, he ignored the Aristotelian constraints involved. The Blessed in the Empyrean would, he said, move about inside it by miracle and would

---

[19] This was taken from St Thomas Aquinas. Cf. above, Chapter 1, p.22.

[20] Leonard Lessius, *op. cit.* pp.526–528. While mentioning Lessius' fluid Empyrean in his *Diatriba de coelo beatorum* (Gorichemi [=Gorkum], 1666), p.143, the Dutch Protestant Gijsbert Voet (1589–1676) said he was wary of arguments over the nature of the Empyrean since they were baseless.

[21] See Chapter 1 above, p.10–11.

[22] Adam Tanner, *op cit.* p.200. (*Per aquas superiores probabilissimè intelligitur corpus cæleste simplex, diaphanum, liquidum, & spirabile, beatorum habitationi destinatum.*) As we have already seen, this idea can be traced to Origen. See above, Chapter 1, p.11.

enjoy the faculties of vision, hearing, speech, smell and touch. They would have haloes, but no clothes, since the climate would be mild (*neque iniuriæ æris erunt*) and there would be no immodesty in their [naked] bodies (*neque ulla ex corpore verecundia*), '... for their bodies', said Barradas, quoting Psalm 103, *Amictus lumine sicut vestimenta* (*Who cover yourself with light as with a garment*), 'would be clothed in light of different colours, some shiningly dressed in green, others in gold, others in white, others in blue'. In the Empyrean, the Blessed '... would have houses as the Gospels tell us. Why not palaces, some bigger than others, in which, without being confined, for they would be transparent, they would be honoured and separated and distinguished from one another according to their rank, as is said in John 14: 2, *In domo Patris mei mansiones multa sunt* (*In my Father's house there are many mansions*)?'[23] Inside the Empyrean, right up to its convex surface, said Barradas, palaces would be built by hand and so situated that some would be higher, others lower and some more beautiful and luxurious than the others. At the very top would be the palace of Christ; below it that of the Virgin Mary, followed by an infinite number assigned to angels and to men. Finally, examining the problem of what language the Blessed would speak, Barradas answered that they would speak a single language as had been the case throughout the earth before the building of the tower of Babel, such as the Hebrew spoken by Adam and Eve in the Garden of Eden.[24]

'Pious and florid' (*Piè & floridè*) was how half a century later the Spanish Jesuit Gabriel Henao qualified the author of this extravagant piece of imaginative speculation. Barradas' allusion to the Blessed having dwellings according to merit should, said Henao, be understood metaphorically.[25]

In his *De Æterna Felicitate Sanctorum* (1616), a work which went into two editions and was reprinted a dozen times, Cardinal Robert Bellarmine, S.J. (1542–1621), already referred to above,[26] avoided the word 'Empyrean', preferring instead Saint Augustine's term 'City of God'. Dividing the cosmos into five 'provinces', he made the first the 'Dwelling place of the Saints' (*Habitatio Sanctorum*) a '... most spacious region, in comparison to which the orb of the earth was like a point'. It was, he said, '... the first province of the Kingdom of God'. The second province he called the 'æthereal' one in which were the stars. The third one was that of the air, winds and clouds, the fourth that of the water, the fifth of the earth.[27]

---

[23] Sebastião Barradas, *Commentaria in concordiam & historiam quatuor Evangelistarum*, IV vols, lib.X, cap.IV (Coimbra, 1599–1611), edn (Lyons, 1608), vol.III, pp.651–653.

[24] *Ibid.* pp.653–654.

[25] Gabriel Henao, *Empyreologia seu Philosophia Christiana de Empyreo Cœlo*, lib.IV, ex.XIII, sect.IV (Lyons, 1652), vol.I, p.303. On Henao see below, pp.146–149.

[26] See above, Chapter 2, pp.44–46.

[27] Robert Bellarmine, *De Æterna Felicitate Sanctorum Libri Quinque* (Antwerp, 1616), pp.15–17.

Bellarmine said nothing about the Empyrean being solid, or fluid inside to enable breathing.

In his remarks on the enjoyment of the physical senses by the Blessed, he avoided references to medieval scholastic writers. Relying exclusively on the authority of Scripture or of the Church Fathers, he made no mention of the constraints of Aristotelian physics which had so preoccupied previous scholars. Quoting the words of the Angel Raphael, *I use invisible food and drink which cannot be seen by men*,[28] food and drink in the City of God will not, said Bellarmine, be corporeal things but spiritual ones. The Blessed will not require clothes, but will be dressed in light. 'The preaching of the word of God will cease in heaven where the uncreated word itself will be plainly spoken to all. Sacraments and sacrifices will not be necessary where sin will not have to be expiated. In the City, God will be openly seen and heard by all without a temple in the place being necessary'.[29]

> Everyone will always see God everywhere and be with Him and speak with Him face to face, whether they be Seraphim and Cherubim, Apostles and Prophets, or minor Angels and minor Saints.[30] [...] There will indeed be different lodgings in Heaven, some bigger and some smaller and there will be different haloes, some more distinguished, others less so, according to varying merits. [...] In the Kingdom of Heaven and the City of God all our Saints whether great or small are truly sons of God and brothers in Christ, heirs of God and joint heirs of Christ and through this they are brothers to each other and the greater ones do not look down on the smaller, nor is there among them any jealousy or hate. [...] The dwelling of the Saints will have many decorations in its halls, rooms and bedrooms which no other city has. Not only will the interior be lavishly decorated, but so also will be the outside of the building itself with rich marble and marble columns; the entry hall will be gilded and painted, and there will be hanging gardens and other things of the same kind too long to enumerate.[31]

Taking his cue from Matt. 13: 43, *Then the righteous will shine forth as the sun in the kingdom of their Father*, Bellarmine described the joy of vision in the City of God. 'What a pleasing spectacle the eyes of the Blessed will see', he declared, 'when their hands and feet and all their members are outlined by the rays of light given forth from them. Nor will their eyes be dazzled or hurt by the extraordinary brightness, for the eyes of the Blessed will be impassible and immortal. [...] In the Kingdom of Heaven the

---

[28] Tobias 12:19–20.

[29] Robert Bellarmine, *op. cit.* pp.89–95. Cf. Rev. 21: 22. *Et templus non vidi in ea: Dominus, enim Deus omnipotens templum illius est, et Agnus.* (But I saw no temple in it, for the Lord God Almighty and the Lamb are its temple.)

[30] On the conditions of the beatific vision, see Saint Augustine, *The City of God*, bk XXII, #29, trans. by Marcus Dods, ed. (New York, 1993), pp.859–864.

[31] Robert Bellarmine, *op. cit.* pp.123–126.

Blessed will be able to hear and speak as Saint Paul heard Christ speaking to him and hearing Him, replied to Him.'[32] Quoting Tobias 13: 23 and Rev. 19: 1, Bellarmine added that in the City of God there would be '... the sweetest singing in which God would be praised and the ears of the Blessed wonderfully entertained'. While recognizing that Holy Scripture had nothing to say about the delight of odour in the Heavenly City, Bellarmine declared on the basis of the testimony of Saint Jerome and Saint Gregory, that '... the bodies of the Saints will give out a sweet smell. If the dead bodies of Saints after the glorification of their souls give out sweet odours, how much more will the living glorified bodies of Saints give forth the sweetest odours. [...] Though the Blessed do not use the food of mortals, they will however enjoy the sense of taste for it not to appear superfluous. All will enjoy the sense of touch since there is no doubt that the bodies of the Blessed can be touched. However, impure contact producing carnal desire (*concupiscentiam generandi*) will disappear from their bodies', said Bellarmine, quoting Matt. 20: 30, *For in the Resurrection they neither marry not are given in marriage, but are like Angels of God in Heaven.* 'But', he added, 'we do not want to waste time on these things which are discussed in the schools. [...] The Blessed', concluded Bellarmine, 'will move about with no difficulty or effort, going very swiftly up and down, backwards and forwards and penetrating whatever places they wished, as if they were not bodies but spirits.'[33] If Bellarmine carefully avoided getting embroiled in the contradictions between theology and Aristotelian physics, his account of the conditions of the future life of the Blessed in Heaven, though a little less colourful than Barradas', remains typical of the Baroque age.

In 1624, the Spanish Jesuit Martin de Roa (1561–1637) published in Seville a vernacular work on the physical conditions enjoyed by the Blessed in the Empyrean: *Estado de los Bienaventurados en el Cielo*. The work went into fourteen editions in the seventeenth century, eight in Spanish, two in Italian, one in Portuguese, one in German and one on French. At the Resurrection, said Roa, the Blessed will recover their bodies intact in a state of complete and robust youth, without loss of limbs or deformities which they had suffered in life; little children would be resuscitated with the development and vigour they would have had, had they grown up. Men and women will be sexually distinguished and the latter will recover their virginity.[34] Whites and Blacks will retain the colour of their skins, that of Blacks shiny and bright. Whites on the other hand will lose their tans acquired working in the sun. Christ will recover his foreskin, but martyrs will retain

---

[32] Acts 1, 9, 22, 26.
[33] Robert Bellarmine, *op. cit.* pp.193–204.
[34] Martin de Roa, *Estado de los Bienaventurados en el Cielo* (Seville, 1624), ff.5^v–8^v.

the scars of torture.[35] The lower part of the Empyrean serves as a firm floor to be walked upon; the upper part, like a vault, serves as a roof. The interior, said Roa, following Lessius and Tanner, is breathable, bright and like a gentle tide (*liquido, respirable, clarissimo, como una marea suave*).[36] The Blessed will retain their sense of vision and the vision of God will not damage their eyesight. Their eyes will be able to contemplate both Christ and the Holy Virgin and they will not only see her pure and beautiful body, but also the inside of her womb where God spent nine months in mortal flesh.[37] Roa discussed the remaining functions of speech and hearing, smell, taste and touch, but, like Bellarmine, he abandoned all reference to the Aristotelian constraints that had so preoccupied previous writers. Roa's work was more of a purely devotional nature than an attempt to reconcile theology and natural philosophy.

Seventeenth-century writers dealing with the Empyrean rarely ventured into attempts at quantifying its dimensions. Two such, however, can be found in the late Renaissance. Measurements of the Empyrean in the works of Giovan Maria Bonardo (?–1585) and Giuseppe Rosaccio, both aimed at a popular reading public and published respectively at Venice (1563) and at Treviso (1595), were based on fanciful extrapolations from medieval distances of the fixed stars, equivalent to the distance of the inner surface of the sphere of Saturn.[38] The only seventeenth-century writer who speculated on the size of the Empyrean was the Bohemian Capucin astronomer and mystic Anton Maria Schyrlaeus de Rheita (1597–1660) in his work *Oculus Enoch et Eliæ* (1645). 'Since God's works are perfect in number, weight and measure, […] it is possible for us to reason out what the enormous distance lying between the earth and the Firmament and Empyrean is likely to be.'[39] From his calculations Schyrlaeus de Rheita estimated that one of the Blessed would not be able to walk round it in 10,000 million years, a figure which enabled him to quote the prophet Baruch, 'O Israel how great is the house of God!'[40]

The majority of the writers on the Empyrean prudently avoided trying to give any indication of its size, concentrating on its theological and natural

---

[35] *Ibid.* ff.10ᵛ–13ʳ. With the exception of explicit mention of the colour of the skins of Whites and Blacks and of the recovering of his foreskin by Christ, these points all appear in Saint Augustine, *op. cit.* bk XXII, #15–20, pp.838–845.

[36] Martin de Roa, *op.cit.* f.59ᵛ.

[37] *Ibid.* ff.65ᵛ–67ᵛ.

[38] Giovan Maria Bonardo, *La grandezza et larghezza, et distanza, di tutte le Sfere […]* (Venice, 1563), edn 1570, p.62 (seven editions between 1563 and 1611) and Giuseppe Rosaccio, *Teatro del cielo e della terra* (Treviso, 1591), edn (Venice, 1595), p.53 (eleven editions between 1591 and 1693).

[39] Anton Maria Schyrlaeus de Rheita, *Oculus Enoch et Eliæ, sive radius sydereomysticus*, pars I, lib. IV, cap. I, membrum VI (Antwerp, 1645), p.193.

[40] *Ibid.*, pars I, lib. IV, cap. I, membrum VI, pp.193–195.

philosophical characteristics. The latter preoccupation remained the principal concern of three Jesuit writers who, at the turn of the second half of the seventeenth century, each wrote, in France, Spain and Italy, substantial works which contained descriptions of the nature of the Empyrean and the condition of the Blessed in it. The first two by Nicolas Caussin (1583–1651) and Gabriel Henao (1612–1704) were books of theology-cum-natural philosophy; the third, by Giovanni Battista Riccioli (1598–1671), was a work largely of technical astronomy into which the author sought to include a theological dimension. Theirs were to be the last systematic attempts to defend the role of the Empyrean as a real place in the Christian cosmos. Henao and Riccioli held more closely to the scholastic tradition than had Bellarmine. Caussin, though not as radical as Bellarmine, showed a scepticism that was more truly French.

Domus Dei was the title of the work published by Nicolas Caussin in Paris in 1650. Caussin was for a time confessor to King Louis XIII of France until as a result of court intrigue he was relegated to Quimper in Brittany by Cardinal Mazarin, who had also been displeased by his book. He was only able to return to Paris after the Cardinal's death.[41] Caussin followed Pereyra's interpretation of the physical nature of the heavens, abandoning like Pereyra the Crystalline Heaven of the Isidorian model.[42] He quoted Pena and Rothmann on refractions and Galileo (though without naming him) on Jupiter's satellites and on Saturn's rings as providing evidence that the heaven of the planets was fluid; the heaven of the fixed stars he left solid.[43] He adopted a tripartite division of the heavens into the *aëreum*, the *sidereum* and the *paradisum*.[44]

Caussin, who wrote in a more classical and literary style than most of the theologians we have studied so far, took up the old question of whether Christ and the Blessed were to be inside the Empyrean or outside on its convex surface. 'But I ask you', he wrote, 'would all those of whom it is said that they have been raised to the temple of God have to walk on top of its roof? Would they only live comfortably in the dwellings of God if they are to be lifted above the nests of swallows to climb on to the cornices of roofs? For what else is standing on the convex surface of the heaven than being outside the heaven? Thus only their feet would take advantage of the dwelling of the Blessed, their heads and their other members being banished outside the world and outside nature. What is there beyond the convex surface of the world except an enormous void where there is only horror and

---

[41] See Pierre Bayle, *Dictionnaire historique et critique*, 5th edn (Amsterdam, 1734), vol. II, pp.375–378 and Ch. Daniel, S.J., *Une vocation et une disgrace à la cour de Louis XIII* (Paris, 1861).

[42] See above, Chapter 2, p.47.

[43] Nicolas Caussin, S.J., *Domus Dei*, lib.I, capsI–XII (Paris, 1650), pp.2–7.

[44] *Ibid.* lib.IV, cap.I, p.123.

darkness? And what should we think of the inhabitants of heaven standing with their whole body in a place of terrifying shades and eternal sorrow?'[45]

Caussin was for keeping everyone inside the Empyrean. 'It would be much better', he said, 'to lay down a solid heaven in the form of a pavement for the Blessed, to set up arches of crystal built as vaults in the immense spaces and to fill the interior of the Empyrean with a breathable substance, than to get entangled in other opinions. This is the view of our Lessius, a man of very careful judgement. Indeed the solidity of the heavens suited the ancients more and fluidity has only been brought in by recent scholars to explain certain movements of stars. Since there is no need for this in the uppermost heaven, nothing prevents us from accepting the heaven as solid on the sides where it surrounds the Blessed, with its inside fluid so as to assure conveniently the functions of the senses.'[46]

But Caussin refused to accept that the functioning of the senses was corporeal; it could only be intellectual. For him the immortality of the soul is not proven by the breathing of air, which is absurd, but by reason and intelligence. The immortality of the soul does not require bodily vitality. The soul is not corporeal or material for, if it were, it would not be incorruptible. It is pointless to imagine that a soul cannot exist without being able to see or hear or smell or taste. Separation from the body would indeed much help counting, dividing, distinguishing and judging. It was ridiculous to ask whether the seat (*sedes*) of the Blessed (i.e. the Empyrean) was big enough for them, even if of a tenuous and airy substance as some would have it, or whether the Blessed would have clothes.[47] Caussin's scepticism regarding the physical enjoyment of the senses in the Empyrean reveals how much the French classical mind was diverging from the Baroque spirit of southern Catholic Europe.

In marked contrast to Caussin both in mentality and style was the work of Gabriel Henao. A Spanish Jesuit, born in Valladolid, Henao was professor of theology at the Jesuit College at Salamanca. His *Empyreologia seu Philosophia Christiana de Empyreo Cœlo* (1652) was noticeably less fettered by the strict Aristotelian tradition perpetuated by Francisco Suarez and Pedro Hurtado de Mendoza.[48] In Henao's work the influence of Lessius is visible. Except that he was considered to be 'one of the most learned men of Spain, frequently consulted',[49] there appears to be relatively little information available about his place in the Spanish intellectual *milieu* of his time.[50]

---

[45] *Ibid.* lib.IV, cap.II, p.124.
[46] *Ibid. loc. cit.*
[47] *Ibid.* lib.IV, cap.VIII, p.130.
[48] On Pedro Hurtado de Mendoza, S.J. (1578–1651) see below Chapter 7, p.169–170.
[49] *Mémoires de Trévoux*, vol.15, 1704, pp.1455-1457. The authors praised Henao for his care in being accurate in his statements, as well as for his tolerance and his modest way of life.
[50] On Henao see Pierre Bayle, ed. *Dictionnaire historique et critique* (Paris, 1830), vol. IX, note

Quoting their arguments at length, Henao followed the contention of Maloni and Lessius that the Empyrean had solid inner and outer surfaces with an interior that was fluid. However, he rejected Tanner's claim, following Origen and William of Auvergne, that the interior of the Empyrean was filled with the Supercelestial Waters. But following Tanner he made all the other heavens solid. Henao then proceeded to examine in great detail, laboriously refuting them, all the possible Aristotelian arguments against a fluid interior to the Empyrean. The latter he claimed was filled with what he termed an *aura Empyrea*, 'more rarefied than the upper region of the elementary air', a proof here of Kepler's influence through Lessius. To objections that the Blessed would have difficulty in breathing in such air, objections founded on mountain sickness experienced at high altitudes (St Augustine's reference to Mount Olympus and Fr José de Acosta's vividly recounted experience on the *Sierra de Pariacaca* in the Andes (1590)),[51] Henao responded, rather more hopefully than convincingly, that for the Blessed in the Empyrean, '... the heart, enjoying the very gentle atmosphere (*suavissima gaudens temperie*), would not require cooling by a thicker and damper air (*refrigeratione auræ crassioris & humidioris*)'.[52]

Citing Pliny, who had said that it was folly to try, as some had done, to calculate the size of the world, it was likewise, said Henao, folly to hope to set down the size of the Empyrean.[53] As a good follower of the Tridentine tradition, he excoriated Francesco Patrizi for having '... invented, at the cost of constant and jumbled repetitions, an infinite Empyrean penetrated by all the other parts of the universe. [...] These ideas are so monstrous and incoherent that I feel ashamed at having to marshall a [counter] argument.'[54] Although often called immense, the Empyrean's finite and limited size had, concluded Henao, been dealt with by certain Fathers of the Church in detail.

In the second volume of his work, Henao dealt with the place of God in relation to the Empyrean. Together with Christ, he located Him inside the Empyrean. Although God is present in the whole universe, He is, said Henao, especially present in the Empyrean. Should it be argued that if God is within the Empyrean, it must necessarily have existed from all eternity,

---

V, p.331. Cf. also the few remarks of Lynn Thorndike, *History of Magic and Experimental Science*, VII, pp.61–62.

[51] St Augustine, 'De Genesi ad Litteram Libri Duodecimi', lib. III, cap.III, in *Œuvres de Saint Augustin*, vol.48 (Paris, 1972), p.217 and José de Acosta, *Historia Natural y Moral de las Indias*, lib.III, cap.IX (Seville, 1590), edn Biblioteca de Autores Españoles (Madrid, 1954), p.65.

[52] Gabriel Henao, *Empyreologia seu Philosophia Christiana de Empyreo Cœlo*, lib.IV, ex.XIV, sect.I (Lyons, 1652), vol.I, pp. 307–312.

[53] *Ibid.* lib.IV, ex.XIII, sect.II, p.298.

[54] *Ibid. loc. cit.*

he replied that there is no reason to think that the Empyrean co-existed with God from eternity.[55] Although the Blessed can go outside above the convex surface of the Empyrean, that is not their usual place.[56] Henao agreed with Barradas that for clothes the Blessed will be dressed in light.[57] Henao then dealt with the functioning of the four remaining senses in the Empyrean, largely following Lessius.

For the transmission of sound, said Henao, '… the inside of the Empyrean, because of its fluidity, will be a convenient medium either for sound to be carried to the ears of the Blessed just as it is now carried to ours through air and water, or for sound to be produced from the striking of the other two hard and solid bodies of the Empyrean itself [i.e. its outer and inner surfaces]'.[58]

Odours in the Empyrean, said Henao, will not have to be purified. Since they lack a contrary, they will be perpetual and will be spread through the liquid interior of the Empyrean as easily as now in our air. But they will then be spread without the evaporation or exhalation of any body. The body itself of the Empyrean will not be odoriferous, but will only serve as a vehicle of odours.[59]

If in the Empyrean there will be no proper sense of taste from the external flavour of food and drink, theologians, said Henao, generally hold with Saint Thomas that the tongue and palate of the Blessed will be delighted by the addition of some flavoured liquid (*humore sapido*). The latter, he added, following the suggestion of John Major,[60] might be the manna of the Hebrews.[61]

On touch, Henao began by quoting Lessius' claim that the Blessed will feel a much greater pleasure from touching the *aura* of the Empyrean than is felt from the touch of a gentle breeze or from the contact of water. He then noted among the objections to this that the *aura* of the inside of the Empyrean would not be felt by touch (*non sentietur per tactum*) unless it were pushed and shaped to deliver an impact to the glorified body (*nisi fingatur imprimere impulsum corpori glorificato*), just as we do not feel air by the sense of touch as long as it not propelled by being for some reason deprived of heat or humidity. To this objection Henao responded that even if the *aura* of the inside of the Empyrean did not actually receive an impact, it would still be subtly sensed (*sentiendam*) by the touch (*per tactum*) of the glorified body,

---

[55] *Ibid.* lib.VI, ex.XVII, sectsI–III, vol.II, pp.25–27.
[56] *Ibid.* lib.VI, ex.XVIII, sect.II, pp.31–37.
[57] *Ibid.* lib.VII, ex.XXVII, sect.II, p.215.
[58] *Ibid.* lib.VIII, ex.XXIX, sect.I, p.271.
[59] *Ibid.* lib.VIII, ex.XXX, sect.V, p.282.
[60] John Major, *In Quartum Sententiarium quæstiones* …, dist.49, qu.14, conclus.5, ed. (Paris, 1521), f.cclxxxiii^v. Cf. Num. 11: 7; Deut. 8: 16.
[61] Gabriel Henao, *op. cit.* lib.VIII, ex.XXX, sect.V, vol.II, p.284.

though the latter would not palpate it (*licet non palpandam*). For any body to be palpated (*palpetur*), an impact is not enough; it requires solidity and consistency as well.[62]

Although Henao made an intense and careful effort to bring together evidence of every sort taken from early Christian and medieval and even classical authorities both in favour of and against his adopted conclusions, his laboriously compiled work, often supported by superfluous or redundant quotations, reveals a limited critical sense and has considerably less originality than that of his predecessors of nearly half a century before.

Discussion of the physical senses of the Blessed in the Empyrean has practically no place in Giovanni Battista Riccioli's *Almagestum Novum*, another vast labour of scholarship published at Bologna in 1651. Riccioli, a professor of astronomy at the Jesuit College at Bologna, shows, in his two volumes, a technical mastery of his subject as well as a thorough knowledge of both classical and medieval sources together with the new physics of the heavens expounded by Tycho, Rothmann, Kepler and Galileo. In his work we find the last serious attempt by a professional astronomer to maintain the integration of the story of the Creation in Genesis with an account of the astronomical structure of the cosmos.

By reintroducing the Empyrean in its medieval light-filled version in a quite original way, Riccioli's interpretation of the Creation stands in contrast to the Spanish Jesuits for whom Neoplatonism was anathema. In his conclusions there is little discernible reference to Aristotle. Rejecting Pereyra's interpretation of Genesis, he restored the Crystalline Heaven, a consolidated part of the Supercelestial Waters lying above it. 'It is indeed much more probable', wrote Riccioli, 'and an act more worthy of God the Creator to have created all the heavens and the elements the First Day and then the Second Day, out of condensed water, the Firmament or the heaven of the fixed stars, thus separating the Empyrean from the æther and the air by means of a firmly placed boundary and interval, the setting of which was the work of a whole day.'[63]

At the beginning of the Creation, continued Riccioli,

> ... God drew upwards [out of the abyss] a part of the waters, placing them immediately below the splendour of the Empyrean so that, from a mixing of its light with the opacity of the water, He formed a very beautiful and perpetual rainbow to delight the eyes of the Blessed with the incredible variety of its colours, far more pleasing than our own and which acts besides as a sort of mirror in which and out of which the bodies of the Blessed and their radiance can be reflected in a wonderful and variegated spectacle. It is thus

---

[62] *Ibid.* lib.VIII, ex.XXXII, sect.I, pp.287–288.
[63] Giovanni Battista Riccioli, *Almagestum Novum, Pars Posterior Tomi Primi*, lib.IX, sect.I, cap.II (Bologna, 1651), p.224.

possible to imagine this aqueous heaven below the Empyrean placed as a sort of vast rainbow all round the Firmament of which the blue and darker part below is turned downwards towards us, the red part lies in the middle and the yellow or golden part is at the top. God then consolidated the remaining part to become the Crystalline Heaven, the density and opacity of which He set as a limit between the invisible heavens, the Aqueous and the Empyrean which concern the after life, and the visible or perceptible heavens, the heaven of fire (*igneum*) and the heaven of air (*aëreum*).[64]

Riccioli's very poetic cosmos appears to have been unique and without successors. In saying that the heaven in which the planets 'move *per se*' was fluid, its matter 'probably igneous in nature' although 'called *æther*',[65] by some, he seems to have followed Tycho. In declaring that the Firmament of the fixed stars formed the '... outer walls of the world (*extrema mundi moenia*)', '... like the shell of an egg or a vault over the world (*sicut testa ovi aut fornix mundi*)', was Riccioli implying that the Empyrean lay outside the Creation?[66] Although he discussed at length the opinions of ancient and modern authors, quoting without hesitation Copernicus, Gilbert, Marsilio Ficino, Descartes, Kepler, Bruno and Galileo for their diverse views on the finiteness or infiniteness of the universe, he prudently (or pusillanimously) avoided any references to the theological problems involved in this issue. Saying that 'mathematical and metaphysical evidence should be kept separate',[67] Riccioli preferred to restrict himself to astronomical and physico-mathematical arguments relating to the outward extension of celestial bodies whose movements could be observed, rather than to engage in philosophical or theological speculations on the infinite spatial extension of the universe. 'What occurs in the part of the heaven above the fixed stars and whether it moves and is finite or is infinite and immobile does not concern this argument', he wrote.[68]

In conclusion, it may be said of the Empyrean that, aside from the Protestant astronomers of the late Renaissance who only referred to it in symbolic terms, the consistent attempts made by Catholic theologians to achieve a plausible coherence concerning the physical conditions inside the Empyrean give way, after the 1630s, to a certain hollowness, the result of the waning of Aristotelian scholasticism. Very soon the Empyrean is found to disappear completely in the wake of the Cartesian revolution.

---

[64] *Ibid.* cap.V, p.236.
[65] *Ibid. loc. cit.*
[66] *Ibid. loc. cit.*
[67] *Ibid.* lib.IX, sect.IV, cap.V, #VI, p.316.
[68] *Ibid. loc cit.*

7

The cosmos in university textbooks

This chapter will deal essentially with Latin Catholic Europe where the content of university textbooks of natural philosophy has been less studied than in the Protestant regions to the north, that is, in England, in the Low Countries and in Germany.[1]

The structure of the cosmos in the Baroque age as usually taught in the universities of Catholic Europe occupied a limited but important place in the manuals of traditional scholastic Aristotelian philosophy. As the seventeenth century advanced, selected parts of the new experimental evidence from astronomy brought forward by Tycho Brahe, Kepler and Galileo became slowly incorporated. The vehicle into which this material was integrated was the *Cursus Philosophicus*, though the actual title could often be different. Basically a commentary on the Aristotelian encyclopedia, it could also be preceded by a Hexaëmeron. University professors who taught it often published their individual courses, the content of which could vary quite considerably within a standard framework. Numerous examples can be found printed all over Europe from the 1630s until well into the eighteenth cen-

---

[1] In England, where the teaching of natural philosophy in the universities remained for most of the seventeenth century officially committed to Aristotelianism, editions of continental textbooks were often used. At Oxford the textbook of the German Protestant, Christoph Scheibler (1589–1653), *Philosophia Compendiosa* (Giessen, 1617), was reprinted six times between 1628 and 1685. See John L. Russell, 'The Copernican System in Great Britain', in *Studia Copernicana* V (1972), pp.217–220. At Cambridge the textbook of Aristotelian philosophy of the French Cistercian, Eustache de St Paul (1543–1640), *Summa Philosophiæ* (Paris, 1609), was reprinted twice in 1640 and 1648. Marc Friedrich Wendelin's *Contemplationum Physicarum Sectiones Tres* (Hannover, 1625–28) was also reprinted in 1648. After 1650 the situation changed rapidly. For the Low Countries, see Paul Dibon, *La philosophie néerlandaise au siècle d'or* (Paris, Amsterdam, London and New York, 1954), vol. I. For Germany, see Peter Petersen, *Geschichte der Aristotelischen Philosophie im Protestantischen Deutschland* (Leipzig, 1921), reprint (Stuttgart–Bad Cannstatt, 1964) (mainly on metaphysics and somewhat dated) and the few suggestive remarks in John Dillenberger, *Protestant Thought and Natural Science* (New York, 1960), reprint (Westport, Connecticut, 1977), pp.93–103.

tury.[2] It was through the model of the *Cursus Philosophicus* that the youth of Catholic Europe's elite acquired a vision of the cosmos in which they lived.[3]

A closer knowledge of what was actually taught to students can be achieved by analysing their class notebooks, when they can be recovered, but research in this direction is only just beginning.[4] For the present all that is aimed at is a rapid survey of published editions of the *Cursus Philosophicus* or works with a similar title, taking an average of three examples from successive periods in the seventeenth century.

An examination of the section on the heavens in the *Cursus Philosophicus* as it was taught in different countries of Catholic Europe reveals the widely varying degrees to which traditional medieval scholasticism was stubbornly perpetuated by some writers, and by others modified to accommodate the new ideas of the scientific revolution. In general a slow trend can be observed up until the last third of the seventeenth century during which the inevitability of accepting the new evidence was progressively recognized, though without as yet any full realization that the entire old Aristotelian framework had to go. While in no way aiming at exhaustivity, the following analysis seeks only to characterize each author sufficiently to identify his place in an evolving trend.

France (Paris)

For France, the works of three professors of philosophy at Paris will be considered: Charles d'Abra de Raconis, François Le Rees and Jean Du Hamel; later we look at one at Toulouse, Jean Vincent, and one at Bordeaux, Jean Bauduer.[5]

---

[2] A number of them are mentioned by B. Jansen, S.J., 'Die scholastische Philosophie des 17. Jahrhunderts', in *Philosoph. Jahrbuch der Görres-Gesellschaft*, 50. Bd 4. Heft. (1937), pp.401–444. Jansen, however, does not expressly address the physics or natural philosophy content of these works.

[3] See the pioneering study by Sister Patricia Reif, 'The Textbook Tradition in Natural Philosophy 1600–1650', *Journal of the History of Ideas* XXX (1969), pp.17–32.

[4] See Anthony Grafton, 'Teacher, Text and Pupil in the Renaissance Classroom: A Case Study from a Parisian College', *History of Universities* I (1981), pp.37–70; Ann Blair, 'The Teaching of Natural Philosophy in Early Seventeenth-Century Paris: The Case of Jean Cécile Frey', *History of Universities* XII (1993), pp.95–158.

[5] For Paris and the north of France the content of the *Cursus Philosophicus* has been studied by L.W.B. Brockliss, 'Aristotle, Descartes and the New Science: Natural Philosophy and the University of Paris, 1600–1740', *Annals of Science* XXXVIII (1981), pp.33–69; idem, *French Higher Education in the Seventeenth and Eighteenth Centuries* (Oxford, 1987), chap. 7, pp.337–390; idem, 'Copernicus in the university: the French experience', in John Henry and Sarah Hutton, eds, *Festschrift for Charles Schmitt* (London, 1990), pp.190–213 and idem, 'Pierre Gautruche et l'enseignement de la philosophie de la nature dans les collèges jésuites français vers 1650', in Luce Giard, ed., *Les jésuites à la Renaissance. Système éducatif et production du savoir* (Paris, 1995),

Charles d'Abra de Raconis (1580–1646) taught in Paris at the Collèges of Le Plessis and Les Grassins from c.1610 to c.1620. His *Totius Philosophiæ, hoc est logicæ, moralis, physicæ et metaphysicæ brevis, et accurate, facilisque et clara methodo disposita tractatio*, first published in 1617, went into seven editions by 1651.[6] In the section on the heavens Abra de Raconis noted that while it was adequately demonstrated that they were of '... a fifth substance distinct from the four elements', the main controversy was on the number of the heavens. Adopting the Isidorian model, he admitted that while some claimed that there were eleven mobile heavens and one immobile, '... the seat and home of the Blessed', 'the truest and most received opinion' postulates ten mobile heavens 'to which we add an eleventh, the Empyrean of the theologians, the outer surface of which', he declared, 'is square'.[7] Abra de Raconis added nothing about the functioning of the senses in the Empyrean. The heavens were 'hard' (*duros*), he asserted, quoting Job 31 [=37: 18].[8] The celestial orbs were not moved by angels but by 'their own form' (*a propria forma*).[9] For the movement of the planets in the fifth essence, Abra de Raconis followed the so-called '*Theorica* compromise' of the Middle Ages, made widely known at the end of the fifteenth century by George Peurbach.[10] The planets in 'partial orbs' (*partiales orbes*) were, he unhesitatingly claimed, moved by solid epicycles (*epicyclus est sphærula quædam solida*).[11]

Compared to similar manuals of the same or even earlier date, the degree of mediocrity of Abra de Raconis' superficial treatment of the physics of the heavens was only equalled by the scarcely justified number of the editions of his work. Not even in the last emended edition, published after the author's death, did there appear the slightest allusion to the new celestial phenomena revealed by Tycho or by Galileo.

Such was not the case with the *Cursus Philosophicus* of François Le Rees (?–c.1640) who taught in the 1630s at the Paris College of La Marche. This

---

pp.187–219. Brockliss refers to the first three authors, but not to the last two. No recent studies exist for the south west or south east of France.

[6] Of which six are in the Bibliothèque Nationale, Paris and one (1651) is in the Bibliothèque Municipale at Bordeaux. On Abra de Raconis, see the notice in Charles H. Lohr, *Latin Aristotle Commentaries – II Renaissance authors* (Florence, 1988), p.3.

[7] Charles d'Abra de Raconis, *Tertia Pars Philosophia seu Physica, editio ultima prioribus auctior & emendatior* (Lyons, 1651), *Disputatio Unica De Celo et Sphæra*, pp.303–305. His assertion that the outer surface of the Empyrean was square came from Rev. 21: 16.

[8] Charles d'Abra de Raconis, *op. cit.* p.328. On Job see above, Chapter 1, p.27.

[9] *Ibid.* pp.331–332.

[10] The '*Theorica* compromise' was an attempt to reconcile the eccentrics and epicycles of Ptolemaic astronomy with the Aristotelian doctrine of the fifth essence by making the planets move in cavities placed within the solid orbs. See Michel-Pierre Lerner, *Le monde des sphères*, vol.I, *Genèse et triomphe d'une représentation cosmique* (Paris, 1996), pp.74–81, pp. 115–130 and Edward Grant, *Planets, Stars and Orbs. The Medieval Cosmos 1200–1687*, chap. 13, pp.284–286.

[11] Charles d'Abra de Raconis, *op. cit.* pp.309–311.

work was published posthumously in 1642, went into four editions by 1660, and shows signs of a new attitude. After noting Aristotle's definition of the heavens that they were incorruptible and consisted of a fifth essence, Le Rees observed that this was incompatible with the description in Genesis of their watery nature. Taking refuge, like the Conimbricenses, in a proclaimed ambiguity,[12] he concluded that '... both opinions are probable, the first because of the authority of the Philosopher [Aristotle] the second because of the Fathers [of the Church], but neither opinion can be proved'.[13]

Le Rees first discussed arguments in favour of the solidity of the heavens, then those defending their liquid nature. The solidity of the heavens was assumed, he said, in the Copernican system and in the classic eleven-sphere system of 'Clavius and the ancients'. The Copernican system, although 'clever' (*ingeniosum*), he rejected for three reasons: the first because it clashed with Holy Scripture and for this he cited Josh. 10: 13 (*steteruntque sol et luna*); the second because the Copernican system made the sphere of the fixed stars so vast that the orbit of the earth in relation to it became insensibly small, which was 'absurd'; his third reason was that 'the heavy and sluggish earth was not suited to perpetual and very rapid movement'. He next described the classic system of eleven solid mobile heavens and one immobile one, the Empyrean. It was not, he said, worth wasting time in argument to disprove it. Working out how to explain the differences in the heavenly motions in this system was a fruitless business since they could be much more easily explained otherwise, that is in accordance with the Tychonic system, the one he preferred.

The fluidity of the planetary heavens in which the planets moved '... like fish in water or like birds in the air', was, declared Le Rees, a requirement of the Tychonic system. In defence of it he cited proofs given by 'outstanding astronomers' from the evidence of comets, Jupiter's satellites and Saturn's rings. It was more appropriate, he said, that the Firmament of the fixed stars be solid, as suggested by the constant order they maintained with regular distances between each other. A solid Firmament would save there having to be a great number of angels to move each star when one would be sufficient; its solidity also would serve like the roof of a vault to support the Supercelestial Waters. Le Rees adopted the tripartite division of the heavens: the Empyrean, the heaven of the fixed stars and the heaven of the planets. Each planet, he said, was moved by an angel. The Empyrean was usually held to be solid, '... but it would perhaps be better to make it fluid and permeable so that, without recourse to a miracle, the Blessed could move about in it and talk to each other'.[14]

---

[12] See above, Chapter 4, p.92.

[13] François Le Rees, *Quarta pars summæ philosophiæ quae est physica* [=fourth part of his *Cursus Philosophicus*] (Paris, 1642), vol.III, pp.433–439.

[14] *Ibid.* pp.441–451 and p.456.

In choosing against Aristotle to adopt Tycho's and Galileo's new evidence on the nature of the heavens, Le Rees was no doubt aware of expected professional loyalties as a teacher of Aristotelianism. He prudently sought to cover himself by stating that just as Aristotle '... had followed the common opinions of the mathematicians of his time, so we, following his example, follow the opinions of the mathematicans of our time'.[15] In spite of his scholastic style Le Rees did show that he had some superficial knowledge of the new astronomy. But the section on the heavens in his *Cursus*, like that of Abra de Raconis, is nevertheless below the intellectual level of similar works being published at similar dates elsewhere.

Jean Du Hamel (?–c.1734)[16] taught in Paris at the Collège de Le Plessis between c.1670 and c.1690. His five-volume *Cursus*, published in Paris in 1705, was set in the traditional Aristotelian mold and showed only a very reluctant acceptance of the new evidence on the nature of the heavens. He began by declaring that celestial matter was not the same as sublunary matter and that the heavens consisted of an incorruptible fifth essence.[17] Incorruptibility, however, was not for him an obstacle to fluidity and he readily admitted from the evidence of Jupiter's satellites, Saturn's rings and comets observed above the moon that the planetary heaven was fluid and not solid. If comets were observed to be 'generated and corrupted' in the region above the moon, this was only 'apparently so and for us' (*apparenter et quoad nos*), but not physically in so far as they themselves were concerned (*physicè & quoad se*). It was probable that both the Firmament of the fixed stars and the Empyrean were fluid, though nothing certain could be said about them. Those who held the Firmament to be solid so that the fixed stars could be set in it like nails in a wheel and the Empyrean to be solid for the whole universe to be enclosed and contained by a solid body could not be demonstrably refuted. If some said that the Empyrean was fluid so that the Blessed could move about and talk to each other after the Resurrection, this was of no moment since after the Resurrection, on account of the rarefied nature of their bodies, the Blessed will move around just as easily in a solid medium as in a fluid one and talk to each other without any sensible production of the voice, just by the 'directing of concepts', like the angels.[18]

In his section on mathematics, Du Hamel dealt succinctly in four pages with the Copernican, Tychonic and Ptolemaic systems, describing them in that order. The Copernican system, consisting of seven spheres counting the Firmament and six planets including the earth had, he noted, been

---

[15] *Ibid*. pp.452.
[16] He is not to be confused with the Oratorian Jean-Baptiste Du Hamel (1624–1706).
[17] Jean Du Hamel, *Philosophia universalis sive commentarius in universam Aristotelis philosophiam ad usum scholarum comparata* (Paris, 1705), vol.V, p.20.
[18] *Ibid*. pp.26–30.

readily embraced by Descartes. The only difference between the Copernican and Cartesian systems was that Copernicus put the fixed stars at varying distances from us and not in the same plane, whereas for Descartes each had its own vortex. Descartes, said Du Hamel, held that, though the visible world might have boundaries and limits, there were none for the universe as a whole. The Ptolemaic system, whose heavens were solid, had twelve heavens including the Empyrean, the *Primum Mobile* and the Crystalline Heaven. In his description of the other two systems, he dropped all reference to the Empyrean. His preference went to the Tychonic system, because it assured the immobility of the earth. He quoted Scripture in favour of a motionless earth, but he made no mention of the Church's condemnation of heliocentrism. 'If the earth revolved, mountains, woods and towns would revolve driven along by winds. But it is not true', he added, 'that the earth is moved by winds, even if the non-uniform and irregular movement of the earth is attributed to the winds not blowing regularly and uniformly.'[19] With this simplistic comment, Du Hamel concluded his rapid and superficial treatment of the heavens, showing the relative indifference, even in the latter part of the seventeenth century, of this Paris university professor to the crucial issues in the astronomical revolution under way around him.

Southern France (Toulouse and Bordeaux)

Jean Vincent (1606–after 1677), a member of the Congrégation des Doctrinaires, taught at the Collège de l'Esquille at Toulouse in the south of France where his *Cursus philosophicus*, published between 1658 and 1671, served the professors there for dictating their courses.[20] More vigorous in mind than the scholars just dealt with, in the third of his six volumes published in 1662 he nevertheless proceeded to justify with a systematic rigour the traditional Aristotelian doctrine of the heavens. Starting as a Hexaëmeron, his work continued as a commentary on the Aristotelian encyclopedia.

He began by defending the incorruptibility of the heavens with arguments against the evidence of comets and of the 1572 supernova. That they proved the fluidity of the heavens was an opinion that might be sustained, though it appeared to him difficult. Fluidity did not prove corruptibility: these phenomena could be the work of God's will by which parts of the fluid heaven had been condensed.[21]

---

[19] *Ibid.* vol.V, pp.16–19 (separate pagination from above).

[20] See R. Corrazé, 'L'Esquille, Collège des Capitouls (1550–1654)', in *Mémoires de l'Académie des Sciences, Inscriptions et Belles Lettres de Toulouse*, 12ᵉ série, vol.16 (1938), p.220. This is the author's only reference to Vincent.

[21] Jean Vincent, *Cursus philosophicus*, lib.II, quæstio. I, sect.VI (Toulouse, 1662), vol.III, pp.193–202.

Vincent then proceeded to refute the arguments for fluid heavens. He refused to accept the evidence of Tycho's observations of comets on the grounds that they differed widely from those of previous astronomers and there was no reason to prefer them to Ptolemy's or King Alphonso's or to those of many others who placed comets below the Moon. Astronomers in their use of instruments could err in giving the altitude of comets. Although it could be said in favour of Tycho that his expertise in such an important discipline deserved praise, the appearance of comets in the celestial region could be ascribed to divine intervention. Sunspots could likewise have the same origin. If Jupiter is alleged to have satellites, why, asked Vincent, are there none round the Moon, Venus and the other planets and even in other parts of the heavens? Apparent spots on the Moon are none other than rarer parts of it unable to return light to us, and allowing it to pass through.

In response to Pena's argument (his name is not mentioned) that Aristotelian physics cannot be reconciled with astronomy, Vincent first summarized it as follows.

> If the heavens were composed of solid and distinct orbs, then the sphere of the Moon would be more tenuous, rare and subtle than that of the sphere of the fire, the sphere of Mercury more subtle than that of the Moon and so on with the other planets. Thus rays of light, passing through so many media unequal in density and placed obliquely so that among these numerous orbs there would have to be what they call eccentric ones, would be repeatedly refracted and as a result stars would appear out of their true places. This is what the science of perspective [sic] tells us, but astronomers report that it is false, no refraction of the rays being observed [by them] till the surface of the air.

For his counter-argument expressed in somewhat muddled fashion, Vincent first granted that

> ... if the heavenly orbs have the same specific nature (*species*) they will have the same tenuity and subtlety [i.e. transparency] and clinging to one another with the greatest contiguity [so as to avoid a vacuum], they will cause no refraction of light. If however they differ specifically in nature nothing obliges us to accept that they differ in subtlety [transparency], since this difference is material and accidental. Hence, in accordance with the opinion of many, the stars and the other parts of the firmament can have the same specific nature (*species*), though be different in density [i.e. optical transparency]. In the same way the heavens may all have an identical tenuity [transparency] though their specific nature be different. It follows from this that it is difficult to claim that light is only first refracted in the air and not in the heavens themselves, given that there are so many and such varied opinions of astronomers on the subject.[22]

---

[22] *Ibid.* sect.VII, prima pars, pp.203–208.

Vincent was here only repeating the argument given by Tycho before him.

Turning to examine the arguments for solid heavens, the solution he favoured, Vincent naturally began by quoting Job 37: 18.[23] In the first place it could be taken that the Empyrean was solid. Secondly, said Vincent, trying no doubt to emphasize Thomist Aristotelianism as opposed to Genesis, '... the Firmament was not to be understood as a hard and solid body, but as a stable and firm one, that is incorruptible, maintaining its state without alteration and corruption'. The Firmament he identified with the eighth sphere which '... protects, consolidates and contains all the other heavens and everything else that exists in the world'. If the stars and planets were being carried through a fluid heaven at great speed, it was not to be denied that there would be collisions between them and parts of the heaven, and the friction would produce a terrific noise. This is contrary to experience and rejected by Aristotle.[24]

That there were three heavens, the Empyrean, the heaven of the air and the heaven of the fixed stars and the planets, was an opinion defended by the Fathers of the Church. If we set aside the air and the Empyrean and turn to the heaven as such, we will find, said Vincent, some astronomers postulating ten heavens, others eleven to take account of four different movements found in the Firmament of the fixed stars. All such opinions were very probable except for the one in which the planets moved in canals inside solid heavens. This theory should be refuted since a vacuum in the canals would imply the absence of a medium for the transmission of light and hence the stars would not be seen, which was contrary to experience. If it were argued that the canals were filled with some sort of fluid and subtle body, this should also be refuted since light rays from stars would be refracted by the two different media and the stars would not appear in their right places. All the above enabled Vincent to comfort his Aristotelian conviction regarding the seven planets, that each required its own orb to move it according to its own movement, since the planets could not be carried by themselves (*per se*) on account of the solidity of the heaven.[25]

To conclude, Vincent turned to the Empyrean. Its existence, he said, could not be physically demonstrated. It could only be perceived through the intellect. It was probable that it was globelike (*globosum*) on its underside in order to contain the other heavens. Its upper side was square as described in the Book of Revelation. From figures given in the latter, he calculated its surface to cover nine thousand square leagues (French leagues). In the Empyrean, where there was no air, how could the Blessed, asked

---

[23] See above, Chapter 1, p.27.
[24] *Ibid.* sect.VII, secunda pars, pp.209–214. Cf. Aristotle, *On the Heavens [De Cælo]*, II X 291a, ed. Guthrie, p.197.
[25] Jean Vincent, *op. cit.* quæstio II, sectio I, pp.215–222.

Vincent, give voiced praise to God? To this question, Vincent, following Saint Thomas to the letter, declared that they would praise God with the air already existing in their lungs, since Aristotle had said that vocalization does not require expulsion and intake of air. If that were not sufficent, one could add the 'fracturing and striking' (*confractio et percussio*) of the Empyrean itself, as Saint Thomas himself had suggested.[26]

The sustained deliberateness of Vincent's methodical attack on the new astronomy in order to preserve the old scholastic synthesis no doubt reveals a presentiment of the rising pressure to do away with Aristotelianism. But Vincent lacked the competence in astronomy capable of persuading his readers of the justness of his cause. Pierre Bayle, in a letter to the latter's brother dated 12 January 1678, was not far off the mark when he wrote of Vincent that he had seen his 'big course in four volumes in which there is a lot of hotch-potch (*son gros cours en quatre volumes où il y a bien de fatras*)'.[27] It was nevertheless from this work that Toulouse students at the Collège de l'Esquille were to derive their knowledge of the cosmos in the Baroque age.[28]

At the opposite extreme from Vincent stands Jean Bauduer (1630–1702), a native of Auch in south-western France.[29] Bauduer taught philosophy and mathematics in the second half of the seventeenth century at the Collège de Guyenne in Bordeaux. Little is known of his career apart from the fact that he stood out among his colleagues for his competence in teaching.[30] Bauduer's only known work, *Philosophiæ clavis, seu cursus philosophicus ad usum studiosæ juventutis* (1649?), the second edition of which appeared at Bordeaux in 1685, was conceived in the traditional framework of a commentary on the Aristotelian encyclopedia. In the section on the heavens there appeared an unusually acutely developed analysis of the Ptolemaic, Copernican and Tychonic astronomical systems, the competence and thoroughness of which sets the author apart from his contemporaries.[31]

---

[26] *Ibid.* section II, pp.222–228.

[27] Pierre Bayle, Lettre LVII, 21/1/1678, in *Nouvelles Lettres de Mr P. Bayle* (The Hague, 1739), vol.I, p.381.

[28] Vincent was succeeded at the Collège de l'Esquille by Joseph Rivalier whose four-volume *Propugnatio philosophiæ thomisticæ c2ontra Cartesium, Gassendum, Cabeum*, published at Toulouse in 1683, followed in the steps of Vincent's *Cursus*.

[29] The parish records of the parish of Saint Orens, Auch, conserved in the *Archives Départementales* at Auch, record the baptism of Jean Bauduer, son of Guillaume Bauduer and Jeanne de Tissier as of 14 April 1630. Assuming that it is the same person, the date of the death of the author Jean Bauduer (1702) is noted in the card index of the Bordeaux bookseller and bibliophile Ernest Labadie, conserved in the Bibliothèque Municipale, Bordeaux.

[30] Ernest Gaulhieur, *Histoire du Collège de Guyenne* (Paris, 1874), p.441.

[31] In his card index Ernest Labadie dates the first edition of his work, 4 vols in 4° (Bordeaux 1649), and the second edition, 4 vols in 8° (Bordeaux, 1685). There appears to be no extant copy of the first edition and its date remains problematical since the author would have

Bauduer began by giving an account of the Ptolemaic system to which he attributed eleven spheres, consisting of the spheres of the seven planets, the sphere of the fixed stars, the Second Crystalline Heaven, the First Crystalline Heaven and the *Primum Mobile*. 'Above these eleven mobile heavens is assigned', he said, 'a twelfth motionless heaven, the solid seat of the Blessed, or the Empyrean, round on the inside surrounding the *Primum Mobile* and on the outside limited by square surfaces as described in Revelations 21: 16: *Civitas in quadro posita [And the City is laid out as a square].*' 'Regarding the Empyrean', noted Bauduer, 'there are differences among the theologians; the philosophers and cosmographers just explain the phenomena of the mobile heavens.' This was his only reference to the Empyrean and when he came to analysing the Tychonic and Copernican systems he dropped all mention of it.

Marshalling arguments in favour of the latter system, Bauduer cited the corroboratory evidence of sunspots, Jupiter's satellites and Saturn's rings. Although he did not use the term, Bauduer seems to have been thinking of Kepler's magnetic *species* when he wrote that, 'If the solar rays have the power to change bodies near us and cause them to break up into component parts, how much more so can the planets, which are neither heavy nor light, nor by their nature destined to be either in motion or at rest but rather indifferent to both constraints, be moved by the vibration of solar rays and carried round, floating as it were in the most liquid æther.'[32]

Bauduer then proceeded to examine and refute one by one objections to the motion of the earth postulated in the Copernican system. To the objection that Holy Writ declared the earth to be at rest and the sun in motion, 'the Copernicans', said Bauduer, 'answer that what is read in the Bible is not always to be understood in a rigorous literal sense, but according to the opinion of the common herd and an outward meaning. Thus the Holy Spirit, which does not intend to teach men astronomy and physics but only to help them achieve salvation, adapted itself to be understood by the untutored populace.' Bauduer made no reference to the Church's condemnation of the Copernican system.

To objections that if the earth moved, heavy bodies thrown upwards would not fall back to the place from which they were thrown, that flying birds and clouds would be left to lag westwards by the earth moving east-

---

written it at the age of nineteen, if the Bauduer baptized in 1630 is the same. Ernest Gaulhieur had never seen a copy of the first edition. Cf. idem, *op. cit. loc.cit.* The Bibliothèque Nationale in Paris has no copy of his work, the copy used here being that of the second edition (1685) in the Bordeaux Municipal Library. Bauduer's commentary on Aristotle's encyclopedia is divided into vol.1 on the Logic, vol.2 on the Physics, vol.3 on Generation and Corruption, and vol.4 on the Heavens and the Meteorologica.

[32] Jean Bauduer, *Philosophiæ clavis seu cursus philosophicus ad usum studiosæ juventutis* (Bordeaux, 1685), vol.IV, p.69.

ward, and that cannon balls fired in opposite directions east and west would have different ranges, Bauduer cited the Copernicans' answer that the motion of the earth was common to all bodies originating from it and that they shared naturally in its motion. To the objection that, if parts of the earth thrown upwards fall back by their innate gravity towards the centre of the universe, the earth cannot be moving round the sun as the centre of the universe, Bauduer gave the Copernican answer that the whole earth was no less heavy nor light than the other planets and that therefore it did not have to be in the lowest place or at the centre of the universe. To the objection that if the earth moved we would, on horseback, feel a blast of air in our faces, something which we do not experience, the answer is that we move with the earth and the air moves with us.

Although very fluid, the air no doubt moves somewhat more slowly than the earth and this could be why, at the equator where the movement of the earth towards the west is most rapid, the air resists slightly and seems to flow westward. It is thus that ships there are carried westward by a perpetual and uniform wind and are able to sail from east to west much more easily and more rapidly than from west to east. The same cause could explain ocean currents. To the objection that if the earth moved, the speed attributed to it by the Copernicans would throw off earthly bodies, living beings and buildings into the Firmament, the latter, said Bauduer, answer that since the earth is like a very great magnet to all earthly bodies, it would in fact pull them and hold them in so that they could not be separated from it without force.

To the objection that it would be absurd to make the earth one of the planets because of the unevenness of its surface, its lack of light and the corruptibility of parts of it, it can be answered that the surfaces of the planets are no less uneven than the earth, as is revealed by the telescope in the case of the moon. The Copernicans, said Bauduer, deny that the planets are more luminous than the earth, for just as the planets receive their light from the sun, so likewise is the earth illuminated by solar rays. The planets are no less corruptible than the earth is, although we on earth do not see the corruptions in them on account of the great distance, just as the inhabitants of the moon and of Jupiter, if such exist, would not see the corruptions which occur on earth. To objections that the heliocentric hypothesis would raise difficulties in relation to observations of parallax, planetary oppositions and conjunctions, Bauduer responded with technical explanations citing the Copernican argument that, in the case of stellar parallax, the orbit of earth is as a point in comparison to the Firmament of the fixed stars.[33]

Bauduer's rebuttals of the natural philosophical objections to the Copernican system seem to have been drawn from a reading of Book I of Kepler's

---

[33] *Ibid.* pp.78–87.

Epitome Astronomiæ Copernicanæ.[34] On the other hand his discussion of criteria for choosing between alternative astronomical hypotheses which closes his discussion of the Ptolemaic, Tychonic and Copernican systems, and which is analysed below, may have been inspired by Kepler's introduction to his *Astronomia Nova* (1609).[35]

Of the three systems, only one, said Bauduer, can be true; the other two are false.

> Although by no natural [philosophical] reason can it be known with certainty which of them is true, for perhaps they are all false since all the phenomena can be understood and explained in other ways than by the Ptolemaic, Copernican and Tychonic systems, it can however be investigated and known by natural [philosophical] reason whether one of them is false. Those which should always be considered to be false are those which go against certain and evident experience. On the other hand those which agree with all the experimental evidence should not be considered false. It is for these reasons that today the Ptolemaic hypothesis is rejected as false by all astronomers. The Copernican and Tychonic hypotheses cannot be rejected because nothing has revealed them to be false, that is to say that there is nothing in them which is contrary to observations.
>
> And once the Ptolemaic system has been rejected, there remains the great problem of which hypothesis, the Copernican or the Tychonic appears truer, for each equally satisfies the celestial phenomena and neither goes against experience. There remains only one way to seek an answer to this question. Obviously, by examining these two hypotheses one can evaluate which fits better rationally or is more simple. For given that reason persuades that it is of no avail to argue with many points what can equally well be argued with fewer, reason also convinces that out of two hypotheses by which the same phenomena are explained, the one that appears truer is the one which is the simpler or the one which is based on fewer assumptions rather than the one based on a greater number. It is this which has influenced most modern writers and nearly all the careful learned authors who regard the Copernican hypothesis as simpler than the Tychonic one.

Bauduer ended with three conclusions: (1) that it is evident that the Ptolemaic system is false since it goes against experience; (2) that it is probable that the Tychonic one is false because, although it explains the motions of the heavens, it is in contradiction with physics in that it makes the whole vast mass of the heavens of the planets move round the sun while

---

[34] Johannes Kepler, *Epitome Astronomiæ Copernicanæ* (Linz, 1618), lib I, pp.103–140; *GW*, VII, pp.23–100.

[35] Johannes Kepler, *Astronomia Nova* ([Heidelberg], 1609), ff.2ʳ–6ᵛ (separate pagination); see Eng. trans. by William H. Donahue: Johannes Kepler, *New Astronomy* (Cambridge,1992), Author's Introduction, pp.45–69. There is a copy of the 1609 edition of Kepler's *Astronomia Nova* in the Bordeaux Municipal Library.

the minute earth remains motionless in the middle; (3) that there is no natural [philosophical] reason to believe the Copernican one to be false, as is shown by arguments taken from both astronomy and physics. 'All the celestial phenomena and motions are neatly explained and any natural [philosophical] reason that can be brought up against it is easily refuted.'[36]

Bauduer's account of criteria for choosing a hypothesis to approach scientific truth stands out in marked contrast to anything encountered among the teachers in universities in the period here studied. If it was to Kepler that Bauduer owed the unfettering of his mind from the hold of the Aristotelian doctrine of the heavens, his abandoning of all reference to the biblical foundations of the medieval cosmos and his silence regarding the Empyrean in his accounts of the Tychonic and Copernican systems were left without justification or explanation. It remains a pity that so little is known about Bauduer and his career.

Catholic Germany

Athanasius Kircher, S.J. (1602–80) was a celebrated figure of the Baroque age who wrote on a great number of diverse subjects. He taught for a time in the early seventeenth century at the Jesuit University at Würzburg and was later followed there by his student Melchior Cornäus, S.J. (1598–1665).[37] Although Kircher left Germany in 1633 to spend the rest of his life as a professor of mathematics at the Jesuit College of Rome where his work on the heavens, *Itinerarium Exstaticum*, was published in 1656, the two other editions of his work published in Würzburg in 1660 and 1671 suggest that it was used there for university teaching. It also became widely known throughout Europe.[38]

The *Itinerarium Exstaticum* is divided into two parts, in the first of which Kircher discusses whether the heavens are solid or fluid. In maintaining, in contrast to most of the Jesuits, that besides the heaven of the planets, the

---

[36] Jean Bauduer, *op. cit.* pp.91–94.
[37] See below, pp.165–166.
[38] On Kircher's life and work see Joscelyn Godwin, *Athanasius Kircher: A Renaissance Man and the Quest for Lost Knowledge* (London, 1979) and the article in the *Dictionary of Scientific Biography*, VII (1973) pp.374–378. The *Itinerarium Exstaticum* ran into problems with the internal Jesuit censorship both before and after publication. Kircher carried out the necessary corrections to the manuscript before publication and survived the criticisms after the work appeared. Neither the author nor the work was ever formally condemned. See Carlos Ziller Camenietski, 'L'extase interplanétaire d'Athanasius Kircher', *Nuncius* 10 (1995), pp.3–32. Cf. also John E. Fletcher, 'Astronomy in the life and correspondence of Athanasius Kircher', *Isis* 61 pt 1 no. 206 (1970), pp.52–67. Except to note (p.58) of the *Itinerarium Exstaticum* that its 'reception was strangely mixed' and (p.59) that Huygens called it 'nothing but a heap of idle unreasonable stuff', Fletcher has little to say of its content.

heaven of the fixed stars was fluid also, he cited the evidence of *Novae* being seen among the fixed stars. When '... some philosophers, unduly attached to the theories of Aristotle and his opinion concerning the solidity of the heavens, say that they were miraculously produced and destroyed by God, it smacks', declared Kircher, obviously thinking of Clavius,[39] 'more of stubbornness than sound philosophy'.[40] As further proof of fluid heavens, Kircher cited, together with other observed astronomical phenomena, the behaviour of comets, the phases of Venus, Jupiter's satellites, Saturn's rings and the argument that if the heavens were solid, the refraction of light from stars would produce 'wonderful colours and continuous rainbows'.[41] There was only one heaven containing the planets and the fixed stars; the latter were not all on the same surface, but some were higher than others and 'more distantly immersed (*profundius immersae*)'.

On the material nature of the heaven, Kircher said that he 'believed the whole of the heaven of the planets and the fixed stars as far as the Supercelestial Waters to be nothing other than the most pure and liquid æther which is essentially and in fact the purest and most refined air and which accordingly you will rightly call fire, as many rightly call fire the pure air which is situated between the lower surface of the sphere of the moon and our impure air. Calling the heaven either fire or air comes to the same thing. Yet in fact it is air', he declared. 'The heaven of the fixed stars and the planets (*cælum sidereum*) is the same as the Spirit of God which lay upon the waters and this Spirit of God was indeed air and æther', he concluded, claiming he would provide proof in a later work, *Mundo Mirabili*. Kircher's words here appear to recall something of Steuco's exegesis of Genesis.

Declaring that '... the corruptibility of the heaven of the planets and the stars was today a very common opinion contrary to Aristotle and his followers', Kircher added that the planets had their own atmospheres (*atmosphæras*) and the sun its spots, all of which argued for the corruptibility of celestial bodies. The celestial bodies (*stellæ*), he declared, with an eclectic generosity, were moved either according to God's laws, or by their own forms, or by intelligences, or immediately by God Himself.[42] Whether because of his residence in Rome, or in spite of it, Kircher shows himself much freer of Aristotelian prejudices for a Jesuit than his contemporaries in most European universities.

---

[39] Cf. above, Chapter 4, pp.92–93.
[40] Athanasius Kircher, S.J., *Itinerarium Exstaticum* (Rome, 1656), 2nd edn (Herbipoli [=Würzburg], 1660) (with title *Iter Exstaticum*), p.30.
[41] Although he did not mention rainbows, Ismael Boulliau had claimed that light refracted through solid orbs would colour them. Cf. Ismael Bouillau, *Astronomia Philolaica* (Paris, 1645), lib.I, p.9.
[42] Athanasius Kircher, *op. cit.* pp.30–34.

The second part of Kircher's *Iter Exstaticum* consists of a voyage by two angels through the cosmos, in which the master Cosmiel explains its secrets to the disciple Theodidactus. To Theodidactus' surprise that he cannot feel the Supercelestial Waters, neither their flow nor their waves, Cosmiel replies explaining this 'arcane mystery' according to the Basilian model. These waters are 'extremely rarefied, transparent and thoroughly purged of all mixing through contact with the earth'. They are 'true waters' and of an elementary nature.[43]

Kircher insisted, through his character Cosmiel, that the Empyrean is '... part of the universe and not outside it, but is like a boundary set for the whole'. Declaring that it was a corporeal place, he added that it was '... nothing other than the surface of a lodged body (*superficies corporis locati*)'. 'It could in no way be called a place, if, as some incorrectly believe, it consisted of a spiritual substance.' Here Kircher may have been thinking of Steuco's Basilian Empyrean. But he then continued, stating that, 'it is indeed called *Empyrean* which is the same as fire, which is the highest form of light and it shines brightly above all the bodies of the universe. It does not blind nor cause any discomfort, but rather, on account of its inestimable beauty, delights the eyes of the Blessed with an inconceivable joy and a charm that defies description.'[44]

Given that the Empyrean was part of the universe, it would, said Kircher, '... be absurd and contrary to the design of the Creator for there to be no physical functioning of the senses, no seeing of colours, no hearing of sounds, no hardness, softness, condensation, rarefaction, and no feeling for quantity; but that all would then be invisible, spiritual and reachable only through the intellect'.[45] Kircher saw the Empyrean as enabling all the material senses to function and the Blessed in it as conserving their physical faculties as on earth.

Melchior Cornäus, S.J. was a student of Kircher who taught at the University of Würzburg and published there in 1657 his *Curriculum Philosophiæ Peripateticæ*, offering a much more succinct treament of the heavens than his master's. Taking issue with Clavius for his eleven solid astronomical heavens, Cornäus divided the heavens into three, the *Aëreum*, the *Sidereum* and the *Empyreum*. In the *Sidereum* heaven, which was 'fluid and liquid', both the fixed stars and the planets were moved by angels, '... like birds in the air or like fish in water'. Angels maintained the constant distances of the fixed stars between one another. Following Kircher, Cornäus described the upper part of the Firmament as consisting of fire and its lower part of air. The Empyrean, not made the Second Day out of water, but right at the begin-

---

[43] *Ibid.* pp.426–427.
[44] *Ibid.* p.429.
[45] *Ibid.* p.430.

ning of the Creation, consisted of matter of a different kind, though this was not 'a pressing subject'. The Empyrean, according to Cornäus, was '... the roof and top of the universe'. Following Lessius he described its lower part as a pavement and floor for the Blessed to walk on. The middle part was liquid and breathable (*liquida & spirabilis*) enabling breathing and speech. The upper part held in the *auram spirabilem* like the roof of a church.[46] If Cornäus appears more aware of the new views of the heavens than some of his other European contemporaries, it was rather more because of his following closely in the steps of his master, than through any gift of individual originality.

Italy

In Italy there were wide differences of approach depending on the regions or the universities concerned. We shall consider as examples two teachers of philosophy who published in the early and later parts of the seventeenth century, Raffaello Aversa and Sigismondo Serbelloni.

Raffaello Aversa (c.1589–1649), a professor of theology at Rome and a member of the Order of Regular Minor Clergy (*Caracciolini*), remained very much a conservative in his analysis of the nature of the heavens in his *Philosophia metaphysicam physicamque complectens quæstionibus contexta*, published at Rome in 1625–27.[47] None the less he did eliminate all the mobile heavens above the sphere of the fixed stars, both the *Primum Mobile* and the Crystalline Heaven. Adopting a tripartite division of the heavens into the *Empyreum*, the *Sidereum* and the *Aereum*, he placed the Empyrean directly above the fixed stars, from which he declared it was separated by an 'opaque curtain' (*opaca cortina*) to prevent us from seeing its vast splendour. The sphere of the fixed stars was moved by an 'assisting intelligence' (*intelligentia assistente*), which he also termed the *primum mobile*. The planets were impelled by two opposite motions, one in an east/west direction by the motion of the sphere of the fixed stars and the other in the opposite direction by each planet's own motion (*motu proprio ... per se*). He accepted Lessius' Empyrean with solid outer surfaces and a fluid interior to enable the Blessed to move and to breathe. Its fluidity, he said, would not prevent it being incorruptible.[48]

---

[46] Melchior Cornäus, S.J., *Curriculum philosophiæ peripateticæ* (Herbipoli [=Würzburg], 1657), disput.II, quaest.I & II, pp.488–500.

[47] The influence on Aversa of Francisco Suarez is noted by B. Jansen, *art. cit.* pp.419–422. See also on Aversa: Lynn Thorndike, *History of Magic and Experimental Science*, VII, pp.393–396 and the article in *Dizionario Biografico degli Italiani*, IV (1962), pp.668–669.

[48] Raffaello Aversa, *Philosophia metaphysicam physicamque complectens quæstionibus contexta* (Rome, 1625–27), vol.II, quæst.XXXII, sect.IV, pp.52–57.

Aversa reveals a certain knowledge of astronomy and was fully conversant with the new evidence brought forward by Tycho and Galileo regarding the heavens, as well as with Tycho's work on refractions. He conceded the justness of Tycho's argument against Rothmann that an identity in the transparency of two media is no guarantee that their material nature is the same,[49] yet he nevertheless rejected Tycho's claims for fluid heavens, opposing to them both Aristotelian doctrine and quotations from Scripture, in particular Job 37: 18.[50] It would be much better, he concluded, to think of the whole heaven as *firmum & solidum*,[51] extending according to the pseudo-Clementine model from the earth to the Empyrean,[52] and consisting of Aristotle's fifth essence.[53] Aware of the controversy over the nature of comets, he asserted that they were not born in the heavens, nor did they move in them. Sunspots were moved round the sun and Jupiter's satellites were moved round the planet on 'firm and solid epicycles'.[54] Aversa's stubborn perpetuation of traditional orthodoxy reappeared in a second edition of his work published at Bologna in 1650.

Sigismondo Serbelloni (c.1619–62), a member of the Order of the Regular Barnabite Clerics, taught both philosophy and theology in a college of the order at Monza.[55] He dealt with the heavens in the second volume of his *Philosophia Ticinensis* published posthumously in 1663.[56] Besides being thoroughly conversant with scholastic method, he shows a certain competence in technical astronomy, for which he relied on the work of Argoli, whom he quotes.[57]

Serbelloni discussed whether the heavens were solid or liquid. The Empyrean, a matter for the theologians, was evidently solid for it to serve as the eternal home of the Blessed. The Firmament was likewise solid, for Scriptural reasons,[58] and because the fixed stars maintained a constant distance between each other. It would require too many intelligences to guide each star, one being sufficient to guide them all. The planetary heaven was fluid, as evidenced by the behaviour of comets, for if the heavens were solid, comets would not be seen in them as the common experience of astrono-

---

[49] *Ibid.* quæst.XXXIII, sect.I, p.80.
[50] *Ibid.* quæst.XXXII, sect.VI, pp.66–67. On Job cf. above, Chapter 1, p.27.
[51] *Ibid.* p.66.
[52] *Ibid.* p.67 and quaest.XXXIII, sect.I, p.79.
[53] *Ibid.* quæst.XXXIII, p.77.
[54] *Ibid.* quæst.XXXII, sect.VI, p.69.
[55] On Serbelloni, see G. Boffito, *Biblioteca Barnabitica. Scrittori Barnabiti* (Florence, 1933–37), vol.III, pp.515–517.
[56] Sigismondo Serbelloni, *Philosophia Ticinensis*, 2 vols (Milan, 1657–63). According to Boffito, a second edition appeared in Vienna, but he gives no date for it.
[57] On Argoli see above, Chapter 4, p.102.
[58] Serbelloni here quoted Job 37: 18. See above, Chapter 1, p.27.

mers had proved. If the heavens were solid, Jupiter's satellites, as revealed by Galileo, could not revolve above and below the planet without breaking through the solidity.[59] In view of the evidence of the new phenomena, the use of epicycles and eccentrics could no longer be defended. The planets moved easily in fluid heavens, each with its own movement.[60]

Serbelloni next discussed the number of the heavens. Having reviewed the system of twelve heavens followed by Clavius, he rejected it in favour of a single planetary heaven, æthereal in nature, each planet being moved by its own intelligence. The heavens as a whole he divided into three, the *Æthereum*, the *Sidereum* and the *Empyreum*. The æthereal region he then divided into four sections, the first and lowest for the Moon, the second for the Sun, Mars, Mercury and Venus, the third for Jupiter and its satellites and the fourth for Saturn and its rings. Above the æthereal region of these 'imaginary heavens' lay the Sydereal heaven of the fixed stars, solid in nature. The *Primum Mobile* he eliminated. Taking issue with Argoli's view that the æthereal region was not the same as the air, being a lighter and more subtle body, Serbelloni, possibly following Rothmann, declared that it was of the same 'entity' as the air, not only because they were of the same matter but also because they had the same form. Since air and æther were both fluid and transparent, they were therefore of the same entity.[61] Serbelloni said nothing about the activities of the Blessed in the Empyrean, nor did he discuss the finiteness or infinity of the universe. In spite of his full awareness of the astronomical developments of the period in which he wrote, Serbelloni was still unable to shake himself free of the framework of analysis imposed by the conventional Aristotelian method. His *Cursus Philosophicus*, although it did not carry this title, was not untypical of its kind.

Spain

In the Iberian peninsula the reticence of Spanish scholars to accept the new vision of the heavens appears in marked contrast to the greater readiness of their Portuguese counterparts. For Spain we shall examine the works of the Jesuits Pedro Hurtado de Mendoza, Rodrigo de Arriaga and Francisco de Oviedo. The works of these three Jesuits, unlike those of their Portuguese contemporaries, became widely known north of the Pyrenees mainly through editions printed at Lyons.

---

[59] There was no general consensus on the evidence of comets until the later part of the seventeenth century. Cf. above, Chapter 4, p.81. From his observations of Jupiter's satellites, Galileo never himself drew this conclusion attributed to him.
[60] Sigismondo Serbelloni, *op. cit.*, vol.II, *De Coelo*, disput. unica, quæst.II, art.IV, pp.25–26.
[61] *Ibid.* quæst.II, art.V, pp.28–32.

Pedro Hurtado de Mendoza, S.J. (1578–1651), who taught theology at Valladolid and then for thirty years at Salamanca, had his *Disputationes a Summulis ad Metaphysicam* sumptuously printed at Valladolid in 1615. It was followed by five other editions with the title of *Disputationes de Universa Philosophia* at Lyons, 1617 and 1624; Toulouse, 1617; Mainz, 1619 and Salamanca, 1621. He wrote with a noticeably literary style which contrasts with that of the majority of the scholastics of his time.[62]

A disciple of Suarez, Hurtado de Mendoza sought like his master to achieve a re-Aristotelianization of the heavens. He began by taking issue with Benito Pereyra, elaborately refuting his interpretation of Steuco's Basilian model. He then refuted the Isidorian one, which he called the 'Commentary of certain Catholics'. His preference was for the pseudo-Clementine interpretation which he expounded as follows: out of the abyss of the waters extending from the earth up to the Empyrean created the First Day of the Creation, God created on the Second day the *Cœlum Stellatum* below the Empyrean. Between these two heavens, He left a good part of the waters (to become the Supercelestial Waters). God then created the fire and the air, and below them the sublunary waters covering the earth. The waters occupying the space of the Firmament (i.e. between the earth and the Empyrean) '... were not eliminated (*non fuere annihilatæ*)', but '... converted into the Firmament which was made from the waters (*conversæ fuerunt in firmamentum quod factæ fuit ex aquis*)'. The *cœlum stellatum* was '... produced from its privation (*cœlum stellatum fuit productum ex privatione sui*)'.[63] It was generated (*generatum*) but '... not indeed by a generation carrying with it a tendency to corruption (*non quidem generatione requirente dispositiones corruptivas*)', '... for the heaven is ungenerable just as it is incorruptible (*sic enim cœlum est ingenerabile, sicut & incorruptibile*)'.[64] Though hastily argued and with little subtlety, such a forthright Aristotelianization transforming part of the waters of the Creation into the incorruptible fifth essence of the astronomical heavens left no ambiguities.

Hurtado divided the heavens into the *aëreum*, the *stellatum* and the *empyreum*. He rejected the *Primum Mobile* and the ninth sphere. The planets he said were moved by intelligences. How did the planets move through the solid and impenetrable scholastic heaven? To explain this he had recourse to the medieval '*Theorica* compromise' theory referred to above. The planets, said Hurtado, moved in 'canals' (*canales*) or 'cavities' (*cavitates*) which were, he

---

[62] On Hurtado de Mendoza see the few remarks of B. Jansen, S.J., *art. cit.* pp.424–426; mainly on his Logic and Metaphysics.
[63] On Aristotle's concept of privation or 'shortage' see Aristotle, *Physics*, I vii and viii, ed. Wicksteed and Cornford, pp.66–89.
[64] Pedro Hurtado de Mendoza, S.J., *Disputationes de Universa Philosophia*, edn (Lyons, 1617), disput.III, 'De Opere sex dierum', sectsII–III, pp. 550–556.

said, like '... vaults or triumphal arcs through which the planets moved triumphantly and show their beauty'.[65] Hurtado was the only Jesuit of his generation to defend this solution. His Aristotelianism led him to be suspicious of astronomers' methods and their instruments. He imprudently mocked Jerónimo Muñoz, when he came to teach at Salamanca, for claiming to measure astronomical distances.[66] It should be noted that Hurtado published his work too early to take account of the evidence of Tycho's and Galileo's astronomical observations as many of the Jesuits were led to do later.

Rodrigo de Arriaga, S.J. (1592–1667), who had studied philosophy and theology under Hurtado de Mendoza, taught in Spain for only two years. The rest of his life, from 1626 to his death in 1667, he spent at Prague where he became Professor and Chancellor of the University, and where his reputation was so great that there ran a saying: *Pragam videre, Arriagam audire*, 'See Prague and hear Arriaga'.[67] Arriaga's *Cursus Philosophicus*, first published in 1632, went into five editions and eight printings by 1669, published in Antwerp, Paris and Lyons. It was widely used throughout Europe. The last edition, 'corrected and augmented', contains however only very slight changes.[68]

Whereas the corruptibility or fluidity of the heavens '... had been an opinion, completely banished from the Schools', wrote Arriaga, '... now only a few years ago, through the careful observations of mathematicians and astronomers with the aid of the highly accurate instruments which they have constructed and particularly with the help of the telescope, the structure of the heavens has begun to be radically changed. Some have held that the heavens are fluid, others that they are corruptible and they have been compelled to explain the phenomena observed in these years in no other way. And in order not to have to bring in a completely new opinion, they have been led to go back and claim that this was the view of the ancient Fathers of the Church. Others, enthusiastically championing the opinion of the ancients, have not hesitated to stigmatize these novelties as rash and wrong. It is not', said Arriaga, whose prime interest was elsewhere, 'my

---

[65] *Ibid.* disput.II, sect.I, pp.532–536.

[66] *Ibid.* disput.II, sect.II, p.537. On Muñoz see above, Chapter 4, p.99–100.

[67] B. Jansen, S.J., *art. cit.* p.426.

[68] On Arriaga, see Pierre Bayle, *Dictionnaire historique et critique*, 5th edn (Amsterdam, 1734), vol.I, pp.513–514; (On his theology: 'On trouve qu'il réussissait beaucoup mieux à ruiner ce qu'il niait, qu'à bien établir ce qu'il affirmait.' On his physics: 'Ses efforts, ses instances, ses souplesses [...] font regretter qu'il ait couru avec tant de force hors du bon chemin.') See the wide-ranging study on Arriaga and the milieu he worked in by Karl Eschweiler, 'Roderigo de Arriaga, S.J., Ein Beitrag zur Geschichte der Barockscholastik', in *Spanische Forschungen der Görresgesellschaft*, Bd I. Reihe III (1931), pp.253–285; also Lynn Thorndike, *History of Magic and Experimental Science*, VII, pp.399–402 and Charles Schmitt, 'Galileo and the 17th century textbook tradition', in P. Galluzzi, ed., *Novità Celesti e Crisi di Sapere* (Florence, 1984), pp.223–224.

intention to deal here with the whole of this question *ex professo* and to review and weigh up the arguments on both sides.'[69]

His words sum up succinctly how the crisis undergone in the previous decades had been experienced. Against the varieties of evidence put forward by Tycho and Galileo in favour of fluid heavens (the behaviour of comets, the unevenness of the moon's surface, Jupiter's satellites and sunspots), Arriaga, influenced by Tanner, marshalled lengthy counter-arguments. Although finally forced, despite himself, to admit the fluidity of the planetary heavens, he still either prudently or obstinately maintained that '... even if there is some probability of the planetary heavens being liquid, it would not however thus appear obviously proven from this evidence, as some recent scholars believe, who consider that without fluid heavens the [phenomena described] above can be explained in no other way'.[70]

The only argument retained by Arriaga, which for him rendered unlikely the existence of solid planetary spheres, was the disproportion between the 'almost infinite size' of the sphere of Saturn and the minuteness of the planet itself into which it '... was fixed like a point or a drop of water in comparison with the sea'. 'There was no point and no use', he said, 'in making Saturn move the whole vast system of the seven heavens. Making a drop of water move the Ocean did not seem a thing wisely conceived. And this same argument would be true for all the other planets as well.'[71] Rejecting the *Primum Mobile* and the Crystalline Heaven, Arriaga adopted Pereyra's pseudo-Clementine model and a tripartite division of the heavens into the Empyrean, the planetary heaven and the heaven of the air. The solidity of the Empyrean was, he declared, beyond controversy. If the planetary heaven seemed to him '... more probably liquid', the heaven of the fixed stars he apparently considered solid, though he did not make himself very clear about this. And if the planetary heavens were fluid, they could be at once fluid and incorruptible since the two things were not the same. Arriaga rejected Hurtado de Mendoza's theory of 'canals' in solid heavens since the vacuum in them would render impossible the transmission of the light by which we observe the heavenly bodies. The planets, said Arriaga, were moved by angels who would hold them up in fluid heavens to prevent them from falling. On the nature of the matter of the heavens, he avoided having to make a clear choice between Genesis and Aristotle by declaring that it was neither aqueous nor a *materia prima*, but rather '... a different substantial form (*formam substantialem diversam*)'.[72]

---

[69] Rodrigo de Arriaga, S.J., *Cursus Philosophicus* (Antwerp, 1632), *Disputatio unica cælestis, De Cælorum natura, numero & motu*, sectio III, p.499.

[70] *Ibid.* subsectio tertia, p. 502.

[71] *Ibid.* sectio IV, subsectio prima and subsectio secunda, p.504.

[72] *Ibid.* pp.504–505.

On the whole, Arriaga does not give the impression of having very thoroughly thought out what he was prepared to defend as true, or condemn as false in astronomy. His whole style reveals a mind still steeped in the involved methods of Aristotelian scholasticism, a mind wholly unprepared to handle the consequences of the astronomical evidence with which he was presented. His embarrassedly ambiguous handling of the evidence for the fluidity of the heavens was treated with little indulgence by the Toulouse Professor Jean Vincent, whose mind, as we have seen, had remained more Aristotelian than Arriaga's. In his *Cursus philosophicus* Vincent remarked how '... surprised' he was, that 'on this subject the imagination of this author lay so far from the truth and by his illusory and false answers he went to the point of throwing into confusion a widely recognized doctrine [i.e. Aristotle's]'.[73]

Unlike Arriaga, Francisco de Oviedo, S.J. (1602–51) spent all his life in Spain teaching the humanities, philosophy and theology in various institutions all over the country. His *Integer Cursus Philosophicus*, published at Lyons in 1640, went into two other editions in 1651 and 1663, also published at Lyons.[74] Still typical of the scholastic tradition, his style is no clearer nor less involved than that of Arriaga's. His method of analysis was closely copied from the latter, but some of his conclusions were different.

Discussing the nature of heavenly matter, Oviedo, in contrast to the Conimbricenses and Arriaga, came down on the side of Genesis and the Church Fathers, declaring that, with the exception of the Empyrean, it was the same as sublunary matter. On this point Aristotle's opinion, he said, was not of the slightest importance (*Aristotelis sententia flocci habenda est*). He had shamefully erred (*erravit enim turpiter*) on the matter of the heavens, imagining a fifth substance different from the rest. Examining the claim of mathematicians (Oviedo had Galileo in mind though he never mentions his name) that, from the evidence of the 'new phenomena' and of sunspots, the heavens were fluid and that they were as a result corruptible, Oviedo argued, like Arriaga, that they could be both fluid and incorruptible. Although he did not think the incorruptibility of the heavens was '... a matter of great moment', he deferred to the authority of those who asserted their incorruptibility, as being for him of greater weight.[75]

Oviedo then proceeded, following Arriaga, to analyse three hypotheses on the physical nature of the heavens, presenting simultaneously counter-arguments to them. The first was that they were all solid, the second that they were all fluid and the third that the heaven of the planets was fluid, but that of the fixed stars solid.

---

[73] Jean Vincent, *Cursus philosophicus*, lib.II, qu.I, no.195 (Toulouse, 1662), vol. III, p.207.

[74] On Oviedo see the few remarks of B. Jansen, *art. cit.* pp.429–431.

[75] Francisco de Oviedo, S.J., *Integer Cursus Philosophicus* (Lyons, 1640), vol.I, *De Cælo Controversia Unica, punctum II*, pp.463–464.

Regarding the first hypothesis, if there was no doubt about the solidity of the Empyrean whose upper surface, he said, was square, the alleged solidity of the other heavens could be questioned. Attacking Tanner for his defence of their solidity, he quoted Pereyra's evocation of the Basilian model and his use of the term *rakiah* to prove that the Firmament was an expansion and a fluid body. Tanner's theory of an Empyrean filled with the Supercelestial Waters was, he said, 'useless and insufficient' (*inefficax & insufficiens*); no such waters existed above the Firmament of the fixed stars or '... if they did, they would have no weight, being beyond the sphere of the Moon and outside the world'.

For the second hypothesis Oviedo enumerated at length the evidence from the newly observed celestial phenomena: mountains observed on the Moon's surface, comets seen in the sphere of the fixed stars (sic), sunspots, Jupiter's satellites and Saturn's rings. He then discussed the counter-arguments, mostly taken from Tanner, against the fluidity of the heavens that these phenomena were held to prove.

For the third hypothesis that the heavens of the planets was fluid and that of the fixed stars solid, Oviedo marshalled support not only from Scripture and from the Church Fathers but also from the observed phenomena and the reasonings of astronomers. Inclined to adopt it, he yet admitted that the sphere of the fixed stars might indeed also be fluid on the grounds that 'strange new stars' (*stellæ alienæ novæ*) were claimed by some to appear in it.[76] For Oviedo comets and *novæ* were the same.

In subsequent paragraphs Oviedo did not hesitate to grant a fluid nature to the sphere of the fixed stars. Following the tripartite division of the heavens into the *Cælo Aëreo, Stellato & Empyreo*, the planets and the fixed stars, he said, together occupied only one heaven, in the upper part of which the fixed stars '... always kept their position', while in the remaining part the planets moved '... like fish in water or like birds in the air'. He refuted Hurtado de Mendoza's theory of 'canals' for the same reasons as those given by Arriaga. Since the planets were moved by intelligences, the *Primum Mobile*, said Oviedo, served no purpose.[77] Concerning the Empyrean, he said nothing about the physical conditions of the Blessed in it or the functioning of the senses, except to affirm that the interior was filled with light, a light which was prevented by the opaque lower surface of the Empyrean from reaching us.

Although Oviedo's conclusions about the nature of the heavens correspond by and large with those adopted by other authors of the *Cursus Philosophicus* at the date at which he wrote, his whole approach leaves an impression of the cautious hesitation and extreme prudence of one unfamil-

---

[76] *Ibid. punctum III*, pp.466–469.
[77] *Ibid. punctum IV*, pp.469–472.

iar with astronomy and, like Arriaga, unprepared to handle the consequences of the new evidence seen in the heavens.

Portugal

In Portugal the new vision of the heavens was received much more readily than in Spain, a fact explained by the stay in Portugal of a singular personality, Cristoforo Borri (1583–1632), an Italian Jesuit of Milanese origin.[78] Borri's influence appears markedly in the works of two other Portuguese Jesuits whom we shall examine: Balthasar Tellez (1596–1675) and Francisco Soares Lusitano (1605–59) and for this reason we shall place Borri within the context of university teaching in Portugal.

The ultimately tragic career of Cristoforo Borri, S.J. began when, after entering the Jesuit order in 1601 and becoming a teacher at the Jesuit Colleges of Mondovi and of Brera in Milan, he was discovered by his superiors to be expounding the 'novel doctrine' of fluid and corruptible heavens. For this he was removed from his chair (probably in 1612) and sent as a missionary to the Orient in 1615.[79] On arrival in China he found his fellow members of the Society being persecuted by the Chinese authorities, one of the reasons being the printing by a Jesuit missionary of a book of astronomy describing the Ptolemaic doctrine of the heavens, whereas, '… centuries before the Arabs [sic] introduced into Europe the doctrine of hard multiple spheres', the Chinese had been teaching that there was '… only one heaven, rarefied and liquid (*tenue e liquido*)'.[80] Borri was at once ordered by his superior to write a treatise persuading his fellow missionaries to abandon the Ptolemaic doctrine and follow that of the Chinese. When Borri showed surprise that what he had been censured for teaching in Europe now became his duty to expound in China, he was told that the reason was the same. Just as for teaching a new doctrine he had had to leave Europe, so for teaching novel opinions to the Jesuits he risked being expelled from China.

---

[78] In Portugal Cristoforo Borri adopted the name of Cristovão Bruno on account of the unfortunate similarity of his name in Italian to 'ass' in Portuguese.

[79] On Borri see Domingos Maurício Gomes dos Santos, S.J., 'Vicissitudes da Obra do Pe Cristovão Borri' in *Anais da Academia Portuguesa da História*, II série, vol.II (Lisbon, 1951), pp.118–150.

[80] Borri refers to this fact in his work *Collecta astronomica* (Lisbon, 1631), p.232. In a letter of 28 October 1595 the Jesuit Missionary Matteo Ricci had written that the Chinese believed 'the heaven to be one and liquid, that is to say of air and other quite absurd things'. See Francesco D'Arelli, 'P. Matteo Ricci S.J., "le cose absurde" dell'astronomia cinese. Genesi, eredità ed influsso di un convincimento tra i secoli XVI-XVII' in I. Iannaccone and A. Tamburello, eds, *Dall'Europa alla Cina: contributi per una storia dell'astronomia*, Università degli studi Federico II, Istituto universitario orientale (Naples, 1990), pp.85–123, esp. p.89.

In 1624 Borri was able to return to Europe. At the University of Coimbra in Portugal he was offered a chair of mathematics and astronomy and there from 1626 to 1627 he taught the doctrine of fluid heavens with, so he says, the '... general approval of the whole College not only of the mathematicians but also of the philosophers and the theologians'. Seeking to publish his course, he obtained the unanimous consent of his colleagues both in Coimbra and in Lisbon, with the sole exception of one, Sebastião Couto (1567–1639), a professor of logic, whose retaliatory animosity had been aroused through having been contradicted by Borri for asserting that mathematics was not a science. Couto was thus able to prevent the publication of the book. Borri then set out for Rome in search of support.[81] There, for unexplained reasons he left the Jesuit Order in 1632, tried first to enter the Cistercian Order of the Holy Cross of Jerusalem and, failing to be accepted, that of another Cistercian order. In the face of their refusal, he brought an ecclesiastical action against both and won his case, but then died suddenly, neither Jesuit nor Cistercian.

His book, entitled *Collecta astronomica*, was meanwhile published in 1631 in Lisbon *sub correptionem Sanctæ Romanæ Ecclesiæ*.[82] The work appears to have been written in Portuguese and later translated into Latin by a Frenchman Fr Le Jeunehomme, for Borri, according to the latter, had 'forgotten his Italian and scarcely remembered his Latin'.[83]

Borri's work is divided into three parts, the first on astronomy, the second on the physics of the heavens and the third a Hexaëmeron. He sought to relate the three parts together by coming back in each one, to themes evoked many times in each of the other two. His is one of the last thorough

---

[81] Borri describes his experiences in a long undated letter to the General of the Jesuit Order Muzio Vitelleschi, printed by Domingos Maurício dos Santos, S.J., in *op cit.* Appendix, pp.143–150.

[82] On Borri, besides Domingos Maurício Gomes dos Santos, *art cit.* see the article in Sommervogel, *Bibliothèque de la Compagnie de Jesus* (Bruxelles–Paris, 1890), vol.I, cols1821–1822 and António Alberto de Andrade, 'Antes de Vernei nascer [...] Borri nas escolas', *Brotéria*, XL fasc. 4 (1945), pp.369–379. On Borri's discussion of heliocentrism, see Luís de Albuquerque, 'Sobre o conhecimento de Galileu e de Copérnico em Portugal no século XVII', *Vertice* XXV (1965), pp.14–27. On Borri's travels in the East see Francesco Surdich, 'L'attività di Padre Cristoforo Borri nelle Indie Orientali in un resoconto inedito', in idem, *Fonti sulla penetrazione europea in Asia* (Genoa, 1979), pp.67–122.

[83] Fr Le Jeunehomme, 'Relation d'un voyage de la Flesche à Lisbonne' [1627], in *Documents inédits concernant la Compagnie de Jésus*, vol. IV (Poitiers, 1864), pp.39–40. A manuscript version in Portuguese of his *Collecta Astronomica* is in the University Library of Coimbra: *Nova astronomia na qual se refuta a antiga da multidão de 12 céus pondo só tres: aereo, sidereo e empireo*, Ms 44. It is not clear whether this is a copy of Borri's draft in Portuguese or a retranslation from the Latin. Another manuscript treatise by Borri in Latin entitled: *De astrologia universa ...*, written in 1612, is in the Biblioteca Nazionale, Rome, Fondo Gesuitico, No. 587. See Michel-Pierre Lerner, 'L'entrée de Tycho Brahe chez les Jésuites, ou le chant du cygne de Clavius', in Luce Giard, ed., *Les jésuites à la Renaissance* (Paris, 1995), pp.157–163.

attempts by a Catholic astronomer to integrate astronomy with the Bible. Closely aligning himself with Pereyra and the latter's interpretation of Genesis, Borri consistently took a view opposed to the rigid Aristotelianism of Suarez. Fully aware of the observations made by Tycho and Galileo, he followed them in the conclusions they had drawn concerning the material nature of the heavens. He described the Ptolemaic, Tychonic and Copernican planetary systems, opting like all the Jesuit astronomers for the Tychonic.[84] Although the Copernican system saved the phenomena for astronomy, it was not, he said, acceptable on physical grounds for it was absurd to imagine the earth carried round from west to east in the space of 24 hours. If the earth were thus to be surrounded by a soft and fluid body, by the air, by what body could it be carried? For if the body were hard there would be no problem.[85] Borri rejected Kepler's recourse to magnetic force (*virtus*) to drive the planets as being 'hidden and mysterious (*tecta et arcana*)'.[86] The Copernican system, Borri finally concluded, was further to be condemned for being incompatible with Holy Scripture.[87]

Denying the existence of the *Primum Mobile* and of the Crystalline Heaven,[88] Borri declared that both the heavens of the planets and of the fixed stars were fluid.[89] The heavens he divided into the *Aëreum*, *Sidereum* and *Empyreum*. The *Aëreum* extended to where the 'vapours and terrestrial exhalations reached, where the third region of the air is'.[90] The *Sidereum* extended in the form of 'pure and limpid æther' as far as the highest fixed stars, above which God had placed the Supercelestial Waters.[91]

In his definition of the Firmament, Borri followed Pereyra, while refuting Suarez.[92] Consisting of ordinary breathable air progressively purified and rarefied to become an *aura ætherea*, the Firmament derived, he said, from the same misty and aqueous matter in which God had set the courses of the planets and stars on the First Day of the Creation.[93]

After reviewing various definitions of the nature of the æther, Borri ended by giving his definition of the *cælum æthereum* or *sidereum* in which there appears not a trace of any reference to Aristotle's fifth essence. He defined the æther as 'a very pure and most limpid continuation of the air itself', divided into 'two regions' which were '... not specifically and essentially different',

---

[84] Cristoforo Borri, S.J., *Collecta Astronomica* (Lisbon, 1631), pp.186–188.
[85] *Ibid.* pp.42–43.
[86] *Ibid.* p.173.
[87] *Ibid.* p.43.
[88] *Ibid.* p.223.
[89] *Ibid.* p.161 and p.229.
[90] *Ibid.* p.258. Cf. Aristotle, *Meteorologica*, I iii 340b, ed. Lee, pp.19–20.
[91] Cristoforo Borri, *op. cit. loc. cit.*
[92] *Ibid.* pp.414–415.
[93] *Ibid.* pp.433–440.

but 'accidentally so', one '... our ordinary thick, vaporous air (*nostro crasso & vaporoso aere*)' and the other '... that most limpid *aura ætherea*'.[94] Apart from his obscure recourse to scholastic distinctions in his division of the air/æther into two regions, Borri's definition can be clearly seen to be inspired by his reading the works of Tycho and Kepler. Whereas Kepler, as we have seen, had simply used the term *aura ætherea*, Borri spoke of the *aura ætherea sive æther*, seeking to give it a respectable origin by attributing it to the Venerable Bede (c.673–735). He quoted Bede as saying that, 'The name Firmament also refers to the æther which is that upper part of the space of the air ... (*Firmamenti nomine etiam æther intelligitur, hoc est superius illud aeris spatium* ...)'.[95] Thus, concluded Borri, '... this opinion seems also to be that of all those who, quoting both sacred and profane sources, say that the heaven consists of *æther* or of an *auram æthereum*'.[96] No doubt acutely aware that the term *aura ætherea* was Kepler's and that Bede had used just the term *æther*, Borri may have been trying to hide the fact that his source was a Protestant.

Borri insisted at length on the real existence of the Supercelestial Waters lying between the *cælum sidereum* and the Empyrean. Their nature, he said, following the Basilian interpretation, was 'watery and vaporous' (*aqueam et nebulosam*)[97] and on this point he took issue with Molina who had seen them as 'heavy and fluid (*graves & fluidas*)'.[98] Angels, said Borri, moved both the planets and the fixed stars.[99] One angel would be sufficient to carry the latter and maintain the regular distances between them.[100]

Although he recognized that there was no physical or mathematical proof of its existence, the Empyrean was for Borri a generally received truth in the Church. On its material nature, he said he was no more persuaded by the reasons advanced by Suarez for it being solid than by those advanced by Maloni for it being fluid. The Empyrean, he declared, was 'solid, hard and incorruptible'. Christ and the Blessed would not all walk on its upper convex surface, as claimed by Suarez, but they would be able to move about inside it, '... going through it or going round the outside of the Empyrean, just as we can in the air in our houses'.[101] Was the Empyrean square in shape as the Book of Revelation described it,[102] or round like the rest of the

---

[94] *Ibid.* pp.258–259.
[95] Cf. Venerable Bede, 'Liber quatuor in principium Genesis ... I i 21–23', in *ed. cit.* pp.21–22 (... *firmamento caeli, quia hoc nomine etiam æther indicetur, hoc est superius illud aeris spatium*). In this quotation Bede is in contradiction with his words quoted above in Chapter 1, p.3.
[96] Cristoforo Borri, *op. cit.* pp.324–325.
[97] *Ibid.* pp.450–452.
[98] *Ibid.* p.462. Cf. Luis de Molina, S.J., *De opere sex dierum* (Lyons, 1621), disp.X, p.678.
[99] Cristoforo Borri, *op. cit.* pp.169–174.
[100] *Ibid.* pp.225–227 and pp.235–237.
[101] *Ibid.* pp.268–275.
[102] Rev. 21: 16: 'And the city [the New Jerusalem] is laid out as a square.'

cosmos? Borri marshalled arguments in favour of both theories, leaving the reader to choose and providing diagrams to show both possibilities.[103]

In his *Summa Universæ Philosophiæ* (1642), Balthasar Tellez shows clearly the influence of Borri, though not quite to the same extent as his fellow Portuguese Francisco Soares Lusitano, whom we shall come to.[104] Besides Borri, Tellez relied on two fellow Jesuits, one a Scot and the other an Englishman, as authorities on mathematical astronomy and mathematics: Hugo Semple (Hugh Sempill) (1596–1654)[105] and Ignatius Stafford (1599–1642).[106] Tellez taught grammar, rhetoric and philosophy for eight years at Coimbra and then theology for another eight in Lisbon. He was also Superior of the Irish Seminary and the College of St Anthony in Lisbon. He adopted a decidedly different stance from the Spanish theologians, distancing himself in particular from the views of Hurtado de Mendoza. After a long analysis of the nature of the heavens in which he presented a full account of the evidence gathered from their observations by Tycho and Galileo, Tellez declared himself firmly in favour of the fluidity, not only of the planetary heavens, but also of that of the fixed stars. The matter of the heavens, said Tellez, for whom Aristotle's fifth essence was a thing of the past, was of an elementary nature. The lower part of the heaven was of air and the upper part, in which the planets and fixed stars moved, of fire.[107] Quoting Borri, he divided the heavens into three: the *aëreum*, *sidereum* and the *empyreum* and, like Borri, he recognized that there was no physical or mathematical proof of the latter's existence.[108] Tellez said nothing about whether its interior was fluid or solid, or anything about the physical condition of the Blessed in it. In a long discussion of the nature of the movers of the planets, in which he took issue with Saint Thomas Aquinas regarding the latter's claim that they were moved by angels, Tellez concluded by claiming that they were moved by their own innate driving power (*virtute motrice sibi intrinsece inhærente*).[109] Although endowed with a broad classical education in the humanities and an accomplished humanist style which

---

[103] Cristoforo Borri, *op. cit.* pp.276–293.

[104] See below, p.179.

[105] Hugo Semple (Hugh Sempill), S.J., *De Mathematicis Disciplinis Libri Duodecim* (Antwerp, 1635), See esp. lib.X, cap.I–cap.II, pp.195–199. Semple declared that he did not want to get involved with philosophical questions concerning the heavens, preferring to keep to pure mathematical astronomy. Born at Craigevar in Scotland, Semple entered the Society of Jesus at Toledo in 1615, later becoming rector of the Scots College at Madrid.

[106] Ignatius Stafford was the author of several works on pure mathematics published in Portuguese in Lisbon.

[107] Balthasar Tellez, S.J., *Summa Universæ Philosophiæ* (Lisbon,1642), vol.I (1st pagination), pars II, lib.I, disp.XXXX, sect.I, pp.327[=333]–337.

[108] *Ibid.* disp.XXXXIV, sect.III, p.354.

[109] *Ibid.* sect.IV, pp.356–359.

contrasts with the run-of-the-mill scholasticism usually encountered in the *Cursus Philosophicus*, Tellez nevertheless shows nothing of the intellectual energy displayed by Borri in his attempt to defend and maintain a synthesis between astronomy and the Bible.

Francisco Soares, known as Francisco Soares (Lusitano) to distinguish him from his celebrated Spanish namesake Francisco Suarez (Granatense), taught philosophy and theology in Lisbon, Coimbra and finally at Evora where he became Rector of the University from 1658 until his death in 1659. He was imprisoned twice, suspected of infidelity to the Portuguese crown because his brother had defected to Spain when Portugal recovered her sovereignty in 1640. Eventually pardoned, he was allowed to continue his university teaching at Evora. He died tragically when, called up together with students and colleagues of Evora University to fight a Spanish army at Elvas, a powder magazine accidentally blew up, killing them all.[110]

Soares' *Cursus Philosophicus* was published in Lisbon in 1651 in four volumes and was followed by two other editions at Evora in 1670 and 1701-3. In it he shows a thorough knowledge of the sources then available on the heavens, writing with a clear style well suited to handling the material. His was a mind distinctly above the average.

Quoting Tycho and Borri, he declared that the planetary heavens were fluid. Among the proofs of fluidity he cited the behaviour of *novae* and of comets and the evidence of refractions. 'If the heavens were solid', said Soares, 'the stars could not shine through them, for how could the light of the stars penetrate such solid and dense bodies. It may be argued that these bodies are transparent, but against this, it can be answered that transparency would not occur in such a thick and deep quantity as each heaven would have, if it were solid.'[111] This argument, as we have seen, was also Gassendi's. 'If the heavens were solid', continued Soares, 'there would either be no day or no night. There would be no day because the light of the sun could not reach us through the spheres, or, if it could, there would be no night because

---

[110] On Francisco Soares see the notice on his life in António Franco, S.J., *Imagem da Virtude* (Coimbra and Evora, 1717-19), vol.III, pp.615-629 (pp.624-626 contain a letter from him to Muzio Vitelleschi, the General of the Jesuit Order); also Francisco Rodrigues, S.J., 'Um Mártir da Restauração de 1640', *Trabalhos da Associação dos Arqueólogos Portugueses* VI (Lisbon, 1940), pp.54-73 and idem, 'A Companhia de Jesus e a Restauração de Portugal 1640', *Anais da Academia Portuguesa da História* VI (Lisbon, 1952), pp.398-401. But see what seems, in our view, the excessively reserved judgement on Soares by J.S. da Silva Dias, 'Cultura e obstáculo epistemológico do Renascimento ao Iluminismo em Portugal', in Francisco Contente Domingues and Luís Filipe Barreto, eds, *A Abertura do mundo. Estudos de história dos Descobrimentos portugueses* (Lisbon, 1986), vol.I, pp.44-46. Soares is not mentioned by Lohr in his bibliography. Cf. Charles H. Lohr, *Latin Aristotle Commentaries* (Florence, 1988).

[111] Francisco Soares, S.J., *Cursus Philosophicus* (Lisbon, 1651), *Ad Libros Aristotelis de Cælo Tractatus Unicus*, disp.I, sect.I, §2, p.273.

at night bright light would return, since the light of the sun, just as it illuminates the moon, would in the same way illuminate the whole sky and the remaining orbs of the other planets.'[112] The latter argument had likewise been advanced by the French astronomer Ismael Boulliau in 1645.[113]

Although many said that the heaven of the fixed stars was also fluid, Soares thought that it was more probably solid and this perhaps explains his rather different tripartite division of the heavens into the *Cælum Æthereum*, the *Cælum Stellatum* and the *Empyreum*. 'For if', said Soares, 'the *Cælum Stellatum* consists of the same *aura ætherea* as that of the *Cælum Planetarum*, it would not be a different heaven.' If the heaven of the fixed stars were fluid, the fixed stars would have to be guided by a countless number of angels in order to maintain the constant distances between them. 'A sort of large wheel or globe to which each star was fixed would be more convenient and could be moved by one angel.' The solidity of the heaven of the fixed stars also conveniently prevented the waters above the heavens from flowing downward.[114]

In discussing the nature of the matter of the heavens, Soares declared that the planets moved in an *aura ætherea*, an opinion he ascribed to Bede (as quoted by Borri), to Pena and Rothmann (as quoted by Tycho), and to Bruno (cited from Tycho).[115] He made no mention of Kepler, the real source of the concept. The heaven of the fixed stars, which Soares regarded as solid, consisted, he said, of water compacted and made 'more solid than adamant, more pure than silver, and more precious than gold'.[116]

On the Empyrean, Soares followed Lessius. Only the inner and outer surfaces of the Empyrean, he said, were solid, the inside being fluid to facilitate breathing and speech. Discussing after Borri whether the Empyrean was round or square, he concluded that it was spherical on both its inner and outer surfaces. The assertion in the Book of Revelation that it was square should be understood as being allegorical.[117]

In discussing the nature of the movers of the heavenly bodies, Soares refused solutions such as Kepler's 'magnetic force', or other hypotheses claiming that they were moved by 'their own intrinsic forms'. Refuting at length objections that, if they were moved by angels, the task over so many

---

[112] *Ibid. loc. cit.*

[113] Ismael Boulliau, *Astronomia Philolaica* (Paris, 1645), p.9 (*Addo nusquam fore noctem si coeli solidi essent*).

[114] Francisco Soares, *op. cit.* disp.I, sect.I, §5, p.275.

[115] I am grateful to Michel-Pierre Lerner for drawing my attention to the fact that Soares only knew Bruno through Tycho's mention of him, since he refers to him using Tycho's uncomplimentary pun on his name, though without realizing that it was a pun: 'Ioannes Iordanus Nullanus'.

[116] Francisco Soares, *op. cit.* disp.I, sect.III, §1–2, pp.281–283.

[117] *Ibid.* disp.II, sect.II, §1–3, pp.291–294.

thousands of years would, like Sisyphus pushing his rock, be beyond their strength, Soares had no doubt that their strength would be fully sufficient.[118]

Abandoning Borri, Soares refuted at length the Basilian model in which the Supercelestial Waters were held to be clouds. These waters were 'fluid as in the sea' (*fluidas per modum earum quae sunt in mari*), and existed both to put out the conflagration at the end of world and to wash its blackened and burnt state. They were not corrupt, but whether they were sweet or salty could only be decided by those who have tasted them.[119] In spite of his recognizably Baroque mind, Soares can be seen as one of the last of a generation of Jesuits to apply considerable effort to maintaining a coherent cosmological synthesis.

Conclusion

The above analysis suggests the following very general conclusions. In the early decades of the seventeenth century, the Aristotelian tradition in the university textbooks remained as yet unaffected by the impact of Tycho's and Galileo's experimental evidence concerning the nature of the heavens. By mid-century, its irrefutable character had forced almost all the authors of the *Cursus Philosophicus* to modify their representation of the cosmos. Whereas up until the 1620s the heavens were generally assumed to be solid, by the 1640s they were, with the exception of the heaven of the fixed stars, recognized by the majority to be fluid. The Empyrean, with its hard outer and inner shells and its interior now granted to be fluid, remained henceforth the sole guarantee of the finite nature of the medieval cosmos. Whereas the existence of the Empyrean had previously been guaranteed both metaphysically and theologically, it now came to depend on a definition that was exclusively theological.

Three important exceptions to this general trend of evolution in the course of the seventeenth century appear in the case of the untypical yet influential figure of Cristoforo Borri in Portugal, in that of the systematically backward-looking stand of Jean Vincent at Toulouse and in that of the enigmatically precocious modernity of Jean Bauduer at Bordeaux.

These figures apart, a relative indifference and, if anything, a limited competence in absorbing the lessons of observational astronomy is apparent among the Paris professors. A more careful attention is observable among those in Italy and especially among those in Catholic Germany. The Spanish Jesuits give the impression of uneasy embarrassment in their handling of the question and stand in singular contrast to their lesser-known colleagues

---

[118] *Ibid.* disp.III, sect.I, §1–4, pp.294–299.
[119] *Ibid.* disp.IV, sect.VI,§ 4–6, pp.316–317.

in Portugal, more readily disposed to accept the new evidence. Except for the intriguingly bold open-mindedness of Jean Bauduer in Bordeaux, the Copernican system is rejected by all, if not automatically because of its condemnation by the Church, occasionally with the adjunction of natural philosophical counter-arguments.

8

The impact of Cartesianism and Copernicanism and the end of the medieval cosmos

The spread of Cartesianism into European culture from Holland and France in the last third of the seventeenth century occasioned everywhere a deep and acrimonious crisis, placing the protagonists of the mechanical philosophy at loggerheads with the guardians of the old order. In France Cartesianism spread through literary *salons* and in certain religious orders, the university and the state being violently opposed to it. Whereas in Holland it was propagated from the start in the universities (though not without considerable internal resistance),[1] only towards the end of the seventeenth century was Cartesian philosophy taught at the University of Paris and then with theological reservations concerning Descartes' assimilation of space and matter.[2]

After a first enthusiastic reception at the Catholic University of Louvain,[3] letters were received from Rome in 1662 expressing surprise at the spread there of the errors of Cartesian philosophy, stating that they led to atheism. On 1 July of the same year, the Papal Pronuncio wrote criticizing the Faculty of Arts for allowing 'the pernicious Cartesian philosophy to be taught to Catholic youth'. He wrote again on 27 August to the Rector of the University, earnestly recommending that, if theses were found with propositions containing the errors of Descartes, either proscribing the theses in their entirety, or at least ordering that propositions 'containing Cartesian novelty, or tainted with it' be expurgated. The Faculty of Theology gave full satisfaction, specifically recognizing five errors of Cartesian philosophy. Two related to cosmology, one asserting the indefinite extension of the universe, the other denying the possibility of a plurality of worlds.[4]

---

[1] See the thorough study by Ernst Bizer, 'Die reformierte Orthodoxie und der Cartesianismus', *Zeitschrift für Theologie und Kirche* (1958), pp.306–372; also Paul Dibon, 'Descartes et ses premiers disciples hollandais', in idem, *Regards sur la Hollande du siècle d'or* (Naples, 1990), pp.600–611.

[2] See below.

[3] See Paul Mouy, *op. cit.* p.97.

[4] See Jean Du Hamel, *Philosophia universalis sive commentarius in universam Aristotelis philosophiam ad usum scholarum comparata* (Paris, 1705), vol.V, pp.11–15 (3rd pagination).

In southern Europe, where the philosophies of Descartes and Gassendi were often conflated as one and termed that of the *novatores*, university authorities were, largely because of the suspect northern origin of these philosophies, able to restrain their subversive effect for some decades longer. At the 15th General Meeting of the Jesuit Order in Rome in 1706, a list was laid down of thirty propositions, the teaching of which became prohibited in Jesuit schools everywhere. Three of them were aimed at Descartes' concept of cosmic space: that 'above the heaven' there was real space filled with matter; that 'the extension of the world was indefinite' and that 'there could be only one world'.[5] The condemnation of the latter proposition obviously did not imply that other worlds really existed, but only that God had power to create them if he wished.

Following the country-by-country analysis as above, this chapter will concentrate first on the study of the impact of Cartesianism in France, where it considerably overshadowed that of Gassendi, then on the spread of the doctrines of both Descartes and Gassendi in the southern Latin countries. Alongside the purely philosophical expositions of Cartesianism and the theologians' refutations of it, Descartes' cosmology is discussed in the textbooks of the *Cursus Philosophicus* in the section customarily devoted to reviewing the three astronomical systems of Ptolemy, Copernicus and Tycho Brahe. The majority of authors, while admitting the technical superiority of the Copernican system, either avoided endorsing it formally, on account of it being still banned by the Church, or else they evasively adopted an attitude of general scepticism regarding the truth of any astronomical system. Both groups dropped any positive reference to the Empyrean. As the eighteenth century advanced, Copernicanism obtained a foothold notably in southern Europe, through the work of Newton, towards whom the Church remained oddly indifferent. In view of the many studies already available, the history of Cartesianism associated with Copernicanism in northern Europe, in Holland, in England and in Germany has been left aside.[6]

---

[5] See Gaston Sortais, 'Le cartésianisme chez les Jésuites français aux XVIIe et XVIIIe siècles', *Archives de philosophie* 6 Pt 3 (1929), pp.36–40.

[6] For Cartesianism (associated with Copernicanism) in northern Protestant Europe, besides the study of Ernst Bizer, *art. cit.*, see Reyer Hooykaas, 'The reception of Copernicanism in England and the Netherlands', in idem, *Selected Studies in the History of Science*, Acta Universitatis Conimbrigensis (Coimbra, 1983), pp.635–663 (esp. pp.661–663 on Cartesiano-Copernicanism). For Cartesianism in Holland, besides Paul Dibon's article cited above, see idem, 'Connaissance révélée et connaissance rationelle: aperçu sur les points forts d'un débat épineux', in *Regards sur la Hollande du siècle d'or* (Naples, 1990), pp.693–719; idem, 'Notes bibliographiques sur les cartésiens hollandais' in E.J. Dijksterhuis *et al.*, *Descartes et le cartésianisme hollandais, Etudes et Documents* (Paris and Amsterdam, 1950), pp.261–300; C. Louise Thijssen-Schoute, 'Le cartésianisme aux Pays Bas', in E.J. Dijksterhuis *et al.*, *op. cit.* pp.183–260; J.A. van Ruler, *The Crisis of Causality. Voetius and Descartes on God, Nature and Change* (Leiden, New York, Köln, 1995). For England, M.H. Nicolson, 'The early stages of Cartesianism in England', *Studies in*

France

In France the philosophy of René Descartes was treated distinctly by three different groups of scholars. The first concentrated on expounding and publicizing it, ignoring the challenges left by its incompatibility with the traditional medieval cosmos or with scholastic interpretations of the Creation in Genesis. The second consisted of the traditionalists who rejected Cartesianism outright for these very reasons. The third, adopting a critical approach, sought to accommodate as many of the features of Cartesianism as possible within the basic theological principles of the medieval cosmos.

In the first group we find Jacques Rohault (c.1620–72), and Pierre-Sylvain Régis (1632–1707), the two foremost publicists of Descartes' philosophy in France.[7] Jacques Rohault's *Traité de Physique* (1671) went into seven editions by 1730, all published in Paris. Pierre-Sylvain Régis' *Système de Philosophie* appeared in Paris in 1690 and again in Paris and Lyons in 1691.

On the relation of Descartes' cosmology to traditional theology, Rohault limited himself to stating that, '... we consider the idea of extension to be so independent of any created Being, that it is almost impossible for us to banish it from our mind, even when we try to conceive the void which we believe came before the creation of the world. This shows that it [extension] does not depend on it [creation] at all, that it is neither a consequence, nor a property nor even less an accident, nor a simple way of being, but that it is everywhere a true substance.'[8] Rohault's pronouncement left no doubt that he understood extended substance as existing prior to and independent of the Creation. Pierre-Sylvain Régis followed Rohault as a spreader of Cartesianism, but he made no apparent allusion in his *Système de Philosophie* to the traditional system which Descartes' philosophy was seen to replace.

Among the traditionalists who wholly rejected Descartes' cosmology was the Oratorian Jean-Baptiste de La Grange (1641–84). After teaching philosophy at Montbrison, at Le Mans and theology at Troyes, he returned to the Oratorian house in Paris in 1675 to write *Les principes de la philosophie contre les nouveaux philosophes, Descartes, Rohault, Regius, Gassendi, le P. Maignan,*

Philology XXVIII (1929), pp.356–374; G.A.J. Rogers, 'Descartes and the English', in J.D. North and J.J. Roche, eds, *The Light of Nature. Essays in the History and Philosophy of Science presented to A.C. Crombie* (Dordrecht/Boston/Lancaster, 1985), pp.281–302 and A. Koyré, *From the Closed World to the Infinite Universe*, chaps V and VI (on Descartes and Henry More). For the English anti-Cartesians, Samuel Gott Armiger (1670) and Robert Fergusson (1675), see Ernst Bizer, *art. cit.* p.357, n.1. On the reception of Cartesianism in relation to astronomy in northern Europe generally, see William Donahue, *The Dissolution of the Celestial Spheres* (New York, 1981), pp.280–294.

[7] On Rohault and Régis, see Paul Mouy, *op. cit.* chap. I, pp.108–138 (Rohault) and pp.145–157 (Régis). Mouy does not address the theological problems involved in Descartes' physics of the heavens.

[8] Jacques Rohault, *Traité de Physique* (Paris, 1671), p.38.

&c. (Paris, 1675), a work that went into four editions by 1684, all published in Paris. Untypical of his order and realizing that he lacked support from his superiors in his resolute defence of tradition, he left the Oratorians, taking a benefice at Chartres where he remained until his death.[9]

In his attack on Descartes' identification of matter with extension, La Grange wrote that, '... what shows how much the doctrine of this philosopher encourages Godlessness (*impiété*) is that one may draw on his principles to claim that matter is eternal and independent of God. [...] If it is true that space and that which we call void is an extended substance as Descartes claims in article 16 of the second part of his *Principles*,[10] the infinite spaces which lie beyond the heavens consist of a matter that is infinitely extended and because these spaces have been, and are, a nothing (*un rien*) which is independent of God, and which God can neither produce nor destroy, there is no doubt that one must conclude that [for Descartes] matter is eternal and independent of God.'[11] La Grange's criticism of Descartes was the same as that which Isaac Barrow levelled at Gassendi, but oddly La Grange showed greater tolerance for Gassendi than for Descartes. Gassendi's thought was 'very far removed from that of Descartes' and, he said, '... would never be accused of favouring heresy or Godlessness'.[12]

On the nature of the heavens La Grange remained a surprisingly die-hard traditionalist and this may to some extent explain the attitude of his superiors. 'One must hold with the Ancients that the heavens are solid',[13] he wrote, adding: 'I consider celestial matter from the convex surface of the sphere of the air as far as the [fixed] stars to be a solid material which touches the Heaven of these same stars, but which is nevertheless separated from them'.[14]

In 1677 Jean Vincent of the Collège de l'Esquille in Toulouse published a detailed refutation of Cartesianism in his *Discussio Peripatetica in qua Philosophiæ Cartesianæ Principia per singula fere capita, seu articulos dilucidé examinantur.* In a section devoted to the discussion of Descartes' indefinite extension of the universe, Vincent quoted Descartes' identification of mat-

---

[9] On La Grange see Francisque Bouillier, *Histoire de la philosophie cartésienne* (Paris, 1854), 3rd edn (Paris 1868), vol.I, pp.554–556, and E. Batterel, *Mémoires domestiques pour servir à l'histoire de l'Oratoire*, ed. Auguste-Marie-Pierre Ingold and E. Bonnardet (Paris, 1904), vol.III, pp.377–379. Grateful thanks are expressed to M. Joseph Barley, Archivist of the Oratorian Order in Paris, for kindly providing relevant information concerning La Grange's life.

[10] Cf. René Descartes, *Principes*, Pt II, #16, *ed. cit.* vol.IX-2, pp.71–72 ('... we must conclude of the space which we imagine to be void that, since it has extension, it must also have substance').

[11] Jean-Baptiste de La Grange, *Les principes de la philosophie contre les nouveaux philosophes, Descartes, Rohault, Regius, Gassendi, le P. Maignan &c.* (Paris, 1675), edn (Paris, 1682), vol.2, chap. I, pp.4–5.

[12] *Ibid.* pp.13–14.

[13] *Ibid.* vol.2, chap. XL, p.592.

[14] *Ibid.* chap. XLIV, p.640.

ter with extension in his *Principes* : 'We know that this world or the extended matter of which the universe consists has no limits, because wherever we imagine these limits to be, we can still imagine beyond them indefinitely extended spaces which we not only imagine, but which we also perceive as something imaginable, that is as real and which thus contain in them an indefinitely extended corporeal substance.'[15]

Vincent commented,

> A thoroughly bad idea indeed and much worse than Plato's. From this idea of Descartes' it can indeed be seen how easy it is to tumble into many errors where one has consequently strayed from the right path. For first of all it follows that God could not have made the universe smaller or greater than he did. For if you say that he could have confined it within the concave surface of the sphere of the Moon in such a way that each element could have been smaller and all of the heavens no greater than a cavity such as that of the moon's sphere, we shall [yet] perceive truly real spaces beyond such a cavity and hence God was not able to so limit the universe. And the same would follow however much smallness or extension you might assign to it. Who would dare commit this outrage to divine freedom and omnipotence?

Next Vincent pointed out the incompatibility of Descartes' identification of matter and space with Christian eschatology.

> Secondly it follows that this universe could not be destroyed by God leaving behind only the earth or only one man [i.e. as a witness]. That man could not but conceive, beyond the limits and boundaries of the earth or in the space in which the universe was previously, a certain extension or indefinitely extended spaces, or have the apprehension of other spaces and hence of a certain corporeal substance. From this it is to be concluded that this universe is a necessary entity indestructible by God. How false and erroneous this is, is obvious to anyone.

Vincent then showed that Descartes' cosmology was incompatible with the Church's doctrine of a creation *ex nihilo*. 'Further, it would clearly follow that God did not create the universe, but that he formed and assembled it from essentially extended matter, necessarily existing and eternal, giving to it only motions and different shapes, different settings and arrangements between its various parts.' This, declared Vincent, was the heresy of the Valentinians and the Seleucians denounced by Tertullian.[16]

---

[15] Translated from Vincent's quotation of Descartes' Latin text. For the French text see René Descartes, *Principes*, pt II, no.21, *ed. cit.* vol.IX-2, p.74.

[16] Vincent gave references to Tertullian's works, *Adversus Hermogenem* and *Adversus Valentinianos*, containing denunciation of the ideas of pagan writers of Antiquity in which the world was held to be eternal and uncreated. Cf. Tertullian, 'Adversus Hermogenem', in *Tertulliani Opera*, Corpus Christianorum Series Latina, *ed. cit.*, vol.I, I,1, p.394 and Tertullian, 'Adversus Valentianos', in *ibid.* vol.II, XV,1, p.765.

In contending that the space in which the universe was created was nothing other than extended matter, Descartes, said Vincent, had fallen into the error of admitting that matter was uncreated and independent of God. 'For if we grasp through imagination that the space, which is above the heavens or which was before the creation of the universe where we now understand the universe to be, has real extension and had it previously and hence is nothing but extended matter, then, since it is certain that such space was not produced by God before the creation of the universe and consequently never came into being, it follows', concluded Vincent, 'that matter is uncreated and independent of God.'

Vincent now pointed out that Descartes' indefinite extension of the universe took no account of the fact that it would have to be finite to distinguish it from a Creator, infinite by principle. Descartes claims, said Vincent, '... that this universe is in a positive sense infinite in its mass and extension'.

> Not us but God himself would either see boundaries in it or he would not. If He did not, He would have to set them [i.e. to distinguish Himself from His Creation]. And what then? Let us imagine a man created by Him, who himself conceives, according to Descartes' idea, such real spaces beyond those limits and as a result an indefinitely extended corporeal substance. Hence it is wrongly held that God does see certain limits in it and that it is consequently positively infinite.

Vincent ended on an ironic note.

> Since nothing has now been left [unresolved] by Descartes concerning the contentious matter on whether God can produce an infinite, a great many philosophers have now thus given up raising such long questions and there now remains no difficulty concerning this so celebrated question!

In his final conclusion Vincent emphasized his adherence to Christian orthodoxy asserting that Descartes' view that 'the universe is eternal or was produced from eternity, [...] is heretical and against the common view of the Fathers of the Church'.[17]

Though aware that Descartes' exposition of the formation of the world appeared incompatible with the traditional account in Genesis, Jean Bauduer of the Collège de Guyenne in Bordeaux showed himself considerably more open to Cartesianism than Vincent. In his *Philosophiæ clavis* (1685), examined in the previous chapter, Bauduer added to his analysis of the Ptolemaic, Tychonic and Copernican astronomical systems an appendix on 'the Cartesian system', in which he acknowledged that as far as the sun, the earth and the planets were concerned, it fitted well enough with the Copernican. 'But

---

[17] Jean Vincent, *Discussio peripatetica in qua philosophiæ cartesianae principia per singula, seu articulos dilucidé examinantur* (Toulouse, 1677), pp.70–73. On Vincent see F. Bouillier, *op. cit.* vol.I, pp.553–554.

the two systems', he said, 'clashed, in that Copernicus denied all motion to the Firmament, regarding it as the highest sphere in which its stars were seen to form the ... immobile vault of the universe surrounding the region of the planets'.

'Descartes', said Bauduer, 'moreover holds the universe to be indefinitely extended because human understanding cannot set any limits to it, nor [according to Descartes] does divine revelation lay down any. However', noted Bauduer, 'our mind, however far carried to a limit, finds beyond, a long, wide and deep space which according to Descartes is a real body.' 'Furthermore', he continued, resuming Descartes' argument, 'God's infinite power and goodness would persuade us that his works are so vast and so magnificent that they should not be confined by any limits. It is for this reason that the universe is held [by Descartes] to be indefinite [in extent] and not infinite, because the word "infinite" is reserved for God alone and because something can be finite without the human mind recognizing its finiteness.'[18]

In giving his assent to Descartes' postulation of the indefinite extent of the universe, Bauduer nevertheless noted, on the other hand, the difficulty of reconciling his theory of the formation of the universe with the doctrine of simultaneous Creation, borrowed from Saint Augustine.[19] Descartes, asserted Bauduer, had not been unaware of this difficulty.

Analysing the question, Bauduer first noted that Descartes had deduced

> ... the way in which all the bodies of this universe could have originated from matter of a varied and undefined sort (*varia & indefinenti*), created by God by being set in motion (*agitatione*), [...] [Descartes] otherwise certainly knew, and Christian faith teaches it, that the bodies of the universe did not come into existence in this way, but that they were [each] produced in a perfect state by God himself at the beginning, as were the heavens, the sun, the fixed stars, the moon, the earth, Adam and Eve, the animals, planets and so forth, just as the great and most powerful Creator teaches that they would have existed at once in their perfection. But this does not prevent Descartes from claiming that, with God allowing and helping, all bodies could have been brought into being in the following way.[20]

With these last words Bauduer introduced his abreviated account of Descartes' theory of the formation of the universe, which he apparently readily accepted without further ado.

Bauduer's successor at the Collège de Guyenne, Guillaume Sabbatié, showed no misgivings whatever in his *Institutiones philosophicæ* (1716–18) over an

---

[18] Jean Bauduer, *Philosophiæ clavis seu cursus philosophicus ad usum studiosæ juventutis* (Bordeaux, 1685), vol.IV, pp.94–97.

[19] Cf. above, Chapter 5, p.120–121.

[20] Jean Bauduer, *op. cit.* p.99.

incompatibility between Descartes' theory and Saint Augustine's doctrine (or else he failed to recognize the possibility), for he merely quoted Descartes' summary of Saint Augustine's account of simultaneous Creation, adding: 'These are Descartes' words. May those who attack him as an atheist read them and may they see how much they insult him.'[21]

At the turn of the seventeenth century at the University of Paris, Cartesianism was being explained, though not explicitly taught as a true doctrine, by two professors: Edmond Pourchot (1651–1734), Rector of the University of Paris, who taught from c.1690 to 1700, and Guillaume Dagoumer (c.1660–1745), who taught from c.1690 to 1710.[22]

Edmond Pourchot's *Institutio philosophica ad faciliorem veterum ac recentiorum philosophorum lectionem comparata* appeared in Paris in 1695 in five volumes and ran into four further editions: Paris, 1700; Lyons, 1711, 1716 and Lyons and Paris, 1733.

In his second volume, on physics, Pourchot expounded the principles of Descartes' philosophy, his identification of space and matter and his doctrine of the three elements and of his vortices. If, in his third volume, he showed theological qualms about accepting the Copernican system, Pourchot saw nothing ungodly in Cartesianism (*Cartesius ab omni impietate in Deum est immunis*).[23] The third volume, still on physics, opens with an account of the Ptolemaic universe, to which Pourchot attributed twelve spheres: the spheres of the seven planets, the Firmament of the fixed stars (or eighth sphere), two crystalline heavens (the second of the two added by Clavius in deference to Copernicus), the *Primum Mobile* and finally the Empyrean of the theologians, '... the seat of the Blessed, held to be motionless and square'. Since the heavens were now recognized to be fluid in nature, the Ptolemaic system could, he said, be no longer defended on any grounds.[24] Pourchot then turned to describing the Copernican system '... embraced by, among others, Gilbert, Kepler and Galileo and after them by Descartes who almost made it his own, since with the help of this new method, he leaves almost nothing to be desired'. 'All the phenomena in the Copernican or Cartesian hypotheses', said Pourchot, 'can now be explained.' However he recognized that '... the system of Copernicus, or of Descartes [sic], can be defended as an *hypothesis*, though not as a *thesis* on account of the evidence of Holy Writ. Although the evidence of Holy Writ has been explained more positively in

---

[21] Guillaume Sabbatié, *Institutiones philosophicæ ex veterum et recentiorum placitis ad usum collegii aquitani*, vol.IV (Bordeaux, 1718), p.33.

[22] On Pourchot and Dagoumer see Francisque Bouillier, *op. cit.* vol.II, pp.637–639. On the dates during which these two professors were teaching, see L.W.B. Brockliss, *French Higher Education in the Seventeenth and Eighteenth Centuries* (Oxford, 1987), p.350 and pp.463–465.

[23] Edmond Pourchot, *Institutio philosophica ad faciliorem veterum ac recentiorum philosophorum lectionem comparata* (Paris, 1695), vol.II, cap.V, pp.84–93.

[24] *Ibid.* vol.III, cap.II, pp.11–20.

favour of Copernicus by great men and by Catholics, yet, accepted to the letter, it stands contrary to this system.'[25]

Pourchot next dealt with the Tychonic system, which he appears to have reluctantly fallen back upon. 'Since the Ptolemaic system appears to go against reason and experience and the Copernican one to go against authority and preconceived judgements, Tycho Brahe', he said, 'had, out of both of them, invented a third one.' But in the Tychonic system Pourchot found greater difficulty in accommodating the Empyrean than in Descartes' division of the universe into three different vortices or heavens.[26]

> Regarding the number of the heavens the followers of Tycho generally acknowledge the Empyrean, the Firmament and the Planetary Heaven which they then divide into the various regions destined for the motion of the planets. This [threefold] number of the heavens is confirmed by the authority of the Apostle [Paul] who speaks in 2 Cor. 12: 2, of [a man] being caught up to the third heaven (*raptus ad tertium cœlum*), or, as they interpret it, to the Empyrean. But among these heavens, those who place the *Primum Mobile* above the Firmament have to count at least four heavens and thus they cannot base themselves on the Apostle's text, which the Copernicans or the Cartesians can effectively use for grounding their hypothesis. For to them *our vortex* is the *first heaven*. The whole *region of the fixed stars*, visible to us, makes up the *second heaven* in relation to our heaven and finally the immense region beyond, as far as it extends, can be held to be the *third heaven*, the *Empyrean*.[27]

In his final acceptance of the Tychonic system, Pourchot said it could be more safely defended than the Copernican, since it satisfied the phenomena just as well and did no violence to Holy Writ either in word or meaning. His parenthetic attempt to reconcile the doctrine of the medieval Empyrean with Descartes' cosmology appears to have been the first and only one. He apparently conceded an indefinite extension to the universe, for he stated that '... philosophers and astronomers have now admitted as most probable [...] that the fixed stars are spread through indefinite spaces and that the stars are scattered in them'.[28] It remains more than likely that Pourchot was privately a Copernican as well as a Cartesian, and only settled for the Tychonic system out of obedience to ecclesiastical authority.[29]

Where Pourchot had made a passing gesture in defence of the Empyrean, Guillaume Dagoumer sought to save a universe created by God, in his *Philosophia ad usum scholæ accomodata*, published in Paris in 1702, later fol-

---

[25] *Ibid.* vol.III, capIII, pp.20–31.
[26] Cf. René Descartes, *Principes*, pt III, no.53, *ed. cit.* vol. IX–2, pp.129–130.
[27] Edmond Pourchot, *op. cit.* pp.40–41.
[28] *Ibid.* p.47.
[29] None the less in 1770, the University of Salamanca in its reproval of Cartesianism explicitly excluded the use of Pourchot's work as a possible textbook. See Jean Sarrailh, *L'Espagne éclairée de la seconde moitié du XVIIIe siècle* (Paris, 1954), p.91.

lowed by two other editions at Lyons, 1746 and 1757. 'The difficulty concerning creation', said Dagoumer in the third volume of his work, 'is that the atheists do not recognize a creator; they merely maintain that substance is necessary and therefore uncreated (*improducibilem*).' Rather than the ideas of atheists such as the Epicureans and others, 'in the shades and in the shadow of death', it was the ideas of certain among the Christians which disturbed Dagoumer more, '... not only those of Hermogenes discussed by Tertullian,[30] but those of many who now state them out loud and in their writings'. 'Descartes', he said,

> teaches that body is a three-dimensional measurable extension. This opinion should be rejected on many counts and above all on what to me would seem [to make] space necessary and uncreated. Hence from Descartes' point of view it appears to follow that matter itself is uncreated, a corollary which Descartes, who postulated that God created matter, never admitted. Thus, had he stood out for it, one of these counts could be laid against him. But what of certain of his disciples? They openly recognize that matter is uncreated.[31]

Dagoumer then mentioned a text in French which had come into his hands: *De l'Infini créé* (*The created infinite*), in which the author, whom he did not identify, '... holding matter to be extension, likewise holds that it is necessary and uncreated'. 'He maintains', reported Dagoumer, 'that an infinite number of vortices have existed from eternity, exist now and will exist forever. These vortices have a beginning and they come to an end, others following upon others so that in any instant an infinite number perish and an infinite number are reborn and thus our vortex has a beginning from the collapse of another. It itself will perish, but others will come after it, hence God has created heaven and earth in the beginning and nothing except God could create anew another mechanical arrangement of the parts.'[32] Noting that '... nothing prevented the writer of the text from validating his system by grounding it in biblical truth, as well as by reasoning it out from the principles of the theologians', Dagoumer asserted that he would meet him with philosophical arguments.[33] The elaborate reasonings he then presented to defend the concept of a unique creation were entirely based on metaphysics, and there appeared in them no appeal to revealed truth.[34]

---

[30] A reference to the doctrine that the world is uncreated and eternal. Cf. Tertullian, 'Adversus Hermogenem' in *Tertulliani Opera*, I,1, Corpus Christianorum, Series Latina I, *ed. cit.*, p.397.

[31] Guillaume Dagoumer, *Philosophia ad usum scholiæ accomodata* (Paris, 1702), edn (Lyons, 1746), vol. III, pp.367–368.

[32] The text of *De l'Infini créé*, later printed at Amsterdam in 1769, is attributed by Francisque Bouillier to the Abbé Jean Terrasson. See F. Bouillier, *op. cit.* vol.II, pp.610–16.

[33] Guillaume Dagoumer, *op. cit.* pp.368–369.

[34] *Ibid*. pp.369–374.

CARTESIANISM AND COPERNICANISM

In the fourth volume of his work Dagoumer reviewed the astronomical systems of his time. Following Pourchot, he first described the Ptolemaic system of twelve spheres: the spheres of the seven planets, the Firmament of the fixed stars, the *Primum Mobile*, the two crystalline spheres and finally the Empyrean enclosing all the rest. He rejected it on the grounds that it went against mechanical laws, astronomical observations and physical principles. He then described, with no mention of the Empyrean, the Tychonic system. He rejected it since it went against mechanical and physical principles.[35]

Turning to the Copernican system, Dagoumer said it was '... rather an astronomical invention than a physical machine. None bold enough, among the [natural] philosophers, had searched out the physical principles by which such a vast work of divine art might have emerged.'[36]

> One alone, René Descartes, whose cleverness is almost equal to the vastness of the orb, in describing, through deep pondering, both the interior of the earth as well as the planets and the fixed stars, has depicted the natures of their bodies, their shapes, structures, positions, and ordering, and has mastered their ruling principles in order to fully set out in a truly consistent manner, what he admitted had been invented and thought up by him [as a fiction] in order to explain it to us.[37]

'Since it has seemed to some', continued Dagoumer, 'that the Copernican system ties in with mechanical laws, satisfies astronomical principles and does not go against physical phenomena, they have held that God actually arranged the universe as described by Copernicus. Others, who teach the Copernican system together with those just mentioned, hold that, unless [otherwise] persuaded, Holy Writ has declared in clear terms that the earth stands still and that the sun moves. The Copernican system cannot be refuted by philosophical arguments, but it can be by theological ones.'[38] Dagoumer's conclusion was that

> ... the Copernican system can never be defended as a true thesis, for besides, it is enough that there may be [an] infinite [number of] possible ways by which the same phenomena may be apprehended and we cannot, by means of an elaborate argument (*argumento vastissimo*), twist the arm (*coactare brachium*) of God Almighty, nor can we, from what these ways keep hidden from us, justly deny that they exist. Indeed how can we know that God has decided this, rather than that? Who was his counsellor? Who has had access to his powers? No one indeed, and hence we cannot know whether God has decided on the Copernican system. Therefore this system cannot be defended

---

[35] *Ibid.* vol.IV, pp.371–385.
[36] Dagoumer had apparently never read the works of Johannes Kepler, or of Newton.
[37] Guillaume Dagoumer, *op. cit.* p.385.
[38] *Ibid.* p.398.
[39] *Ibid.* pp.402–403.

as a definite thesis, even were it not to clash with Holy Writ, and therefore at the most it can [only] be defended as a hypothesis.[39]

Dagoumer then proceeded with a critical analysis of Descartes' theory of the universe. Descartes' postulation that matter was created by God could not, he said, be reconciled with his identification of matter with extension. Dagoumer denied absolutely that extended substance (*res extensa*) could be created.[40] In admitting that matter extended indefinitely, Descartes was implying that God had had to produce it indefinitely and hence that it was impossible for us to conceive of his having produced only a limited amount of matter, for instance of the size of a fly (*muscæ æqualem*), let alone of the size of the earth. Dagoumer said that in the past he used to refute this idea because the notion that matter was 'necessarily immense' made him 'shudder at the thought (*horresco referens*)'. 'That its parts are a substance and yet that it is a continuum (*connexio*) so that God himself cannot produce a certain and definite part, unless he produces others, this I do not understand.' However he conceded that '... if extension is itself matter, or steps in the differentiation of matter, these Cartesian principles apply very satisfactorily'.

The term 'world' (*mundus*), said Dagoumer, was highly ambiguous, referring either to the entire collection of corporeal bodies (*collectio rerum corporearum*), or to the earth inhabited by men. To him the entirety of all the corporeal bodies (*universitatem rerum corporearum*) was 'one world' (*unum mundum*) and it appeared to him '... certain that the celestial region has an infinite extension. Its great size is in no way incompatible with a created actual infinite (*creata infinita actu*), or with created matter of the magnitude of an actual infinite (*seu materia creata quae sit infinitæ actu magnitudinis*).' Dagoumer however concluded sceptically (and prudently), 'I doubt whether God would have produced this. He could have, or he could not have.'

Quite disposed to entertain seriously the possibility of a plurality of inhabited planets, Dagoumer cited the works of Huygens[41] and Fontenelle,[42] though he put aside Cyrano de Bergerac's *Voyage dans la Lune* (1657) which he said was just fit to amuse the spectators of Italian theatre.[43] If it were argued that the existence of other inhabited planets raised the problem of how they had been peopled by the sons of Adam, or of how the Apostles could have brought Christianity to them, it could be answered that the same question had occurred in relation to the Antipodes. Holy Writ, he declared, neither affirms nor denies their being inhabited.[44]

---

[40] *Ibid.* p.424.
[41] Christian Huygens, *Kosmotheôros sive de terris cœlestibus* ... (The Hague, 1698); French trans., *Nouveau traité de la pluralité des mondes* (Paris, 1702).
[42] Bernard Le Bouyer de Fontenelle, *Entretiens sur la pluralité des mondes* (Paris, 1686).
[43] Guillaume Dagoumer, *op. cit.* pp.432–435.
[44] *Ibid.* p.440.

To sum up our examination of the works of Pourchot and Dagoumer, it may be said that by the beginning of the eighteenth century in France, the rôle of the Empyrean, when mentioned in connection with the Ptolemaic and Tychonic systems, had become merely symbolic, having lost its hold as a theological reality. The Creation, as described in Genesis, had been reduced to a purely philosophical argument over God's ability to create an actual infinite, or a creation of infinite size, a subject on which Dagoumer was careful not to commit himself. Neither of the two, although tempted, endorsed the Copernican system.

Italy

One of the first in Italy to spread the new philosophies from the north, though with critical reservations, was Tommaso Cornelio (1614–86), a philosopher and doctor of medicine from Cosenza who brought Descartes' works to Naples from Rome at the early date of 1649.[45] Cornelio taught philosophy and theoretical medicine at Naples from 1653 until 1670. His *Progymnasmata physica*, published in Venice in 1663, was widely reprinted in Europe in six other editions: Frankfurt, 1665; Venice, 1683; Leipzig, 1683; Jena, 1685; Copenhagen, 1685 and Naples 1688.[46]

In his discussion of the origins of the universe, after reviewing the doctrines of the pre-Socratics and of Aristotle, Cornelio noted how in his time philosophy had been freed from the former tyranny of the universities by Gilbert, Stelliola,[47] Campanella, Galileo, Bacon, Gassendi, Descartes and Hobbes. All had taken up the principles of the Ancients and especially those of Democritus. Of them all, the one who stood out most was the *ingeniosissimus* Descartes. While full of praise for Descartes' method in philosophy, he observed that it did not explain all the phenomena of nature satisfactorily enough. 'Activating force' (*vim efficientem*) never seemed to be adequately explained. In advancing this concept that nature was divided into two principles, one being matter from which a thing is produced and the other being an activating force producing each thing, Cornelio claimed to find them expounded by the pre-Socratics, by the Stoics, by Plato (certainly not by Aristotle), also by Telesio and Paracelsus and finally by some

---

[45] See Eugenio Garin, *Dal Rinascimento all'Illuminismo* (Florence 1993), pp.82–83.

[46] On Cornelio see M. Torrini, *Tommaso Cornelio e la ricostruzione della scienza* (Naples, 1977), esp. pp.62–69; also Eugenio Garin, *op. cit.* pp.82–114; the extensive article by V. Comparato in *Dizionario Biografico degli Italiani* 29 (1983), pp.136–140 and Claudio Manzoni, *I Cartesiani Italiani* (Udine, 1984), pp.15–35.

[47] Nicola Antonio Stelliola (1547–1623), a Neapolitan scholar, wrote among other things an *Encyclopedia Pytagorea* (Naples, 1616) and *Il Telescopio o ver Ispecillo celeste* ... (Naples, 1627). See G. Gabrielli, 'Intorno a Nicola Antonio Stelliola, Filosofo e Linceo Napoletano', *Giornale Critico della Filosofia Italiana* X (1929), pp.469–485.

who, '... led by the authority of Holy Writ, make the beginnings of the universe (*rerum naturæ*) to be heaven and earth. They believe heaven to be fire and because of this, to have the power of movement and activation, the earth being receptive and almost passive.' This theory, he said, had been expounded by Agostino Doni for whom '... the primary bodies are the earth and the fine æther by which the earth is surrounded on all sides'.[48] In preferring to Descartes' account of the origins of the formation of the universe the theory of active and passive principles, it is possible that Cornelio may have sought to play down its inspiration from the heterodox work of Telesio by bringing in Doni's accommodation of the doctrine with the Creation.[49] Unlike Telesio's, Doni's work was never put on the Index of prohibited books.[50]

In his discussion of the universe, Cornelio began by assenting to the concept of an infinite universe. 'It is rightly held that this universe (*rerum universitatem*) by which everything is contained is absolutely immense and surrounded by no circumscribing limit. It must be accepted that it is greater and more splendid than what the understanding of the human mind can grasp. There is no argument by which we can give to it any definite limits or boundaries. For what bourne shall be conceived to be in them beyond which there is no place, no space, nothing able to contain?'

The size of the universe, Cornelio went on, was a question that was extremely obscure. 'Who', he asked, 'has dared to define its limits?' 'While Descartes in fact makes the size of the universe indefinite, it is human intelligence rather than the limits of the universe that seems to be defined [by him].' Bruno, noted Cornelio, had written of innumerable worlds similar

---

[48] Tommaso Cornelio, *Progymnasmata physica*, Venice, 1663, 'De initiis rerum naturalium, Progymnasma II', pp.33–43. Agostino Doni (born mid-sixteenth century in the Cosenza region – died after 1583) was a doctor of medicine and a naturalistic philosopher who had fled religious persecution in Italy to find temporary refuge in Switzerland and finally in Poland. His major work, little known in his day, was his *De natura hominis* (Basle, 1581). Doni recognized, as Cornelio had quoted him, that, 'God had in the beginning created the world and nature, [...] that he had created it and then given it form and structure.' There were, 'only two primary bodies, one was the earth, the other the rarefied æther which moves through the upper region. [...] The earth was inert, heavy, opaque and cold. [...] The æther was mobile, rarefied, bright, transparent and by nature hot.' Agostino Doni, *De natura hominis libri duo* (Basle, 1581), Lat. edn and Italian trans. by Luigi de Franco, in idem. *L'eretico Agostino Doni, medico e filosofo cosentino del '500* (Cosenza, 1973), Appendice, Liber Secundus, Praefatio, p.298 and cap.II, p.310. On Doni's life see Luigi de Franco, *op. cit.* chap. I, pp.15–33; Delio Cantimori, *Eretici italiani del Cinquecento* (Florence, 1939), reprint (Turin, 1992), p.333, n.3; E. Garin, *op. cit.* pp.15–16 and the notice by A. Rotondò, in *Dizionario Biografico degli Italiani* 41 (1992), pp.154–158.

[49] On Telesio's physical theory, see the illuminating article by Michel-Pierre Lerner, 'Aristote "oublieux de lui-même" selon B. Telesio', *Les Etudes Philosophiques*, No. 3 (1986), pp.371–389.

[50] Cf. Luigi de Franco, *op. cit.* p.164.

to ours, but '... anyone who has observed the heaven, will easily recognize how far off the mark and away from truth are Bruno's systems'. Descartes, thought Cornelio, '... falls into the same difficulties, for his innumerable vortices appear to be a counterpart to Bruno's systems'. In his hypotheses, Descartes, however, was 'cleverer in the precautions he took'. 'But who', asked Cornelio, '... does not see that this and similar imagined inventions (*opinionum commenta*) derive rather from prophetic utterances (*hariolantibus*), than from informed conjectures [based on] intelligent judgements.' Rejecting Descartes' theory of multiple vortices, Cornelio commented: 'Indeed I more easily perceive the whole immense work of the Creator of nature as just one world (*uno mundo*)'. He concluded sceptically, 'Truly I consider the assemblage of so great a work to be above human comprehension.'[51] Cornelio then proceeded to discuss the three astronomical systems, of Ptolemy, Tycho and Copernicus.

First he described the Ptolemaic system, 'very well known and once almost generally accepted', which placed the earth in the centre of the universe round which each planet was carried attached to its orb. 'Beyond was the last and highest sphere of the fixed stars which held the whole world in its embrace.'[52] Cornelio made no mention whatever of the Empyrean in his account of the Ptolemaic system nor in the other two.

The second system, the Copernican, placed the sun in the middle of the universe round which the planets revolved. Beyond them was the outer limit of the sphere of the fixed stars, '... thought to be attached to the heaven'. 'This system, first put forward by the Pythagoreans, was brought out of oblivion by Copernicus who owed his entire knowledge of it to Italy.' A certain Hieronymus Tallavia of Calabria, asserted Cornelio, '... had written something on this system and his notes had come into Copernicus' hands after the former's death'.[53]

The third system described by Cornelio was Tycho Brahe's geo-heliocentric hypothesis. While all these systems were to a high degree in accord with all the celestial phenomena, they were not, he said, in every way in agreement with nature and reason. The Ptolemaic hypothesis with its 'impenetrable orbs', 'homocentric to the earth' (sic), was easily refuted by the phases of Venus and Mercury, by sunspots, by Jupiter's satellites, by the variations in Mars' declination, by the trajectories of comets and by other phenomena '... proving the nature of the heaven to be rarefied (*tenuem*) and

---

[51] Tommaso Cornelio, *op. cit.* 'De universitate, Progymnasma III', pp.45–47.
[52] *Ibid.* p.48.
[53] *Ibid. loc cit.* In his study on Cornelio, M. Torrini, noting that Cornelio is silent on Tallavia in both his unpublished *De Mundi structura* and in his *Astronomia*, suggests that his evocation of the mysterious Calabrian scholar amounts to no more than an attempt to allege past Italian primacy in scientific invention. See M. Torrini, *op. cit.* p.36, n.21.

permeable (*perviam*)'. 'Copernicus' system not only went against Holy Writ, but it also introduced imaginary orbs, incompatible with physical reason, to explain the uneven velocities and declinations of the sun and the moon and it said nothing certain about the place (*loco*) of the fixed stars and how they were disposed.' 'No less absurd', said Cornelio, 'is Tycho's hypothesis. For [...] how can it occur that the sun drives and carries round five planets in its annual motion, while the earth and the moon, which are contained inside the orbits of Mars, Jupiter and Saturn, completely escape the sun's force and drive?'[54]

In his evaluation of the three systems, Cornelio took refuge in a renunciatory pyrrhonism. 'These sorts of hypotheses therefore', he concluded, 'although apparently suited to explaining the movements of the stars, address physical reason much less. It must thus be recognized that, as yet, the structure of the world is, and probably will be, incomprehensible, so that it will be always be hidden in obscurity. For indeed such a work is greater and more admirable than we can grasp with the mind.'[55]

Turning to consider the matter of the universe, Cornelio, following Descartes,[56] distinguished three sorts, the first 'fiery and bright (*ignea & lucida*)', the second 'æthereal and transparent (*ætherea ac perlucida*)' and the third 'earthy and opaque (*terrea atque opaca*)'. Of the first kind consisted the sun and the fixed stars, of the second the æther spread all around, and of the third the earth together with the planets.

Cornelio then examined the nature and properties of the æther. 'The nature of the æther', he said, 'is transparent to the highest degree (*summé perlucida*), light (*levis*) and liquid (*liquida*), although in places it is less transparent on account of the exhalations and mixing of vapours together with the heaviness and thickness which it sometimes has.' He recognized, following Kepler,[57] that '... if the æther did not allow light to pass through it freely (*lumini non omnino pervius esset*), the possibility of observing all the stars and especially the fixed stars contained in the highest and remotest embrace of the heaven would be rendered impossible for us'. As Boulliau had done before him,[58] he noted that were the æther not transparent '... the whole of the region [of the fixed stars] illuminated by the sun, would shine forth in the darkness of night with a certain light'. This, said Cornelio, would occur in a similar manner to the twilight produced by the solar depression angle, '... just as when the brightness of the stars near the horizon is dulled by the air around the earth, producing morning and evening

---

[54] Tommaso Cornelio, *op. cit.* 'Progymnasma III', pp.48–49.
[55] *Ibid.* p.49.
[56] René Descartes, *Principes*, pt III, #52, *ed. cit.* vol. IX-2, p.129.
[57] See above, Chapter 3, p.78.
[58] Cf. Ismael Boulliau, *Astronomia Philolaica, ed. cit.* p.9.

twilights on account of the existence in it of numerous particles which refract and reflect the light of the sun and of the stars'.

'Furthermore', continued Cornelio, 'the æther not only allows light to pass through it freely, but also bodies of any kind, as is obvious from the vapours and exhalations passing freely through it.' 'Such indeed is the fineness (*tenuitas*) of the æther that its reality (*natura*) has been doubted.' Some, he said, had seen the æthereal region '... not to be in any way part of corporeal nature, but to be rather a space or a capaciousness suited for containing bodies'. But, he argued, '... a void of this kind, that is absolutely nothing, besides being incompatible with physical reason, appears utterly unsuited to the propagation of light'. Cornelio admitted that '... others, in defining body as that which is touched (*tangitur*) [i.e. which can be touched] and which hinders and impedes things which move, have said that the æther is empty and void because it neither allows touch, nor does it offer physical resistance to moving bodies'. However, he refused to entertain the postulate of a void, conceiving the æther to be such that, though rarefied enough to carry light, it in no way impeded the motion of the planets. The latter were, he said, '... easily carried round just as ships, at a standstill in stagnant waters, are shifted by hardly any effort or are moved by a very slight wind'.[59] In ending his discussion of the nature of the æther with this scarcely enlightening example, Cornelio gave no clue regarding his position on the subject of celestial dynamics, such as whether the planets were moved by angels or driven by Kepler's magnetic species.

In Cornelio's work, there remains, in his allusion to Doni, little more than a token acknowledgement of the biblical roots of the medieval cosmos. If, in his treatment of the heavens, he readily adopted the concept of a universe without limits, he avoided being entrapped by the fantasies of Bruno's infinite worlds or of Descartes' vortices. His pyrrhonic attitude regarding astronomical hypotheses was doubtless a consequence of his thorough classical education. Although he showed a certain awareness of the contributions of Tycho and Kepler, his apparent indifference to, or his incompetence in, mathematical astronomy resulted in his inability to advance a debate that had still to await the renewal undertaken by Newton.

The introduction of Cartesianism in Italy met with a violent response from the Neapolitan Jesuit Giovanni Battista De Benedictis (1622–1706), who saw in it a grave threat to the whole scholastic outlook. De Benedictis taught philosophy and theology at the Jesuit College at Lecce and later for thirteen years at the Collegio Massimo in Naples.[60] Between 1688 and 1692 he published in Naples a *Cursus Philosophicus* in four volumes entitled

---

[59] Tommaso Cornelio, *op. cit.* 'De Universitate, Progymnasma III', pp.49–51.

[60] On De Benedictis, see Eugenio Garin, *op. cit.* pp.95–98 and the article by A. de Ferrari in the *Dizionario Biografico degli Italiani* 33 (1987), pp.368–371.

Philosophia Peripatetica, in which he attacked the modern ultramontane philosophies.[61] Seeking to reach a wider public, he renewed his assault in a vernacular work, published under the name of Benedetto Aletino, *Lettere Apologetiche in Defesa della Teologia Scolastica, e della Filosofia Peripatetica*, Naples, 1694 and Rome, 1703. In the third Letter, *Contra il Cartesio creduto da più di Aristotele*, he accused Descartes of being a follower of Democritus and Epicurus (sic), 'names to appal every Christian ear'. Gassendi's christianization of Epicurus he called a vain attempt 'to whiten an Ethiopian'. Cornelio, 'a worshipper' of Descartes, he took to task for saying that Descartes had raised his head above all the Ancients. 'What did this mean', asked De Benedictis, 'if he is their disciple?'[62] Cartesianism he associated with Protestants, saying that these heretics liked Descartes, in the same way that Martin Luther had made them hate Aristotle.[63]

Descartes' identification of matter with extension, said De Benedictis, '… was turning divine substance into necessity, or making it corporeal, or making non-being immense. For either [divine substance] is not present throughout space and cannot be called immense or, if it is present and is extended, it is therefore body.' 'Where', asked De Benedictis, 'does this new philosophy lead? First it requires admitting that the universe has no boundaries, and that what ordinary philosophers call imaginary spaces are true real bodies and hence that either the world is infinite as Descartes in fact holds, or, as Epicurus would have it, that there are an infinite number of worlds.' This, declared De Benedictis, was one of the errors of Origen. Furthermore, if we imagine extension in the spaces beyond all the heavens and it is held (in Cartesian terms) to be body, why do we not similarly imagine extension in time, which would necessarily mean that it has always been body? 'But what is this', said De Benedictis, 'if not making the world eternal, a condemnable notion of Aristotle's and which no Christian ear can ever hear without horror?' 'Either God would not be the creator of matter, or in other terms, only by the necessity of nature.' 'In producing a body, God would not be a free agent, but a necessary one.'[64] Descartes, concluded De Benedictis, '… identifies extension with body to the shame of reason and faith. He makes God sit at managing the universe with the sole job of a miller in a mill (*fà seder Dio al governo del mondo col solo ufficio di mugnajo al mulino*)'.[65]

---

[61] It has not been possible for us to consult this work, which is apparently neither in the Biblioteca Vaticana nor in the Biblioteca Casatanense in Rome.

[62] Benedetto Aletino [Giovanni Battista De Benedictis], S.J., *Lettere Apologetiche in Difesa della Teologia Scolastica, e della Filosofia Peripatetica* (Naples, 1694), *Lettera Terza apologetica, Contra il Cartesio creduto da più di Aristotele*, pp.122–124 and p.180.

[63] *Ibid.* p.121.

[64] *Ibid.* pp.148–151.

[65] *Ibid.* p.187.

Some thirty years after this withering attack on Cartesianism, and some seventy years after Cornelio's precociously modern reflections, there appeared a *Cursus Philosophicus* by Eduardo Corsini (1702–65), a teacher of philosophy at Florence. Corsini's *Institutiones philosophicæ ad usum scholarum piarum*, published in Florence in six volumes in 1731–34, was still relatively traditional for its date, showing little overall change in the picture of the heavens. Two further editions appeared at Bologna, 1741–42 and at Venice, 1764.[66]

To a wealth of classical erudition deployed in his analysis of the nature of heavens in the third tome of his work, Corsini added brief references to Descartes' cosmology. While admitting that Descartes' vortices made the existence of only one world difficult to uphold, he nevertheless declared in favour of the commonly received opinion. Descartes' postulation of an indefinitely extended universe could not be defended. There was nothing in nature that could strictly speaking be called indefinite. The world created by God, who was infinite, must have definite limits, as was laid down in Holy Writ. 'The common opinion', declared Corsini, 'held that all the stars did not move in a void, as Gassendi held, but in a very rarefied celestial substance and that, between the stars and the outer limits of the heaven and the world, there was nothing other contained than the seat of the Blessed, the heaven which is called the Empyrean because of its fiery splendor.'

The definition of the Empyrean in the Book of Revelation, there called the City of God, was treated by Corsini with a rational scepticism. Theologians and philosophers, reading in the Book of Revelation that the City of God was 'laid out as a square', have thought that this refers literally to the Empyrean and have held the outer surface of the universe to be square. In the same verse the City of God has 'a circumference of twelve thousand stades', which would give the Empyrean or the Universe a circumference of about 375 Italian miles, equivalent to the distance between Milan and Naples. 'Nothing', said Corsini, 'could perhaps be imagined as more absurd or more foolish.'

After citing a number of classical sources to show that the figure of the universe was spherical, Corsini then, without naming either Descartes or Copernicus, envisaged the consequences of a Cartesio-Copernican infinite universe.

> What then if the heavens are thus motionless and the stars are not placed on the same surface and do not have a round figure and do not move circularly and if it is said that the outer bodies of the world [i.e. forming a boundary to it] do not exist, but that beyond the fixed stars and the bounds of the Empy-

---

[66] On Corsini's life and career see the article by Ugo Baldini in the *Dizionario Biografico degli Italiani* 29 (1983), pp.620–625.

rean there still lies above them an immense mass (*molem*). [...] Indeed all the binding force and idea of truth, which all those reasons appear to support that we invoke in claiming the spherical figure of the world, would collapse and it would be clearly shown how few they are that are made known to us for certain and which we might suppose are clearly and freely given to us if we apprehend something merely by conjectures.[67]

Having said this, Corsini refrained from exploring further the consequences of his speculation.

Refuting Aristotle's claim that the world existed eternally, Corsini asserted that the Creation took place in time *ex nihilo* as expounded in Holy Writ. Holding to the traditional hexaëmeral interpretation, he rejected both Saint Augustine's doctrine of simultaneous creation and Philo's claim that the Creation in six distinct days should be understood allegorically and not literally.[68]

Corsini then discussed in turn the Ptolemaic, Copernican and Tychonic astronomical systems. The Ptolemaic system, to which he attributed twelve spheres, consisted of the Empyrean, two crystalline spheres, the *Primum Mobile*, the Firmament of the fixed stars and the seven planets. In describing the other two systems he ignored the Empyrean.[69] The Copernican hypothesis had been, he said, '... embraced to an amazing degree by Rheticus, Maestlin, Reinhold, Gilbert, Kepler, Galileo, Boulliau, Gassendi, and, together with many others, by Descartes'. 'There were however many things which were alleged against the Copernican system by the defenders of the Ptolemaic and Tychonic systems partly on physical grounds, partly on astronomical grounds and partly on grounds of Holy Writ.' 'Many believe that the immobility of the earth and the motion of the sun are not articles of faith. [...] Others answer more readily that the words of Holy Writ do not have a binding force because it very often speaks according to the common opinion of men and in order to be understood by the common herd.' Corsini dismissed Descartes' notion of an earth remaining motionless while carried round the sun in its own vortex. Descartes, he said, was 'playing with words or deceiving us'.[70] Turning to the Tychonic hypothesis, he declared that it was nothing other than the Copernican hypothesis reversed so that the sun and the earth changed places. The general opinion was, however, that it went against physical laws.

Distinguishing between a thesis and a hypothesis in astronomy, Corsini said the word hypothesis should be understood as nothing more than a

---

[67] Eduardo Corsini, *Institutiones philosophicæ ad usum scholarum piarum*, Tractatus Primus, disputatio prima, cap.I (Florence, 1732), vol. III, pp.8–21.
[68] *Ibid*. disp.I, cap.II, pp.29–49.
[69] *Ibid*. disp.I, cap.VI, p.75.
[70] *Ibid*. disp.I, cap.VII, pp.95–101.

supposition concerning the order and motion of the stars. Hence in a hypothesis truth was not required. A thesis on the other hand was the arrangement of the stars, not only as they are conceived by us, but as they are claimed and held to be existing in nature. Corsini declared that he maintained absolutely that '... although, in relation to all the others which have been invented up till now, the Copernican opinion as a hypothesis is agreed to be more accurate, easier and simpler and would seem almost to be the divine judgement of the wisest of men, it however cannnot, either, as invented by Pythagoras, or as taken up again by Nicolas of Cusa, or as enlarged upon by Copernicus or, in short, as clarified by Descartes, be defended by any argument as a thesis'.

Recalling that the immobility of the earth had been laid down not by the Pope but by the Cardinals, and was not therefore an article of faith, that the Pope had no power in defining these things and that Holy Writ had no authority in matters pertaining to natural phenomena, Corsini said he would show 'by the light of reason and on the basis of natural laws' that the Copernican theory could not be defended as a thesis.[71]

Corsini then, like Cornelio before him, adopted an attitude of Pyrrhonism. He agreed that in the Copernican hypothesis all the phenomena were successfully explained so that nothing seemed to need correcting, refuting or to be desired. 'But should it', he asked,

> therefore be thought that another hypothesis which could explain everything with the same or a greater success was impossible? Therefore out of the innumerable and even infinite number of guiding principles by which the Divine Architect had been able to arrange the celestial bodies and each of the parts of the universe in order to fully display to us the same phenomena which are at present observed, was this, the one worked out by Pythagoras, the one that he chose? [...] Someone in the future might devise a new hypothesis, much more remarkable than the Copernican and someone might also in the future reveal new stars, new planets and even new celestial bodies whose motion and phenomena could not be explained in the Copernican hypothesis.
>
> Indeed the Ptolemaic hypothesis itself had been seen to be the best, had not the received solidity of the heavens and the old order of the heavenly bodies been upset by comets freely crossing the heaven, the varying declination of Mars in relation to Mercury, the phases of Venus, Jupiter's satellites and Saturn's rings. Thus on the same principle, the Copernican opinion has so far been able to be held and defended as the better and more plausible hypothesis, just as long as another has not been invented that is better grounded, in which the same phenomena are explained, or until there has

---

[71] The texts of the 1616 condemnation of Copernicus and of the 1633 condemnation by the Cardinals of Galileo are given in Giovanni Baptista Riccioli, S.J., *Almagestum Novum* (Bologna, 1651), pp.496–500.

been worked out another hypothesis to explain the motions of other stars which this one is not equal to.[72]

Corsini's proclaimed indifference to the ecclesiastical censure of heliocentrisim, coupled with his Pyrrhonic stance regarding the status of the Copernican astronomical system, may indeed have been the product of a sincere mind, yet it might also represent an ultimate attitude of prudent precaution. While apparently still not ready to abandon the concept of a finite universe, his work can be said to retain fewer traces of the medieval cosmos than those that continue to appear in the writings of the more modernist of the Spanish scholars of the same period.

Spain

The revolutionary philosophies from northern Europe reached Spain later than in the case of Italy, being introduced in the south of the country at Seville and, as at Naples, by doctors of medicine. They spread mainly through private associations known as *tertulias* in the face of violent opposition from the universities.

In a letter dated 8 June 1700, the Rector of the University of Seville wrote to the Rector of the University of Osuna (near Seville) calling upon him '... to use his great influence to help in the extermination of a society or *tertulia* which had recently set itself up in the city and was seeking to spread modern Cartesian and paraphysical doctrines as well as others, both Dutch and English, whose object was to pervert the well known doctrine of Aristotle, so widely accepted in the Roman-Catholic schools (*Escuelas cathólico-romanas*)'. Such societies, he said, were causing grave prejudice not only to the University of Seville but to all the others in Castille for '... they were being set up everywhere'. 'They were in touch with each other solely with the object of joining together to get Spanish universities to abandon the doctrines of Aristotle and Galen.' The incriminated doctrines, 'practised only by heretics', were 'very ancient and thoroughly condemned' and they were being 'resuscitated today under the veil of new philosophy and medicine'.[73] The Rector's alarmed plea was in fact directed against the founding in 1700 of the Royal Society of Medicine in Seville.[74]

The new philosophies continued nevertheless to spread, often, to begin with, in the form of selected aspects of them, without necessarily any immediate and entire acceptance. It was the University of Valencia that showed

---

[72] Eduardo Corsini, *op. cit.* disp.I, cap.VIII, pp.102–113.

[73] Letter reproduced by Ramón Ceñal, 'Cartesianismo en España. Notas para su historia (1650–1750)', *Revista de la Universidad de Oviedo* (1945), pp.34–35.

[74] See José María López Piñero, *Ciencia y Técnica en la Sociedad Española de los siglos XVI y XVII* (Barcelona, 1979), pp.425–429.

itself the most open to the ideas of the *novatores*.[75] The two universities which maintained the most obdurate resistance, and well into the latter part of the seventeenth century, were the University of Salamanca and the Faculty of Theology at Santiago de Compostella.[76]

The first critical evaluation of the Cartesian view of the universe is to be found as early as 1675 in the work of the Spanish Jesuit Joseph Zaragoza (1627-79). Born at Alcalà de Xivert, Zaragoza studied at the University of Valencia. He first taught at the Jesuit College of Palma de Majorca, benefiting from contact there with the astronomer Vicent Mut. He then returned to teach at the University of Valencia, where he worked together with other astronomers and mathematicians, before finally moving to teach mathematics at the Imperial College at Madrid.[77]

In his vernacular work *Esphera en commun celeste y terraquea*, published at Madrid in 1675, Zaragoza reviewed the astronomical systems of Antiquity, of Tycho and of Copernicus. The latter's system, condemned by the Church, was, he said, acceptable as a hypothesis for calculations, though not as reality.[78] The heavens, he asserted, were corruptible and of the same species as sublunary matter. They were also fluid, except for the Firmament. Zaragoza reluctantly accepted the Supercelestial Waters: '... although it is beyond us to know why God put them there [...] we cannot deny the truth [of them], Divine authority being greater than human capacity'. Zaragoza claimed that it had been Copernicus (sic) who had assumed an 'indefinite heaven' and had in this been followed by both 'Gilbert and Descartes'. But philosophers and the Fathers of the Church had rightly asserted a contrary opinion. 'It was the outer surface of the Empyrean, either square or spherical, which limited the heaven.' Zaragoza advanced two further counter-arguments. Firstly, '... the infinite [he made no distinction between "infinite" and "indefinite"], lacking boundaries, had no definite figure'. Secondly an infinite universe precluded

---

[75] See José María López Piñero and Victor Navarro Brotóns, *Història de la Ciència al País Valencià* (Valencia, 1995), p.294.

[76] See Jean Sarrailh, *op. cit.* pp.91-92.

[77] On Zaragoza's life and work, see Victor Navarro Brotóns, 'Los Jesuitas y la Renovación científica en la España del siglo XVII', *Studia Historica. Historia Moderna* 14 (1996), pp.35-40; José María López Piñero and Victor Navarro Brotóns, *op. cit.* pp.214-233; José María López Piñero, *op. cit.* pp.439-443 and A. Cotarelo Valledor, 'El Padre José de Zaragoza y la astronomia de su tiempo', in *Estudios sobre la ciencia espanola del siglo XVII* (Madrid, 1935), pp.65-223.

[78] That Zaragoza inwardly accepted the Copernican system as true is argued by Juan Vernet from the fact that he was also the author of an *Astronomia nova methodo iuxta Lansbergii hypothesim ad meridianum Matritensem accomodata* (1670), in which he followed Lansberg's version of heliocentrism. See Juan Vernet, 'Copernicus in Spain', in J. Bukowski ed., *Colloquia Copernicana I, Etudes sur l'audience de la théorie héliocentrique*, Conférence du Symposium de l'Union Internationale d'Histoire et de Philosophie des Sciences (Torún, 1973), in *Studia Copernicana*, V (Warsaw, 1973), pp.284-285. Vernet's opinion had earlier been expressed by A. Cotarelo Valledor, *op. cit.* pp.161-162.

the possibility of a void in which God might create other worlds. 'God', said Zaragoza, 'has not created all that he could have and it is certain that he can create new heavens beyond the Empyrean in the infinite imaginary space that philosophy acknowledges.'[79] With these arguments Zaragoza held Cartesianism at bay, so preserving his conception of the closed medieval cosmos.

How seriously the threat of Cartesianism was perceived at a conservative university such as that of Salamanca appears in the extensive and systematic rebuttal of Descartes' philosophy undertaken by Francisco Palanco (1657–1720), of the Order of Minims, in the fourth tome of his *Cursus Philosophicus* published at Madrid in 1714, a work of over four hundred pages. Palanco, a professor of philosophy and theology at the University of Salamanca and a sometime member of the Holy Inquisition, entitled his tome *Dialogus physico-theologicus contra philosophiæ novatores sive thomista contra atomistas*.

In dealing with Descartes' ideas concerning the universe, Palanco argued that the reason which had led Descartes to postulate an indefinite extension of the universe must inevitably lead him to hold the correlative proposition that the universe has existed eternally (*a parte ante*). 'According to Descartes', declared Palanco,

> the universe is immense and indefinite because whatever space we imagine beyond the world cannot be void and empty, since space and body do not differ in themselves and because of this, space empty of body implies a contradiction. [...] Therefore this space in which we imagine the universe to have been created by God, or the space which the universe in fact fills, has never been empty of body. Therefore it has been a body from eternity and has had no beginning to its formation. If indeed space empty of body beyond the universe is unacceptable, likewise space empty of body anterior to the universe is unacceptable. Again, if Descartes, in extending all about him (*circumcirca*) his imagination and his mind, cannot find space empty of body, neither can he therefore, in extending his imagination and mind backwards (*a parte antea*) or forwards (*a parte post*), likewise find space empty of body in which the universe might have been created.
>
> God would never be able to find space that was empty or unoccupied in which he could create a world. The universe therefore, according to Descartes was not only indefinite spatially (*circumscripta*), but also indefinite temporally (*a parte antea*), in such a way that no beginning can be assigned to it because the imaginable space existing previously in which it might have been created had already been occupied by an indefinitely extended body. Descartes therefore sincerely holds the universe to have existed eternally (*ab æterno*).

If it were objected that Descartes never actually says this, but that he affirms, in accordance with Holy Writ, that the universe was created in the beginning, as a Catholic admits, Palanco replied that

---

[79] Joseph Zaragoza, S.J., *Esphera en commun celeste y terraquea* (Madrid, 1675), pp.43–52.

he sometimes does so, but so briefly and in passing (*per transellam*) and that if we pay close attention to his principles which he follows to justify fully and consistently the immensity of the universe, it is not easy to discern whether he sincerely admitted in his mind that the universe had a beginning, or whether he may have really been trying to avoid the censure of the Church. But whatever it may be regarding this, it is most certain that his principle, by which he states that the universe all about is indefinite, leads us, with an equal or greater effectiveness, to believing the universe to have had no beginning to its formation in the past (*a parte antea*) and hence encourages, on this point of his doctrine, the error of Epicurus and other pagans who asserted that the matter of the universe has eternally existed (*ab æterno*) and is co-eternal with God.[80]

To those who recognized that the universe was created by God (and few, as yet, were prepared to dispute this), Palanco's argument against Descartes' assimilation of matter and space appeared perfectly logical.

While Spanish scholars such as Palanco set about combating the new ideas from the north with implacable argumentation, largely taken from the works of the Church Fathers, the Oratorians of Valencia were exceptional in that they showed a much greater readiness to examine these ideas critically, selecting from among them those which seemed theologically admissible. The Oratorian Tomás Vicente Tosca (1651–1723) is held to have been significantly influential in spreading the doctrines of Descartes and Gassendi in Spain.[81] If, however, he accepted Gassendi's christianized atomism, his Catholic orthodoxy led him to refute the principles of Descartes' cosmology. Born at Valencia, Tosca studied at the university there, later entering the order of the Oratorians. He created a school of mathematics for his order and eventually became Vice-Rector of the University. His major work was a nine-volume *Compendio Mathematico* written in Spanish and published at Valencia in 1707–15. There were three further editions published at Madrid in 1727, and at Valencia in 1757 and 1760. Tosca followed this work with a single-volume *Compendium philosophicum* written in Latin and published at Valencia in 1721; a second edition appeared there in 1754.[82] In his *Compendio Mathematico*, Tosca dealt succinctly with the heavens in volume VII in the section on 'Astronomy'.[83] In his later *Compendium philosophicum* he repeated

---

[80] Francisco Palanco, *Dialogus physico-theologicus contra philosophiæ novatores sive thomista contra atomistas, Cursus Philosophici, Tomus Quartus* (Madrid, 1714), Dialogus XCII, pp.427–429. Palanco's work was the object of a rebuttal by the French fellow Minim Jean Saguens, *Atomismus demonstratus et vindicatus ab impugnationibus philosophico-theologicis Reverendi admodum Patris Francisci Palanco* (Toulouse, 1715). Saguens however does not address the points dealt with above.

[81] Cf. José María López Piñero and Victor Navarro Brotóns, *op. cit.* pp.246–256.

[82] *Ibid. loc. cit.*

[83] On Tosca's treatment of astronomy in this work, see Roberto Marco Cuéllar, 'El "Compendio Mathematico" del Padre Tosca y la Introducción de la Ciencia Moderna en

the general outline, set forth in the former work, filling it out in greater detail and with added material.[84] It is this latter work that will be examined. Tosca began his section on the heavens in the *Compendium philosophicum* with an account of the Creation in the form of a Hexaëmeron into which he introduced the christianized atomism of Gassendi, thus giving it a different colouring from the traditional form.[85] He evoked Saint Augustine's doctrine of a simultaneous creation only to put it aside, declaring that he held to the general opinion that the Creation had taken place in 'six real and distinct days' and that they should not be seen in allegorical terms.

In introducing Gassendi's atomism into his account of the First Day of the Creation, 'God', said Tosca,

> the First Day created *ex nihilo* corporeal and spiritual substances, the latter being the Angels. The corporeal substance consisted of an infinite number of corpuscles, beyond our understanding and which was incapable of existing separately in the form of a further division and which we can justly call atoms. This mass of atoms, enclosed within the very vast space of the Empyrean heaven, also created at the same time, we believe to have been the prime matter of all corporeal things. [...] From these atoms, or corpuscles, [...] God produced other corpuscles. As these basic atoms joined together in different ways, innumerable molecules were produced which, although they were bigger than atoms, remained completely imperceptible to our senses. [...] To these particles so formed, God gave different motions and to a great number of them he impressed an innate impetus, by which they moved rapidly, according to nature, towards the middle of the above mentioned space. It hence occurred that, as they pressed from all sides towards that one point, the more solid and hard formed the globe of the earth and those which remained acquired the fluidity of water. The latter did not indeed form the pure element of water, but they were in number similar to real water mixed with very different substances. Moses [i.e. Genesis] describes this multitude of flowing waters as the 'deep' (*Abyssi*) when he says, 'And darkness was on the face of the deep' (*& tenebrae erant super faciem abyssi*).[86]

The Second Day of the Creation, '... this upper chaotic mass was condensed so that an enormous space unfolded between the upper and lower

---

España. II La Astronomia', in *Actas del Segundo Congreso Español de la Historia de la Medicina* (Salamanca, 1965), vol.I, pp.333–343.

[84] On Tosca's *Compendium philosophicum*, see Victor Navarro Brotóns, 'El Compendium Philosophicum (1721) de Tosca y la introducción en España de la ciencia y la filosofía modernas', in *La Ilustración Española, Actas del Coloquio Internacional celebrado en Alicante 1–4 Octubre, 1985* (Alicante, 1986), pp.51–70.

[85] For Gassendi's christianization of the atomism of Epicurus, see Pierre Gassendi, *Syntagma philosophicum*, in *ed. cit.* vol.I, pars II, sect.I, lib.III, cap.VIII, p.280.

[86] Tomás Vicente Tosca, *Compendium philosophicum* (Valencia, 1721), vol.III, tract V, lib.I, cap.I, prop.IX, pp.366–367.

waters filled only with very fine corpuscles. This was what Scripture calls the Firmament'.[87]

Arguing that there was only one world (*Mundus unicus est*), Tosca recognized that there could be many possible worlds since Divine Omnipotence was 'infinite and inexhaustible'. He took issue with Descartes for denying, in the *Principia*, the possibility of a plurality of worlds and for stating that the matter of this world is immense and spread out indefinitely. 'In this way it would already occupy all the imaginable spaces everywhere in which these other worlds should have to be. This', said Tosca, 'is false, for it would follow from this that the universe is actually infinite in extension.' Descartes' contention that the universe is indefinitely extended, declared Tosca, '... is beyond all our comprehension. The universe moreover, as such, is actual, and therefore either finite or infinite. If it were actually infinite, this would be an absurdity. If actually finite, God could then produce a great number of worlds beyond it'. 'Our assertion', ended Tosca, '[that there is only one world] can be definitely proved only by divine revelation.'[88]

Tosca divided his universe into two regions: elemental and æthereal; the latter occupying the entire space from the Moon to the Empyrean. Declaring that the Empyrean belonged more to theology than to philosophy, he would, he said, deal first with the *Caelum sidereum*. In examining the three opinions that the heavens were all solid, that they were all fluid, or that the heaven of the planets was fluid while that of the fixed stars was solid, Tosca opined in favour of the second opinion. The whole space in which the heavenly bodies moved was a most fluid and subtle æther which he identified as the *rakiah* of the Hebrews or a spread-outness (*expansum*). There was nothing in the realm of nature, even the pores of a solid body, that it did not pervade.[89]

Tosca envisaged three possibilities by which the motion of heavenly bodies was assured: the first that the whole of the 'breathable aura' (*spirabilis aura*) between the region of the Moon and the Empyrean moved, carrying with it the heavenly bodies (*moveatur secum deferet Astra*); the second that they were carried by an impetus given to them in the beginning by God; the third that they were carried by angels.[90] In the first one can be seen an allusion to Descartes' concept of a vortex, but Tosca rejected this, preferring the second solution.[91]

The heaven (*Caelum sidereum*) consisted, said Tosca, of a subtle and most fluid substance that was incorruptible. It was nothing other than a subtle

---

[87] *Ibid.* p.369.
[88] *Ibid.* prop.XI, pp.374–375.
[89] *Ibid.* lib.II, cap.I, prop.I, p.381.
[90] *Ibid.* prop.II, pp.388–389.
[91] *Ibid.* prop.XII, p.417.

aggregate of atoms or corpuscles making up the body of the most fluid æther. Tosca sought to circumvent the difficulty involved in rendering an incorruptible heaven compatible with the tradition of its aqueous origin in Genesis by the hardly plausible assertion that '... water is held not to be corrupted when divided into very minute drops provided that they keep the same property (*ratio*) and nature as water. It can therefore be said to be of the same substance as the very fluid æther.'[92] Tosca followed the Baroque tripartite division of the heavens into the *Aëreum*, the *Sidereum* and the *Empyreum*, 'the seat of the Blessed reigning with Christ'. On the Supercelestial Waters he inclined to the Basilian model, it seeming to him 'more probable' that they were 'rarefied waters spread out like vapour and mist'.[93]

Describing in turn the astronomical systems of the ancients and the moderns, he included the Empyrean in the classic Ptolemaic system, to make up a total of twelve spheres, but in his description of the Copernican and Tychonic systems he omitted any mention of it. His acknowledged preference was for the Tychonic system. 'Each of these two systems', he said, 'can be considered on an equal basis, either as an absolute thesis, or only as an hypothesis. One or the other can be accepted as an absolute thesis when it is affirmed to exist as such in the universe.' 'Both the Copernican and Tychonic systems can be accepted as hypotheses. Anyone who claims that a particular system actually exists absolutely in the universe would be philosophizing wrongly.'[94]

Noting that Copernicus' book had '... first been prohibited by the Holy Inquisition, then afterwards allowed if the passages in it, where it was assertively stated that the sun was motionless and that the earth moved, were expurgated and deleted, it must therefore be held', said Tosca, 'that the earth is motionless and that the sun moves round it. Though it is false that the earth moves and that the sun is motionless, the Copernican opinion, if however accepted only as a reasoned hypothesis (*tantum in ratione hypothesi*), is simpler than the Tychonic one and it explains the heavenly phenomena with fewer motions. But enough of this.'[95]

Although Tosca examined the Copernican system attentively and with a certain sympathy, there seems however no apparent reason to surmise that, had it not been condemned by the Church, he would have adopted it. The Empyrean, referred to elsewhere, he dropped without a word from the two systems he took seriously. On the other hand his presentation of the Creation in the form of a Hexaëmeron reveals an attachment to a tradition long abandoned north of the Pyrenees in the period. If, like his contemporaries,

---

[92] *Ibid*. prop.IV, p.392.
[93] *Ibid*. prop.XIII, pp.423–428.
[94] *Ibid*. cap.II, props XIV-XX, pp.435–442.
[95] *Ibid*. prop.XXIII, p.459.

he maintained theological reservations regarding Descartes' cosmology, also like others of his time, he allowed a certain eclecticism to weaken the coherence of his treatment of the cosmos.

By the middle of the eighteenth century, in Spain, influenced by the vogue in favour of Newtonianism, the Gallician Benedictine, Benito Jerónimo Feijoo (1676–1764) openly declared in favour of Copernican heliocentrism. In his *Cartas eruditas* (1742–60), Feijoo, a professor of theology at the University of Oviedo and Spain's most celebrated publicist of the Enlightenment, can be seen progressively throwing off his theological reticence regarding the Copernican system. Most revealing of the change in the intellectual climate in Spain, closely aligned to one then occurring in Rome, is the comparison of Feijoo's analysis of the Copernican system in *Carta* XX in the third volume of his *Cartas* (1750), with his later assessment of Newton's cosmology in *Carta* XXI in the fourth volume (1753).[96]

The only argument *à ratione* against the Copernican system, said Feijoo in his earlier text, was the impossibility of proving the parallax of the fixed stars, 'though this had been attempted an infinite number of times with the greatest application'.

> For my part I declare that, if on this matter judgement be made only on philosophical and mathematical grounds, I would be the most thorough Copernican in the world. But the unfortunate thing is that after having gone through all that there is of philosophy and mathematics on the matter, there remains an argument on a higher level than all those which have been, or are, put forward. It is that which is taken from the authority of Scripture. I am aware that the Copernicans answer that Scripture, in matters purely concerning nature and completely unconnected with everything that is theological or moral, uses expressions suited to the understanding of the common people, although in reality they are false. But this solution can only be accepted when Scripture is entirely devoid of arguments in favour of the Copernican opinion, and that is not the case. It should be recognized that the Ptolemaic system is absolutely indefensible and that it is only maintained in Spain on account of the great ignorance in our schools of matters astronomical, but it could be abandoned together with the Copernican system, by embracing that of Tycho Brahe, in which the celestial phenomena are explained well enough. I am quite aware that the latter are explained better and more simply in the Copernican system than in Tycho's. [...] But I do not see why God should be obliged to construct a world according to a system which seems the most convenient to us. Doubtless for the designs of Divine Providence of which we are ignorant, the system which seems to us the most convenient, may be the most inconvenient of all.[97]

---

[96] José Gavira's comments on Feijoo's two *Cartas* appear to miss the contrast between them. See José Gavira, *Aportaciones para la Geografía Española del siglo XVIII* (Madrid, 1932), pp.51–53. Neither of the two *Cartas* carries a date.

[97] Benito Jerónimo Feijoo, *Cartas eruditas*, vol. III (Madrid, 1750), Carta No. XX, 3rd printing (Madrid, 1754), pp.237–252.

If Feijoo's cautiously sceptical conclusion in the above letter, published in 1750, is not very different from that of Tosca, the much more confident position adopted in his letter on Newton published in 1753 appears in significant contrast.[98] Feijoo now turned to quoting the French Jesuits in their publication *Mémoires de Trévoux* (1746) as asserting that '... modern physicists were nearly all Copernicans'.[99] The progress of the Copernican system, noted Feijoo, was essentially due to the prodigious spread of Newton's system, in which was included that of Copernicus. In fact Feijoo's interest in Newton was more in using him as a surrogate for Copernicus than for the originality of his thought. The works of Copernicus and of Galileo remaining under the ban of the Church in this period, certain Jesuits had ventured to expound heliocentrism, though in an oblique manner, through the work of Newton, to which the Church manifested no opposition. Feijoo quoted the French Jesuits as noting that in Rome the Jesuit Fathers Noceti and Boscovitch had written on the doctrine of heliocentrism in their work *De Iride et Aurora boreali* (1747), inspired by Newton's work on light.[100] Covering himself with the authority of the French Jesuits' report, Feijoo asserted that the Copernican system, '... far from being an affair restricted to heretics, or to philosophers suspect as regards the Faith, is followed by innumerable Catholic writers and is taught in Rome itself, within the view and knowledge of the Pope and the College of Cardinals'. It was 'an erroneous conception' that knowledge of the Copernican doctrine came from 'the pestilential airs of the north (*ayres infectos de el norte*)'.[101] Although ready to accept the Copernican system, Feijoo still held to a finite universe.[102] He said nothing about Newton's concept of space or about the status of the biblical account of the Creation in an infinite universe.

---

[98] Enrique Lopez, instead of seeing in this contrast a reflection of the historical evolution of Feijoo's position, mistakenly to us sees it as an example of his paradoxical mind. See Enrique Lopez, 'Feijoo y la Biblia, o la gran paradoja', *Studium Ovetense* IV (1976), pp.187–247, esp. pp.200–204. John D. Browning likewise appears to fail to recognize Feijoo's change of position on the subject of heliocentrism. See John D. Browning, '"Yo hablo como Neutoniano", El Padre Feijoo et el neutonianism', in *II Simposio sobre el Padre Feijoo y su siglo*, 'Catedra Feijoo', Universidad de Oviedo (Oviedo, 1981), vol.I, pp.221–230.

[99] See *Mémoires de Trévoux* (1746), art.XLVIII, p.908. (The occasion was a review of Robert Vaugondy's book, *Abregé des differens systèmes du monde* (Paris, 1745). The Jesuits did not, however, say whether they considered the view of the physicists acceptable.)

[100] See *Mémoires de Trévoux* (1749), art.XVII, pp.304–324.

[101] Benito Jerónimo Feijoo, *Cartas eruditas*, vol. IV (1753), Carta No. XXI, 3rd printing (Madrid, 1765), pp.331–347.

[102] *Ibid.* p.340.

Portugal

On the whole, the new ideas reaching Portugal from northern Europe at the close of the Baroque age were at first resisted and then selectively filtered in much the same way as in Spain.[103] In the late seventeenth century, however, the vigorous approach to analysing the nature of the heavens, initiated by Cristoforo Borri and maintained by Francisco Soares Lusitano, appears sadly absent in the work of the Azorean Jesuit António Cordeiro (1640–1722). Rising to become Professor of Philosophy and Theology at Coimbra from 1676 to 1696, Cordeiro was in the end relieved of his post for propagating ideas considered too innovative. Whatever might have been considered innovative in his thought certainly did not concern cosmology, for in his treatment of the heavens in the third volume of his *Cursus Philosophicus*, published after much delay in Lisbon in 1714, there appears no reference to the new observations of the astronomers or to Cartesian physics.

For Cordeiro, the heavens (except for the Empyrean) and the elements (except for fire derived from primordial light) are of a corruptible nature, and were all created at once on the First Day. The Firmament of the Second Day is not solid, but a spread-outness (*expansum*) or a stretched-outness (*extensum*), consisting of a fluid æther, 'not a *quinta substantia*, but the air itself', reaching as far as the fixed stars. The Firmament, together with the planets, was not a new creation but was, in accordance with the Basilian interpretation of the pseudo-Clementine model, formed by air being placed by God between the earth and the Supercelestial Waters 'which are the waters of the clouds'.[104]

Abandoning Clavius' system of twelve spheres, Cordeiro adopted the tripartite division of the heavens into the *Aereum*, *Sidereum* and *Empyreum*, but he made no reference to the Tychonic system generally associated with it. If the heaven of the planets was fluid, the heaven of the fixed stars and that of the Empyrean were solid. Many doubted that new stars and comets could be seen in the former. Such things, he said, are only seen below it. The Empyrean, probably consisting of a fifth essence or *quinta substantia*, was rounded on its underside, but the shape of its upperside was unknown. The inside was filled with a very pure air to enable the Blessed to breathe and speak.[105] Cordeiro added nothing further about the conditions of the Blessed in the Empyrean. Though his work has been evaluated variously,

---

[103] On the ideas from the north and on the Cartesianism of Portuguese natural philosophers generally, see A.A. de Andrade, 'Descartes em Portugal nos séculos XVII e XVII', *Brotéria* LI fasc. 5 (1950), pp.432–451 and A. Coxito, 'Para a história do cartesianismo e do anticartesianismo na filosofia portuguesa (sécs XVII–XVIII)', *Cultura, história e filosofia* VI (1987), pp.23–38.

[104] António Cordeiro, *Cursus Philosophicus* (Lisbon, 1714), Pars secunda, in physicam. Tractatus tertius, disp.I, quæst.3, art.2, p.615 and disp.II, quæst.I, art.I, pp.617–620.

[105] *Ibid.* quæst. I, art.I, pp.626–629.

there can be no doubt that his superficial treatment of the heavens remains far below the level of critical awareness attained by his predecessors.[106]

Almost half a century later the intellectual climate in Portugal, as in Spain, had changed considerably. The Portuguese Jesuit Ignácio Monteiro (1724–1812), a professor of mathematics at the University of Coimbra, while quoting the second of Feijoo's two *Cartas* mentioned above, showed however a much more prudent caution in sharing Feijoo's enthusiastic reading of the French Jesuits' account of the liberal climate in Rome.

In his *Compêndio dos elementos de mathemática*, published in Coimbra in 1754–56, Monteiro, well aware of the work of contemporary European astronomers, described the Copernican and Tychonic systems.[107] He noted that astronomers were divided into two camps, but that most of them declared in favour of Copernicus.[108] Of the latter's system he said that neither mathematical nor physical reasons showed it to be false, nor were there natural causes that went against it. It satisfied astronomical phenomena and observations with greater simplicity than the other [systems], as Riccioli himself had admitted. The Inquisition in Rome had however forbidden it and allowed it only as a hypothesis for purposes of calculation. The same prohibition had been published by the Inquisition in Portugal so that no Portuguese philosopher or mathematician might defend or affirm publicly that the earth moved. The reason for these prohibitions was certain texts of Holy Writ which, taken literally as the Church Fathers had later taken them, were very much against the motion of the earth. But, continued Monteiro,

> the learned Benedictine Fr Feijoo, quoting the Jesuit writers in the *Mémoires de Trévoux*, says that in Rome the heliocentric system is regarded with other eyes. There are two points which remain beyond doubt in this matter: The first is that, in the Church's defining that one of the above mentioned texts be understood literally, the immobility of the earth remains quite certain and all the arguments of the Copernicans pure paralogisms. The second is that so far the Church has neither declared, nor proposed as an article of faith, that the texts concerned be understood literally, nor [declared] that the earth is immobile.[109]

---

[106] The dismissive judgement of J.S. da Silva Dias appears more relevant than that of Manuel Moraes, S.J., who ignores Cordeiro's treatment of the heavens. See J.S. da Silva Dias, 'Cultura e obstáculo epistemológico do Renascimento ao Iluminismo em Portugal', in Francisco Contente Domingues and Luís Filipe Barreto, eds, *A Abertura do Mundo. Estudos de História dos Descobrimentos Europeus* (Lisbon, 1986), vol.I, pp.46–47 and Manuel Moraes, S.J., *Cartesianismo em Portugal. António Cordeiro* (Braga, 1966).

[107] On Monteiro's familiarity with works of contemporary European astronomers see João Pereira Gomes, 'A cultura científica de Ignácio Monteiro', *Brotéria* XLIII (1946), pp.268–287.

[108] Ignácio Monteiro, *Compêndio dos elementos de mathemática* (Coimbra, 1756), vol. I, p 128.

[109] *Ibid.* pp.216–218.

Monteiro's remarks make it fairly clear that he was a convinced Copernican from a scientific point of view and was only held by obedience to his order from affirming the truth of heliocentrism.

The Portuguese Oratorian Teodoro de Almeida (1722–1804) was a much more widely known figure than his Jesuit contemporary. While he was not a member of any university, his career was spent in teaching in his order or in giving public lectures in Lisbon.[110] Between 1751 and 1800, he published a vernacular encyclopedia of natural philosophy in ten volumes destined for a popular audience with the title of *Recreaçaõ filosofica, ou dialogo sobre a filosofia natural para instrucçaõ de pessoas curiosas, que naõ frequentaraõ as aulas.* In it he reveals the considerable influence of the fellow members of his order in France (Bernard Lamy)[111] and Spain (Tosca).[112] Almeida's encyclopedia in Spanish translation proved a popular success both in Spain and in Spanish America.[113]

In the sixth volume of his encyclopedia, entitled *Tratados dos Ceos e do Mundo*, Lisbon, 1762, Almeida dealt with the heavens in the form of a dialogue between three characters, Silvio, Eugenio and Teodosio, the last representing the author himself. Having settled that the heavens were fluid in nature,[114] Almeida turned to the vortices of that 'great and incomparable man of his century, Descartes, the beauty of whose ideas has almost drawn after him half the world of letters'. However, because he lacked adequate instruments and the large number of observations made later, his reputation had 'considerably declined'. His system had been abandoned by the best specialists, having been invalidated by the evidence from comets, whose vortices would perturb the orbits of the planets, or the vortices of the comets would have their own orbits perturbed by the planets. Where Descartes had proposed a universe that was 'full', Newton, said Almeida, proposed one that was 'void' and '... it happens that he is much closer to the truth'.[115]

It was quite impossible, continued Almeida, for any body to move freely in Descartes' space full of matter, however subtle and fluid it might be. The

---

[110] Francisco Contente Domingues, *Ilustração e Catolicismo, Teodoro de Almeida* (Lisbon, 1994), p.43 and pp.76–77. This excellent little work gives a thorough overview of Teodoro de Almeida in the context of eighteenth-century Portugual.

[111] Bernard Lamy, *Entretiens sur les sciences* (Grenoble, 1683), (Lyons, 1694), (Lyons, 1724). Mod. critical edition by F. Girbal and P. Clair Girbal (Paris, 1966).

[112] On the influences on Almeida see Francisco Contente Domingues, *op. cit.* p.69.

[113] See Robert Ricard, 'Sur la diffusion des œuvres du P. Theodore de Almeida', *Boletim Internacional de Bibliografia Luso-Brasileira*, IV No. 4 (1963), pp. 626–630 and Marie Hélène Piwnik, 'Une entreprise lucrative: Les traductions en Espagnol du Père Teodoro de Almeida', *Arquivos do Centro Cultural Português*, Fundação Calouste Gulbenkian (Lisboa–Paris), XXXI (1992), pp.199–206.

[114] Teodoro de Almeida, *Recreação Filosofica* ..., vol.VII, 'Tratado dos ceos e do mundo' (Lisbon, 1762), Tarde XXIX, §II, pp.15–21.

[115] *Ibid.* §III, pp.22–27.

planets had revolved 'for seven thousand years' without being noticeably retarded and it was evident that the fluid in these immense spaces where they moved was so rarefied that they could be said to be void. The resistance experienced by the planets was negligible, or almost negligible, and no astronomer comparing the most ancient observations with modern ones had so far observed any. In accepting that these spaces were 'totally void or almost void', Almeida admitted that light, 'which in Newton's opinion is a substance', remained a problem. Here he resigned himself to again insisting on the extremely rarefied nature of the fluid which was held to fill space.[116]

Almeida then discussed in turn the Ptolemaic, Tychonic and Copernican systems. Declaring that no one now followed the Ptolemaic, he went on to criticize the Tychonic system, saying that it did not have 'the beauty and uniformity of the Copernican one', which was 'much simpler and easy to understand'. In his discussion of three systems, there appeared no mention whatever of the Empyrean.

The Copernican system, as a thesis, had been forbidden by the Roman Inquisition 'for very good reasons', said Almeida, it being permitted only as a hypothesis. 'Whoever says that *the earth moves as a planet round the sun, and that this is so in reality*, does not speak rightly, for there is no evident argument that proves it. [...] However whoever says that *on the supposition that the earth moves and that the sun is motionless, everything that has been so far discovered in physics and astronomy concerning this subject is beautifully explained*, speaks rightly.' [...] 'What God has determined, I do not know and that', asserted Almeida with prudent humility, 'is not the only thing that I do not know.'[117] 'Speaking with Christian sincerity', he declared that he did not 'truly know the secrets of God, nor the highly ingenious mechanism according to which God had thought out the motion of the celestial bodies. However, if He had thought out the motion of the celestial bodies, which we observe, according to the same laws of motion which He had determined for those on earth, I am persuaded', said Almeida, 'that they would move as they are supposed to do in this [Copernican] system.'[118] 'Today if the astronomers were to find evident reasons that the earth moved, the Church would be ready to accept such an opinion. This had been the answer given by the Jesuit Honoré Fabri to a Copernican who had raised the subject with him.'[119] 'As long as the matter lies in doubt in that which concerns astronomy and the laws of physics, we should follow the literal understanding of the relevant passages in Scripture', was his final conclusion.[120]

---

[116] *Ibid.* §IV, pp.27–41.
[117] *Ibid.* Tarde XXXII, §III, pp.227–229. Almeida's italics.
[118] *Ibid.* §III, p.237.
[119] *Ibid.* §IV, p.240.
[120] *Ibid.* §IV, p.246.

Almeida now turned to the 'beautiful Newtonian system'. Ever respectful of the Church's condemnation of heliocentrism, he carefully reminded his readers that it represented 'a mere hypothesis'. Nevertheless he enthusiastically pronounced it to be 'the most ingenious thing that had ever been described in all physics'.[121] Having been apparently unable to consult Newton's works in the original, he relied on the account given by Willem Jacob 'sGravesand (1688–1742) in his *Physices elementa mathematica experimentis confirmata, sive introductio ad philosophiam Newtonianam* (Leiden, 1720–21). In relatively simple mathematical terms, but probably still above the heads of a popular audience, Almeida expounded Kepler's first and second laws, together with Newton's inverse square law that 'Gravity decreases and diminishes in proportion to the increase of the square of the distance at which the body lies.'[122]

Although obviously much attracted to the heliocentric systems of Copernicus and Newton, both Monteiro and Almeida can be seen to maintain a dutiful deference to the decisions of the Catholic hierarchy.

To sum up this chapter, it may said that during the later part of the Baroque age and as it drew to a close in the first half of the eighteenth century, the university figures we have analysed show, with very few exceptions, a general rejection of Descartes' identification of space and matter on the grounds that it failed to distinguish the Creation from the Creator and that it implied that matter was independent of God.

In the relatively standardized analysis of the three astronomical systems of Ptolemy, Tycho and Copernicus undertaken by all the authors of a *Cursus Philosophicus*, the Empyrean, formally included in the description of the Ptolemaic system, is dropped in those of the other two. The Copernican system, while praised for its simplicity and recognized as being superior to the Ptolemaic or Tychonic ones, is rejected, either on the grounds that it had been condemned by the Church for being incompatible with Scripture, or, from a sceptical point of view, it is maintained that there can be no certainty that any system corresponds with reality. It can be surmised that the latter explanation was a way of avoiding ecclesiastical censure, without having to recognize explicitly the Church's authority on the matter.

It was only after the middle of the eighteenth century, with the increasing regard for the Newtonian system and with the liberalization of the intellectual climate in Rome following the accession of the 'Enlightenment' Pope Benedict XIV in 1740 and the rescinding in 1757 of the ban on the publication of works expounding heliocentrism,[123] that teachers in Catholic

---

[121] *Ibid.* Tarde XXXIII, §I, pp.281.
[122] *Ibid.* § II–III, pp.301–316.
[123] The text of the deliberation of the Congregation of the Index in 1757 was as follows: *Quod, habito verbo cum Sanctissimo Domino Nostro omittatur Decretum quo prohibentur libri omnes*

institutions were officially given the freedom to discuss the motion of the earth, thereby bringing to an end the medieval cosmos.[124] It was not, however, until after 1835 that all Copernican works were finally removed from the Index.[125]

By the end of the eighteenth century the Empyrean as a real place had been reduced to being referred to in Catholic theology in the following terms employed by the Abbé Bergier in his *Dictionnaire de théologie* (1789–92): 'The conjectures of philosophers, theologians and even of some of the Fathers of the Church on the creation, situation and nature of this pleasant dwelling tell us nothing. It should be the object of our desires and of our hopes and not of our speculations.'[126]

---

docentes immobilitatem solis et mobilitatem terrae. Text in *OG* XIX, p.419. See Walter Brandmüller, *Galilei und die Kirche. Ein 'Fall' und seine Lösung* (Aachen, 1994), pp.184–185; Pierre-Noël Mayaud, S.J., *La condamnation des livres coperniciens et sa révocation à la lumière de documents inédits des Congrégations de l'Index et de l'Inquisition* (Rome, 1997), pt III, chap.3, esp. p.197 and pp.203–206.

[124] See Paolo Casini, *Newton e la coscienza europea* (Bologna, 1983), pp.143–155; John H. Russell, S.J., 'Catholic astronomers and the Copernican system after the Condemnation of Galileo', *Annals of Science* 46 (1989), pp.383–385.

[125] Pierre-Noël Mayaud, S.J., *op. cit.* chap.6, pp.271–274.

[126] Abbé Nicolas Bergier, *Dictionnaire de théologie* (Liège, 1789–92), edn (Paris, 1829), vol.3, p.52.

Conclusion

The sustained endeavour over many centuries to integrate the structure of Greek astronomical science with the Creation story of the Bible endowed the Christian West with a more rational cosmology than the enigmatically succinct and at times contradictory account in the Book of Genesis. To the ahistorical structure of Greek science, Christian eschatology brought the fecund notion of collective hope, a crucially dynamic factor in medieval civilization. On the other hand the Aristotelian component in Catholic theology enabled the Church to rein in the latent tendencies to chiliastic excess in Christian eschatology, that is the belief that the end of world was imminent.

Borrowing features from Antiquity and modifying them in such a way as to render them specifically Christian, theologians added to the Biblico-Hellenistic synthesis begun by the Church Fathers, progressively shaping it to create the medieval cosmos. Aristotle's doctrines, recovered by the West from the twelfth century on, enabled them to transform the Neoplatonic concept of the Empyrean to become a precisely situated place housing the Blessed, the Middle Ages' most authentic invention. The icy or crystalline solidity attributed to the Supercelestial Waters was conflated with Aristotle's celestial fifth essence, thus providing a rigid encasement to the cosmos.

As long as the fundamental Christian belief in a world created *ex nihilo* at a given instant in time and destined to come to an end in the future was maintained against Aristotle's doctrine that the world was eternal, and as long as Aristotle's principle of a finite cosmos was used to support the finiteness of the Creation in Genesis, the medieval cosmos was able to survive through many centuries, until the Renaissance and the Reformation. However, the protracted efforts of medieval theologians to discover ways of overcoming the difficulties of enabling the senses, as defined by Aristotle, to function for the Blessed in his incorruptible fifth essence of which the Empyrean was held to consist, may perhaps have served, over the long term, to lift some of the paralysing constraints in the Stagirite's tightly coherent thought.

Reformation theologians, in the wake of Luther's revolt against scholastic Aristotelianism, tended to reject the whole concept of the Empyrean, which except for a few isolated authors practically disappeared from Protestant thought. The Catholic theologian Agostino Steuco stands out in the Renaissance for his proposal of three modifications of the medieval cosmos. The first was his adoption of a reinterpretation, by the Venetian hermeticist Francesco Giorgio, of the meaning of the Hebrew *rakiah*, the 'Firmament' in Genesis, as signifying not 'solidity' but 'stretched-outness' (*extensum*) or 'spread-outness' (*expansum*). The second was his resuscitation from the early Christian era of Saint Basil's Neoplatonic definition of the Empyrean as an infinite spiritual light existing before the Creation; the third was his adoption of Saint Basil's identification of the Supercelestial Waters as the clouds and vapour of the hydrological cycle. If the heterodox notion of an uncreated infinite Empyrean was summarily rejected, the remaining two features came to be definitively incorporated into the thought of both Catholic and Protestant theologians.

While admitting the fluid nature of the Firmament, Steuco and the majority of his Catholic successors failed to shake themselves sufficiently free of Aristotle's doctrine of the heavens to abandon the rigid orbs carrying the celestial bodies. Only at the turn of the sixteenth century was this feature finally eliminated when the Stoic concept of the celestial bodies moving freely in a fluid heaven came to be corroborated by evidence gathered by two Protestant astronomers in northern Europe, Tycho Brahe and Christoph Rothmann, in the course of their experiments in applied optics. Intrigued by the peremptory assertion by the Frenchman Jean Pena, that Aristotle's doctrine of the physics of the heavens could not be defended in the face of the optical theory of Euclid and Ptolemy, they were each able, by measuring the refraction of light rays from stars with specially designed astronomical instruments of great precision, to accumulate proof of the justness of his claim and of the non-existence of the solid spheres once believed to carry the celestial bodies. They further added support for this conviction from their observations of the trajectories of comets. Theirs was the first major breakthrough of the Renaissance in which empirical evidence from observations with instruments was used to show up errors in Aristotelian doctrine. While both astronomers were satisfactorily agreed on the fluid nature of the astronomical heavens, Tycho Brahe's reluctance to accept that identical optical characteristics furnished sufficient proof of material identity, and his consequent refusal to abandon the Aristotelian distinction between air and æther, showed a more truly scientific rigour than Rothmann's forthright assertion that his measurements of refracted light rays adequately proved the non-existence of an æther different from air.

If Tycho's prudent approach came to be taken up by a number of Catholic natural philosophers, Rothmann's more audacious claim was followed by

Protestant natural philosophers and astronomers. Later, Kepler proposed a fluid, though otherwise imprecisely defined, *aura ætherea* situated above the atmosphere and allowing the unhindered frictionless passage of both light rays and celestial bodies. The difficulty of explaining how the fixed stars maintained constant distances between one another in a fluid cosmos, however, led most Catholic natural philosophers to retain for a time a solid sphere to hold them, while admitting a fluid heaven for the planets.

During the Baroque age the members of the Jesuit Order occupied the forefront of the intellectual scene in Catholic Europe. Instrumental in an attempted revival of Aristotelian philosophy in the form of the Second Scholasticism, the Jesuits were to play a crucial rôle in endeavouring to reconcile experimental astronomical evidence with biblical revealed truth. In this they were to find themselves faced with a singularly delicate choice. The medieval geocentric astronomical system of solid spheres was recognized, even by the foremost Jesuit astronomer Christoph Clavius just before he died, as being no longer tenable; but the alternatives were the Copernican heliocentric system or the Tychonic geo-heliocentric system. The former, condemned by the Church for being incompatible with Holy Writ, furthermore clashed with the physics of Aristotle and lacked conclusive astronomical proof. Tycho's system, though difficult to sustain on both astronomical and physical grounds, and in spite of its Protestant author being branded as a heretic, satisfied the theological condition of a motionless earth and hence came to be adopted by Jesuit astronomers. Their decision can be seen as the first major capitulation by the Catholic Church in its slow relinquishing of the medieval cosmos.

The continuing retreat from Aristotelianism left Catholic theologians less able to defend Thomist arguments justifying the functioning of the senses in an Empyrean that was still held to be solid. It thus came to be admitted that only its upper and lower surfaces were solid, the interior being filled with a fluid respirable body like air, enabling the Blessed to breathe and move about. The consequences of this development resulted in the disappearance of the last Aristotelian guarantee of the finiteness of the cosmos, the existence of its outer 'shell' being henceforth solely determined by theological dogma.

There was now a general recognition of the fluid nature of the heavens; certain other parts of Aristotle's doctrine on the celestial region put into question by the evidence of Galileo's telescopic observations were dropped too. Otherwise, however, the Tridentine culture of the Counter-Reformation proved relatively successful, throughout the Baroque age, in delaying a complete abandonment of the medieval cosmos, especially in the universities. It further succeeded in hindering the spread of 'subversive' ideas of pre-Socratic origin resuscitated from Antiquity by Italian heterodox thinkers such as Giordano Bruno and Francesco Patrizi.

Among these ideas, the doctrine of an infinite cosmos proved the greatest threat to the foundations of the medieval cosmos. While Bruno forthrightly made his infinite cosmos a material plenum, in Patrizi's the corporeal and the incorporeal interpenetrated. Where Bruno's thought led directly to Descartes' identification of matter and extension, Patrizi's led to Gassendi's concept of uncreated space and to Henry More's only slightly less unorthodox identification of God and space, later to be taken up by Newton. Both the philosophies of Bruno and Patrizi, as well as of those who followed them, ignored the crucial Christian distinction between the Creator and his Creation, which the Aristotelian principle of a finite cosmos had so effectively supported.

During the later part of the Baroque age, a violent crisis, caused by the spread of Cartesianism from Holland into France and from thence outward, shook the whole of Catholic Europe. Throughout the first half of the eighteenth century, Church and State in Catholic countries everywhere battled the materialistic cosmology it proposed. By the middle of the century, the growing regard for the importance of the Newtonian synthesis, as it was carried across Europe to Italy, at last led the ecclesiastical authorities in Rome to allow it to be discussed and taught. Newtonianism, more tolerantly received in Catholic Europe than Cartesianism, besides demonstrating the obsolescence of the latter, led in 1757 to the final lifting of the ban on the teaching of the heliocentric doctrine in Copernican works. At this point the Church can be said to have come to abandon the medieval cosmos.

If in the above we have traced out how the medieval cosmos slowly came to its end, there remains the more difficult question of the causes of its decline. Without attempting to cover the wide reach of all the possible causes, two factors may be suggested.

Having furnished for the organization of the practice of the Christian religion a coherent framework explanatory of the whole of nature, Aristotle's philosophy became, through the flood of ever more refined scholastic commentaries over the course of centuries, drained of its earlier promised capacity to provide a rational account of the natural world. It was the sterile uses to which the scholastics had put Aristotle's thought that drove Renaissance and Reformation thinkers to an exasperated revolt against what had once appeared as a stepping stone to the understanding of nature and which to them had now become a stumbling block. The failing Aristotelian programme led them to seek alternatives in Neoplatonism and later among the pre-Socratics.

At the close of the twelfth century, there was introduced into Europe, simultaneously with the Aristotelian encyclopedia, another totally independent component of the Greek heritage, the science of optics, in which light in the form of rays was analysed with the methods of geometry. At about the same time, a development of this tradition by the Arab astronomer and optician Ibn al-Haytham was also to reach the West.

From the thirteenth to the sixteenth century, the two strands of originally Greek thought remained so compartmentalized in separate disciplines that only in the middle of the sixteenth century was the incompatibility of their theoretical bases confronted for the first time. A theory choice imposed by this sudden new awareness was made possible by the improved precision of Renaissance optical measuring instruments. To Aristotle's qualitative analysis of nature there began to be progressively substituted an accumulation of quantitative knowledge, its empirical character ensuring its triumph.

Except in Catholic universities, held back by the Counter-Reformation's revival of Aristotelianism, the quantification of natural phenomena proceeded paradoxically hand in hand with the Renaissance's resuscitation of pre-Socratic doctrines in which the corporeal and the incorporeal overlapped in defiance of Aristotelian principles. The resulting divinization of space was claimed by Newton as a medium to carry his gravitational force, without at the same time hindering the motion of the planets and upsetting the planetary laws of his astronomical system. Though preceded by the destructive effects of the Cartesian interlude, it was the unlikely alliance of mysticism and measurement in the Newtonian heliocentric synthesis, replacing the geocentric one founded on Genesis and Aristotle, which finally brought down the medieval Christian cosmos.

Bibliography

Abbreviations

GW   Johannes Kepler, *Gesammelte Werke*, ed. W. von Dyck, M. Caspar, F. Hammer and C.H. Beck (in course of publication, Munich, 1937–).

OG   Galileo Galilei, *Le Opere di Galileo Galilei*, Edizione Nazionale, ed. Antonio Favaro, 20 vols (Florence, 1899–1909). Reprinted 1929–39, 1964–66 and 1968.

Pat. Grec.   *Patrologie Grecque*, ed. J.P. Migne (Paris, 1857–66), 162 vols.

Pat. Lat.   *Patrologie Latine*, ed. J.P. Migne (Paris, 1844–64), 221 vols.

TBOO   Tycho Brahe, *Opera Omnia*, ed. J.L.E. Dreyer, 15 vols (Copenhagen, 1913–29), reprint, Amsterdam, 1972.

Epist.   Tycho Brahe, *Epistolarum astronomicarum libri* (Uraniborg, 1596); also in *TBOO*, VI.

*   Copy in the Bordeaux Municipal Library.

Bibliographies, Biographical Dictionaries, Source Books, Encyclopedias, Collections and Books of Reference

Aguilar Piñal, Francisco, *Bibliografía de Autores Españoles del siglo XVIII*, Consejo Superior de Investigaciones Científicas, 10 vols (in course of publication) vol. III (Madrid, 1984), pp.272–300: studies on Feijoo.

Bayle, Pierre, *Dictionnaire historique et critique*, 1st edn (Rotterdam, 1697); 5th edn 5 vols (Amsterdam, 1734); edn 16 vols (Paris, 1820–24).

Bergier, Abbé Nicolas, *Dictionnaire de théologie*, 8 vols (Liège, 1789–92); other edns (Paris, 1829), (Besançon, 1830–31), (Paris, 1852), (Paris, 1864).

Boffito, G., *Biblioteca Barnabitica. Scrittori Barnabiti*, 4 vols (Florence, 1933–37).

Catalogue des livres composant la Bibliothèque de Bordeaux, 9 vols (Bordeaux, 1830–87), vol. *Sciences et Arts*, 1830; vol. *Théologie*, 1852.

Cohen, M.R. and Drabkin, I.E., *A Source Book in Greek Science*, Harvard University Press (Cambridge, Mass., 1958).

Denifle, H. and Chatelain, A., *Chartularium Universitatis Parisiensis*, vol. 1 (Paris, 1889).

Dictionary of Scientific Biography, ed. Charles C. Gillispie, 18 vols (New York, 1970–80).

Dictionary of the History of Science, eds W.F. Bynum, E.J. Brown and Roy Porter (London, 1982).

Dictionnaire de la Bible, ed. Fulcran-Grégoire Vigouroux, 5 vols (Paris, 1895–1912).

Dictionnaire de théologie catholique, eds A. Vacant, E. Mangenot and É. Amann, 15 vols (Paris, 1926–50).

Dizionario Biografico degli Italiani (vol. I, 1960), in course of publication.

Grant, Edward, ed., *A Source Book in Medieval Science*, Harvard University Press (Cambridge, Mass., 1974).

Mémoires de Trévoux, 254 vols (Trévoux, 1701–64).

Lohr, Charles H., S.J., *Commentateurs d'Aristote au Moyen Age Latin. Bibliographie de la littérature secondaire récente*, Vestigia 2, Etudes et Documents de philosophie antique et médiévale (Fribourg, Suisse and Paris, 1988).

Lohr, Charles H., S.J., *Latin Aristotle Commentaries, II, Renaissance Authors* (Florence, 1988).

Reusch, Heinrich, *Die Indices Librorum Prohibitorum des Sechzehnten Jahrhunderts* (Tübingen, 1886), reprint (Nieuwkoop, 1961).

Silva, Innocêncio Francisco da, *Diccionário Bibliográfico Portuguez* (continued by Brito Aranha), 23 vols (Lisbon, 1858–1923); reprint (Lisbon, 1972).

Sommervogel, Carlos, S.J., *Bibliothèque de la Compagnie de Jésus*, 12 vols (Brussels and Paris, 1890–1930); reprint (Héverlé–Louvain, 1960).

Primary sources

Abra de Raconis, Charles d', *Totius Philosophiæ, hoc est logicæ, moralis, physicæ et metaphysicæ brevis, et accurate, facilisque et clara methodo disposito tractatio* (Paris, 1617, 1622, 1625, 1628, 1630–31, 1637; Lyons, 1651*).

Acosta, José de, S.J., *Historia Natural y Moral de las Indias* (Seville, 1590), ed. Biblioteca de Autores Españoles, LXXIII (Madrid, 1954).

Aegidius Romanus, see Giles of Rome.

Albert the Great (Albertus Magnus), 'Summæ Theologiæ Pars segunda', in idem, *Opera Omnia*, ed. Auguste Borgnet, vol. 32 (Paris, 1895).

Albert the Great (Albertus Magnus), 'Commentaria in II Sententiarum', in idem, *Opera Omnia*, ed. Auguste Borgnet, vol. 27 (Paris, 1895).

Albert the Great (Albertus Magnus), 'De sensibus corporis gloriosi', ed. F.M. Henquinet, 'Une pièce inédite du commentaire d'Albert le Grand sur le IVe livre des Sentences', *Recherches de théologie ancienne et médiévale*, 7 (1935), pp.273–293.

Albertus Magnus, see Albert the Great.

Albert of Saxony, *Questiones et decisiões physicales insignium virorum: Alberti de Saxonia [...] tres libros De Celo et Mundo [...]* (Paris, 1518).

Aletino, Benedetto (De Benedictis, Giovanni Battista), S.J., *Lettere Apologetiche in Difesa della Teologia Scolastica, e della Filosofia Peripatetica* (Naples, 1694); (Rome, 1703).

Alexander of Aphrodisias, *Commentary on the Meteorologica of Aristotle (Commentaire sur les Météores d'Aristote)*, Lat. trans. by William of Moerbeke, ed. A.J. Smet (Louvain, 1968).

Alhazen, see: Ibn al-Haytham.

Almeida, Teodoro de, *Recreaçaõ filosofica, ou dialogo sobre a filosofia natural para instrucçaõ de pessoas curiosas, que naõ frequentaraõ as aulas*, 10 vols (Lisbon, 1751–1800), vol. VI = *Tratado dos ceos e do Mundo* (Lisbon, 1762).

Ambrose, Saint, 'Hexaëmeron', in Migne, *Pat. Lat.* vol.14.

Amerpoel, Johannes, *Cartesius Mosaizans seu evidens & facilis conciliatio Philosophiæ Cartesii cum historia Creationis primo capite Geneseos per Mosem tradita* (Leovardiæ [=Leeuwarden], 1669).

Anselm, Saint, 'Proslogion', in Migne, *Pat. Lat.* vol.158.

[Anselm of Laon], 'Glossa ordinaria', in Migne, *Pat. Lat.* vol.113.

Apian, Petrus, *Cosmographicus Liber* (Landshut, 1524).

Argoli, Andrea, *Astronomicorum libri tres* (Rome, 1629); (Padua, 1648); (Lyons, 1659*).

Aristotle, *Physics*, ed. and Eng. trans. by Philip H. Wicksteed and Francis M.

Cornford, Loeb Classical Library, 2 vols (London and Cambridge, Mass., 1934–57).

Aristotle, *On the Heavens*, ed. and Eng. trans. by W.K.C. Guthrie, Loeb Classical Library (London and Cambridge, Mass., 1939).

Aristotle, *Meteorologica*, ed. and Eng. trans. by H.D.P. Lee, Loeb Classical Library (London and Cambridge, Mass., 1952).

Aristotle, *On the Soul, Parva Naturalia, On Breath*, ed. and Eng. trans. by W.S. Hett, Loeb Classical Library (London and Cambridge, Mass., 1957).

Arriaga, Rodrigo de, S.J., *Cursus Philosophicus* (Antwerp, 1632); (Paris, 1637) [= 2nd edn]; (Paris, 1639); (Lyons, 1644 [= 3rd edn], (Lyons, 1647, 1651); (Lyons, 1653) [= 4th edn], (Lyons, 1669) [= 5th edn].

Aslachus, Conrad, *De natura cæli triplici libelli tres*, Sigenæ (Nassoviorum [=Siegen], 1597).

Aslaksen, Cort, see: Aslachus, Conrad.

Augustine, Saint, 'De Genesi ad litteram libri duodecim. La Genèse au sens littéral (Livres I–VII)', Latin text and French trans. by P. Agaësse and A. Solignac, *Œuvres de Saint Augustin*, 48, 7ᵉ Série: Exégèse, Bibliothèque Augustinienne (Paris, 1972).

Augustine, Saint, *The City of God*, trans. by Marcus Dods (New York, 1993).

Averroës (Ibn Rushd), see Aristotle, *Libri tres de anima [...] cum Averroes Cordubensis fidiss. interprete ac apostillis. Ant. Zimara philosophi consummatiss. [...]* (Lyons, 1530*).

Aversa, Raffaello, *Philosophia metaphysicam physicamque complectens quæstionibus contexta*, 2 vols (Rome, 1625–27); 3 vols (Bologna, 1650).

Baer, Nicolai Reymers (Nicolaus Raimarus Ursus), *Fundamentum astronomicum* (Strasbourg, 1588).

Baillet, Adrien, *Vie de Monsieur Des-Cartes*, 2 vols (Paris, 1691).

Barradas, Sebastião, S.J., *Commentaria in concordiam & historiam quatuor Evangelistarum*, 4 vols (Coimbra, 1599–1611), followed by numerous other editions published at Lyons, Mainz, Brescia, Venice and Antwerp.

Barrow, Isaac, *Lectiones Mathematicæ* [1665] (London, 1684).

Basil, Saint, *Homélies sur l'Hexaémeron*, French trans. with Greek text and introduction by Stanislas Giet, Sources chrétiennes 26bis (Paris, 1968).

Basil, Saint, *Exegetic Homilies*, trans. Sister Agnes Clare Way, C.D.P. (The Catholic University of America, Washington, DC, 1963).

Bauduer, Jean, *Philosophiæ clavis seu cursus philosophicus ad usum studiosæ juventutis*, 2nd edn 4 vols (Bordeaux, 1685*). No known extant copy of the 1st edn.

Bayle, Pierre, *Nouvelles Lettres de Mr. P. Bayle*, vol. I (The Hague, 1739).

Bede, Venerable, 'Liber quatuor in principium Genesis ...' in *Bedae Venerabilis Opera*, Corpus Christianorum, Series Latina, CXVIIIA, Pars II, I (Turnhout, Belgium, 1967).

Bellarmine, Robert, S.J., 'The Louvain Lectures (Lectiones Lovaniensis) of Bellarmine and the autograph copy of his 1616 Declaration to Galileo', texts in the original Latin (Italian) with English translation, Introduction, Commentary and notes by Ugo Baldini and George Coyne, S.J., Vatican Observatory Publications, Special Series, *Studi Galileani*, 1 2 (Città del Vaticano, 1984).

Bellarmine, Robert, S.J., *De Æterna Felicitate Sanctorum, Libri Quinque* (Lyons, 1616); (Antwerp, 1616). French trans. (Paris, 1656). There were two editions of the work and twelve printings.

Berkeley, George, 'A Treatise concerning the Principles of Human Knowledge', in A.A. Luce and T.E. Jessup, eds, *The Works of George Berkeley Bishop of Coyne*, vol.II (London and New York, 1949).

Biancani, Giuseppe, S.J., *Aristotelis loca mathematica* (Bologna, 1615).

Biancani, Giuseppe, S.J., *Sphæra Mundi seu Cosmographia* (Bologna, 1620*); (Modena, 1630, 1635 and 1653).

Biel, Gabriel, *Commentaria in quartum librum sententiarum* (Tübingen, 1501); (Brescia, 1574*).

Blancanus, Josephus, S.J., see: Biancani, Guiseppe.

Blaeu, Joan, *Le Grand Atlas ou Cosmographie Blaviane* (Amsterdam, 1663). Vol. I contains coloured engravings of Tycho Brahe's instruments.

Bocarro Francês, Manuel, *Tratado dos cometas que appareceram em Novembro passado de 1618* (Lisbon, 1619) (Biblioteca Nacional, Lisbon, 235A).

Bonardo, Giovan Maria, *La grandezza et larghezza, et distanza, di tutte le Sfere [...]* (Venice, 1563) (seven editions between 1563 and 1611).

Borri, Cristoforo, *Collecta astronomica* (Lisbon, 1631). There is a Portuguese manuscript translation in the University Library, Coimbra, Portugal: Ms 44: *Nova astronomia na qual se refuta a antiga da multidão de 12 céus pondo só tres: aereo, sidereo e empireo*. It is not clear whether this is a copy of Borri's draft in Portuguese or a retranslation from the Latin version. Another manuscript treatise by Borri in Latin entitled *De astrologia universa* ..., written in 1612, is in the Biblioteca Nazionale, Rome, Fondo Gesuitico, No. 587.

Bossuet, [J.B.], *Correspondance*, 15 vols (Paris, 1909–25).

Boulliau, Ismael, *Astronomia Philolaica* (Paris, 1645*).

Brahe, Tycho, *De Nova et Nullius Ævi Memoria Prius Visa Stella iam pridem Anno a nato Christo 1572 mense Novembri primum conspecta Contemplatio Mathematica* (Copenhagen, 1573), British Library: [C.54.66.36]. Microfilm in the Bordeaux Municipal Library; facsimile edn (Copenhagen, 1901), also in *TBOO*. Eng trans., Tycho Brahe, *Learned Tico Brahe his astronomical coniecture of the new and much admired* * [star] *which appeared in the year 1572* (London, 1632).

Brahe, Tycho, *De Mundi Ætherei Recentioribus Phænomenis liber secundus* (Uraniborg, 1588); (Prague, 1603); (Frankfurt, 1610, 1648). Also in *TBOO*, IV, pp.155–162. Partial Eng. trans. in Marie Boas and A. Rupert Hall, 'Tycho Brahe's system of the world', *Occasional Notes of the Royal Astronomical Society* 3 21 (London, 1959), pp.257–263.

Brahe, Tycho, *Epistolarum astronomicarum libri* (Uraniborg, 1596*); (Nuremberg, 1601); (Frankfurt, 1610*). Also in *TBOO*, VI.

Brahe, Tycho, *Astronomiæ Instauratæ Mechanica* (Wandesburg [Wandsbeck], 1598); (Nuremberg, 1602). Partial Eng. trans. with reproductions of engravings of the instruments in Elis Strömgren and Bengt Strömgren, *Tycho Brahe's Description of his Instruments and Scientific Work* (Copenhagen, 1946).

Brahe, Tycho, *Astronomiæ Instauratæ Progymnasmata* (Prague, 1602), (some copies are dated 1603); (Frankfurt, 1610*), (Frankfurt, 1648*). Also in *TBOO*, II (1915); III (1916).

Brenz, Johann, *De Majestate Domini nostri Iesu Christi ad dextram Dei patris et de vera praesentia corporis et sanguinis ejus in Coena* (Frankfurt, 1562); (Frankfurt, 1563).

Bruno, Giordano, *De l'Infinito Universo et Mondi* ([London], 1584). Eng. trans. by Dorothy Waley Singer, in Singer, Dorothy Waley, *Giordano Bruno: His Life and Thought* (New York, 1950). French edition, *De l'infini, de l'univers et des mondes*; texte italien établi par Giovanni Aquilecchia; notes de Jean Seidengart; traduction française de J.-P. Cavaillé, revue et corrigée par A. Ph. Segonds, Y. Hersant, N. Ordine and J. Seidengart; introduction par Miguel Angel Granada, *Œuvres complètes [de Giordano Bruno]* IV (Paris, 1995).

Bruno, Giordano, 'De Immenso et Innumerabilibus' (1591), in idem, *Opera Latine conscripta*, ed. F. Fiorentino, I (Bks 1–3), II (Bks 4–8), (Naples, 1879–84).

Buridan, Jean, *Quaestiones super Libris Quattuor De Caelo et Mundo*, ed. E.A. Moody (Cambridge, Mass., 1942), reprint (New York, 1970).

Cajetan, Cardinal, see: Vio, Thomas de.

Calvin, John, *In quinque libros Mosis commentarii* (Geneva, 1595*). (1st edn Geneva, 1551). Eng. trans. by Rev. John King MA, John Calvin, *Commentaries on the First Book of Moses called Genesis*, 2 vols (Edinburgh, 1847–50).

Campanus of Novara, *Tractatus de Sphera*, edn (Florence, 1518).

Campanus of Novara, 'Theorica Planetarum', Eng. trans. in F.S. Benjamin and G.J. Toomer, *Campanus of Novara and Medieval Planetary Theory* (Madison, Wisconsin 1971).

Cardanus, Hieronymus, *De subtilitate libri XXI* (Nuremberg, 1550).

Caussin, Nicolas, S.J., *Domus Dei* (Paris, 1650).

Celaya, Juan de, *Expositio magistri ioannis de Celaya Valentini in quattuor libros de celo & mundo Aristotelis cum questionibus eiusdem* (Paris, 1518).

Cesi, Federico, 'De Caeli unitate, tenuitate fusaque et pervia stellarum motibus natura ex sacris litteris epistola (1618)', in Christoph Scheiner, S.J., *Rosa Ursina sive Sol* (Bracciano, 1630*), pp.775–784. Mod. edn of Cesi's Latin text with introduction, Italian trans. and notes by Maria Luisa Altieri Biagi and Bruno Basile, eds, in *Scienziati del Seicento* (Milan–Naples, 1980), pp.1–38.

Cicero, *De Natura Deorum*, ed. and Eng. trans. by H. Rackham, Loeb Classical Library (London and New York, 1933).

Clavius, Christoph, S.J., *In Sphæram Ioannis de Sacrobosco commentarius* (Rome, 1570); (Rome, 1581 [augmented edition]); (Rome, 1585*); (Lyons, 1593*); (Lyons, 1607*); (Venice, 1596); (Venice,1601); (Rome, 1607); (Saint Germain, 1608*); (Mainz 1611) [= Vol. 3 of *Opera Mathematica*]; (Lyons, 1618*).

Copernicus, Nicolaus, *De Revolutionibus Orbium Cælestium Libri VI* (Nuremberg, 1543*); (Basle, 1566*); (Amsterdam, 1617*). Eng. trans. by A.M. Duncan, *Copernicus: On the revolutions of the heavenly spheres*, A new translation from the Latin with introduction and notes (London, Vancouver and New York, 1976).

Cordeiro, António, S.J., *Cursus Philosophicus*, 3 vols (Lisbon, 1714).

Cornäus, Melchior, S.J., *Curriculum philosophiæ peripateticæ* (Herbipoli, [=Würzburg], 1657*).

Cornelio, Tommaso, *Progymnasmata physica* (Venice, 1663) (Microfilm in the

Bordeaux Municipal Library); (Frankfurt, 1665); (Venice, 1683); (Leipzig, 1683); (Jena 1685); (Copenhagen, 1685); (Naples, 1688).

Corsini, Eduardo, *Institutiones philosophicæ et mathematicæ ad usum scholarum piarum*, 6 vols (Florence, 1732*); (Bologna, 1741–42); (Venice, 1764).

Dagoumer, Guillaume, *Philosophia ad usum scholæ accomodata* (Paris, 1702); (Lyons, 1746*); (Lyons, 1757).

Dante, *Divina Commedia (Paradiso)*, in *Œuvres complètes*, French trans. by André Pézard (Paris, 1965).

De Benedictis, Giovanni Battista, S.J., see: Aletino, Benedetto.

Descartes, René, *Œuvres de Descartes*, Charles Adam and Paul Tannery, eds, 12 vols (Paris, 1897–1913); 2nd edn (Paris, 1964–78); reprint (Paris, 1996).

Descartes, René, *Principia Philosophiæ* (Amsterdam, 1644), in *Œuvres de Descartes*, etc., Vol.VIII-1.

Descartes, René, *Principes de la Philosophie* (Paris, 1647) (French translation of the first Latin edition, 1644, reviewed and added to by Descartes), in *Œuvres de Descartes*, etc., Vol.IX-2.

Descartes, René, *Le Monde (Traité de Lumière)* (written in 1633, and published Paris, 1664, 1667), in *Œuvres de Descartes*, etc., Vol.XI.

Descartes, René, *L'entretien avec Burman*, Latin text with French translation and notes by Jean-Marie Beyssade (Paris, 1981).

Diogenes Laertius, *Lives of Eminent Philosophers*, Greek text with Eng. trans. by R.D. Hicks, Loeb Classical Library (London and New York, 1925).

Doni, Agostino (Augustini Donii Cosentini Medici & Philosophi), *De natura hominis libri duo* (Basle, 1581), Lat. edn and Italian trans. by Luigi de Franco, in idem, *L'eretico Agostino Doni, medico e filosofo cosentino del'500* (Cosenza, 1973), Appendice, pp.191–425.

Du Hamel, Jean, *Philosophia universalis sive commentarius in universam Aristotelis philosophiam ad usum scholarum comparata*, 5 vols (Paris, 1705).

Durandus of Saint-Pourçain (Durandus de Sancto Porciano), *In Sententias theologicas Pet. Lombardi commentariorum libri quatuor* (edn Lyons, 1587).

Euclide, *L'Optique et la catoptrique*, French trans. by Paul Ver Eecke (Paris, 1959).

Feijoo, Benito Jerónimo, *Cartas eruditas*, 5 vols Madrid, T.I (1742); T.II (1745); T.III (1750); T.IV (1753); T.V (1760).

Fokkes, Johannes, see: Holwarda, Johannes Phocylides.

Fontenelle, Bernard Le Bouyer de, *Entretiens sur la pluralité des mondes* (Paris, 1686).

Frisius, Gemma, *De Radio Astronomico* (Antwerp, 1545).

Froidmont, Libert, *Meteorologicorum libri sex* (Antwerp, 1627, 1631); (Oxford, 1639); (Louvain, 1646); (London, 1646, 1655, 1670).

Fromondus, Libert, see: Froidmont, Libert.

Fyens, Thomas and Froidmont, Libert, *De cometa anni MDCXVIII, Dissertationes Thomae Fieni [...] et Libert Fromondi* (Antwerp, 1619*).

Galileo Galilei, *Sidereus Nuncius* (Venice, 1610); (Frankfurt, 1610*); (London, 1653*); (Bologna, 1655/56*); (Amsterdam, 1682). Eng. trans. by Albert van Helden (Chicago, 1989). Modern edition of Latin text with French trans., introduction (94pp) and notes by Isabelle Pantin, *Le Messager Céleste* (Paris, 1992).

Galileo Galilei, *Dimostrazioni intorno alle macchie solari e loro accidenti, comprese in tre lettere scritte al [...] Marco Velseri* (Rome, 1613*). Partial Eng. trans. in *The Discoveries and Opinions of Galileo*, trans and introduction by Stillman Drake (New York, 1957).

Galileo Galilei, *Lettera a Madama Cristina di Lorena, Gran Duchessa di Toscana* [1615] (with trans. into Latin) (Strasbourg, 1636); also in *OG*, V, pp. 309–348. Eng. trans. 'Letter to the Grand Duchess Cristina' (1615), in *Discoveries and Opinions of Galileo*, trans. Stillman Drake (New York, 1957), pp.177–216. French trans. with introduction by François Russo, 'Lettre de Galilée à Christine de Lorraine Grande Duchesse de Toscane (1615)', *Revue d'histoire des sciences* XVII 4 (1964), pp.331–366.

Galileo Galilei, *Il Saggiatore* (Rome, 1623); Eng. trans. *The Assayer*, in Stillman Drake and C.D.O'Malley, *The Controversy on the Comets of 1618* (Philadelphia, 1960). French trans. by Christiane Chauviré, *L'Essayeur de Galilée*, Annales Littéraires de l'Université de Besançon (Paris, 1980).

Galileo Galilei, *Dialogo sopra i due massimi sistemi del mondo* (Florence, 1632); Latin trans. *Systema cosmicum* (Strasbourg, 1635); (Lyons, 1641); (London, 1663). 3rd edn of Italian original, Turin, 1979. Eng. trans. by Stillman Drake: Galileo, *Dialogue Concerning the Two Chief World Systems*, 2nd edn (Berkeley, Los Angeles, London, 1953); 2nd rev. edn, 1967.

Gassendi, Pierre, *Institutio Astronomica* (The Hague, 1646*); (London, 1653).

Gassendi, Pierre, *Syntagma Philosophicum* = Vols I & II in idem, *Opera Omnia*, 6 vols (Lyons, 1658*); (Florence, 1727); reprint, (Stuttgart–Bad Canstatt, 1964).

Gilbert, William, *De Magnete* (London, 1600*).

Giles of Rome (Aegidius Romanus), *Hexaëmeron*, edn (Venice, 1521); (Padua, 1549); (Rome, 1555).

Giles of Rome (Aegidius Romanus), *Super segundo libro Sententiarum*, 1st edn n.p.n.d.; 2nd edn (Venice, 1482), 3rd edn with title: *In Secundum Librum Sententiarum, Quæstiones* (Venice, 1581).

Giorgio, Francesco, *De Harmonia mundi totius cantica tria* (Venice, 1525*), (Paris, 1545, 1566); French trans. (Paris, 1578*).

Giorgio, Francesco, *In Scripturam Sacram Problemata* (Venice, 1536*); (Paris, 1574, 1575, 1622, 1624).

Gloriosi, Giovanni Camillo, *De Cometis Dissertatio Astronomico-Physica* (Venice, 1624*).

[Góis, Manuel de, S.J.], *Commentarii Collegii Conimbricensis, Societatis Iesu in quatuor libros De Cœlo* (Lisbon, 1593); (Lyons, 1594, 1598*); (Lyons, 1608, 1616); (Cologne, 1596, 1599, 1603, 1618, 1631); (Venice, 1606, 1616).

Gorlaeus (van Goorle), David, *Exercitationes Philosophicæ*, n.d.n.p. [Leyden, 1620].

Gretzer, Jacob, S.J., *Disputatio de variis coelis Lutheranis, Zwinglerianis, Ubiquetariis, Calvinianis &c. Sanctorum vel veris vel fictiis receptaculis et habitaculis* (Ingolstadt, 1621), also in idem, *Opera Omnia*, vol. V (Ratisbon, 1734), pp.206–260.

Guericke, Ottonis de, *Experimenta nova (ut vocantur) Magdeburgica de Vacuo Spatio* (Amsterdam, 1672). Reprint Otto Zeller (Aelen, 1962). German trans. by Hans Schimank: Otto von Guericke, *Magdeburgica Versuche über den Leeren Raume* (Düsseldorf, 1968). Eng. trans. by Margaret G.F. Ames: Otto von Guericke, *The New (so-called) Magdeburg Experiments* (Dordrecht, 1993).

Guilielmus Alvernus see William of Auvergne.

Heckius (van Heeck), Joannes, *De nova stella disputatio* (Rome, 1605*).

Henao, Gabriel, S.J., *Empyreologia seu Philosophia Christiana de Empyreo Cœlo* (Lyons, 1652*).

Hilary of Poitiers, Saint, 'Tractatum super psalmos', in Migne, *Pat. Lat.* vol.9.

Holwarda, Johannes Phocylides (Johannes Fokkes), *Philosophia Naturalis seu Physica Vetus-Nova* (Franeker, 1651).

Horrocks, Jeremiah, *Opera Posthuma* (London, 1673).

Huet, Pierre-Daniel, *Censura philosophiæ cartesianæ* (Paris, 1689).

Hurtado de Mendoza, Pedro, S.J., *Disputationes de Universa Philosophia* (Valladolid, 1615); (Lyons, 1617*); (Lyons, 1624); (Toulouse, 1617); (Mainz, 1619); (Salamanca, 1621).

Huygens, Christian, *Kosmotheôros sive de terris cœlestibus* (The Hague, 1698). French trans., *Nouveau traité de la pluralité des mondes* (Paris, 1702).

Ibn al-Haytham, 'De Aspectibus', in Friedrich Risner, ed., *Opticæ Thesaurus Alhazeni Arabis libri septem [...]* (Basle, 1572*); reprint (New York, 1972).

Isidore of Seville, *De Rerum Natura*, ed. Lat. text with French trans. by Jean Fontaine (Bordeaux, 1960).

Jean Mair, see: John Major.

Jerome, Saint, 'Commentariorum in Ezechielem prophetam libri quatuordecim', in Migne, *Pat. Lat.* vol.25.

Joannes Majoris, see: John Major.

Johannes de Sacrobosco, see John of Holywood.

John of Damascus, Saint, 'De Fide Orthodoxa', in Migne, *Pat. Grec.* vol.94.

John of Holywood (Johannes de Sacrobosco), 'Tractatus de Spera', ed. Lynn Thorndike, *The Sphere of Sacrobosco and its Commentators* (Chicago, 1949).

John Major (Joannes Majoris) [Jean Mair], *Le Traité de l'infini [Propositum de Infinito]*, nouvelle édition avec traduction et annotations par Hubert Elie (Paris, 1937). 1st edn (Paris, 1506). Other editions: (Lyons, 1508, 1513, 1516), (Toulouse, 1513); (Caen, n. d.).

John Major (Joannes Majoris), *In Quartum Sententiarum quæstiones ...* (Paris, 1516*); (Paris, 1521).

Kepler, Johannes, *Opera Omnia*, ed. Christian Frisch, 9 vols (Frankfurt–Erlangen, 1858–71).

Kepler, Johannes, *Mysterium Cosmographicum* (Tübingen, 1596); also in *GW*, I; German trans., Johannes Kepler, *Das Weltgeheimnis* (Augsburg, 1923). 2nd edn (Frankfurt, 1621) (with added notes by Johannes Kepler); also in *GW*, VIII. Modern edn of 2nd edn, Latin text and Eng. trans. by A.M. Duncan, *The Secret of the Universe*, Introduction and Commentary by E.J. Aiton, with Preface by I. Bernard Cohen (New York, 1981). French trans. of 2nd edn by Alain Segonds, *Le Secret du Monde*, with introduction of 49pp, 4 appendices and notes (Paris, 1984).

Kepler, Johannes, *Ad Vitellionem Paralipomena quibus Astronomiæ Pars optica traditur* ... (Frankfurt, 1604*); also in *GW*, II (1939). Partial French trans. by Catherine Chevalley: *Les fondements de l'optique moderne: Paralipomènes à Vitellion*, with introduction and notes (Paris, 1980).

Kepler, Johannes, *De Stella Nova in pede serpentarii* ... (Prague, 1606*); also in *GW*, I (1938).

Kepler, Johannes, *Astronomia Nova* (Prague, 1609*); also in *GW*, III (1937). German trans. by Max Caspar, Johannes Kepler, *Neue Astronomie*, Munich, 1929. Eng. trans. by William H. Donahue, Johannes Kepler, *New Astronomy* (Cambridge, 1992).

Kepler, Johannes, *Dissertatio cum Nuncio Sidereo* (Prague, 1610), also in *GW*, IV. Eng. trans. by E. Rosen, *Conversation with Galileo's Sidereal Messenger* (New York, 1965). Modern French edition: *Dissertatio cum Nuncio Sidereo. Narratio de Observatis Jovis Satellitibus*, Latin text with French trans., introduction (116 pp) and notes by Isabelle Pantin (Paris, 1993).

Kepler, Johannes, *Dioptrice* (Augsburg, 1611*) (London, 1653*), also in *GW*, IV (1941). Reprint of Augsburg, 1611 edn with introduction by M. Hoskin (Cambridge, 1962).

Kepler, Johannes, *Appendix Hyperaspistis seu Spicilegium ex Trutinatore Galilei*, in Tycho Brahei, *Hyperaspistes*, ed. Johannes Kepler (Frankfurt, 1625* and 1635*); also in *GW*, VIII. Partial Eng. trans. by C.D. O'Malley: Johannes Kepler, 'Appendix to the Hyperaspistes [1625]', in Stillman Drake and C.D. O'Malley, *The Controversy on the Comets of 1618* (Philadelphia, 1960).

Kepler, Johannes, *Epitome Astronomiæ Copernicanæ*, Lib. I, II & III (Linz, 1618*); (Frankfurt, 1635); also in *GW*, VII.

Kepler, Johannes, *Epitome Astronomiæ Copernicanæ*, Lib. IV (Linz, 1620, 1622*); also in *GW*, VII.

Kepler, Johannes, *Epitome Astronomiæ Copernicanæ*, Libri V, VI, VII (Frankfurt, 1621*); also in *GW*, VII.

Kepler, Johannes, 'Fragmentum Orationis de Motu Terrae', in *Collectanea ex codicibus Pulkoviensibus*, in *Opera Omnia*, ed. Ch Frisch (Frankfurt, 1858–78), vol.VIII, pp.266–268.

Kepler, Johannes, *Apologia pro Tichone contra Ursum* (1600), Ms edited with Eng. trans. by Nicolas Jardine, *The Birth of History and Philosophy of Science, Kepler's Defense of Tycho against Ursus* (Cambridge, 1984), pp.85–207.

Kircher, Athanasius, S.J., *Itinerarium Exstaticum* (Rome, 1656); 2 vols (Herbipoli [=Würzburg], 1660*) with title *Iter Exstaticum* as with following edition (Herbipoli [=Würzburg], 1671*).

La Grange, Jean-Baptiste de, *Les principes de la philosophie contre les nouveaux philosophes, Descartes, Rohault, Regius, Gassendi, le P. Maignan &c.*, 2 vols (Paris, 1675); 2nd edn (Paris, 1681, and 1682); 3rd edn (Paris, 1684).

Lamy, Bernard, *Entretiens sur les sciences* (Grenoble, 1683); (Lyons, 1694); (Lyons, 1724). Mod. critical edition by F. Girbal and P. Clair Girbal (Paris, 1966).

Le Jeunehomme, Fr, 'Relation d'un voyage de la Flèche à Lisbonne [1627]', in *Documents inédits concernant la Compagnie de Jésus* (Poitiers, 1864), vol.IV, pp.39–40 (on Cristoforo Borri).

Le Rees, François, *Cursus Philosophicus* (Paris, 1642); 2nd edn (Paris, 1648); 4th edn (Paris, 1660).

Lessius (Leys), Leonard, S.J., *De Summo Bono* (Antwerp, 1616*); in *Opuscula* (Paris, 1626); (Lyons, 1651–53).

Longomontanus, Christian Severinus, *Astronomia Danica* (Amsterdam, 1622*, 1640*); (Amsterdam, 1663).

Lucretius, *On the Nature of Things [De Natura Rerum]*, Latin text and Eng. trans. by W.H.D. Rouse, revised by Martin F. Smith, Loeb Classical Library (Cambridge, Mass. and London, 1992).

Luther, Martin, *In primum librum Mose enarrationes* (Nuremberg, 1544, 1550*); Eng. trans. by George V. Schick in Martin Luther, 'Lectures on Genesis', Chapters 1–5, in Jaroslav Pelican, ed., *Luther's Works*, vol.I (Saint Louis, 1958).

Luther, Martin, 'Enarrationes Martini Lutheri in Epistolas D. Petri duas ... (1525)', in idem, *Opera*, vol.V (Wittenberg, 1554*), ff.439^r–500^v.

Lydyat, Thomas, *Prælectio astronomica de natura cœli & conditionibus elementorum* (London, 1605).

Magini, G. Antonio, *Novæ Cælestium Orbium Theorica congruentes cum observationes Copernici* (Venice, 1589*).

Maloni, Daniel, *Scolasticae Bibliothecae in secundum librum Sententiarum, Tomus Primus* (Venice, 1596).

Martianus Capella, *De Nuptiis Philologiae et Mercurii*, ed. A. Dick (Leipzig, 1925). Eng. trans. with commentary, 'The Marriage of Philology and Mercury', in W.H. Stahl and Richard Johnston, *Martianus Capella and the Seven Liberal Arts* (New York, 1977) vol.II.

Melanchthon, Philipp, *Initia doctrinae physicae* (Wittenberg, 1549); *Doctrinae physicae elementa, sive initia* (Lyons, 1552*); also reprinted in *Corpus Reformatorum*, vol.13 (Halle, 1834).

Mersenne, Marin, *Quæstiones celeberrimæ in Genesim* (Paris, 1623).

Michael Scot, 'Super auctore spere cum questionibus', in Lynn Thorndike, ed., *The Sphere of Sacrobosco and its Commentators* (Chicago, 1949).

Molina, Luis de, S.J.,'Tractatus de Opere sex dierum', in *In primam D. Thomæ partem, in duos tomos divisa* (Lyons, 1593); (Lyons, 1621).

Monteiro, Ignácio, S.J., *Compêndio dos elementos de mathemática*, 2 vols (Coimbra, 1754–56).

More, Henry, *Enchiridion Metaphysicum* (London, 1671*).

Morin, Jean-Baptiste, *Responsio pro telluris quiete ad I. Lansbergi Apologiam pro telluris motu* (Paris, 1634).

Morin, Jean-Baptiste, *Astrologia Gallica* (The Hague, 1661*).

Müler, Nicolaus, *Institutionum astronomicarum libri duo* (Groningen, 1616*, 1649).

Mulerius, Nicolaus, see: Müler, Nicolaus.

Muñoz, Jerónimo, *Libro del Nuevo Cometa y del lugar donde se hazen; y como se vera por las Parallaxas quan lexos estan de tierra; y del Prognostico deste* (Valencia, 1573*). French trans. (Paris, 1574); Latin trans. (Antwerp, 1575). Modern edn, transcription in modern Spanish with Eng. trans. and facsimile of Spanish original with introduction, notes and appendices by Victor Navarro Brotóns (Valencia, 1981).

Muñoz, Jerónimo (Hieronymi Munnos), *Commentaria Plinii libri segundi De Naturali Historia*, in Victor Navarro Brotóns and Enrique Rodriguez Galdeano, *Matemáticas, cosmología y humanismo en la España del siglo XVI. Los Comentarios al segundo libro de la Historia Natural de Plinio de Jerónomo Muñoz*, Latin text with Spanish trans. and introduction by Victor Navarro Brotóns (Valencia, 1998).

Nabod, Valentin, *Primarum de Coelo et Terra Institutionum [...] libri tres* (Venice, 1573).

Nancelius, Nicolaus, *Petri Rami Vita* (Paris, 1595), ed. with Eng. trans. by Peter Sharrat, *Humanistica Lovaniensia* XXIV (1975), pp.161–277.

Neander, Michael, *Elementa sphæricæ doctrinæ seu de primo motu* (Basle, 1561).

Newton, Isaac, *De Gravitatione et Aequipondio Fluidorum*, Eng. trans. with Latin text in *Unpublished Scientific Papers of Isaac Newton: A Selection from the Portsmouth Collection in the University Library, Cambridge, chosen, edited and translated by A. Rupert Hall and Marie Boas* (Cambridge, 1962), pp.89–156. French edition with Latin text, French trans., introduction and notes by

Marie Françoise Biarnais (Paris, 1985). The *De Gravitatione* is dated by Madame Biarnais to between 1662 and 1665. B.J.T. Dobbs gives substantial reasons for dating it to '1684 or early 1684/5'. Cf. B.J.T. Dobbs, *The Janus Faces of Genius, the Role of Alchemy in Newton's Thought* (Cambridge, 1991), pp.141–144.

Newton, Isaac, *Philosophiæ Naturalis. Principia Mathematica*, Eng. trans. from the 2nd edn 1713, by Andrew Motte, 1729, ed. Florian Cajori (Berkeley and London,1934), new edn (1962).

Nicolas of Cusa, *Of Learned Ignorance [De Docta Ignorantia]*, Eng. trans. Fr Germain Heron with introduction by Dr D.J.B. Hawkins (New Haven, 1954).

Nicolas of Cusa, 'Complementum theologicum', [1453] in idem, *Opera Omnia*, chap. VI (Basle, 1565).

Oreggi, Agostino (Augustinus Oregius), *De Opere sex dierum tractatus quattuor* (Rome, 1625, 1632).

Origen, see Origène.

Origène, *Homélies sur la Genèse*, I, 2, texte latin, trad. fr. et notes de Louis Doutreleau, S.J., Sources chrétiennes, No. 7bis (Paris, 1976).

Oviedo, Francisco de, S.J., *Integer Cursus Philosophicus* (Lyons, 1640*); 2 vols (Lyons, 1651, 1663).

Palanco, Francisco, S.J., *Dialogus physico-theologicus contra philosophiæ novatores siue thomista contra atomistas, Cursus Philosophici, Tomus Quartus* (Madrid, 1714) (microfilm in the Bordeaux Municipal Library).

Paracelsus, Theophrastus Philippus Aureolus Bombastus von Hohenheim, *De Meteoris liber unus* (Basle, 1569*).

Patrizi, Francesco, *De Rerum Natura libri II priores. Alter de spacio physico; alter de spacio mathematico* (Ferrara, 1587). Both sections were republished in Patrizi's *Nova de Universis Philosophia*. The section *De Spacio Physico* has been translated into English by Benjamin Brickman, 'On physical space. Francesco Patrizi', *Journal of the History of Ideas* 4 (1943), pp.224–245.

Patrizi, Francesco, *Nova de Universis Philosophia libris quinquaginta comprehensa* (Ferrara, 1591); (Venice, 1593).

Pena, Jean, *De Usu optices Præfatio*, in Jean Pena, ed., *Euclidis Optica et Catoptrica* (Paris, 1557). Pena's preface was reprinted in Peter Ramus, *Collectaneæ Præfationes Epistolæ Orationes* (Marburg, 1599), pp.140–157.

Peñafiel, Ildephonso de, S.J., *Cursus integri Philosophici* (Lyons, vol.I, 1653*; vols II & III, 1655*; vol.IV, 1670*).

Pereyra, Benito, S.J., *Prior tomus Commentariorum et Disputationum in Genesim* (Lyons, 1590, 1607); (Ingolstadt, 1590); (Rome, 1591); (Cologne, 1601, 1607, 1622, 1685); (Venice, 1607); (Mainz, 1612).

Petau, Denis, S.J., 'De sex primorum mundi dierum Opificio', in idem, *Theologica dogmata* (Paris, 1644). Also in idem, *Opus de theologicis dogmatibus*, vol.III (Antwerp, 1700).

Peter Lombard, see: Petri Lombardi.

Petri Lombardi, Magistri, *Sententiae in IV libris distinctae*, Liber I & II, Spicilegium Bonaventurianum, ed. PP. Collegii S. Bonaventurae Ad Claras Aquas, Grottaferrata, vol.I, pars II, Liber I et II (Rome, 1971).

Peucer, Caspar, *Historia carcerum et liberationis divinæ* (Zurich, 1605).

Philo of Alexandria, *De Somnis*, Greek text with Eng. trans. by F.H. Colson and G.W. Whitaker, Loeb Classical Library (London and Cambridge, Mass., 1949).

Pierre d'Ailly, 'Quatuordecim questiones in Spheram', in *Spheram noviter recognita* (Florence, 1518).

Pliny, *Natural History*, Latin text with Eng. trans. by H. Rackham, Loeb Classical Library (London and Cambridge, Mass., 1949).

Pourchot, Edmond, *Institutio philosophica ad faciliorem veterum ac recentiorum philosophorum lectionem comparata*, 5 vols (Paris, 1695*); (Paris, 1700); (Lyons, 1711 and 1716); (Paris and Lyons, 1733).

Procopius of Gaza, 'Commentaria in Genesim', in Migne, *Pat. Grec.* vol.87.

Pseudo-Clement, *Die Pseudoklementinen, II Rekognitionen in Rufins Übersetzung*, ed. Bernhard Rehm (Berlin, 1965).

Pseudo-Dionysius (Denys l'Aréopagite), *La hiérarchie céleste*, intr. par René Roques, étude et texte critiques par Günther Heil, trad. et notes par Maurice de Gandillac, Sources chrétiennes 58 (Paris, 1958), 2nd edn (Paris, 1970).

Ptolemy, Claudius, *L'Optique de Claude Ptolémée dans la version latine d'après l'arabe l'Emir Eugène de Sicile*. Critical edition of Latin text by Albert Lejeune (Louvain, 1956).

Ptolemy, Claudius, 'Optics, V'. Extract on atmospheric refraction, Eng. trans. in M.R. Cohen and I.E. Drabkin, *A Source Book in Greek Science* (Cambridge, Mass., 1958), pp.281–283.

Raban Maur, 'Commentaria in Genesim', in Migne, *Pat. Lat.* vol.111.

Régis, Pierre-Sylvain, *Système de Philosophie contenant la logique, la métaphysique, la physique et la morale* (Paris, 1690); 7 vols in-12° (Paris/Lyons, 1691).

Riccioli, Giovanni Baptista, S.J., *Almagestum Novum*, 2 vols (Bologna, 1651*).

Risner, Friedrich, ed., *Opticæ thesaurus Alhazeni Arabis libri septem [...] Item Vitellionis [...]* (Basle, 1572*); reprint (New York, 1972).

Rivalier, Joseph, *Propugnatio philosophiæ thomisticæ contra Cartesium, Gassendum, Cabeum*, 4 vols (Toulouse, 1683*).

Roa, Martin de, S.J., *Estado de los Bienaventurados en el Cielo* (Seville, 1624, 1626); (Gerona, 1627); (Huesca, 1628); (Lisbon, 1630); (Barcelona, 1631); (Madrid, 1645, 1653); (Alcalà, 1663). Italian trans. (Orvieto, 1626); (Milan, 1628). Portuguese trans. (Lisbon, 1628). French trans. (Lyons, 1631). German trans. (? 1639).

Robert Grosseteste, *Hexaëmeron*, ed. Richard Dales and Servus Gieben, O.F.M. Auctores Britannici Medii Aevi VI (Oxford, 1982). Eng. trans., *On the six days of Creation. A translation of the Hexaëmeron*, by C.F.I. Martin, Auctores Britannici Medii Aevi, VI (2) (Oxford, 1995).

Rohault, Jacques, *Traité de Physique* (Paris, 1671, 1672, 1675, 1682, 1705, 1723, 1730).

Rosaccio, Giuseppe, *Teatro del cielo e della terra* (Treviso, 1591) (eleven editions between 1591 and 1693).

Roslin, Helisäeus, *De Opere Dei Creationis seu de Mundo Hypotheses* (Frankfurt, 1597).

Rothmann, Christoph, 'Mathematici descriptio accurata cometæ anni 1585', in Willebrord Snell, *Descriptio cometæ qui anno 1618 mense Novembri effulsit* (Leiden, 1619), pp.69–154.

Rothmann, Christoph, *Observationum stellarum fixarum liber primus*, Murhardsch Bibiothek der Stadt Kassel, 2° Ms Astr. 5 nr 7, cap.23, ff.68^v–71^v partially printed in 'Appendice', in Miguel Angel Granada, 'Il problema astronomico-cosmologico e le sacre scritture dopo Copernico: Christoph Rothmann e la "teoria dell'acccomodazione"', *Rivista di storia della filosofia* 51 (1996), pp. 823–828. Idem. *Ms cit.*, cap 18, ff.51v–58v, printed by Miguel Angel Granada, 'Eliminazione delle sfere celesti e ipotesi astronomiche in un inedito di Christoph Rothmann. L'influenza di Jean Pena e la polemica con Pietro Ramo', in *Rivista di storia della filosofia* 52 (1997), pp.799–821.

Rupert of Deutz, 'In Genesim', in *De Trinitate et operibus eius*, Corpus Christianorum Continuatio Medievales, ed. H. Haake, XXI (1971).

Sabbatié, Guillaume (also spelt Sabatier), *Institutiones philosophicæ ex veterum et recentiorum placitis ad usum collegii aquitani*, 4 vols (Bordeaux, 1716–18*); 4 vols (Bordeaux, 1724*).

Saguens, Jean, *Atomismus demontratus et vindicatus ab impugnationibus philosophico-theologicis Reverendi admodum Patris Francisci Palanco* (Toulouse, 1715*).

Scheiner, Christoph, S.J., *Refractiones Coelestes, sive Solis Elliptici Phænomenon Illustratum* (Ingolstadt, 1617).

Schyrlaeus de Rheita, Anton Maria, *Oculus Enoch et Eliæ, sive radius sydereomysticus* (Antwerp, 1645).

Semple, Hugo (Hugh Sempill), S.J., *Mathematicis Disciplinis Libri Duodecim* (Antwerp, 1635*).

Serbelloni, Sigismondi, *Philosophia Ticinensis*, 2 vols (Milan, 1657–63*).

Snell, Willebrord, *Descriptio cometæ qui anno 1618 mense Novembri effulsit* (Leiden, 1619).

Soares (Soares Lusitano), Francisco, S.J., *Cursus Philosophicus*, 2 vols in-fol. (Coimbra, 1651); (Evora, 1670, 1701–3).

Steuco, Agostino, *Recognitio veteris testamenti ad hebraicam veritatem* (Venice, 1529*); (Lyons, 1531).

Steuco, Agostino, *Enarrationum in Psalmos pars prima* (Lyons, 1533, 1548*).

Steuco, Agostino, *Cosmopoeia* (Lyons, 1535*).

Steuco, Agostino, *De Perenni Philosophia* (Lyons, 1540); (Basle, 1542*); reprint Johnson Reprints (New York, 1972).

Steuco, Agostino, *Opera Omnia* (Paris, 1577–78*); 3 vols (Venice, 1591).

Stevin, Simon, *Hypomnemata*, Latin trans. from the Dutch by Willebrord Snell (Leyden, 1605–08).

Suarez, Francisco, S.J., *Commentariorum ac Disputationum in tertiam partem D. Thomæ, Tomus Secundus* (Alcalá, 1592); (Lyons, 1594); (Madrid, 1598); (Mainz, 1616).

Suarez, Francisco, S.J., *Metaphysicarum Disputationum* (Salamanca, 1597); (Mainz, 1600, 1605, 1614, 1630); (Paris, 1605*); (Paris, 1619); (Geneva, 1608, 1614, 1636); (Cologne, 1608, 1620); (Venice, 1610, 1619). Reprint (Hildesheim, 1965).

Suarez, Francisco, S.J., *De Opere sex dierum* (Lyons, 1621).

Tanner, Adam, S.J., *Dissertatio peripatetico-theologica de coelis* (Ingolstadt, 1621).

Tellez, Balthasar, S.J., *Summa Universæ Philosophiæ* (Lisbon, 1642); (Paris, 1644); 2 vols (Lisbon, 1651–52).

Tertullian, Quintus Septimius, 'De præscriptionibus hæreticorum', in *Tertulliani Opera*, Corpus Christianorum, Series Latina I (Turnhout, Belgium, 1954), pp. 187–224.

Tertullian, Quintus Septimius, 'Adversus Hermogenem' in *ibid.*, pp.397–435.

Tertullian, Quintus Septimius, 'Adversus Valentianos' in *ibid.*, Series Latina II, pp.753–778.

Theodoretus, 'Beati Theodoreti in loca difficili Scriptura Sacræ questiones selectæ', in Migne, *Pat. Grec.* vol.80.

Thierry of Chartres, 'Magister Theodorici Carnotensis Tractatus', in N. Haring, 'The Creation and Creator of the World according to Thierry of Chartres and Clarenbaldus of Arras', *Archives d'histoire doctrinale et littéraire du Moyen Age* 30 (1955), pp.184–200.

Thomas Aquinas, *Summa Theologiæ*, 1ª, 65–74, Latin text, Eng. trans. and notes by William Wallace, O.P. vol.10, 'Cosmogony' (London and New York, 1967).

Thomas Aquinas, *Summa Theologiæ*, 3ª, Latin text, Eng. trans., notes and glossary by C. Thomas Moore, O.P. vol.55, 'The Resurrection of the Lord' (London and New York, 1976).

Thomas Aquinas, *Scriptum super libros sententiarum*, ed. R.P. Mandonnet, vols I & II (Paris, 1929).

Thomas Aquinas, *Scriptum super libros sententiarum*, ed. Maria Fabianus Moos, vol. III (Paris, 1933).

Thomas Aquinas, *Commentum in quatuor libros sententiarum*, volumen secundum, pars altera, edn (Parma, 1858).

Tolosani, Giovanni Maria, 'Opusculum quartum de coelo supremo immobili et terra infima stabili, ceterisque coelis et elementis intermediis mobilibus', [1546/47], a fourth appendix later added to his *De Veritate S. Scriptura* (completed in 1544), Biblioteca Nazionale di Firenze, Ms Conventi Sopressi, J.I.25, f.340ʳ, printed by Eugenio Garin, 'Alle origini della polemica anticopernicana', *Studia Copernicana* VI (1973), pp.31–42.

Tosca, Tomás Vicente, *Compendio Mathematico*, 9 vols (Valencia, 1707–15); 9 vols (Madrid, 1727).

Tosca, Tomás Vicente, *Compendium philosophicum*, 5 vols (Valencia, 1721); 7 vols (Valencia, 1754). Portuguese edn 5 vols (Lisbon, 1752–54).

Tostado de Rivera Madrigal, Alphonso de, *Opera omnia* (Venice, 1507–30, 1547, 1596, 1615); 13 vols (Cologne, 1613*).

Ursus, see Baer, Nicolai Reymers.

Vespasiano da Bisticci, *Vite di Uomini Illustri* [15th century], 3 vols (Bologna, 1893).

Vincent, Jean, *Cursus philosophicus*, 5 vols (Toulouse, 1662*).

Vincent, Jean, *Discussio peripatetica in qua philosophiæ cartesianæ principia per singula, seu articulos dilucidé examinantur* (Toulouse, 1677*).

Vio, Thomas de (Cajetan), 'In posteriorem D. Pauli Epistolam ad Corinthios commentarii', in idem, *Opera Omnia*, vol.V, cap.XII (Lyons, 1639*).

Vio, Thomas de (Cajetan), *Tertia Pars Summæ Totius Theologiæ Sancti Thomæ Aquinatis [...]* (Lyons, 1581*).

Voet, Gijsbert, *Diatriba de cœlo beatorum* (Gorichemi [=Gorkum], 1666).

Wendelin, Marc Friedrich, *Contemplationum Physicarum Sectiones Tres*, 3 vols (Hannover, 1625–28); 3 vols (Cambridge, 1648).

William of Auvergne (Guilielmus Alvernus), 'De Universo Pars I', in *Opera Omnia*, vol.I (Paris, 1704).

William of Conches, 'De Philosophia Mundi', in Migne, *Pat. Lat.* vol.172, cols 41–102. Text mistakenly attributed to Honorius Augustodunensis by Migne. Cf. P. Duhem, *Le système du monde*, vol. III, p.90.

Witelo, *Perspectiva [=Opticæ libri decem]*, in Friedrich Risner, ed., *Opticæ thesaurus Alhazeni Arabis libri septem [...] Item Vitellionis [...]* (Basle, 1572*); reprint (New York, 1972).

Zanchi, Girolamo, 'De Operibus Dei intra spacium sex dierum creatis' (Neustadt, 1591); (Hannover, 1597), in idem, *Operum theologicum* (Heidelberg, 1605); (Geneva, 1613*) (vol.III); (Geneva, 1617, 1619).

Zaragoza, Joseph, S.J., *Esphera en commun celeste y terraquea* (Madrid, 1675).

Ziegler, Jacob, *In C. Plinii de Naturali Historia librum secundum commentarius* (Basle, 1531*); (Cologne, 1550).

Ziegler, Jacob, *Conceptionum in Genesim Mundi & Exodum, Commentarii* (Basle, 1548*).

Secondary sources

Aiton, E.J., *The Vortex Theory of Planetary Motions* (London and New York, 1972) (on Kepler, Galileo, Descartes and Newton).

Albuquerque, Luís de, 'Sobre o conhecimento de Galileu e de Copérnico em Portugal no século XVI', *Vertice* XXV (1965), pp.14–27 (on Borri).

Andrade, António Alberto de, 'Antes de Vernei nascer ... O Padre Cristovão Borri lança nas escolas, a primeira grande reforma científica', *Brotéria* XL fasc. 4 (1945), pp.369–379.

Andrade, António Alberto de, 'Descartes em Portugal nos séculos XVII e XVIII', *Brotéria* LI fasc. 5 (1950), pp.432–451.

Andrade, António Alberto de, *Curso Conimbricense I*, Instituto de Alta Cultura (Lisbon, 1957).

Baldini, Ugo, 'Christoph Clavius and the Scientific Scene in Rome', in Coyne, G.V., Hoskin, M.A. and Pedersen, O., eds, *Gregorian Reform of the Calendar. Proceedings of the Vatican Conference to Commemorate its 400th Anniversary, 1582–1982* (Città del Vaticano, 1983), pp.137–169.

Baldini, Ugo, 'Uniformitas et Soliditas doctrinæ. Le censure Librorum et Opinionum', in idem, *Legem Impone Subactis. Studi su filosofia e scienza dei Gesuiti in Italia 1540–1632* (Rome, 1992), pp.75–119.

Baldini, Ugo, 'Dal geocentrismo alfonsino al modello di Brahe. La discussione Grienberger–Biancani', in *ibid.*, pp.217–250.

Baldini, Ugo, 'La scuola di Clavio e la crisi della teoria astronomica', in *ibid.*, pp.122–216.

Baldini, Ugo, 'La astronomia del Cardinale', in *ibid.*, pp.285–344.

Baldini, Ugo, *Legem Impone Subactis. Studi su filosofia e scienza dei Gesuiti in Italia, 1540–1632* (Rome, 1992).

Baldini, Ugo, ed., *Christoph Clavius e l'attività scientifica dei Gesuiti nell'età di Galileo*, Atti del Convegno Internazionale (Chieti, 28–30 Aprile, 1993) (Rome, 1995).

Baldini, Ugo, 'La formazione scientifica di Giovanni Battista Riccioli', in Luigi Pepe, ed., *Copernico e la questione copernicana in Italia dal XVI al XIX secolo* (Florence, 1996), pp.123–182.

Barker, Peter, 'Jean Pena (1528–1558) and Stoic Physics in the sixteenth century', *Southern Journal of Philosophy* XXIII (1985), Supplement, pp.93–107.

Batterel, L., *Mémoires domestiques pour servir à l'histoire de l'Oratoire*, ed. Auguste-Marie-Pierre Ingold and E. Bonnardet (Paris, 1904); reprint (Geneva, 1971).

Bedouelle, Guy and Roussel, Bernard, eds, *Le temps des Reformes et la Bible* (Bible de tous les temps), vol.V (Paris, 1989).

Belluci, D., 'Luther et le défi de la Théologie de la Parole à la science contemporaine du ciel', in O. Fatio, ed., *Les Eglises face aux sciences du Moyen Age au XXe siècle* (Actes du colloque de la commission internationale d'histoire ecclésiastique comparée tenu à Genève en Août 1989) (Geneva, 1991), pp.53–63.

Benjamin, F.S. and Toomer, G.S., *Campanus de Novara and Medieval Planetary Theory* (Madison, 1971).

Bernhardt, Wilhelm, *Philipp Melanchthon als Mathematiker und Physiker* (Wittenberg, 1865); reprint Sändig Reprints, Wiesbaden, 1973.

Bizer, Ernst, 'Die reformierte Orthodoxie und der Cartesianismus', *Zeitschrift für Theologie und Kirche* (1958), pp.306–372. Also in Eng. trans., 'Reformed Orthodoxy and Cartesianism', in Robert Funk *et al.*, eds, *Translating Theology into the Modern Age* (New York, 1965), pp.20–82.

Blackwell, Richard J., *Galileo, Bellarmine, and the Bible* (Notre Dame and London, 1991).

Blair, Ann, 'The Teaching of Natural Philosophy in Early Seventeenth-Century Paris: The Case of Jean-Cécile Frey', *History of Universities* 12 (1993), pp.95–158.

Bloch, Olivier René, *La philosophie de Gassendi* (The Hague, 1971).

Boas, Marie and Hall, A. Rupert, 'Tycho Brahe's System of the World', *Occasional Notes of the Royal Astronomical Society* 3, No. 21 (1959), pp.254–263; Contains (pp.257–263) an English translation of the first part of Chapter VIII of Tycho Brahe's *De Mundi Ætherei Recentioribus Phænomenis liber secundus* (Uraniborg, 1588); Cf. Latin text in Tycho Brahe, *Opera Omnia*, ed. J.L.E. Dreyer, vol.IV, pp.155–162.

Bouillier, Francisque, *Histoire de la philosophie cartésienne* (Paris, 1854), 3rd edn, 2 vols (Paris,1868).

Brandmüller, Walter and Greipl, Egon Johannes, *Copernico, Galileo e la Chiesa*, Pontificia Academia Scientiarum (Florence, 1992).

Brandmüller, Walter, *Galilei und die Kirche. Ein 'Fall' und seine Lösung* (Aachen, 1994).

Brickman, Benjamin, 'On Physical Space. Francesco Patrizi', *Journal of the History of Ideas* 4 (1943), pp.224–245. Contains translations from Patrizi's *De spacio physico* and *De spacio mathematico* in his *De Rerum Natura* (1587) and in his *Nova de Universis Philosophia* (1591).

Brockliss, L.W.B., 'Aristotle, Descartes and the New Science: Natural Philosophy at the University of Paris, 1600–1740', *Annals of Science* XXXVIII (1981), pp.33–69.

Brockliss, L.W.B., *French Higher Education in the Seventeenth and Eighteenth Centuries* (Oxford, 1987).

Brockliss, L.W.B., 'Copernicus in the University: the French experience', in *Festschrift for Charles Schmitt*, ed. John Henry and Sarah Hutton (London, 1990), pp.190–213.

Brockliss, L.W.B., 'Der Philosophieunterricht in Frankreich', in *Grundrisse der Geschichte der Philosophie*, founded by Friedrich Ueberweg, new edn by Jean-Pierre Schobinger, *Die Philosophie des 17. Jahrhunderts*, Bd 2 *Frankreich und Niederlande* (Basle, 1993), pp.3–86.

Brockliss, L.W.B., 'Pierre Gautruche et l'enseignement de la philosophie de la nature dans les collèges jésuites français vers 1650', in Luce Giard, ed., *Les jésuites à la Renaissance. Système éducatif et production du savoir* (Paris, 1995), pp.187–219.

Browning, John D.,'"Yo hablo como Neutoniano", El Padre Feijoo et el neutonianismo', in *II Simposio sobre el Padre Feijoo y su siglo*, 'Catedra Feijoo', Universidad de Oviedo, vol.I (Oviedo, 1981), pp.221–230.

Bukowski, J., ed., *Colloquia Copernicana I*, Etudes sur l'audience de la théorie héliocentrique, Conférence du Symposium de l'Union internationale d'histoire et de philosophie des sciences, Toruń, 1973, in *Studia Copernicana* V (Warsaw, 1973).

Burchill, Christopher J., 'Girolamo Zanchi: Portrait of a Reformed Theologian and his Work', *Sixteenth Century Journal* XV No. 2 (1984), pp.185–207.

Cantimori, Delio, *Eretici Italiani del Cinquecento* (Florence, 1939), republished (Turin, 1992).

Cantor, G.N. and Hodge, M.J.S. eds, *Conceptions of the Ether. Studies in the History of Ether Theories* (Cambridge, 1981).

Capek, Milic, ed., *The Concepts of Space and Time* (Boston, 1976).

Carraud, Vincent, 'Descartes et l'Écriture Sainte', in *L'Écriture Sainte au temps de Spinoza et dans le système spinoziste*, Groupe de recherches spinozistes, Travaux et Documents, No. 4 (Paris, 1992), pp.41–70.

Carreras y Artau, Tomas and Carreras y Artau, Joaquin, *Historia de la Filosofía Española, Filosofía Espãnola de los Siglos XIII y XIV* (Madrid, 1943).

Casini, Paolo, *Newton e la coscienza europea* (Bologna, 1983).

Caspar, Max, *Kepler*, Eng. trans. and ed. by C. Doris Hellman (London 1959) (original German edn, Stuttgart, 1948). New Eng. edn with new introduction and references by Owen Gingerich. Bibliographical citations by Owen Gingerich and Alain Segonds (New York, 1993).

Ceñal, Ramón, S.J., 'Cartesianismo en España, notas para su historia, 1650–1750', *Revista de la Universidad de Oviedo* (1945), pp.5–97.

Christianson, John R., 'The Celestial Palace of Tycho Brahe', *Scientific American* 204 No. 2 (1961), pp.118–128.

Christianson, John R., 'Tycho Brahe's Cosmology from the *Astrologia* of 1591', *Isis* 59 (1968), pp.312–318.

Christianson, John R., 'Tycho Brahe's German Treatise on the Comet of 1577: a study in science and politics', *Isis* 70 (1979), pp.110–140.

Copenhaver, Brian P., 'Jewish Theologies of Space in the Scientific Revolution', *Annals of Science* 37 (1980), pp.489–548.

Corrazé, R., 'L'Esquille, Collège des Capitouls (1550–1654)', in *Mémoires de l'Académie des Sciences, Inscriptions et Belles Lettres de Toulouse*, 12e, série 15 (1937), pp.155–227; 16 (1938), pp.181–255; (16, p.220 on Jean Vincent).

Cotarelo Valledor, Armando, 'El Padre José de Zaragoza y la Astronomia de su tiempo', in *Estudios sobre la ciencia española del siglo XVII* (Madrid, 1935), pp.65–223.

Coxito, A., 'Para a história do cartesianismo e do anticartesianismo na filosofia portuguesa (sécs XVII–XVIII)', *Cultura História e Filosofia* VI (1987), pp.23–38.

Cuéllar, Roberto Marco, 'El "Compendio Mathematico" del Padre Tosca y la Introducción de la Ciencia Moderna en España', in *Actas del Segundo Congreso Español de la Historia de la Medicina* vol.I (Salamanca, 1965), pp.325–357.

Daniel, Ch., S.J., *Une vocation et une disgrâce à la cour de Louis XIII* (Paris, 1861) (on Nicolas Caussin, S.J.).

D'Arelli, Francesco, 'P. Matteo Ricci S.J., "le cose absurde" dell'astronomia cinese. Genesi, eredità ed influsso di un convincimento tra i secoli XVI–XVII', in I. Iannaccone and A. Tamburello, eds, *Dall'Europa alla Cina: contributi per una storia dell'astronomia*, Università degli studi Federico II – Istituto universitario orientale (Naples, 1990), pp.85–123.

De Franco, Luigi, *L'eretico Agostino Doni, medico e filosofo cosentino del '500* (Cosenza, 1973).

Dias, J.S. da Silva, 'O Cânone Filosófico Conimbricense (1592–1606)', *Cultura História e Filosofia*, IV (1985), pp.257–370.

Dias, J.S. da Silva, 'Cultura e Obstáculo Epistemológico do Renascimento ao Iluminismo em Portugal', in Francisco Contente Domingues and Luís Filipe Barreto, eds, *A Abertura do Mundo. Estudos de História dos Descobrimentos portugueses*, vol.I (Lisbon, 1986), pp.41–52.

Dibon, Paul, *La philosophie néerlandaise au siècle d'or*, vol.I, Paris, Amsterdam (London and New York, 1954).

Dibon, Paul, *Regards sur la Hollande du siècle d'or* (Naples, 1990).

Dibon, Paul, 'Notes bibliographiques sur les cartésiens hollandais' in E.J. Dijksterhuis *et al.*, *Descartes et le cartésianisme hollandais, Etudes et Documents* (Paris and Amsterdam, 1950), pp. 261–300.

Dillenberger, John, *Protestant Thought and Natural Science* (New York, 1960), reprint (Westport, Connecticut, 1977).

Dobbs, B.J.T., *The Janus Faces of Genius, the Role of Alchemy in Newton's Thought* (Cambridge, 1991).

Dobbs, B.J.T., 'Stoic and Epicurean doctrines in Newton's system of the world', in Margaret J. Osler, ed., *Atoms, 'Pneuma', and Tranquillity; Epicurean and Stoic Themes in European Thought* (Cambridge, 1991).

Dobbs, B.J.T. and Jacob, Margaret C., *Newton and the Culture of Newtonianism* (New Jersey, 1994).

Domingues, Francisco Contente, *Ilustração e Catolicismo, Teodoro de Almeida* (Lisbon, 1994).

Donahue, William H., *The Dissolution of the Celestial Spheres 1595–1650* (New York, 1981).

Drake, Stillman and O'Malley, C.D. (eds and trans.), *The Controversy on the comets of 1618* (Philadelphia, 1960).

Dreyer, J.L.E., *Tycho Brahe: A Picture of Life and Work in the Sixteenth Century* (London, 1890), reprint (Gloucester, Mass., 1977).

Dreyer, J.L.E., *A History of Planetary Systems from Thales to Kepler* (London, 1906), new edn with title *A History of Astronomy from Thales to Kepler*, revised with foreword by W.H. Stahl (New York, 1953).

Duhem, Pierre, *Etudes sur Léonard de Vinci*, 3 vols (Paris, 1906–9), reprint, 3 vols (Paris, 1984).

Duhem, Pierre, *Le système du monde*, 10 vols (Paris, 1913–59).

Elena, Alberto, *Las Quimeras de los Cielos, Aspectos epistemológicas de la revolución copernicana* (Madrid, 1985).

Eschweiler, Karl, S.J., 'Die Philosophie der Spanischen Spätscholastik auf den Deutschen Universitäten des Siebzehnten Jahrhunderts', *Spanische Forschungen der Görresgesellschaft* I (1928), pp.251–325.

Eschweiler, Karl, S.J., 'Rodrigo de Arriaga ein Beiträg sur Geschichte der Barockscholastik', *Spanische Forschungen der Görresgesellschaft* I 3 (1931), pp.253–285.

Feingold, Mordechai, *The Mathematicians' Apprenticeship. Science, Universities and Society in England, 1560–1640* (Cambridge, 1984).

Firpo, L., 'Il processo di Giordano Bruno', *Rivista Storica Italiana* LX (1948), pp.542–597; LXI (1949), pp.5–59.

Firpo, L., 'Filosofia italiana e controriforma', *Rivista di Filosofia* 41 (1950), pp.159–173.

Fletcher, John E., 'Astronomy in the Life of Athanasius Kircher S.J.,' *Isis* 61 (1970), pp.52–67.

Fontaine, Jacques, *Isidore de Séville et la culture classique dans l'Espagne wisigothique*, Etudes Augustiniennes, 2 vols (Paris, 1983).

Fragata, J., 'Soares Lusitano e a Ciência média', *Revista Portuguesa de Filosofia* 20 (1964), pp.131–147.

Freudenberger, Theobald, *Augustinus Steuco aus Gubbio* Reformationsgeschichtlhe Studien und Texte, Heft 64/65 (Münster, 1935).

Furley, D.J., 'The Greek Theory of the Infinite Universe', in idem, *Cosmic Problems. Essays on Greek and Roman Philosophies of Nature* (Cambridge, 1989), pp.1–13.

Gabrielli, Giuseppe, 'Intorno a Nicola Antonio Stelliola, Filosofo e Linceo Napolitano', *Giornale Critico della Filosofia Italiana* X (1929), pp.469–495.

Gabrielli, Giuseppe, 'Un anonimo 'Gesuita Portoghese' del Carteggio Galileiano identificato', in *Atti della Reale Accademia d'Italia. Rendiconto della Classe di Scienze Morali e Storiche*, Serie Settima, Rome, III (1943), pp.103–109 (concerns Cristoforo Borri).

Galluzzi, P., ed., *Novità Celesti e Crisi di Sapere* (Florence, 1984).

Garin, Eugenio, 'A Proposito di Copernico', *Rivista Critica di Storia della Filosofia*, Anno XXVI Fasc. 1 (1971), pp.83–87.

Garin, Eugenio, 'Alle origini della polemica anticopernicana', in *Studia Copernicana* VI (1973), pp.31–42.

Garin, Eugenio, *Dal Rinascimento all'Illuminismo. Studi e Ricerche*, Seconda edizione, rivista e accresciuta (Florence, 1993).

Gaulhieur, Ernest, *Histoire du Collège de Guyenne* (Paris, 1874).

Gavira, José, *Aportaciones para la Geografía Española del siglo XVIII* (Madrid, 1932); (pp.39–54 deal with works on astronomy).

Giard, Luce, ed., *Les jésuites à la Renaissance. Système éducatif et production du savoir* (Paris, 1995).

Gilson, Etienne, *La philosophie au Moyen Age* (Paris, 1952).

Gilson, Etienne, 'A la recherche de l'Empyrée', in idem, *Dante et Béatrice, Etudes dantesques* (Paris, 1974), pp.69–77.

Gingerich, Owen and Westman, Robert S., 'The Wittich Connection: Conflict and Priority in Late Sixteenth Century Cosmology', *Transactions of the American Philosophical Society*, 78 Pt 7 (1988), esp. pp.69–76.

Godwin, Joscelyn, *Athanasius Kircher A Renaissance Man and the Quest for Lost Knowledge* (London, 1979).

Goldstein, Bernard R., 'Refraction, Twilight and the Height of the Atmosphere', ch. IX, pp.105–107, in idem, *Theory and Observation in Ancient and Medieval Astronomy* (London, 1985), Variorum Reprints.

Goldstein, Bernard R., 'Ibn Mucadh's Treatise on Twilight and the Height of the Atmosphere', ch. X, pp.97–118, in idem, *Theory and Observation in Ancient and Medieval Astronomy* (London, 1985), Variorum Reprints.

Goldstein, Bernard R. and Barker, Peter, 'The role of Rothmann in the dissolution of the celestial spheres', *British Journal for the History of Science* 28 (1995), pp.385–403.

Gomes, João Pereira, 'A cultura científica de Ignácio Monteiro', *Brotéria*, Lisbon, XLIII (1946), pp.268–287.

Gonzáles, Justo L., 'Athens and Jerusalem Revisited: Reason and Authority in Tertullian', *Church History* 43 (1974), pp.17–25.

Gouhier, Henri, 'La crise de la théologie au temps de Descartes', *Revue de théologie et de philosophie* 4 (1954), pp.19–54.

Gouhier, Henri, *Cartésianisme et Augustinisme au XVIIe siècle* (Paris, 1978).

Grabmann, M., 'Die "Disputationes Metaphysicæ" des Franz Suarez in ihrer methodischen Eigenart und Fortwirkung', in *Mittelalterliches Geistesleben*, 3 vols (Munich, 1926), vol.I, pp.525–560.

Grafton, Anthony, 'Teacher, Text and Pupil in the Renaissance Classroom: A Case Study from a Parisian College', *History of Universities* I (1981), pp.37–70.

Granada, Miguel Angel, 'Petrus Ramus y Jean Pena: crítica de la cosmología aristotélica y de las hipótesis astronómicas a mediados del siglo XVI', *Revista de Filosofía*, Seville, No. 12/13 (1991), pp.11–72.

Granada, Miguel Angel, *El debate cosmológico en 1588. Bruno, Brahe, Rothmann, Ursus, Roslin*, Istituto Italiano per gli studi filosofici, Lezioni della Scuola di Studi Superiori in Napoli, 18 (Naples, 1996).

Granada, Miguel Angel, 'Il problema astronomico-cosmologico e le sacre scritture dopo Copernico: Christoph Rothmann e la "teoria dell' acccomodazione"', *Rivista di storia della filosofia* 51 (1996), pp.789–828.

Granada, Miguel Angel, 'Eliminazione delle sfere celesti e ipotesi astronomiche in un inedito di Christoph Rothmann, L'influenza di Jean Pena e la polemica con Pietro Ramo', in *Rivista di storia della filosofia* 52 (1997), pp.785–821.

Grant, Edward, 'Place and Space in Medieval Physical Thought', in P.K. Machamer and R.G. Turnbull, eds, *Motion, Time, Space and Matter in the History of Philosophy* (Columbus, Ohio, 1976), pp.137–167.

Grant, Edward, 'Aristotelianism and the Longevity of the Medieval Worldview', *History of Science* 16 (1978), pp.93–106.

Grant, Edward, 'Cosmology', in David C. Lindberg, ed., *Science in the Middle Ages* (Chicago, 1978), chap. 8, pp.265–302.

Grant, Edward, 'The Medieval Doctrine of Place: Some Fundamental Problems', in A. Maierù and A. Paravicini Bagliani, eds, *Studi sul XIV Secolo in Memoria di Anneliese Maier* (Rome, 1981), pp.57–79.

Grant, Edward, *Much Ado about Nothing. Theories of Space and Vacuum from the Middle Ages to the Scientific Revolution* (Cambridge, 1981).

Grant, Edward, 'Celestial matter: a Medieval and Galilean problem', *Journal of Medieval and Renaissance Studies* 13 No. 2 (1983), pp.157–186.

Grant, Edward, 'A new look at Medieval Cosmology 1200–1687', *Proceedings of the American Philosophical Society* 129 (1985), pp.417–432.

Grant, Edward, 'Celestial Perfection from the Middle Ages to the late seventeenth century', in M.J. Osler and P.L. Farber, eds, *Religion, Science and Worldview. Essays Presented in Honor of Richard Westfall* (Cambridge, 1985), pp.137–162.

Grant, Edward, 'Science and Theology in the Middle Ages', in David C. Lindberg and Ronald L. Numbers, eds, *God and Nature. Historical Essays on the Encounter between Christianity and Science* (Berkeley, Los Angeles and London, 1986), pp.49–75.

Grant, Edward, 'Celestial Orbs in the Latin Middle Ages', *Isis* 78 (1987), pp.153–173.

Grant, Edward, *Planets, Stars, and Orbs, The Medieval Cosmos, 1200–1687* (Cambridge, 1994).

Grant, Edward, *The Foundations of Modern Science in the Middle Ages. Their Religious, Institutional and Intellectual Contexts* (Cambridge, 1996).

Gregory, Tullio, 'L'*Apologia* e le *Declarationes* di Francesco Patrizi', in *Medievo e Rinascimento: studi in onore de Bruno Nardi* (Florence, 1955), pp.387–424.

Günther, S., 'Jacob Ziegler, ein Bayerischer Geograph und Mathematiker', *Forschungen zur Kultur und Literaturgeschichte. Bayerns* IV (1896), pp.1–61; V (1897), pp.116–128.

Hackett, J.M.G., 'The Attitude of Roger Bacon to the *Scientia* of Albertus Magnus', in J.A. Weisheipl O.P., ed., *Albertus Magnus and the Sciences, Commemorative Essays, 1980*, Pontifical Institute of Medieval Studies (Toronto, 1980), pp.53–72.

Hahm, David E., *The Origins of Stoic Cosmology* (Columbus, Ohio, 1977).

Hall, A.R., *Henry More and the Scientific Revolution* (Cambridge, 1996).

Hellman, C. Doris, *The Comet of 1577: its Place in the History of Astronomy* (New York, 1944), reprint (New York, 1971).

Hellman, C. Doris, 'Was Tycho Brahe as Influential as he Thought?', *The British Journal of Science* I Pt IV No. 4 (1963), pp.295–324.

Hellman, C. Doris, 'The Rôle of Measurement in the Downfall of a System: Some Examples from Sixteenth Century Comet and Nova Observations', *Vistas in Astronomy* 9 (1967), pp.43–52.

Henry, John, 'Francesco Patrizi da Cherso's Concept of Space and its Later Influence', *Annals of Science* 36 (1979), pp.549–573.

Hine, William L., 'Mersenne and Copernicanism', *Isis* 64 (1973), pp.18–32.

Hooykaas, Reyer, 'The reception of Copernicanism in England and the

Netherlands', in idem, *Selected Studies in the History of Science*, Acta Universitatis Conimbrigensis (Coimbra, 1983), pp.635–663.

Hübner, Jürgen, *Die Theologie Johannes Keplers zwischen Orthodoxie und Naturwissenschaft* (Tübingen, 1975).

Jansen, Bernard, S.J., 'Die scholastiche Philosophie des 17. Jahrhunderts', *Philosophisches Jahrbuch der Görresgesellschaft*, Fulda, 50 (1937), pp.401–444.

Jansen, Bernard, S.J., *Die Pflege der Philosophie im Jesuitorden während des 17./18. Jahrhunderts* (Fulda, 1938), 96pp.

Jardine, Nicholas, 'The Significance of the Copernican Orbs', *Journal of the History of Astronomy* XIII (1982), pp.168–194.

Jardine, Nicholas, *The Birth of History and Philosophy of Science, Kepler's Defense of Tycho against Ursus* (Cambridge, 1984).

Jourdain Cl., *Histoire de l'Université de Paris aux XVIIe et XVIIIe siècles* (Paris, 1862–1866).

Kirk, G.S. and Raven, J.E., *The Pre-Socratic Philosophers* (Cambridge, 1969).

Koyré, Alexandre, 'Le vide et l'espace infini au XIVe siècle', *Archives d'histoire doctrinale et littéraire du Moyen Age* 24 (1949), pp.45–91.

Koyré, Alexandre, *From the Closed World to the Infinite Universe* (Baltimore and London, 1957). French trans., *Du monde clos à l'univers infini* (Paris, 1962).

Koyré, Alexandre, *Newtonian Studies* (Chicago, 1968).

Koyré, Alexandre, *La révolution astronomique* (Paris, 1961, 1974); idem, *The Astronomical Revolution*, Eng. trans. by R.E.W. Madison (Ithaca, NY, 1973).

Koyré, A. and Cohen, I. Bernard, 'The case of the missing *tanquam:* Leibniz, Newton, Clarke', *Isis* 52 (1961), pp.555–566.

Koyré, A. and Cohen, I. Bernard, 'Newton and the Leibniz–Clarke Correspondence', *Archives internationales d'histoire des sciences* 15e Année (1962), pp.63–126.

Krafft, Fritz, *Otto von Guericke*, 'Erträge der Forschung', 87 (Darmstadt, 1978).

Kristeller, Paul Oskar, *Eight Philosophers of the Italian Renaissance* (Stanford, California, 1964).

Kusukawa, Sachiko, *The Transformation of Natural Philosophy. The Case of Philip Melanchthon* (Cambridge, 1995).

Lattis, James M., *Between Copernicus and Galileo, Christoph Clavius and the Collapse of Ptolemaic Cosmology* (Chicago and London, 1994).

Lennon, Thomas M., *The Battle of the Gods and Giants. The Legacies of Descartes and Gassendi (1655–1715)* (Princeton, New Jersey, 1993).

Lerner, Michel-Pierre, 'Aristote "oublieux de lui-même" selon B. Telesio,' *Les Etudes Philosophiques* No. 3 (1986), pp.371–389.

Lerner, Michel-Pierre, 'Le problème de la matière céleste après 1550: aspects de la bataille des cieux fluides', *Revue d'histoire des sciences*, XLII/3 (1989), 255–280.

Lerner, Michel-Pierre, *Tre Saggi sulla cosmologia alla fine del Cinquecento*, Istituto Italiano per gli studi filosofici, Lezioni della Scuola di Studi Superiori in Napoli, 14 (Naples, 1992).

Lerner, Michel-Pierre, 'L'entrée de Tycho Brahe chez les jésuites ou le chant du cygne de Clavius', in Luce Giard, ed., *Les jésuites à la Renaissance. Système éducatif et production du savoir* (Paris, 1995), pp.145–185.

Lerner, Michel-Pierre, *Le monde des sphères*, vol.I, *Genèse et triomphe d'une représentation cosmique* (Paris, 1996); vol.II, *La fin du cosmos classique* (Paris,1997). (The most thorough investigation to date of the history of astronomical doctrines relating to cosmology from earliest Antiquity to Galileo and Descartes.)

Lerner, Michel-Pierre, 'Copernic (Nicolas) (1473–1543)', in Colette Nativel, ed., *Centuriæ Latinæ. Cent figures humanistes de la Renaissance aux Lumières offertes à Jacques Chomarat* (Geneva, 1997), pp.285–292.

Lindberg, David C., *Theories of Vision from Al-Kindi to Kepler* (Chicago and London, 1976).

Lindberg, David C.,'The Genesis of Kepler's Theory of Light: Light Metaphysics from Plotinus to Kepler', *Osiris*, 2nd series, 2 (1986), pp.5–42.

Lindberg, David C. and Numbers, Ronald L., eds, *God and Nature. Historical Essays on the encounter between Christianity and Science* (Berkeley, Los Angeles and London, 1986).

Litt, Thomas, *Les corps célestes dans l'univers de Saint Thomas d'Aquin* (Louvain–Paris, 1963).

Lohr, Charles, 'The Medieval Interpretation of Aristotle', in Norman Kretzmann and Eleanor Stump, eds, *The Cambridge History of Later Medieval Philosophy* (Cambridge, 1982), pp.80–98.

Lopez, Enrique, 'Feijoo y la Biblia, o la gran paradoja', *Studium Ovetense*, IV (1976), pp.187–247.

Lopez Piñero, José Maria, *Ciencia y Técnica en la Sociedad Española de los siglos XVI y XVII* (Barcelona, 1979).

Lopez Piñero, José María and Navarro Brotóns, Victor, *Història de la Ciència al País Valencià* (Valencia, 1995).

McGuire, J.E. and Rattansi, P.M., 'Newton and the "Pipes of Pan"', *Notes and Records of the Royal Society of London* 21 (1966), pp.108–143.

McGuire, J.E., 'Neoplatonism and Active Principles: Newton and the *Corpus Hermeticum*', in Robert S. Westman and J.E. McGuire, *Hermeticism and the Scientific Revolution*, William Andrews Clark Memorial Library (Los Angeles, 1977), pp.95–142.

Mahnke, Dietrich, *Unendliche Sphäre und Allmittelpunkt* (Halle, 1937); reprint (Stuttgart–Bad Canstatt, 1966).

Manzoni, Claudio. *I Cartesiani italiani 1660–1760* (Udine, 1984).

Martinet, Monette and Schobinger, Jean-Pierre, eds, *Die Philosophie des 17. Jahrhunderts (Frankreich und Niederland)* (Basle, 1993).

Maurach, Gregor, 'Coelum Empyreum, Versuch einer Begriffsgeschichte', *Boethius* VIII (Wiesbaden, 1968).

Maurer, H.M. and Ulshöfer, K., *Johannes Brenz und die Reformation im Herzogtum Württemberg* (Stuttgart, 1975).

Mayaud, Pierre-Noël, S.J., *La condamnation des livres coperniciens et sa révocation à la lumière de documents inédits des Congrégations de l'Index et de l'Inquisition*, Miscellanea Historiae Pontificiae edita a Facultate Historiae Ecclesiasticae in Pontificia Universitate Gregoriana, vol.64, Editrice Pontificia Università Gregoriana (Rome, 1997).

Michaud-Quantin, Pierre, *Etudes sur le vocabulaire philosophique du Moyen Age* (Rome, 1970).

Michel, P.H., *La cosmologie de Giordano Bruno* (Paris, 1962). Eng. trans. by Dr R.E.W. Madison, *The Cosmology of Giordano Bruno* (Ithaca, NY, 1973).

Moraes, Manuel, S.J., *Cartesianismo em Portugal. António Cordeiro* (Braga, 1966).

Moran, Bruce T., 'Princes, Machines and the Valuation of Precision in the 16th Century', *Sudhoffs Archiv* 61 (1977), pp.209–228.

Moran, Bruce T., 'Wilhelm IV of Hesse-Kassel: Informal Communication and the Aristocratic Context of Discovery', in T. Nickles, ed., *Scientific*

Discovery: Case Studies, Boston Studies in the Philosophy of Science (Dordrecht and London, 1980), pp.67–96.

Moran, Bruce T., 'Christopher Rothmann, the Copernican Theory and Institutional and Technical Influences in the Criticism of Aristotelian Cosmology', *Sixteenth Century Journal* XIII No. 3 (1982), pp.85–108.

Mouy, Paul, *Le développement de la physique cartésienne 1646–1712* (Paris, 1934), reprint (New York, 1981).

Muckle, J.T., 'Robert Grosseteste's use of Greek sources in his Hexaëmeron', *Medievalia et Humanistica* 3 (1945), pp.33–48.

Nardi, Bruno, 'La dottrina dell'Empireo nella sua genesi storica e nel pensiero dantesco', in idem, *Saggi di filosofia dantesca* (Florence, 1930), new edn (Florence, 1967), pp.167–214.

Navarro Brotóns, Victor, 'El compendium philosophicum (1721) de Tosca y la introducción en España de la ciencia y la filosofia modernas' in *La Ilustración Española, Actas del Coloquio Internacional celebrado en Alicante*, 1–4 Octubre 1985 (Alicante, 1986), pp.51–70.

Navarro Brotóns, Victor, 'Los Jesuitas y la Renovación científica en la España del siglo XVII', *Studia Historica. Historia Moderna* 14 (1996), pp.15–44.

Navarro Brotóns, Victor, 'Las ciencias en la España del siglo XVII: el cultivo de las disciplinas físico-mathemáticas', *Arbor* CLIII, Nos 604–605 (1996), pp.197–252.

Navarro Brotóns, Victor and Rodriguez Galdeano, Enrique, *Matemáticas, cosmología y humanismo en la Espāna del sigle XVI. Los Comentarios al segundo libro de la Historia Natural de Plinio de Jerónomo Muñoz*, Latin text of Muñoz's Commentary on the second book of Pliny's Natural History with Spanish trans. by Victor Navarro Brotóns and Enrique Rodriguez Galdeano; introduction by Victor Navarro Brotóns (Valencia, 1998).

Nicolson, M.H., 'The early stages of Cartesianism in England', *Studies in Philology* 26 (1929), pp.356–374.

North, John, *The Fontana History of Astronomy and Cosmology* (London, 1994).

Osler, Margaret J., ed., *Atoms*, Pneuma *and Tranquillity, Epicurean and Stoic Themes in European Thought. Essays in Honor of Richard S. Westfall* (Cambridge, 1985).

Pantin, Isabelle, 'Galileo Galilei (1564–1642)', in Colette Nativel, ed., *Centuriæ Latinæ. Cent figures humanistes de la Renaissance aux Lumières offertes à Jacques Chomarat* (Geneva, 1997), pp.385–389.

Peset Llorca, Vicente, 'Acerca de la difusión del sistema copernicano en España', in *Actas del Segundo Congreso Español de la Historia de la Medicina*, I (Salamanca, 1965), pp. 309–324.

Petersen, Peter, *Geschichte der Aristotelischen Philosophie im Protestantischen Deutschland* (Leipzig, 1921); reprint (Stuttgart–Bad Cannstatt, 1964).

Piwnik, Marie-Hélène, 'Une entreprise lucrative: Les traductions en espagnol du Père Teodoro de Almeida', *Arquivos do Centro Cultural Português* XXXI (Fundação Calouste Gulbenkian, Lisbon/Paris, 1992), pp.199–206.

Quasten, Johannes, *Initiation aux Pères de l'Eglise* (Paris 1958), French trans. by J. Laporte of Johannes Quasten, *Patrology*, 2 vols (Utrecht/Antwerp, 1953).

Randles, W.G.L., 'Le ciel chez les jésuites espagnols et portugais (1590–1651)', in Luce Giard, ed., *Les jésuites à la Renaissance. Système éducatif et production du savoir* (Paris, 1995), pp.129–144.

Reif, Sister Patricia, 'The Textbook Tradition in Natural Philosophy, 1600–1650', *Journal of the History of Ideas* XXX (1969), pp.17–32.

Ricard, Robert, 'Sur la diffusion des œuvres du P. Theodore de Almeida', *Boletim Internacional de Bibliografia Luso-Brasileira* IV, No. 4 (1963), pp.626–630.

Ricci, Saverio, *'Una Filosofica Milizia' Tre Studi sull'Accademia dei Lincei* (Udine, 1994).

Robbins, Frank, *The Hexaëmeral Literature: A Study of the Greek and Latin Commentaries on Genesis* (Chicago, 1912).

Rochemonteix, Camille, *Un collège de Jésuites aux XVIIe et XVIIIe siècles. Le collège Henri IV de la Flèche*, 4 vols (Le Mans, 1899)

Rochot, Bernard, ed., *Pierre Gassendi, sa vie et son œuvre 1592–1655* (Paris, 1955).

Rodis-Lewis, Geneviève, *L'Œuvre de Descartes*, 2 vols (Paris, 1971).

Rodis-Lewis, Geneviève, *Descartes. Biographie* (Paris, 1995).

Rodrigues, Francisco, S.J., 'Um Martyr da Restauração de 1640', *Trabalhos da Associação dos Arqueólogos Portugueses*, Lisbon, VI (1940), pp.54–73 (on Francisco Soares (Lusitano)).

Rodrigues, Francisco, S.J., 'A Companhia de Jesus e a Restauração de Portugal 1640', *Anais da Academia Portuguesa de História*, Lisbon, VI (1952), pp.327–405.

Rogers, G.A.J., 'Descartes and the English', in J.D. North and J.J. Roche, eds, *The Light of Nature. Essays in the History and Philosophy of Science presented to A.C. Crombie* (Dordrecht–Boston–Lancaster, 1985), pp.281–302.

Rosen, Edward, 'Was Copernicus' *Revolutions* approved by the Pope?', *Journal of the History of Ideas* XXXVI (1975), pp.531–542.

Rosen, Edward, 'The Dissolution of the Solid Celestial Spheres', *Journal of the History of Ideas* XLVI (1985), pp.13–31.

Rotondò, A., 'Cultura umanistica e difficoltà di censori. Censura ecclesiastica e discussioni cinquecentesche sul platonismo', in *Le pouvoir et la plume. Incitation, contrôle et répression dans l'Italie du XVIe siècle*, Centre interuniversitaire de recherche sur la Renaissance italienne, Paris, 10 (1992), pp.20–33 (on Francesco Giorgio).

Ruler, J.A. van, *The Crisis of Causality. Voetius and Descartes on God, Nature and Change* (Leiden, New York, Köln, 1995).

Russell, John L., S.J., 'The Copernican System in Great Britain', *Studia Copernicana* V (1972), pp.189–239.

Russell, John L., S.J., 'Catholic Astronomers and the Copernican System after the Condemnation of Galileo', *Annals of Science* 46 (1989), pp.365–386.

Sabra, I.A., 'The authorship of the *Liber de Crepusculis*', *Isis* LVIII (1967), pp.77–85.

Sambursky, Samuel, *The Physics of the Stoics* (London, 1959).

Santos, Domingos Maurício Gomes dos, S.J., 'Para a história do Cartesianismo entre os Jesuitas Portugueses do século XVIII', *Revista Portuguesa de Filosofia* I fasc. 1 (1945), pp.27–44.

Santos, Domingos Maurício Gomes dos, S.J., 'Vicissitudes da Obra do P^e Cristovão Borri', *Anais da Academia Portuguesa da História*, Lisbon II Série II (1951), pp.118–150.

Sarrailh, Jean, *L'Espagne éclairée de la seconde moitié du XVIIIe siècle* (Paris, 1954).

Schmidt, C., 'G. Zanchi', *Theologische Studien und Kritiken* XXV (1859), pp.697–699.

Schmitt, Charles B., 'Perennial Philosophy from A. Steuco to Leibnitz', *Journal of the History of Ideas* XXVII (1966), pp.505–532.

Schmitt, Charles B., 'Towards a reassessment of Renaissance Aristotelianism', in idem, *Studies in Renaissance Philosophy and Science*, ch. VI, pp.159–193 (London, 1981), Variorum Reprints.

Schmitt, Charles B., 'Galileo and the 17th-century textbook tradition', in P. Galluzzi, ed., *Novità Celesti e Crisi di Sapere* (Florence, 1994), pp.217–228.

Schofield, Christine Jones, *Tychonic and Semi-Tychonic Systems* (New York, 1981).

Schottenloher, K., *Jakob Ziegler aus Landau an der Isar*, Reformationsgeschichtliche Studien und Texte, 8–10 (Münster, 1910) (not seen).

Segonds, Alain, 'Kepler et l'infini', in F. Monnoyeur, ed., *Infini des philosophes, infini des astronomes* (Paris, 1995), pp.21–40.

Segonds, Alain, 'Brahe (Tycho) (1546–1601)', in Colette Nativel, ed., *Centuriæ Latinæ. Cent figures humanistes de la Renaissance aux Lumières offertes à Jacques Chomarat* (Geneva, 1997), pp.175–182.

Segonds, Alain, 'Kepler (Johannes) (1571–1630)', in Colette Nativel, ed., *ibid.*, pp.457–472.

Shea, William R., *Galileo's Intellectual Revolution* (New York, 1977).

Singer, Dorothy Waley, *Giordano Bruno. His Life and Thought* (New York, 1950), reprint (New York, 1968).

Solana, Marcial, *Historia de la Filosofía Española, Epoca del Renascimiento (siglo XVI)*, vol. III (Madrid, 1941).

Solignac, Aimé, S.J., 'Exégèse et Métaphysique. Genèse 1, 1–3 chez saint Augustin', in [Paul Vignaux, ed.], *In Principio. Interprétations des premiers versets de la Genèse*, Etudes Augustiniennes (Paris, 1973), pp.153–171.

Sortais, Gaston, 'Le cartésianisme chez les jésuites français aux XVIIe et XVIIIe siècles', *Archives de philosophie* 6 Pt 3 (1929), pp.1–109, esp. pp.46–86.

Spampanato, V., *Vita di Giordano Bruno*, 2 vols (Messina, 1921); reprint (Rome, 1988).

Spanneut, Michel, *Le Stoïcisme des Pères de l'Eglise: de Clément de Rome à Clément d'Alexandrie* (Paris, 1957).

Stauffer, Richard, 'L'exégèse de Genèse 1, 1–3, chez Luther et Calvin', in [Paul Vignaux, ed.], *In Principio. Interprétations des premiers versets de la Genèse*, Etudes Augustiniennes (Paris, 1973), pp.245–266.

Sticker, Bernhard, 'Landgraf Wilhelm IV und die Anfänge der modernen astronomischen Messkunst', *Sudhoffs Archiv* 40 (1956), pp.15–25.

Strömgren, Elis and Strömgren, Bengt, *Tycho Brahe's Description of his Instruments and Scientific Work* (Copenhagen, 1946). Partial Eng. trans. with reproductions of engravings.

Surdich, Francesco, 'L'attività di Padre Cristoforo Borri nelle Indie Orientali in un resoconto inedito', in idem, *Fonti sulla penetrazione europea in Asia* (Genoa, 1979), pp.67–122.

Taton, René and Wilson, Curtis, eds, *Planetary Astronomy from the Renaissance to the rise of astrophysics. Part A: Tycho Brahe to Newton*, in Hoskin, Michael (gen. ed.), *The General History of Astronomy, Vol. 2A* (Cambridge, 1989).

Teixeira, P.M., 'P. Cristovão Borri', *Boletim Eclesiástico da Diocese de Macau*, LXXII No. 838 Sept. 1974, pp.567–572.

Thijssen-Schoute, C. Louise, 'Le cartésianisme aux Pays Bas', in E.J. Dijksterhuis *et al.*, *Descartes et le cartésianisme hollandais, Etudes et Documents* (Paris and Amsterdam, 1950), pp.183–260.

Thijssen-Schoute, Caroline Louise, *Nederlands Cartesianisme* (Amsterdam, 1954); reprint (Utrecht, 1989).

Thoren, Victor, 'The Comet of 1577 and Tycho Brahe's System of the World', *Archives internationales d'histoire des sciences* XXIX (1979), pp.53–67.

Thoren, Victor, 'New Light on Tycho's Instruments', *Journal of the History of Astronomy* 4 (1973), pp.25–45.

Thoren, Victor, *The Lord of Uraniborg. A Biography of Tycho Brahe* (Cambridge, 1990).

Thorndike, Lynn, *History of Magic and Experimental Science*, 8 vols (New York, 1923–58).

Thorndike, Lynn, *The Sphere of Sacrobosco and its Commentators* (Chicago, 1949).

Torrell, J.P., *Initiation à Saint Thomas d'Aquin* (Fribourg and Paris, 1993).

Torrini, Maurizio, *Tommaso Cornelio e la ricostruzione della scienza* (Naples, 1977).

Van Genderen, J., *Herman Witsius* (Amsterdam, 1953).

Van Helden, Albert, *Measuring the Universe. Cosmic Dimensions from Aristarchus to Halley* (Chicago and London, 1985).

Vasoli, C, 'Francesco Giorgio Veneto', in E. Garin *et al.*, *Testi umanistici su l'ermetismo* (Rome, 1955), pp.81–90.

Verbeke, G., *L'évolution de la doctrine du pneuma du stoïcisme à S. Augustin* (Paris–Louvain, 1945).

Vernet, Juan, 'Copernicus in Spain', in Bukowski, J., ed., *Colloquia Copernicana I*, Etudes sur l'audience de la théorie héliocentrique, Conférence du Symposium de l'Union internationale d'histoire et de philosophie des sciences, Torún, 1973, in *Studia Copernicana* V (Warsaw, 1973).

[Vignaux, Paul, ed.] *In Principio. Interprétations des premiers versets de la Genèse*, Etudes Augustiniennes (Paris, 1973).

Viera y Clavijo, J. de, 'Elogio de D. Tostado', *Memorias de la Academia Española*, Madrid, II (1870), pp.602–628.

Weisheipl, James A., O.P., 'The Life and Works of Saint Albert the Great', in idem, ed., *Albertus Magnus and the Sciences, Commemorative Essays, 1980*, Pontifical Institute of Medieval Studies (Toronto, 1980), pp.13–51.

Wesley, Walter G., 'The Accuracy of Tycho Brahe's Instruments', *Journal of the History of Astronomy* IX (1978), pp.42–53.

Williams, A., *The Common Expositor. An account of the Commentaries on Genesis, 1527–1633* (Chapel Hill, USA, 1948).

Zahlten, Johannes, *Creatio Mundi. Darstellung der Sechs Schöpfungstage und naturwissenschaftliches Weltbilder im Mittelalter*, Stuttgarter Beiträge zur Geschichte und Politik, 13 (Stuttgart, 1979) (important for the iconography of Hexaëmerons).

Ziller Camenietski, Carlos, 'L'extase interplanétaire d'Athanasius Kircher', *Nuncius* 10 (1995), pp.3–32.

Zöckler, Otto, *Geschichte der Beziehungen zwischen Theologie und Naturwissenschaft mit besonderer Rücksicht auf Schöpfungsgeschichte*, 2 vols (Gütersloh, 1877–79).

Index

Abra de Raconis, Charles d' 152–153, 155
Abraham Ibn Ezra *see* Avenezra
Accademia dei Lincei 84, 85
Acosta, José de 147
Adam (& Eve) 18, 22, 121, 122, 141, 189, 194
Aegidius Romanus *see* Giles of Rome
Æther 11, 37, 46, 54, 62, 63, 69, 70, 71, 74, 78, 79, 81, 83, 84, 89, 90, 102, 103, 104, 111, 125, 130, 149, 150, 160, 164, 168, 177, 198–199, 209, 210, 213
Aiton, E.J. 120n.71
Albattani 60
Albertus Magnus *see* Albert the Great
Albert the Great 2, 12–18, 92, 120, 136
Albuquerque, Luís de 175n.82
Aletino, Benedetto *see* De Benedictis, Giovanni Battista
Alexander of Aphrodisias 92–93
Alexander of Hales 2n.2
Alhazen *see* Ibn al-Haytham
Almeida, Teodoro de 215–216
Alphonso de Tostado *see* Tostado, Alphonso de
Ambrose, Saint 6n.21
Amerpoel, Johannes 123–124
Anaxagoras 60, 121n.71
Anaximenes 121n.71
Andrade, António Alberto de 92n.52, 175n.82, 213n.103
Angels 11, 37, 87, 120, 136, 138, 142, 143, 153, 154, 155, 165, 171, 177, 178, 180
Anselm, Saint 14
Anselm of Laon 7, 14
Apian, Peter 12
Aquinas, Thomas *see* Thomas Aquinas, Saint
Aratus 131
Argoli, Andrea 101–102, 167–168
Aristotle
  Meteorologica 74n.63, 78n.81, 92
  On Breath [Parva Naturalia] 137n.10
  On the Heavens [De Cælo] 5n.16, 8, 9n.37, 35n.14, 41, 58n.1, 97n.79

On the Soul [De Anima] 16n.70, 18n.84, 22n.113, 23n.116, 24n.120
Physics 169n.63
Armiger, Samuel Gott 184n.6
Arriaga, Rodrigo de 16, 170–172
Aslachus, Conrad 52–53, 72, 77, 112, 114–115
Athens 1
Atmosphere 78, 101, 164
Augustine, Saint 5, 18, 42n.51, 47n.66, 101, 120–121, 142n.30, 144n.35, 147, 189, 190, 202, 208
Augustinians 24, 34
Aura 89, 90, 139, 140, 148
Aura ætherea 78, 79, 102, 104, 116–117, 176, 177, 180, 221
Aura empyrea 147
Aura spirabilis 139, 166, 209
Avenezra (Abraham Ibn Ezra) 27
Averroes (Ibn Rushd) 17n.79
Aversa, Raffaello 166–167

Bacon, Francis 195
Bacon, Roger 12n.53, 25
Baer, Nicolai Reymers (Ursus), 107, 110
Balbus, Lucilius 62
Baldini, Ugo 46n.61, 90n.48, 93n.57, 95n.67, 99n.86, 201n.66
Baldwein, Eberhardt 64
Barker, Peter 59n.8, 61
Barley, Joseph 186n.9
Barnabite Clerics 167
Barradas, Sebastião 140–141
Barrow, Isaac 126, 186
Basil, Saint 2, 3–5, 6n.22, 8, 9, 40, 42n.49, 43, 44, 127, 220
Basilian model 3–5, 9, 10, 25, 27, 33, 42, 44, 47–48, 49–50, 54, 56, 76, 79, 82, 83, 114, 116, 165, 169, 173, 177, 181, 210, 213
Batterel, E. 186n.9, 188–189
Bauduer, Jean 152, 159–163, 181, 182
Bayle, Pierre 55, 146n.50, 159, 170n.68

Bede, Venerable 3, 12, 177, 180
Beduelle, Guy, 7n.28
Bellarmine, Robert 44–46, 86–88, 93, 95, 141–143
Bellucci, D. 34n.9
Benedict XIV (Pope) 217
Benedictines 211
Bergerac, Cyrano de 191
Bergier, Nicolas (Abbé) 218
Berkeley, George 132
Bernard, P. 19n.91
Bernhardt, Wilhelm 38n.27
Bessel, Friedrich Wilhelm xii
Biancani, Giuseppe 95, 98
Biel, Gabriel 38
'Birds and Fish' metaphor
  Bellarmine, R. 46
  Biancani, G. 95
  Cornäus, M. 165
  Gassendi, P. 125
  Le Rees, F. 154
  Luther, M. 35
  Melanchthon, P. 38
  Oviedo, F. de 173
  Roslin, Helisaeus 53
  Ziegler, J. 35
Bizer, Ernest 183n.1, 184n.6
Blackwell, Richard J. 44n.35, 90n.47
Blair, Ann 152n.4
Blancanus, Giuseppe *see* Biancani, Giuseppe
Blessed (in the Empyrean)
  Abra de Raconis, Charles d' 153
  Albert the Great 15–18
  Amerpoel, J. 124
  Aslachus, C. 52–53
  Aversa, R. 166
  Barradas, S. 140–141
  Basil, Saint 4
  Bauduer, J. 160
  Bellarmine, R. 142–143
  Biancani, G. 97
  Biel, G. 38
  Caussin, N. 145–146
  Cordeiro, A. 213
  Cornäus, M. 166
  Du Hamel, J. 155
  Gassendi, P. 125
  Giles of Rome 26
  Gorlaeus, D. 83
  Henao, G. 147–149
  Horrocks, J. 136
  Isidore of Seville 6
  Kircher, A. 165
  Lessius, L. 138–140
  Luther, M. 38–39
  Maloni, D. 137

Oviedo, F. de 173
Petau, D. 55
Pourchot, E. 190
Riccioli, G.B. 149–150
Roa, M. de 143–144
Robert Grosseteste 9
Rothmann, C. 135
Serbelloni, S. 167–168
Suarez, F. 138
Tellez, B. 178
Thomas Aquinas 21–24
Tosca, T.V. 210
Tostado, Alphonso de 28–31
Vincent, J. 158
William of Auvergne 10–12
Zanchi, G. 50–51
Bloch, Olivier René 125n.87, 126n.93, 127n.101
Bocarro Francês, Manuel 100–101
Boffito, G. 167n.55
Bonaventure, Saint 2n.2
Borri, C. 174–178, 179, 180, 181, 213
Boscovitch, R.G. 212
Bossuet, 123
Boswell, 120
Bouillier, Francisque 186n.9, 188n.17, 190n.22, 192n.32
Boulliau, Ismaël 117, 164n.41, 180, 198, 202
Bradwardine, Thomas 14
Brahe, Tycho 58, 63–79, 80, 81, 82, 83, 84, 85, 88, 89, 90, 93, 95, 98, 100, 101, 102, 103, 111, 113–115, 124, 149, 151, 153, 157, 167, 170, 171, 176, 177, 178, 179, 180, 181, 199, 220
Brandmüller, Walter 217n.123
Brenz, Johann 39
Brockliss, L.W.B. 152n.5, 190n.22
Browning, John D. 212n.98
Bruno, Cristovão (Borri, C.) 178n.78
Bruno, Giordano 106, 107–109, 111–112, 116, 135n.4, 150, 180, 196, 197, 199, 221–222
Bürgi, Jost 64
Burman, François 120, 123
Burchill, Christopher J. 50n.83
Bynum, W.F., Brown, E.J. & Porter, Roy 59n.6

Cajetan, Cardinal (Thomas de Vio) 7n.28, 48n.76, 137
Callipus, 125
Calvin, John 34n.9, 42, 114
Campanella, Tommaso 195
Campanus of Novara 6, 20
Cantimori, Delio 196n.48
Cantor, G.N. 79n.89
Capek, Milic 129n.108
Caracciolini 166
Cardanus, Hieronymus 61

INDEX

Carraud, Vincent 120n.68
Carreras y Artau, Tomas & Carreras y Artau, Joaquin 27n.134
Casini, Paolo 132n.128, 218n.124
Caspar, Max 77n.79
Castelli, Benedetto 123n.78
Castellion, Sebastian 114
Caussin, Nicolas 145–146
Celaya, Juan de 12, 35n.15
Ceñal, Ramón 204n.73
Cesi, Federico 84n.88
Chaix-Roy, Jules 42n.51
Christianson, John 64n.29
Christina of Lorraine (Grand Duchess) 27
Cicero 61, 62, 81
Clavius, Christoph 90–92, 94–95, 97, 154, 164, 165, 168, 190, 213 221
Clement VIII (Pope) 112
Colleges
    Guyenne (Bordeaux) 159, 188, 189
    L'Esquille (Toulouse) 156, 159, 186
    La Flèche 55, 118, 122
    Brera (Milan) 174
    Lecce (Naples) 199
    Mondovi (Milan) 174
    Palma de Majorca 205
    St Anthony (Lisbon)
    S. Rocco (Parma) 95
    Royal (Paris) 59, 102, 103
    Massimo (Naples) 199
    Romano (Rome) 47, 90, 163
    Sapientiae (Collegium) (Heidelberg) 83
    Trinity (Dublin) 80
Comets x, 67, 74, 75, 81, 89, 90, 92, 98, 105, 154, 155, 157, 164, 173, 197, 215
Comparato, V. 195n.46
Conimbricenses 92–93, 118, 154, 172
Copenhaver, Brian P. 129n.110
Copernican system (astronomy)
    Almeida, T. de 216, 217
    Bauduer, J. 159, 160–163, 188–189
    Borri, C. 170
    Cornelio, T. 197–198
    Corsini, E. 202–204
    Dagoumer, G. 193, 195
    Descartes, R. 122–123
    Du Hamel, J. 155–156
    Feijoo, B.J. 211–212
    Gassendi, P. 124–125
    Le Rees, F. 154
    Monteiro, I. 214–215
    Pourchot, E. 190–191, 195
    Tosca, T.V. 210
    Zaragoza, J. 205
Copernicus 60, 97, 122, 124, 133, 150, 190, 193, 197, 203, 205, 210, 214, 217
Cordeiro, A. 213–214

Cornäus, Melchior 163, 165–166
Cornelio, Tommaso 195–199
Corrazé, R. 156n.20
Corsini, E. 201–204
Costabel, Pierre 71, 102n.107
Cotarelo Valledor, Armando 100n.95, 101n.96, 205n.77
Council of Trent 39, 84
Couto, Sebastião 173
Coxito, A. 213n.103
Creation 1, 2, 3, 6, 7, 8, 30, 33, 41, 42, 43, 83, 113, 119, 120–122, 127, 132, 149, 169, 176, 185, 202, 208, 210, 219, 220
Crystalline Heaven (or Sphere) 7, 12, 19, 25, 97, 99, 145, 150, 160, 166, 171, 176, 190, 193, 202
Cuéllar, Roberto Marco 207n.83
Cursus Philosophicus 151, 152, 155, 156, 159, 168, 170, 171, 173, 179, 181, 199, 201, 206, 213

D'Arelli, Francisco 174n.80
Dagoumer, Guillaume 190, 191–194, 195
Daniel, Ch. 145n.41
Dante 21
De Benedictis, Giovanni Battista 199–200
De Ferrari, A. 199n.60
De Franco, Luigi, 196n.48
Democritus 108, 195
Denifle, H. and Chatelain, A. 12n.51
Descartes, René 59n.6, 107, 117, 118–123, 124, 129, 130, 132, 150, 156, 183, 185, 186, 187, 188, 189, 190, 191, 192, 194, 195, 197, 198, 199, 200, 201, 202, 203, 205, 206, 207, 209, 210, 215, 217
Dias, J.S. da 91n.52, 179n.110, 214n.106
Dibon, Paul 118n.56, 120n.69, 151n.1, 183n.1, 184n.6
Dillenberger, John 35n.11, 151n.1
Dini, Monsignor 85
Diogenes, Laertius 121n.71
Dobbs, B.J.T. 130n.118, 131nn.121 & 123
Dominicans 2n.2, 12, 19, 133
Domingues, Francisco Contente 215n.110
Donahue, William H. 80n.1, 82n.13, 98n.85, 184n.6
Dörfel 81
Doni, Agostino 196, 199
Dreyer, J.L.E. 67n.30, 81n.6, 110n.17
Du Hamel, Jean 152, 155–156
Duhem, Pierre 8n.35, 12n.53, 17n.76, 19n.90, 20n.99, 24n.122, 108nn.7, 8, 11 & 12
Durandus of Saint Pourçain 21, 138
Durandus of Sancto Porciano *see* Durandus of Saint Pourçain

Empedocles 59

Empyrean
  Abra de Raconis, Charles d' 153
  Albert the Great 14–18
  Almeida, T. de 216
  Amerpoel, J. 124
  Anselm of Laon 7
  Aslachus, C. 52–53
  Aversa, R. 166–167
  Basil, Saint 3–4, 220
  Bellarmine, R. 44, 141–143
  Biancani, G. 95
  Bocarro Francês, M. 101
  Bonardo, G.M. 144
  Borri, C. 177
  Cajetan, Cardinal 7n.28, 21–22, 97n.78
  Campanus of Novara 20
  Cesi, F. 86–87
  Clavius, C. 95
  Cordeiro, A. 213
  Cornäus, M. 165–167
  Cornelio, T. 197
  Corsini, E. 201–202
  Dagoumer, G. 193
  Du Hamel, J. 156
  Gassendi, P. 125
  Giles of Rome 25–26
  Guericke, O. von 128
  Horrocks, J. 136
  Hurtado de Mendoza, P. 169
  Isidore of Seville 6
  Kepler, J. 135
  Kircher, A. 165
  Le Rees, F. 154
  Lessius, L. 138–140
  Luther, M. 38–39
  Maloni, D. 136–137
  Martianus Capella 7
  Molina, L. de 48–49
  Morin, J.B. 103
  Oviedo, F. de 172–173
  Patrizi, F. 113
  Petau, D. 55–56
  Pereyra, B. 47
  Peter Lombard 7–8
  Pierre d'Ailly 20
  Pourchot, E. 190–191
  Riccioli, G.B. 149–50
  Roa, M. 143–144
  Robert Grosseteste 9
  Rosaccio, G. 144
  Roslin, H. 53–54
  Rothmann, C. 135
  Schyrlaeus de Rheita, A. M. 144
  Serbelloni, S. 167–168
  Soares, F. 180
  Steuco, A. 40–42
  Suarez, F. 48–50, 137–140
  Tellez, B. 178
  Thomas Aquinas 19–20
  Tolosani, G.M. 133
  Tosca, T.V. 209–210
  Tostado, Alphonso de 28–31
  Vincent, J. 158–159
  William of Auvergne 10–12
  Zanchi, G. 50–51
  Zaragoza, J. 205–206
Enlightenment 132, 211
Epicurians 192
Epicurus 200
Eschweiler, Karl 170n.68
Ether 5 *see also* Æther
Etienne Tempier 24
Euclid 15, 31, 58, 59, 64, 220
Eudoxus 125
Eugubinus *see* Steuco, Agostino
Extramission theory of vision 15
Ezekiel 3n.5

Fabri, Honoré 216
Faculty of Theology (Santiago de Compostella) 205
Feijoo, Benito Jerónimo 211–212, 214
Feingold, Mordechai 80n.1
Fergusson, Robert 184n.6
Ficino, Marsilio 32, 150
Field, J.V. 75
Fifth essence (or element) 3, 5, 8, 9, 14, 21, 25, 28, 42, 48, 55, 58, 59, 61, 79, 81, 82, 92, 93, 109, 153, 154, 155, 167, 169, 176, 178, 213
Finite cosmos
  Brahe, T. 114
  Corsini, E. 201–202
  Feijoo, B.J. 212
  Gassendi, P. 125
  Kepler, J. 79,116
  Lydyat, T. 81
  Müler, N. 82
  Riccioli, G.B. 150
  Tosca, T.V. 209
Firmament
  Albert the Great 12
  Amerpoel, J. 124
  Anselm of Laon 7
  Augustine, Saint 5
  Basil, Saint 4–5
  Bede, Venerable 3
  Bellarmine, R. 44
  Borri, C.
  Campanus of Novara 6
  Cesi, F. 86
  Clavius, C. 90
  Cordeiro, A. 213
  Corsini, E. 202

Firmament continued
  Dagoumer, G. 193
  Du Hamel, J. 155
  Hurtado de Mendoza, P. 169
  Giles of Rome 25–26
  Giorgio, F. 33
  Isidore of Seville 6
  Le Rees, F. 154
  Luther, M. 34–35
  Mersenne, M. 89
  Michael Scot 6
  Molina, L. de 49
  Oreggi, A. 54–55
  Oviedo, F. de 173
  Pereyra, B. 47–48
  Petau, D. 56
  Pourchot, E. 190
  Pseudo-Clement 2
  Riccioli, G.B. 149–150
  Robert Grosseteste 9
  Rupert of Deutz 5
  Serbelloni, S. 167
  Steuco, A. 40, 42–43, 220
  Suarez, F. 49–50
  Tanner, A. 140
  Thierry of Chartres 5
  Thomas Aquinas 19
  Tosca, T.V. 208
  Tostado, Alphonso de 27–28
  Vincent, J. 158
  Wendelin, M.F. 83
  William of Auvergne 10
  William of Conches 5
  Zanchi, G. 52
  Ziegler, J. 37
Firpo, L. 112n.26
Fixed stars (fluid medium)
  Argoli, A. 102
  Aslachus, C. 77
  Aversa, R. 167
  Baer, N. R. (Ursus) 110
  Borri, C. 176
  Brahe, T. 76
  Bruno, G. 109
  Du Hamel, J. 155
  Gassendi, P. 103
  Gloriosi, G.C. 102
  Kircher, A. 164
  Oviedo, F. de 173
  Patrizi, F. 113
  Pourchot, E. 191
  Tellez, B. 178
  Tosca, T.V. 209
  Ziegler, J. 37
Fixed stars (solid sphere)
  Arriaga, R. 171
  Aversa, R. 166

  Bellarmine, R. 46
  Biancani, G. 95
  Caussin, N. 145
  Clavius, C. 92
  Cordeiro, A. 213
  Kepler, J. 117
  Le Rees, F. 154
  Mersenne, M. 89
  Morin, J.B. 103
  Müler, N. 82
  Riccioli, G.B. 99, 149
  Serbelloni, S. 167
  Soares, F. 180
  Tanner, A. 93
  Vincent, J. 158
  Zaragoza J. 205
Fletcher, John E. 163n.38
Fokkes, Johannes *see* Holwarda, Johannes
  Phocylides
Fonseca, Pedro 92
Fontaine, Jacques 6n.22
Fontenelle, Bernard Le Bouyer de 194
France 152–163, 185–195
Franciscans 2, 26
Franco, António 179n.110
Freudenberger, Theobald 39n.35
Frisius, Reiner Gemma 61
Froidmont, Libert 89–90
Fromondus, Libert *see* Froidmont, Libert
Furley, D.J. 106n.1
Fyens, Thomas 89

Gabriel Biel *see* Biel, Gabriel
Gabrieli, G. 195n.47
Galileo, (Galileo Galilei) G. 22, 27, 85–86,
  87, 94, 98, 101, 122, 125, 145, 149, 150, 151,
  153, 155, 167, 168, 170, 171, 172, 176, 178,
  181, 190, 202, 212, 221
Garin, Eugenio 134n.3, 195n.45, 199n.60
Gassendi, P. 103–104, 119, 124–127, 128,
  179, 184, 186, 195, 200, 202, 207, 208
Gaulhieur, Ernest 159n.30
Gavira, José 211n.96
Genesis (Book of) 1, 2, 4, 5, 12, 28, 32, 37,
  41, 43, 46, 62, 82, 119, 120, 123, 124, 132,
  149, 154, 171, 176, 185, 195, 210, 219, 223
Genesis (Commentary on)
  Augustine, Saint 5n.13
  Bede, Venerable 3n.5
  Bellarmine, R. 44–46
  Calvin, J. 34n.9
  Luther, M. 34–36
  Molina, L. de 48–49
  Oreggi, A. 54–55
  Pereyra, B. 47–48
  Petau, D. 55–56
  Procopius of Gaza 3n.5

Genesis (Commentary on) continued
  Raban Maur 3n.5
  Robert Grosseteste 8–9
  Roslin, H. 53–54
  Rupert of Deutz 5n.17
  Suarez, F. 49–50
  Tostado, Alphonso de 25
  Zanchi, G. 50–52
  Ziegler, J. 37
Germany (Catholic) 163–166
Giet, Stanislas 3n.6
Gilbert, William 98n.85, 107, 110, 111, 150, 190, 195, 202, 205
Giles of Rome 2, 24–26
Gilson, Etienne 18n.83, 21n.104
Giorgio, Francesco 32–34, 220
Gliozzi, M. 102n.106
Gloriosi, Giovanni Camillo 101–102
Glossa ordinaria 7
Godwin, Joscelyn 38, 163
Góis, Manuel de 92
Goldstein, Bernard, 28n.139, 78n.81
Gomes, João Pereira 214n.107
Gonzales, Justo L. 1n.1
Gorlaeus, David 82–83
Grabmann, M. 98n.83
Grafton, Anthony 152n.4
Granada, Miguel A. 53n.98, 59n.7, 75n.67, 109n.13, 110n.17, 135
Grant, Edward 26n.130, 70n.50, 107nn.3 & 6, 108n.7, 125n.90, 126, 128n.106, 129n.109, 132n.129, 153n.10
Gravesand, Willem Jacob 's 217
Gravity 131–132
Gregory, Tullio 112n.26
Gregory of Nyssa 18
Gretzer, Jacob 39n.33
Grienberger, Christoph 93
Grillo, E. 95n.66
Grosseteste, Robert 2, 8–9, 41
Guericke, Otto von 107, 127–128
Guilielmus Alvernus *see* William of Auvergne
Guillaume de Conches *see* William of Conches
Günther, S. 36n.16

Hackett, J.M.G. 12n.53
Hahm, David E. 46n.62, 117n.53
Hall, A.R. 129nn.108 & 109
Heavens (tripartite division of) (*Empyreum, Æthereum, Aereum*)
  Arriaga, R. 171
  Aslachus, C. 52
  Aversa, R. 166
  Bellarmine, R. 44, 97
  Borri, C. 176
  Cajetan, Cardinal 97n.78
  Caussin, N. 145
  Cordeiro, A. 213
  Cornäus, M. 165
  Hurtado de Mendoza, P. 98, 169
  John of Damascus, Saint 44, 49, 52, 53, 97
  Kepler, J. 116
  Le Rees, F. 154
  Oviedo, F. de 173
  Patrizi, F. 97, 113
  Pourchot, E. 190
  Roslin, H. 53
  Serbelloni, S. 168
  Soares, F. 180
  Steuco, A. 97
  Suarez, F. 49
  Tellez, B. 178
  Tosca, T.V. 210
  Vincent, J. 158
  Zanchi, G. 52
Heavens of the Heavens (*cœlos cœlorum*) 113, 114, 124
Heaven of the Trinity 14, 15
Heckius, Joannes 84–85
Hellmann, C. Doris 53n.98, 63n.23
Henao, Gabriel 141, 145, 146–149
Henquinet, F.M. 15n.66, 18n.83
Henry, John 77n.76, 106n.3, 112n.28
Hermeticism 32
Hermogenes 192
Hevelius 81
Hexaëmerons 6, 40, 48, 50, 54, 55, 88, 151, 156, 175, 202, 208, 210
Hexaëmerons
  Ambrose, Saint 6n.21
  Basil, Saint 3–5
  Giles of Rome 24–26
  Robert Grosseteste 8–9
Hilary of Poitiers 6n.22
Hine, William L. 88n.40
Hipparchus 60
Hobbes, Thomas 195
Holwarda, Johannes Phocylides 118
Hooykaas, Reyer 184n.6
Huet, Pierre-Daniel 119n.60
Hübner, Jürgen 115n.44
Hurtado de Mendoza, Pedro 146, 168, 169–170, 178
Huygens, Christian 163n.38, 194
Hveen 64
Hydrological cycle 4, 43, 44

Ibn al-Haytham (Alhazen) 25, 61n.11, 62, 63, 67, 70, 73, 78n.81, 222
Ibn Mu^{c}adh 78n.81
Ibn Rushd *see* Averroes
Imperial College (Madrid) 205

INDEX

Indefinite extension of universe 119, 124, 126, 184, 189, 191, 196, 201, 205, 206, 207, 209
Index (of prohibited books) 34, 42, 107, 119, 217n.123, 218
Infinity of universe
　Aslachus, C. 52
　Baer, N.R. (Ursus) 110
　Bruno, G. 107–109
　Cesi, F. 87
　Cornelio, T. 196
　Dagoumer, G. 194
　De Benedictis, G.B. 200
　Gloriosi, G.C. 102
　Guericke, O. von 128
　Newton, I. 131–132
　Patrizi, F. 113
Intelligences 164, 166, 167, 169, 173
Intromission theory of vision 16
Isidore of Seville 2, 6, 18
Isidorian model (or interpretation) 6–7, 25, 28, 38, 44, 47, 97, 145, 169
Italy 166–168, 195–204

Jansen, B. 152n.2, 166n.47, 169n.62, 170n.67
Jean Buridan 35n.15, 70
Jean Mair *see* John Mair
Jerusalem 1
Jerome, Saint 3n.5, 14, 37n.22
Jesuit Colleges
　Bologna 149
　Brera 174
　La Flèche 55, 118, 122
　Lecce 199
　Mondovi 174
　Naples 199
　Parma 95
　Rome 47, 90, 163
　Salamanca 146
Jesuits 80, 90–99, 122, 135, 145, 168, 170, 174, 176, 178, 181, 184, 212, 214, 221
Job 27, 34, 49, 153, 158, 167
Johannes de Sacrobosco *see* John of Holywood
Johannes Majoris *see* John Major
John Major 107–108, 148
John of Damascus (Saint) 44, 49, 52, 53, 97
John of Holywood 7, 90
Joshua 154
Jourdain, Charles 119n.66
Jupiter's satellites 94, 125, 145, 154, 155, 157, 160, 164, 168, 173, 197

Kepler, Johann 58, 61, 75, 77–79, 86, 88, 90, 95n.67, 98–99, 101, 102, 103, 104, 107, 111, 115–118, 130, 131, 135–136, 139, 147, 149, 150, 151, 160, 161–162, 163, 176, 177, 180, 190, 193n.36, 198, 199, 202, 217, 221
Kircher, Athanasius 163–165
Kirk, G.S. & Raven, J.E. 106n.2
Koyré, A. 15n.64, 107n.6, 115n.43, 119, 127nn.98 & 101, 129nn.108 & 109, 132n.130, 184n. 6
Koyré, A. & Cohen, I. Bernard 130n.114
Krafft, Fritz 127n.102, 128n.106
Kristeller, Paul Oscar 112n.25
Kusukawa, Sachiko 38n.27

Labadie, Ernest 159n.31
La Grange, Jean-Baptiste 185
Lamy, Bernard 215
Landgrave Wilhelm of Hesse-Cassel *see* Wilhelm IV (Landgrave of Hesse-Cassel)
Lansberg, Philip van 205n.78
Lattis, James M. 91n.49
Le Jeunehomme, Fr 175
Lennon, Thomas M. 126n.96
Le Rees, François 152, 153–155
Lerner, Michel-Pierre 7n.27, 26n.130, 75, 94n.64, 133n.1, 153n.10, 175n.83, 180n.115, 196n.49
Lessius, Leonard 138–140, 147, 148, 166, 180
Leys, Leonard *see* Lessius, Leonard
Leucippus 120
Liber de excentricitate orbium see Thabit ibn Qurra
Lindberg, David 16n.70, 58n.4, 79n.86
Litt, Thomas 19n.91
Lohr, Charles H. 153n.6, 179n.110
Longomontanus, Christian Severinus 76–77, 82, 90, 103, 132
López, Enrique 212n.98
López Piñero, José María 100n.91, 204n.74, 205nn.75 & 77, 207n.81
Lucretius 106n.1
Luther, Martin 34–36, 38–39, 200, 220

McGuire, J.E. and Rattansi, P.M. 130n.115
Maestlin, Michael 202
Magini, G.A. 97
Mahnke, Dietrich 117n.52
Mair, John *see* John Major
Major, John *see* John Major
Majoris, Johannes *see* John Major
Maloni, Daniel 30, 136–137, 139, 147, 177
Manzoni, Claudio 195n.46
Martianus Capella 7
Martinet, Monette 102n.107
Maurach, Gregor 7n.29
Maurer, H.M. & Ulshöfer, K. 39n.34
Mayaud, Pierre-Noël 217–218n.123, 218n.125
Mazarin, Cardinal 145
Melanchthon Philipp 35n.11, 37–38, 114

270   INDEX

Mémoires de Trévoux 146n.49, 212
Mersenne, Marin 88–89, 122
Michael Scot 6
Michaud-Quantin, Pierre 15n.69
Michel, P.H. 106n.3, 112n.23
Molina, Luis de 48–49, 177
Monteiro, Ignácio 214–215, 217
Moon's surface (unevenness of) 94, 171, 173
Moraes, Manuel 214n.106
Moran, Bruce T. 64n.27
More, Henry 107, 128–129, 222
Morin, Jean Baptiste 76, 82, 102–103, 119–120
Moses 41, 43, 82, 124, 208
Mount Olympus 147
Mouy, Paul 119n.65, 183n.3
Muckle, J.T. 9n.37
Müler, Nicolaus 81–82
Mulerius, Nicolaus *see* Müler, Nicolaus
Muñoz, Jerónimo 99–100, 170

Nabod, Valentin 46
'Nails in a wheel, knots in wood' metaphor 35, 125, 155
 Celaya, J. de, 35n.15
 Jean Buridan, 35n.15
 Pierre d'Ailly 35n.15
 William of Auvergne 35n.15
Nancel, Nicolas 59
Nancelius, Nicolaus *see* Nancel, Nicolas
Navarro Brotóns, Victor 100n.91, 205n.77, 208n.84
Neander, Michael 46
Neoplatonism 3, 5, 19, 28, 32, 40, 46, 79, 98, 108, 127, 149, 222
Newton, Isaac 99, 106n.2, 129–132, 184, 196n.36, 199, 211, 215, 216, 217, 222, 223
Nicolas of Cusa 108, 117, 203
Nicolson, M.H. 184n.6
Nimesius 18
Noceti, C. 212
North, John xii
Novae 74, 84, 90, 92, 93, 99, 156, 164, 173
Novatores 205
Nunes, Pedro 78n.83

Odour (in the Empyrean)
 Albert the Great 17
 Barradas, S. 141
 Bellarmine, R. 143
 Caussin, N. 146
 Lessius, L. 140
 Roa, M. de 144
 Thomas Aquinas 22
 Tostado, Alphonso de 30
Oratorians 207, 215
Order of Minims 88, 206, 207n.80
Origen 11, 37n.25, 140, 147

Oreggi, Agostino 54–55
Oregius, Augustinus *see* Oreggi, Agostino
Ostler, Margaret J. 131n.123
Oviedo, F. de 168, 172–174

Palanco, Francisco 206–207
Palla Strozzi 33
Pantin, Isabelle 85n.23
Paracelsus, Theophrastus Philippus Aureolus Bombastus von Hohenheim 79, 195
Parallax 74, 92, 99, 161, 211
Patrizi, Francesco 77, 82n.11, 102, 103, 106, 107, 112–113, 115, 125, 147, 221–222
Paul, Saint 7n.28, 20, 97n.78, 131
Pena, Jean 58–64, 68, 70, 73, 74, 81, 82, 83, 85, 93, 101, 110, 145, 157, 180, 220
Peñafiel, Ildephonso de 98n.82
Pereyra, Benito 47–48, 83, 97, 120, 145, 149, 169, 171, 173, 176
Petau, Denis 55–56
Peter Lombard 2n.2, 7–8, 15, 24
Petersen, Peter 151n.1
Peucer, Caspar 75–76, 113–114
Peurbach, George 153
Phases of Venus 94, 164, 197
Philip III, (King of Spain) 100
Philo of Alexandria 104, 131, 202
Pico della Mirandola 32
Pierre d'Ailly 20, 35n.15
Piwnik, Marie Hélène 215n.113
Plato 5, 195
Pliny 36, 62, 71n.54, 80, 100
Pneuma 36, 62, 71n.54, 76, 106n.2, 117n.53, 131
Poggio 106n.1
Portugal 174–181, 213–217
Pourchot, Edmond 190–191, 193, 195
Presocratics 101, 195, 221, 222, 223
Primum Mobile 7, 8, 19, 25, 97, 99, 101, 103, 109, 128, 133, 160, 166, 168, 169, 171, 173, 176, 190, 191, 193
Procopius of Gaza 3n.5
Protestants 1, 32, 38–39, 80–84, 133, 135–136
 Amerpoel, J. 123–124
 Aslachus, C. 52–53
 Brahe, T. 113–115
 Gilbert, W. 111
 Guericke, O. von 127
 Kepler, J. 115–17
 Lydyat, T. 80–81
 Melanchthon, P. 37–38
 More, H. 128–129
 Müler, N. 81–82
 Peucer, C. 75–76
 Roslin, H. 53–54
 Gorlaeus, D. 82–84

Protestants continued
　Wendelin, M.F. 83–84
　Zanchi, G. 50–52
　Ziegler, J, 36–37
Pseudo-Clement 2, 3, 12, 48
Pseudo-Clementine model (or intepretation) 2–3, 9, 10, 25, 27, 33, 42, 44, 47, 49, 54, 56, 92, 167, 169, 171, 213
Pseudo-Dionysius 139
Ptolemaic system (astronomy)
　Almeida, T. de 216–217
　Apian, P. 12n. 56
　Bauduer, J. 159–162, 188
　Borri, C. 174, 176
　Campanus of Novara 6n.26
　Celaya, J. de 12n.55
　Cornelio, T. 197
　Corsini, E. 202–203
　Dagoumer, G. 193, 195
　Du Hamel, J. 155–156
　Feijoo, B. J. 211
　Gassendi, P. 124–125
　Le Rees, F. 154
　Michael Scot 6n.25
　Pourchot, E. 190–191, 195
　Tosca, T.V. 216
Ptolemy, Claudius
　Almagest 26, 124, 157
　Geography 33
　Optica 58, 59, 62, 63, 70, 220
　Planetary Hypotheses 7n.27, 25
Pythagoras 203
Pythagorians 197

Quasten, Johannes 1n.1

Raban Maur 3n.5
Raka
　Luther, M. 34
　Steuco, A. 40
Rakiah
　Cesi, F. 86
　Giorgio, F. 33
　Kepler, J. 116–117
　Luther, M. 34
　Oviedo, F. de 173
　Pereyra, B. 48
　Steuco, A. 40, 42–43
　Tosca, T.V. 209
　Tostado, Alphonso de 27
　Wendelin, M.F. 83
Ramus, Peter 59, 61
Raphael, (Angel) 142
Recognitiones (Pseudo-Clementine) 2–3
Refractions 59, 62–63, 67–75, 77, 82, 83, 86, 88, 89, 90, 92, 93–94, 95, 101, 105, 157, 164, 167

Régis, Pierre Sylvain 185
Reif, Patricia 152
Reinhold, Erasmus 202
Res extensa 118
Respiration (in the Empyrean)
　Aversa, R. 166
　Caussin, N. 146
　Cordeiro, A. 213
　Cornäus, M. 166
　Henao, G. 147
　Lessius, L. 139
　Maloni, D. 137
　Roa, M. de 144
　Suarez, F. 137
Resurrection 18, 28, 31, 38, 155
Reusch, Heinrich 42n.46
Rheticus, Georg Joaquin 202
Ricard, Robert 215n.113
Ricci, Matteo 174n.80
Ricci, Saverio 84n.20
Riccioli, G.B. 51, 98–99, 145, 149–150, 203n.71, 214
Richard, R. 123n.81
Rivalier, Joseph 158n.28
Roa, Martin de 143–144
Rochemonteix, Camille 123n.77
Rochot, Bernard 127n.101
Rodrigues, Francisco 179n.110
Rogers, G.A.J. 184n.6
Rohault, Jacques 185
Rosen, Edward 69n.43, 134n.3
Roslin, Helisaeus 53–54, 71
Rothmann, Christoph 58, 63–76, 79, 81, 82, 83, 85, 86, 88, 89, 90, 93, 95n.67, 98, 101, 102, 110, 135, 145, 149, 167, 168, 180, 220
Rotondò, A. 34n.7, 196n.48
Rudolf II, (Emperor) 109
Rufinus 2
Ruler, J.A. van 123n.80, 184n.6
Rupert of Deutz 5, 37n.25
Russell, John L. 151n.1, 218n.124

Sabbatié, Guillaume 189–190
Sabra, A.I. 78n.81
Sacrobosco, Johannes de *see* John of Holywood
Saguens, Jean 207
Saint Ambrose *see* Ambrose, Saint
Saint Anselm *see* Anselm, Saint
Saint Augustine *see* Augustine, Saint
Saint Basil *see* Basil, Saint
Saint Bonaventure *see* Bonaventure, Saint
Saint Jerome *see* Jerome, Saint
Saint John of Damascus *see* John of Damascus, Saint
Saint Paul *see* Paul, Saint

INDEX

Saint Paul, Eustache de 151n.1
Saint Thomas Aquinas *see* Thomas Aquinas, Saint
Sambursky, Samuel 36n.18, 46n.62, 62n.19
Santos, Domingos Maurício Gomes dos 174n.79, 180n.82
Sarrailh, Jean 191n.29, 205n.76
Saturn's rings 94, 125, 145, 154, 155, 160, 164, 173
Scheibler, Christoph 151n.1
Scheiner, Christoph 78, 86, 101
Schimank, H. 127n.102
Schmidt, C. 50n.83
Schmitt, Charles B. 40n.36, 170n.68
Schofield, Christine Jones 95n.71
Schottenloher, K. 36n.16
Segonds, Alain 63n.23, 115n.43
Seleucians 187
Seminary, Irish (Lisbon) 178
Semple (Sempill), Hugo 178
Sensibilia 17
Sentences of Peter Lombard (Commentary on)
    Albert the Great 14
    Biel, Gabriel 38
    Durandus of Saint Pourçain 21
    Giles of Rome 26
    John Major 148
    Thomas Aquinas 19
Septuagint 37n.22, 40, 43, 44
Serbelloni, Sigismondo 166, 167–168
Shamaim 43
Shea, William R. 94
Sierra de Pariacaca 147
Silva, Innocêncio Francisco da 100n.95
Simultaneous creation 42n.51, 47n.66, 120–123, 189, 190, 202, 208
Sixth essence
    Albert of Saxony 28n.141
    Tostado, Alphonso de 28
Smell (in the Empyrean) *see* Odour (in the Empyrean)
Snell, Willebrord 59n.6, 67n.37, 68, 78n.83
Soares, Francisco (Lusitano) 174, 178, 179–181, 213
Solana, Marcial 47n.64, 92n.52
Solar depression angle 78n.81, 198
Sortais, Gaston 184n.5
Sound (in the Empyrean) see Voice and hearing
Space
    Descartes, R. 119
    Gassendi, P. 124–127, 222
    Guericke, O. von 128
    More, H. 128
    Newton, I. 130–132
    Patrizi, F. 112, 115

Spain 168–174, 204–12
Spampanato, V. 107n.5
Spanneut, Michel 131n.125
Species 15, 17, 24, 30, 98, 137, 138, 160, 199
Stafford, Ignatius 178
Stauffer, Richard 34n.8
Stelliola, Nicola Antonio 195
Stephen, Friar 11
Stereoma 40, 42, 43
Steuco, Agostino 3n.5, 39–43, 47–48, 51–52, 113, 120, 126, 127, 137, 164, 169, 220
Stevin, Simon 78n.83
Sticker, Bernhard 64n.27
Stjernborg 64
Stoicism 36, 46, 61, 68, 79, 80, 131
Suarez, Francisco 28, 48–50, 120, 137–138, 146, 169, 176, 177
Sunspots 94, 125, 157, 160, 164, 167, 172, 173, 197
Supercelestial Waters
    Albert the Great 12
    Amerpoel, J. 124
    Augustine, Saint 5
    Basil, Saint 4
    Bellarmine, R. 38
    Borri, C. 176, 177
    Brahe, T. 114
    Cajetan, Cardinal 97n.78
    Campanus of Novara 6–7
    Giles of Rome 25
    Gorlaeus, D. 83
    Guericke, O. von 128
    Hurtado de Mendoza, P. 169
    Isidore of Seville 6
    Kepler, J. 79
    Kircher, A. 164–165
    Le Rees, F. 154
    Lydyat, T. 81
    Molina, L. de 49
    Oreggi, A. 54
    Oviedo, F. de 173
    Pereyra, B. 48
    Petau, D. 56
    Peucer, C. 113
    Pseudo-Clement 4
    Riccioli, G.B. 149
    Soares, F. 181
    Steuco, A. 43
    Suarez, F. 49–50
    Tanner, A. 140
    William of Auvergne 10–11
    Zaragoza, J. 205
    Ziegler, J. 37
Surdich, Francesco 175n.82

Tallavia, Hieronymus 197
Tanner, A. 93–95, 98, 140, 147, 171, 173

INDEX

Taste (in the Empyrean)
  Albert the Great 18
  Bellarmine, R. 143
  Caussin, N. 146
  Henao, G. 148
  John Major 148
  Lessius, L. 140
  Roa, M. de 144
  Thomas Aquinas 22
  Tostado, Alphonso de 29
Telescope 64, 87, 94, 170
Telesio, Bernardino 107n.3, 195, 196
Tellez, Balthasar 174, 178–179
Tempier, Etienne *see* Etienne Tempier
Terrasson, Abbé Jean 192n.32
Tertulia 204
Tertullian 1, 187, 192
Thabit ibn Qurra 17, 30
Thales 131
Theodoretus 3n.5
'*Theorica* compromise' 26n.130, 153, 158, 169, 171, 173
Thierry of Chartres 5
Thijssen-Schoute, Caroline 123n.81, 184n.6
Thomas Aquinas, Saint 19–24, 49, 120, 137, 138, 148, 159, 178
Thorndike, Lynn 33n.3, 46n.63, 54n.104, 59n.8, 82n.13, 166n.47, 170n.68
Thoren, Victor 64n.26, 67
Tolosani, Giovanni Maria 133
Torrell, P.J. 19n.89
Torrini, M. 195n.46, 197n.53
Tosca, Tomás Vicente 207–211, 212, 215
Tostado, Alphonso de 2, 26–31, 136, 140
Touch (in the Empyrean)
  Albert the Great 18
  Barradas, S. 141
  Bellarmine, R.
  Henao, G. 148–149
  Kircher, A. 165
  Lessius, L. 140
  Roa, M. de 144
  Thomas Aquinas, Saint 21–22
  Tostado, Alphonso de 29
Tycho Brahe *see* Brahe, Tycho
Tychonic system (astronomy)
  Almeida, T. de 216
  Bauduer, J. 159–160, 162, 163
  Biancani, G. 95
  Borri, C. 176
  Brahe, T. 95n.71
  Cordeiro, A. 213
  Cornelio, T. 197
  Corsini, E. 202
  Dagoumer, G. 193, 195
  Du Hamel, J. 155–156
  Feijoo, B.J. 211

  Gassendi, P. 124–125
  Le Rees, F. 154
  Monteiro, I. 214
  Pourchot, E. 191, 195
  Tosca, T.V. 210
  Zaragoza, J. 205

Urban VIII (Pope) 54
Ubiquistæ
  Aslachus, C. 52–53
  Brenz, Johann 39
  Zanchi, G. 50–51
Universities
  Bologna 39
  Cambridge 151n.1
  Coimbra 92, 175, 179, 213, 214
  Evora 140, 179
  Franeker 118
  Groningen 81
  Heidelberg 50
  Helmstadt 127
  Leyden 127
  Louvain 89, 183
  Osuna (Spain) 204
  Oviedo 211
  Oxford 151n.1
  Padua 101
  Paris 11, 24, 183, 190
    Collège de Montaigu 107
    Collège of La Marche 153
    Collège of Le Plessis 153, 155
    Collège of Les Grassins 153
  Prague 93n.58, 170
  Rome (La Sapienza) 102, 112
  Salamanca 26, 146, 191n.29, 205, 206
  Seville 204
  Tübingen 53
  Utrecht 121n.69
  Valencia 99, 204, 205
  Wittenberg 75
  Würzburg
Uraniborg 64, 67
Ursus, Nicolaus Raimarus *see* Baer, Nicolai Reymers

Valentinians 187
Van Genderen, J. 123n.81
Van Goorle, David *see* Gorlaeus, D.
Van Heeck, Joannes *see* Heckius, Joannes
Van Helden, Albert 107n.4
Vasoli, C. 33n.3
Vaugondy, Robert 212n.99
Verbeke, G. 106n.2
Ver Eecke, Paul 58n.5
Vernet, Juan 205n.78
Vespasiano da Bisticci 33n.6
Viera y Clavijo, J. de 27n.134

Vincent, J. 152, 156–159, 172, 181, 186–188
Vincent of Beauvais 2n.2
Vision (in the Empyrean)
   Albert the Great 15–16
   Barradas, S. 141
   Bellarmine, R. 142
   Caussin, N. 146
   Durandus of Saint Pourçain 21, 138
   Kircher, A. 165
   Lessius, L. 138
   Roa, M. de 144
   Suarez, f. 138
   Tostado, Alphonso de 30–31
Vitelleschi, Muzio 175n.81, 179n.110
Voet, Gijsbert 140n.20
Voice and hearing (in the Empyrean)
   Albert the Great 16–17
   Barradas S. 141
   Bellarmine, R. 143
   Caussin, N. 146
   Giles of Rome 26
   Henao, G. 148
   Kircher, A. 165
   Lessius, L. 138
   Maloni, D. 137

Roa, M. de 144
Suarez, F. 137
Thomas Aquinas 23
Tostado, Alphonso de 30
Vincent, J. 159
Vortices (Cartesian) 121, 192, 197

Weisheipl, James A. 12n.52
Wendelin, Marc Friedrich 83–84, 151n.1
Wesley, Walter G. 64n.26
Wilhelm IV (Landgrave of Hesse-Cassel) 63, 74
William of Auvergne 2, 9–12, 35n.15, 140
William of Conches 5
Witelo 60, 61n.11, 63, 67, 73
Wittich, Paul 64

Ymaginatio modernorum 25–26

Zanchi, G. 50–52
Zaragoza, Joseph 205–206
Ziegler, J. 36–37, 62, 71n.54, 76
Ziller Camenietski, Carlos 163n.38
Zöckler, Otto, 27n.134, 39n.35